Using the STL

MW00445667

Second Edition

Springer

New York
Berlin
Heidelberg
Barcelona
Hong Kong
London
Milan
Paris
Singapore
Tokyo

Robert Robson

Using the STL

The C++ Standard Template Library

Second Edition

With 36 Illustrations

 Springer

Robert Robson
2645 Battleford Road, #1104
Mississauga, Ontario L5N 3R8
Canada
rnrobson@yahoo.com

Library of Congress Cataloging-in-Publication Data
Robson, Robert.
   Using the STL: the C++ standard template library/Robert Robson.
     p. cm.
   Includes bibliographical references.
   ISBN 0-387-98857-2 (softcover: alk. paper)
   1. C++ (Computer program language).   2. Standard template library.
  I. Title.
  QA76.73.C153R625   1999
  005.13′3—dc21   99-26377

Printed on acid-free paper.

Production managed by Francine McNeill; manufacturing supervised by Erica Bresler.
Photocomposed copy prepared from the author's Ami Pro files.
Printed and bound by Hamilton Printing Co., Rensselaer, NY.
Printed in the United States of America.

9 8 7 6 5 4 3 2 1

ISBN 0-387-98857-2 Springer-Verlag New York Berlin Heidelberg   SPIN 10727808

Preface to the Second Edition

A lot has happened since the first edition of this book was written. When the first edition was prepared, there was only one version of the Standard Template Library (STL) available—the Hewlett-Packard version. Since then, several other versions have appeared from major compiler and library vendors. This is in an effort to conform to the recent International Standards Organization/International Electrotechnical Commission (ISO/IEC) C++ standards, which define the STL as part of the Standard C++ Library.

As expected, the STL is becoming widely available and an accepted part of C++ program development. This is good. Unfortunately, the proliferation of implementations makes it difficult to exactly define the STL. We now have multiple implementations, many of which are slightly incompatible with one another. The reasons for this are largely due to different capabilities of the compilers on which they are implemented. Many compilers do not implement the most recent features of the language since production of standards often precedes conforming implementations by many months. This will improve over time as the compilers add the necessary capabilities to support the full STL.

In attempting to revise a book on the STL, I was faced with the question of which definition to use. When there was only a single implementation, the answer was obvious. With several implementations differing in slight ways, there is the possibility of describing the most commercially successful version, describing an idealized version, trying to describe all of the versions, or describing the standard. Describing the most commercially successful version would do a disservice to those running other versions. Describing all versions is just not practical since I do not have access to all of the hardware necessary to run some of the versions out there. Therefore, I decided to describe the STL as defined by the most recent ISO/IEC C++ standard of September 1998. Although I have yet to find an implementation that conforms to this standard, most of the implementations come very close—close enough that the casual user might not even notice the differences. Furthermore, the compiler and library vendors are working on implementations that fully conform to the standard. Thus, by the time you read this, a conforming implementation might be available. Regardless, this is the standard that all vendors will be striving to meet and is the safest implementation to describe.

This book also describes extensions provided by some of the popular implementations. I have not attempted to be rigorous in this, as I merely want to provide you with a glimpse of what is possible and how future development of the STL might proceed. I want to introduce these extensions to those of you who might be using those libraries. The space devoted to these discussions is minimal, and it is clearly indicated that such capabilities are not part of the C++ standard.

All languages evolve, and C++ is no different. Thus, any book describing a language can be no more than a snapshot of the language as it is at some point in time. The C++ standard will change, and the definition of the STL will likely change with it. Fortunately, most of the concepts and basic structure of the language and libraries will remain the same. Therefore, I have hopes that the information in this book will be useful for a period of years.

Thanks are due to the readers who provided comments on the first edition. I have attempted to address their comments in an effort to correct deficiencies in the first edition. My thanks also go to Michelle French, who was an enormous help in editing the manuscript for the second edition.

Robert Robson
Mississauga, Ontario, Canada
1999

Preface to the First Edition

Programming languages evolve in steps. They began with weakly typed languages like FORTRAN and progressed to strongly typed languages like PASCAL. This had the positive effect of moving the detection of many programming errors from run time to compile time. This had the negative effect of limiting the generality of functions since they were now bound to specific data types. This virtually eliminated the writing of reusable software components. The result was that programmers had to reimplement common algorithms and data structures over and over.

Newer languages, such as C++, provide a way to decouple algorithms and data structures from the data types upon which they operate. C++ provides this capability via the template mechanism. Suddenly, it became possible to write generic algorithms and data structures that could be reused. In effect, this provides debugged software components that can be combined to form programs much faster than by reimplementing the components each time they are needed.

At the same time that programming languages were evolving, computer hardware was becoming incredibly inexpensive compared to programmers' salaries. This provided a strong incentive to reduce costs by increasing programmer productivity. Software reuse was seen as one way to increase programmer productivity.

The drive to increase programmer productivity was initially met by the introduction of reusable components by compiler vendors and other software companies. While this was a major step forward, it was flawed by introducing multiple libraries that addressed the problem in different ways. The result was that component reuse meant that a programmer might need to learn several such libraries.

The Standard Template Library (STL) was introduced after several years of studying how a library of reusable components should be designed. As a result, it introduces several new concepts that make the library easier to use and allow the generic algorithms to be applied to data stored in arrays as well as the containers provided by the STL.

The STL has been accepted as a standard by the American National Standards Institute (ANSI) committee for the standardization of the C++ language. This means that it must be provided by all C++ compilers, just like common functions such as `strlen()`. The result is a single, well-defined library of reusable components that is available to all programmers regardless of the compiler or platform they use.

This book introduces the algorithms and data structures that comprise the STL and the philosophy behind their creation. An understanding of the philosophy is crucial since it allows you to see the underlying structure and regularity in the library. An understanding of this regularity reduces the amount of material that you must remember to use the STL effectively.

This book began as a series of notes on the use of the STL for a programming project in which I was involved. As the magnitude of effort and the required detail became apparent, turning it into a book was the natural thing to do.

The resulting book not only describes the components of the STL and the philosophy behind them, but it shows how you can use them. This is done by pointing out some of the pitfalls in the usage of the STL and by showing examples of real-world problems being solved with the STL. An explanation of many of the algorithms implemented by the STL is provided for those readers not familiar with the underlying concepts.

While this book is aimed primarily at professional programmers, it is not restricted to this audience. It is suitable for software managers who need a high-level understanding of the STL as well as students who wish to expand their programming knowledge and skills. A table at the end of the introduction shows which chapters are most appropriate to each type of reader.

I believe that the STL will become an important component in the Standard C++ Library and that it will be vital for programmers to have a good working knowledge of the STL. The result will be decreased tedium in the production of software, higher quality, and increased productivity.

I would like to thank the people who read initial versions of this book especially Heather Collicutt and Brigitte Bonert. I also wish to thank Ross Judd of Atomic Energy of Canada, Ltd., who had the foresight and interest to allow me the time to investigate the STL and write this book. Final thanks go to all of the people at Springer-Verlag who made this book possible.

I wish you well in your programming endeavors and hope that this book helps you achieve your goals.

Robert Robson
Mississauga, Ontario, Canada
1997

Contents

1
Introduction

1.1 What Is the STL?

The Standard Template Library (STL) is a collection of generic data structures and algorithms written in C++. The STL is not the first such library, as most C++ compilers provide libraries with a similar intent, and several commercial libraries are available. One of the problems with the libraries from different vendors is that they are all mutually incompatible, so that programmers are continually learning new libraries as they migrate from one project to another and one compiler to another. The STL has been adopted as a standard by the International Standards Organization, International Electrotechinical Commission (ISO/IEC) and the American National Standards Institute (ANSI), meaning that it is an extension to the language that is supported by all compilers and is readily available.

The STL was not adopted as a standard because of its completeness, lack of ownership by a particular vendor, ease of use, or even by random selection. It was adopted as a standard because it has the following advantages over other generic libraries:

- The STL generalizes the concept of the iterator. The authors recognized that an iterator is a general form of the pointer and implemented it as such. As a result, all data structures can use iterators in the same way that pointers are used to reference elements in an array.

- Since all algorithms are based on a generalization of the pointer, the STL algorithms can be used on regular arrays as well as the container types provided by STL. This greatly increases the applicability of the algorithms.

- The STL pays particular attention to the efficiency of the algorithms used. That is not to say that the other libraries are inefficient—most of them are not—but the STL uses efficient techniques for the implementation of every algorithm and states the speed of each algorithm to give the programmer a basis for selecting among competing algorithms.

The STL provides a collection of generic container data structures and algorithms that can be used to operate upon them. A container data structure is one that can contain instances of other data structures. The STL provides implementations of the vector, list, set, multiset, deque, map, multimap, queue, priority queue, heap, and stack. These containers are said to be generic since they can contain instances of any other type of data. This genericity is gained by extensive use of C++ templates.

The adoption of STL offers several other advantages:

- Since it is a standard, it is available across all compilers and platforms. This allows the same library to be used in all projects and reduces the training time required for programmers to switch between projects. As the STL gains popularity, programmers proficient in its use will be readily available.

- Use of a library of reusable components increases programming productivity since your own programmers do not have to reinvent the wheel by writing their own algorithms. Employing a library of bug-free functions not only reduces development time, but it increases the robustness of the applications in which it is used.

- Applications can be written so that they are faster since they are built from efficient algorithms and the programmers have the ability to select the fastest algorithm for a given situation.

- The readability of the code is increased. The 1970s saw control structures built from `gotos` replaced with structured statements such as the `while` loop, `if-then-else` statement, and the like. This increased the readability and maintainability of the code since programmers no longer had to examine a series of conditions and branches to determine the type of control structure being implemented—they were clearly identified by keyword.

- The STL makes the same contribution to algorithms and data structures. Programmers no longer have to pore over obscure code to identify algorithms—they are identified by function calls with standardized names. This makes the code much easier to read and maintain. It also increases the functionality of reengineering tools since these tools can more readily recognize the algorithms being employed.

- Memory management is improved since the STL relegates memory management to an allocator class. Special-purpose allocator implementations can be written to provide higher performance or to handle non-standard memory models.

1.2 History

The main authors of the Standard Template Library are Alexander Stepanov and Meng Lee, both of whom work for Hewlett-Packard. Stepanov and David Musser of the Rensselaer Polytechnic Institute began working on generic programming in the early 1980s, implementing the ideas in Ada and Scheme. When C++ adopted templates, they began a C++ implementation of the library that had been developed in Ada. Since the original C++ implementation of templates did not support the capabilities required, Stepanov had discussions with Bjarne Stroustrop and the C++ language was extended to provide the necessary capabilities.

Stroustrop suggested to Stepanov that he present his ideas to the ANSI committee for the standardization of C++. This was done at the June 1993 meeting of the committee and, to Stepanov's surprise, they agreed to adopt it as an extension to the C++ library.

The original version of the STL was produced by Stepanov and Lee at Hewlett-Packard and released in October 1995. The standardization committee has made revisions to streamline some of the algorithms and to increase the regularity of the application programming interface. They have also added important classes such as the `string` and the `valarray`. The version of the STL used in this book corresponds to *International Standard ISO/IEC 14882, Programming Languages—C++*, of September 1998.

1.3 STL Components

Large software libraries can generally be broken down into a series of different categories of components. This provides a paradigm to aid in the design and understanding of the library. The STL provides five different component categories, as shown in the following list:

algorithms   The STL provides a wealth of common algorithms including sorts, searches, numerical algorithms, and the like. The algorithms can be used on STL data structures, arrays, or user-defined data structures that provide iterators.

iterators Iterators provide a generalization of the pointer that allows the programmer to visit each element in a container data structure in an orderly fashion.

containers These common data structures contain and manage the storage of other data structures. The containers provided include the vector, list, set, and map.

function objects Many of the algorithms allow the programmer to pass a function to the algorithm to customize its functionality. Function objects are a generalization of the pointer to a function that would be passed by a C programmer.

adaptors Adaptors can take one component and provide a different interface to it. This allows one data structure to be turned into another that requires the same capabilities but whose interface must provide a different set of operations.

1.4 Generic Algorithms

All computer programmers get the feeling of déjà vu when writing code. They often feel as if they have written the same code before—and indeed they have. Computer programs employ the same common algorithms again and again. Often, the situation is slightly different each time they are used, and the programmer must rewrite the algorithm, adapting it to the new situation. Obviously, this is a repetitive task that should be eliminated, but the means for producing a generic algorithm that can be used in a wide variety of situations is not obvious.

Let us begin by taking a look at the commonly available libraries of reusable code that have been successful. The two most common examples that come to mind are libraries of mathematical functions and string handling functions. Almost every compiler provides these, and almost every programmer takes advantage of them. The question is, "What makes these libraries successful while others are doomed to failure?"

Both mathematical and string-handling functions deal with a very limited number of data types. Most mathematical functions deal with integers and floating point values, whereas string-handling functions deal with a representation of a string. This limited range of data types provides a clue about the source of their success. The algorithms do not have to be rewritten to work with other data types since there are no other data types to which they are applicable. Therefore, we can conclude that to produce generic algorithms, we must be able to separate the algorithm from the data representation that it is manipulating.

A simple example serves to illustrate this point. Consider the case of performing a linear search of an array looking for the first occurrence of a specific value. The code for searching an array of integers might look like Listing 1.1:

```
int* LinSearch(int* array, int size, int value)
{
    int *endPoint;

    endPoint = array + size;
    for(;array != endPoint;array++) {
        if((*array) == value) return array;
    }
    return NULL;
}
```

Listing 1.1 — A Linear Search of an Array of Integers

The algorithm is fairly straightforward and works the way we want it to work. The problem is that when we have to search an array of strings looking for a specific string, we find that we must rewrite the algorithm, as in Listing 1.2:

```
char* StrSearch(char* array[], int size, char* value)
{
    char* endPoint;

    endPoint = array + size;
    for(;array != endPoint;array++) {
        if(strcmp(array,value) == 0) return array;
    }
    return NULL;
}
```

Listing 1.2 — A Linear Search of an Array of Strings

These two functions have both great similarities and great differences. Examining them, we find that the algorithm for the search is identical in each case.

The differences lie in the data types and the operations that are performed on them. The different data types require different declarations, necessitating a re-write of the function. The comparison of values is also different. For integers, we can simply use operator==, but strings require the use of strcmp().

To make the linear search algorithm generic, we must separate the representation of the type and the operations on that type from the algorithm itself. One approach to this is to use a generic pointer to pass the data and pass function pointers to perform the necessary operations. The linear search implemented using this technique is shown in Listing 1.3:

```
void* LinearSearch(void*           array,
                   int             elemSize,
                   int             size,
                   CompareFuncType comp,
                   void*           value);
{
    char* ptr, endPoint;

    ptr = (char*)array;
    endPoint = ptr + (size * elemSize);
    for(;ptr != endPoint;ptr+=elemSize) {
        if( 0 == comp(ptr, value)) return ptr;
    }
    return NULL;
}
```

Listing 1.3 — A Generic Linear Search Using void*

Making the function generic requires a little more work than originally planned since the function must know the size of each element in the array to be able to iterate through it correctly. There is no doubt that this technique works, but as it is used, several problems become apparent:

- The parameter list is longer, making it more bothersome to type and more prone to error.

- The user must correctly specify the size of the elements in the array, an implementation detail that is best left to the compiler.

- The use of void* as a generic pointer is not type-safe. The programmer can inadvertently pass an array of one type, a value of another type, and assign the result to a third type. The compiler will happily generate code for this and never notice that anything is amiss. This bypasses all the type checking provided by the language and creates a multitude of potential errors.

A much better way to isolate the data type from the algorithm is to use the template capabilities of C++. Revising our linear search to use templates, we get the Listing 1.4:

```
template <class T>
T* LinearSearch(T* array, int size, T& value)
{
    T* endPoint;

    endPoint = array + size;
    for(;array != endPoint;array++) {
        if((*array) == value) return array;
    }
    return NULL;
}
```

Listing 1.4 — A Generic Linear Search Using a Template

This satisfies the requirements for genericity while not circumventing the type system of the language. Thus, it is a safer, easier-to-use solution to the problem than that provided by using void* to gain independence from the data type. We conclude that the best approach to writing generic functions in C++ is to employ the template facility.

1.4.1 C++ Templates

The C++ template facility provides a way to abstract the data type on which an algorithm operates from the algorithm itself. This separation of type from algorithm allows the creation of generic code that can be reused in a wide variety of situations. This is the true meaning of code reuse, not the trivial reuse of code that is achieved by inheriting methods from a base class. Although this is reusing existing code, it is limited to a single class hierarchy and could be achieved by using plain old structures and functions. The reuse of existing algorithms with different data types will save a lot more effort in the long run than the effort saved by inheritance.

Templates might be unfamiliar to some programmers since they are a recent addition to the language. Although the necessity for a template facility for C++ was recognized from the beginning, its inclusion in the standard was delayed until the problem was better understood and the C++ designers had a chance to try out various solutions.

The result of this effort is a template facility that allows functions and classes to be parameterized with one or more types. These types are enclosed in angle brackets and form a parameter list similar to the ones used with functions. The difference is that in a function, the parameters specify the variables that will be used, whereas in a template, the parameters specify the types that will be used. Consider the declaration of a simple vector class in Listing 1.5:

```
template <class T>
class vector {
public:
    vector();
    ...
private:
    T  storage[VECTOR_SIZE];
};
```

Listing 1.5 — A Simple Vector Class

A class like this allows you to provide operators that can allocate more storage if the vector becomes full or check the validity of subscripts rather than having invalid subscripts result in a run-time error. The trouble with designing a class like this is that we need to know what type of values are to be stored in the vector. Unfortunately, this cannot be known beforehand. We are left with these choices:

- Create a version of the vector class for each type that will be stored in the vector.

- Use a `void*` pointer to store the location of the physical storage.

- Use a template to abstract the type that is to be stored in the vector.

The first solution requires writing a lot of repetitious code and, even if this is done, there will always be a new type that someone will want to store in a vector that will require writing yet another version of the code. The second solution, the use of a `void*`, subverts the type-checking of the language and opens the user to a plethora of new errors. The onus for ensuring that all the little details are correct is shifted from the compiler onto the programmer—not a desirable situation. The third solution is the only one that makes sense. It allows the type to be changed without having to rewrite the code, while maintaining the strong type checking of the language.

The first line of the declaration states that this is a template and will be parameterized by a single type T. (The word *class* is required and does not imply that the type T can only be a class.) Within the class declaration itself, any occurrence of the type T is replaced by the actual type specified as a parameter when the class is created. For example, to create a vector of integers we would write this:

```
vector<int> intVector;
```

This is similar to supplying the actual parameters in a function call. When this object is created, all the instances of type T in the class will be replaced by type int. The way templates are implemented by the compiler is very different than the way parameters are passed to a function. Rather than passing values, the compiler must change types, which must then go through the normal type-checking mechanism of the compiler. The simplest way to do this is to have the compiler write a new version of the class, which then goes through the normal type-checking and compilation process.

At this point, it should be obvious why these are called templates. Although it appeared as if we wrote a vector class, in reality we wrote a template from which such a class could be created once the type information was known. The code for an instance of the vector class for a specific type was actually written by the compiler! The advantage of this is that effort is shifted from the programmer to the compiler without altering the run-time efficiency.

It can be argued that, if a great number of types are used to instantiate a template, the compiler will invisibly generate a lot of code that will inflate the size of the resulting executable. Although this is true, the severity of the problem can be reduced by using smaller classes and moving functionality out of methods and into nontemplate functions whenever possible. The alternative is to achieve a greater degree of physical code reuse by using void* to make the same code work with any type. Given the size of modern computer memories versus the cost of correcting programming mistakes created by the use of void*, it makes sense to sacrifice memory to obtain more reliable software.

One last point to note is that the types passed to a template need not always be types—values can be used as well. This facility is provided mainly to allow programmers to alter the size of data to be allocated in a class by passing the size as a parameter to the template. In the vector class, we have to know how big to make the underlying array used to store the actual values. We could modify our definition of the vector to take advantage of this, as shown in Listing 1.6:

```
template <class T, int size>
class vector {
public:
   vector();
   ...
private:
   T  storage[size];
};
```

Listing 1.6 — A Simple Vector Class with the Size as a Template Parameter

The same effect could be achieved by passing the size as a parameter to the constructor, but that would imply that the space allocation would have to be done at run-time. This could make the use of a class such as this less efficient than a built-in array and would discourage programmers from using such classes.

The STL depends heavily on the template facility of C++ to achieve its goal of providing generic algorithms. This takes us a long way toward achieving our goal of reusability, but as we examine the problem more closely, we find there are still improvements to be made.

What happens if we try to use the linear search function, developed previously, on a linked list? The answer is that it fails miserably since the current implementation assumes that the data are stored in an array in contiguous storage. We need to be able to generalize the addressing of the elements in the data structure being searched. An interesting approach to this problem is the one taken by the STL, which generalizes the concept of the pointer so that it can be used on any kind of container.

1.5 Iterators

One of the most common operations to perform on a container data structure is to traverse all or some of the elements stored in the data structure. Traversal is defined as visiting all or some of the elements in the container in a predefined order. An object that can return a reference to each of the elements in a container in turn is called an iterator.

Our previous version of the linear search algorithm made use of such an iterator—the pointer. It used the address of the beginning of the array to find the first element and added the size of the array to the address of the beginning to find the address of the element just past the end. To advance from one element to the next, it simply incremented the value of the pointer by the size of the elements in the array.

We can rewrite the linear search algorithm once again so that the parameters are expressed in terms of iterators, as shown in Listing 1.7. Now, the function will accept a pointer to the first element it will search and a pointer to the element just after the last one it will search.

```
template <class T>
T* LinearSearch(T* first, T* last, T& value)
{
    for(;first != last; first++) {
        if((*first) == value) return first;
    }
    return NULL;
}
```

Listing 1.7 — A Linear Search Using Iterators

Let us examine the properties of our iterator. This function used the following operators provided by the pointer:

- operator!=
- operator++
- operator*

This is a very simple algorithm. If we examine more complex algorithms, we find that further operations are required to use a pointer as an iterator. Ultimately, an iterator must support all the operations that can be performed on a pointer. These operations are summarized for the iterators x and y and the integer n:

```
x++        x + n       x - y       x > y       *x

++x        x - n       x == y      x <= y      x = y

x--        x += n      x != y      x >= y

--x        x -= n      x < y       x[n]
```

If we can design an iterator that supports the same operations as a pointer, then we will be able to use it just like a pointer, and it will be indistinguishable from one. This is exactly what the designers of the STL have done—created an iterator that generalizes the concept of the pointer by providing the same operations that are provided by pointers. The result is that any STL algorithms that use iterators can use pointers as well.

Because one of the goals of the STL is to be efficient, not all iterators support all operations. Think about how an iterator for a singly linked list would have to be built. Some operations, such as operator++, are easily implemented by simply following the link to the next member of the list. This is a constant time operation and is very efficient. But how would you implement operator--? Since the list has links only in the forward direction, you would have to return to the head of the list and traverse the links until you found the desired element. This is a linear time operation that you might not want to provide. If you provide it, then you offer the users of the list class convenience—but at the same time, you make it easy for them to write very inefficient code. It might be wiser to omit the operations that are inefficient for a particular container, thus encouraging the users of the class to search out another class that supports the operations they require. This will actually encourage the use of a more appropriate and efficient data structure.

The STL designers recognized this problem and provided several different categories of iterators that provide only the operations that can be implemented efficiently. Each of the iterator categories provides a different subset of the operations defined on pointers. Each of the container classes supports one or more iterator types, dependent on the efficiency of the iterator operations for each container. The STL provides these iterator categories:

forward iterators   Iterators that can be moved a single element at a time only in the forward direction.

bidirectional iterators   Iterators that can be moved one element at a time in either the forward or reverse directions.

| random access iterators | Iterators that can be moved either forward or backward and can move by more than a single element at once. |

In addition to these, the STL provides two other iterator classes. It is common for programmers to want to read data from a stream into a container or to write data from a container onto a stream. The designers of the STL noted that if streams could have iterators associated with them, then reading and writing stream data could be handled much more easily with the functions provided by the STL. Of course, the stream iterators cannot have all the operations supported by the other types of iterators. For example, once something is printed on a stream you cannot move backwards and print over it. Similarly, you can dereference an iterator for an input stream to get the value read, but you cannot dereference the iterator for an output stream to find the next value that will be printed. The two additional iterator classes are shown in the following.

| input iterators | Iterators that can be moved one position at a time in the forward direction and allow dereferencing only when used as an r-value (on the right-hand side of an assignment). |

| output iterators | Iterators that can be moved one position at a time in the forward direction and allow dereferencing only when used as an l-value (on the left-hand side of an assignment). |

Input and output iterators are the base classes for the stream iterators: `istream_iterator` and `ostream_iterator`. These iterators can be connected to `cin` and `cout`, respectively, or other input and output streams. This provides a way to have an STL algorithm take its input directly from an input stream or write its output on an output stream.

Virtually all of the STL algorithms use iterators to indicate the range of operands on which they should operate. Similarly, all STL containers provide iterators to allow access to the contained objects. Thus, an understanding of iterators is vital to the effective use of the STL.

1.6 Standard Exceptions

C++ predefines a set of standard exceptions that can be thrown by methods and functions to indicate that something has gone wrong. The standard exceptions are not part of the STL but are thrown by some of the methods and functions in the STL. Thus, it is important to have some understanding of how to interpret these exceptions.

The standard exceptions are defined in the header <stdexcept>, and all are derived from the base class exception. The standard exceptions and their meanings are listed below:

logic_error	Reports errors that can be detected before the program begins execution.
domain_error	Reports errors where the data is of the wrong type.
invalid_argument	Reports invalid arguments to functions and methods.
length_error	Reports an attempt to produce an object that is larger than the maximum size allowed.
out_of_range	Reports an argument that is outside the expected range.
runtime_error	Reports any error that is detectable only at run time.
range_error	Reports range errors that occur in internal computations.
overflow_error	Reports an arithmetic overflow.
underflow_error	Reports an arithmetic underflow.

The exceptions most commonly thrown by the STL are length_error and out_of_range. Most exceptions are thrown by methods and functions dealing with the string class. Good programming practice dictates that exceptions should be caught and handled to avoid unexpected program termination.

1.7 Complexity

The designers of the STL realized the importance of the efficiency of algorithms. They also realized that if the STL were to be widely adopted, the algorithms it offered would have to be as efficient as those programmers could code by hand. The approach they adopted was to select the most efficient algorithm they could find for each operation. Nevertheless, some compromises had to be made to yield a library that was truly generic. Furthermore, there is almost never a single way to solve any problem, so they decided to state the efficiency of each algorithm so that the programmers would have a basis for deciding among

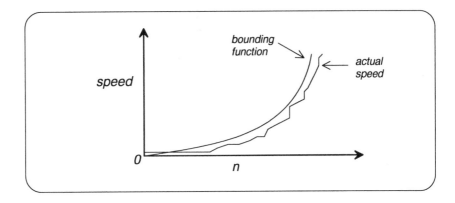

Figure 1.1 — Graph of the Bounding Function for an Algorithm

algorithms. This statement of efficiency is called the complexity of the algorithm. In order for you, the STL user, to make proper use of the library, you must understand the notation used to measure the complexity of an algorithm—big Oh notation.

In the early days of computers programmers had to time their programs against a clock to figure out how fast they were. As machines got increasingly faster over time, this proved to be a meaningless measure since they could halve the speed of a program by doubling the speed of the computer on which it ran. Clearly, what was needed was a measure of the speed of an algorithm that was independent of the speed of the machine on which it was executed.

The first observation computer scientists made was that the speed of most algorithms depends on the amount of data that the algorithm processes. This developed into the idea of finding a function of the number of data items n that approximated the observed speed of the algorithm. After timing algorithms with various amounts of data, scientists found that most algorithms were proportional to some simple functions of n, for nontrivial values of n.

The speed of many algorithms was found to be directly proportional to the amount of data processed by the program and could be expressed as cn, where c is a constant multiplied by the amount of data. Other algorithms were found to be proportional to n^2, and so on. Scientists soon realized that the proportionality constants were not very important since they could double the speed of their computer and eliminate the speed difference introduced by a proportionality

n	$log\ n$	$n\ log\ n$	n^2	n^3
10	3.32	33.22	100	1,000
20	4.32	86.44	400	8,000
30	4.91	147.21	900	27,000
40	5.32	212.88	1,600	64,000
50	5.64	282.19	2,500	125,000
60	5.91	354.41	3,600	216,000
70	6.13	429.05	4,900	343,000
80	6.32	505.75	6,400	512,000
90	6.49	584.27	8,100	729,000
100	6.64	664.39	10,000	1,000,000
500	8.97	4,482.89	250,000	125,000,000
1,000	9.97	9,965.78	1,000,000	1,000,000,000
2,000	10.97	21,931.57	4,000,000	8,000,000,000
3,000	11.55	34,652.24	9,000,000	27,000,000,000
4,000	11.97	47,863.14	16,000,000	64,000,000,000
5,000	12.29	61,438.56	25,000,000	125,000,000,000
10,000	13.29	132,877.12	100,000,000	1,000,000,000,000

Table 1.1 — Values of Common Functions of n

constant of two. Therefore, they started to consider just the order of an algorithm—the function with the proportionality constant removed.

Scientists also observed that the functions were true for nontrivial values of n only. Many algorithms exhibited a different speed for small values of n, usually less than five. Thus, the definition was modified to state that the function had to hold only for values of n greater than some small value. This did not create a

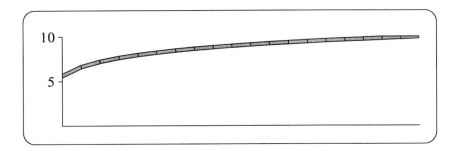

Figure 1.2 — *n* Versus *log n*

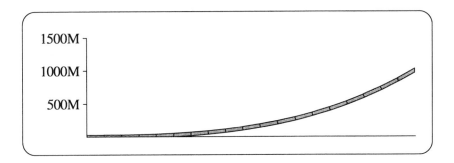

Figure 1.3 — *n* Versus n^3

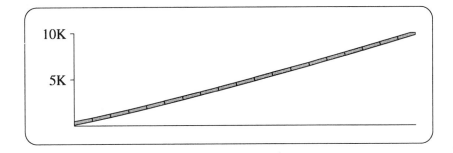

Figure 1.4 — *n* Versus *n log n*

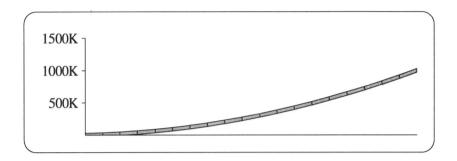

Figure 1.5 — n Versus n^2

problem since most algorithms handled trivial amounts of data so quickly that no one was really concerned about their speed.

It proved far more difficult to find a function to describe the exact speed of some algorithms than others. To simplify the problem, scientsits changed the definition once again to state that the speed could be expressed as a function that formed a minimal upper bound on the actual speed. This means that it is permissible to use a function that is very close to the actual speed—but always greater than it—for nontrivial values of n. This can be seen in the graph of computation time versus n (Figure 1.1).

Experimentally obtained results will not always yield a perfectly smooth curve due to imprecision in timing and a small amount of time taken by periodic activities such as flushing I/O buffers. Notice that the bounding function is indeed greater than or equal to the experimental results for nontrivial values of n. At very low values of n, the two curves may cross, as shown above.

A notation was developed to express this bounding function that is called big Oh notation because it is denoted by an upper case letter O. Thus, an algorithm whose speed was found to be proportional to n would have its speed expressed as $O(n)$, and one proportional to n^2 would be expressed as $O(n^2)$.

Although it is fine to talk about these functions in the abstract, most people need to see some solid figures to truly understand what it all means. Table 1.1 shows values of n and the values of common functions of n.

The values of the logarithmic functions are actually base 2 logarithms. This might seem to be a strange base to use, but it makes a lot of sense when we consider the nature of computer algorithms. The algorithms that exhibit logarithmic

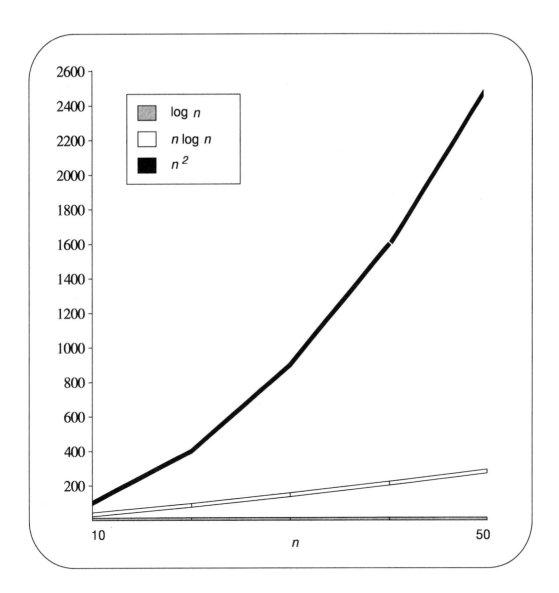

Figure 1.6 — Various Functions of *n*

times typically function by splitting their data in half repeatedly until many small groups of data (often single data units) are obtained. The algorithm then performs calculations on the smaller amounts of data and recombines the smaller results to yield the final result. This is called the divide-and-conquer approach and can be much faster than performing calculations on all the data at once.

To calculate the speed of such algorithms, we are faced with the problem of how many times a value n can be cut in half. Taking a number like 8, we see that it can be divided by 2 once to yield 4, which can be divided to yield 2, which can be divided to yield 1. That is a total of three times that 8 can be divided by 2. This is the same as asking how many times 2 can be multiplied by itself to yield the value n, which is the exact definition of a base 2 logarithm! Although other bases could be used, base 2 gives nice round numbers for the powers of 2 that are commonly encountered in computer science.

The point to notice from Table 1.1 is that as n increases, $\log_2 n$ increases slowly, $n \log_2 n$ increases much faster, n^2 increases faster still, and n^3 goes up astronomically. The raw figures do not tell the whole story, however—it is also useful to examine the shape of the curves to see how the rate of increase changes with increasing values of n. The series of charts in Figures 1.2 to 1.5 show functions of n for the range $50 \ldots 1000$.

Notice the differing shapes of the curves as the value of n changes. In the case of $\log n$, the slope of the curve actually becomes more gentle as the value of n increases. This implies that algorithms whose speed is proportional to a logarithmic function can scale up to higher values of n very well. In fact, the value of $\log n$ is always less than the value of n itself.

All of the other curves are concave upwards indicating that the speed of the algorithm decreases faster and faster as the value of n increases. As the order increases, the curve becomes more pronounced, indicating that the situation is growing worse.

Let's look at one final chart where the functions are shown on the same set of axes (Figure 1.6).

The function n^3 has been omitted since it would make the other functions look like horizontal lines. Note how fast n^2 increases compared to the other functions. This should serve as a demonstration of the amount of time it takes for an n^2 algorithm to execute. Avoid such algorithms whenever possible, particularly when nontrivial amounts of data are involved.

There is one other common speed an algorithm can have—constant. This is for an algorithm that takes the same amount of time regardless of the amount of

Operation	Best Speed
sorting	$O(n \log n)$
searching unsorted data	$O(n)$
searching sorted data	$O(\log n)$
retrieving a value from a binary tree	$O(\log n)$
retrieving a value from a heap	$O(\log n)$
retrieving a value from a hash table (optimal)	$O(1)$

Table 1.2 — Speeds of Common Operations

data being processed. Although such algorithms are rare in practice, constant is often used to indicate the speed of small operations such as multiplying two values together. The notation for an algorithm that takes constant time is $O(1)$.

The notion of complexity can also be applied to the amount of memory an algorithm requires. Many algorithms require no more memory than that needed to store the original data, whereas others require extra storage for intermediate results. Most algorithms will state their memory requirements as constant, meaning that no additional memory is required.

Before you go off to select algorithms based on their performance, you should have some idea of what the best speeds are for some common operations. This is summarized in Table 1.2.

This table demonstrates that if you have to sort some values, there is no excuse for using a sort that offers performance worse than $O(n \log n)$ since the STL provides an easy-to-use function that has that performance. Second, if you have some unsorted values and have to perform multiple searches of them, it might well be worth it to sort them so that the search time will be reduced. If a great number of searches are being performed, then a hash table could be used, although this particular data structure usually needs to be tuned to the particular problem to offer its best performance.

Algorithmic complexity is not that difficult to comprehend, although it is sometimes very difficult to calculate. Paying attention to the complexity of the algorithms you use and how they are combined in your program will result in programs that execute in a fraction of the time required by those where the algorithms are selected in a haphazard fashion.

1.7.1 Analyzing Complexity

Probably the simplest way to measure the complexity of an algorithm is to implement it and then time it with various amounts of data. The problem with this approach is that you have to actually code the algorithm before you can determine its complexity. This is not a lot of trouble for a small algorithm, but it becomes impractical with larger programs.

Another approach is to examine the algorithm and calculate how many times each of the statements, or groups of statements, are executed. To do this we need some simple rules:

- Any statement that is independent of the amount of data executes in constant time and is said to be $O(1)$.

- The complexity of the code in an `if-then-else` statement is the greater of the complexities of the two branches.

- Statements in a loop are executed the maximum number of times permitted by the loop.

When we look at an algorithm, we find that different parts of it have different complexities. To find the overall complexity of the algorithm, these individual complexities will have to be combined. The following rules can be used to combine complexities to find the total complexity of an algorithm:

- If an algorithm is of complexity $O(f(n))$, and $f(n)$ is known to be $O(g(n))$, then the complexity of the algorithm is $O(g(n))$.

- If the speed of an algorithm is $cf(n)$, where c is a proportionality constant, then the constant can be ignored and the algorithm has complexity $O(f(n))$.

- If one part of an algorithm is of complexity $O(f(n))$ and is followed sequentially by another part of the algorithm of complexity $O(g(n))$, then the overall complexity of the two parts is $O(\max(f(n), g(n)))$, which is the larger of the two complexities.

- If one part of an algorithm of complexity $O(f(n))$ surrounds another part of the algorithm that has complexity $O(g(n))$, then their combined complexity is $O(f(n) \times g(n))$.

We see how to apply these rules by examining the following simple algorithm:

```
int SumProd(int n)
{
    int result, k, i;

    result = 0; O(1)                    a          n*O(n) =
    for(k=1; k<=n; k++) {                          O(n²)
        for(i=1; i<=k; i++) {
            result += k*i;      O(1)  n*O(1) = O(n)
        }                                   d
    }                                              b
    return(result); O(1)  c
}
```

Boxes have been drawn around the different portions of the code to break it into logical sections. The top box (a) initializes the value of `result` to zero and is independent of the value of `n`; so is $O(1)$. The same is true of the bottom box (c) which returns the result. The center box (d) contains the multiplication, which is also of $O(1)$. It is, however, in a loop that goes from 1 to `k`. This loop is executed a maximum of `n` times since that is the largest value that `k` can be assigned by the outer loop, and we always assume that a loop is executed the maximum number of times. This means that the inner loop has a complexity of $O(n)$ and the combined complexity of the algorithm in box d is $O(n) \times O(1) = O(n)$ since the inner loop contains the multiplication and we multiply complexities when one is contained in another. The same logic is applied to calculate the complexity of box b as $O(n) \times O(n) = O(n^2)$. Finally, three sequential algorithms are combined by finding the maximum of their individual complexities, $\max(O(1), O(n^2), O(1)) = O(n^2)$, the complexity of the complete algorithm.

The complexity of each of the STL algorithms is clearly stated so that you can use the outlined techniques to calculate the overall complexity of your program. Proper use of this technique will let you select the most efficient STL algorithms and combine them in the most efficient manner.

1.8 Thread Safety

A container is said to be thread-safe if two threads accessing the same container with write access cannot corrupt the container or its contents. This is difficult to ensure since one thread could be appending data to a container and be interrupted, and another thread accessing the same container could be dispatched. Suppose the first thread had written the data but not incremented the container size when it was interrupted. The second thread would try to remove a value from the container and would have an incorrect size. The problem is that the first thread was interrupted before it could complete, leaving the container in an inconsistent state.

The solution to this problem is to make all of the operations on a container atomic. This means that the thread performing an operation on a container cannot be interrupted until the operation is complete. This guarantees that when any thread starts to perform an operation on a container, the container will be in a consistent state.

Most operating systems provide some type of thread synchronization primitives. Often, these take the form of a mutex, or some way to guarantee an area of mutual exclusion so that only a single thread can be executing the code within the area of mutual exclusion. The synchronization primitives vary from one implementation to another, but they usually provide similar capabilities.

C++ was designed for performance. Since the locking required to implement mutual exclusion can be expensive, its use conflicts with the design goals of the language. Further, C++ does not define thread synchronization primitives within the language, so there are no thread operations that could be used that would be portable. The standard does not mandate that the STL containers be thread-safe, leaving this to the library implementor.

Most of the STL implementations define thread-safety as not using nonconstant static data in the containers and not using global data. The Hewlett-Packard (HP) implementation doesn't meet these criteria since both the list and deque share common storage among instances. The Silicon Graphics Inc. (SGI) implementation claims that there is no nonstatic data shared among instances of their containers. SGI further claims that its allocators are thread-safe so that the allocator itself will not cause a problem with threads. Other commercial implementations also claim thread-safety [IG98, RI99].

These thread-safe libraries are ready to be used in conjunction with threads, but they require that thread synchronization primitives be used. The simplest approach to using threads safely is to derive a thread-safe class from an existing thread-safe STL container. This is done by placing the operations that access the container in areas of mutual exclusion. No other operation will be able to start until the operation accessing the container completes, ensuring mutual exclusion.

One further point is that for some higher-level operations on containers, the use of thread-safe container methods will not be sufficient to ensure atomicity. As an example, consider the case of finding a reference to an object in a container and using the reference to modify the object. There must be no interruption between these two operations. Otherwise, there is the possibility that the reference could be invalidated by an operation performed by another thread.

Operations such as this must lock out other operations on the container until they complete.

If you are not sure whether the STL implementation you are using is thread-safe, check the vendor's documentation to see if the implementation is free of nonconstant shared data and global data. You should also check the allocator to ensure that it is thread-safe.

1.9 Namespaces

The C++ standard mandates that all STL data structures and algorithms be placed in the namespace `std`. This means that, in addition to including the appropriate header file, you must qualify the names of STL components or employ the `using` statement to merge all components in the `std` namespace into the global namespace. Further, the relational operator templates (eg, `operator>`) are in the namespace `rel_ops` within the namespace `std`.

1.10 Overview of This Book

A book of this type must serve many different readers. Some of you will be computing professionals with experience in both C++ and template libraries. Others of you will have only recently learned the basics of C++ and will be looking for a library to help you write your first programs. This book assumes that all readers have a good grasp of C++, and the only effort to review the language is a few pages on templates.

Examine your own skill level to determine if there are parts of the book you can skip because they are too easy. Then try to identify what you are looking to get out of the book—a high-level overview of the STL, how to use the containers, how to use the algorithms, or even how to extend the STL. Table 1.3 provides a rough outline of what each chapter covers and guides you to determine which you should read.

Chapter	Content	Type of Reader			
		Novice	Experienced: new to STL	Experienced: knows some STL	Manager
1	• overview of STL • generic algorithms • overview of iterators • exceptions • complexity	✓	✓		✓
2	• iterators • similarity to pointers • iterator classes and operations • stream iterators • iterator functions	✓	✓	✓	✈
3	• operators • function objects • overview of the STL algorithms	✓	✈		✓
4	• nonmutating sequence algorithms • mutating sequence algorithms	✓	✓	✈	
5	• sorting algorithms • searching algorithms • set algorithms • heap algorithms • miscellaneous algorithms	✓	✓	✈	
6	• numeric algorithms • valarray	✓	✓	✈	
7	• vectors • lists • deques • strings	✓	✓	✈	✈
8	• sets • multisets • maps • multimaps	✓	✓	✈	✈
9	• overview of adaptors • stacks • queues • priority queues • reverse iterators • insert iterators • function adaptors	✓	✓	✓	✈
10	• allocators		✈	✓	
11	• writing iterators • writing generic functions • writing containers			✓	
12	• summary • future directions	✈	✈	✓	✓

Chapter	Content	Type of Reader			
		Novice	Experienced: new to STL	Experienced: knows some STL	Manager
A	· header files	📖	📖	📖	
B	· STL reference	📖	📖	📖	

Legend:

✍   should be read in depth

✈   *fly through* or skim the topic

📖   for reference only

Table 1.3 — How to Read This Book

2
Iterators

2.1 Introduction

Virtually all of the STL algorithms and data structures make extensive use of iterators. Therefore, the programmer must have a good understanding of what an iterator is and how it works. Fortunately, since iterators are a generalization of pointers, they share many of the properties of pointers, making them relatively easy to master for the average C programmer.

This chapter begins by using pointers as iterators, showing how they can be used in a variety of STL algorithms, and noting the properties that pointers possess. It then goes on to introduce the different types of STL iterators and to illustrate their use on simple container classes.

I recommend that you read this chapter before continuing on to further chapters if you have no previous experience with the STL.

2.2 Pointers as Iterators

A container is a data structure that contains zero or more instances of other objects. Usually, these objects are all the same type of object. For example, a basket is a container that can contain many different types of objects. Although you could fill the basket with a mixture of apples and peaches, it is simpler to get two baskets and fill one with apples and the other with peaches. Most of the time, this is more convenient than mixing the two fruits in a single basket.

The container makes it much easier to move the fruit around than if you were simply carrying it in your hands. You have a problem, however, when you want to do something with the individual fruits in the basket. Suppose you want to examine each of the apples for worms. You have to reach into the basket, pick up an apple, examine it, and put it back. Now, when you reach for the second apple to check it for worms, you cannot tell which one you already checked. All the apples look alike and the more you check, the worse the problem becomes. You could use another basket to hold the apples you have checked, but baskets cost money and that technique would increase the number of baskets you need. What you really need is an automated tool that will reach into the basket for you, retrieve an apple, hand it to you, then put it back when you are done. This tool would go through the apples in an organized fashion so that each apple was handed to you exactly once. In the world of the fruit picker, no such tool exists; in the world of computer programming, we have such a tool and it is called an iterator.

Computer programmers use containers for much the same reason as do fruit pickers—convenience. It is much easier to move a single object around and keep track of it than to handle many smaller objects. Programmers, like fruit pickers, want to access the contents of a container one at a time without duplication. For this reason, the concept of the iterator evolved.

The simplest type of container is the array. Programmers use arrays to hold many different types of objects including predefined types such as integers, characters, and floating point values as well as user-defined structures and even other arrays. One common use of the array is to contain the characters that constitute a string. Such a string can be declared and initialized:

```
char message[32];
strcpy(message, "Hello World");
```

This creates the string and assigns a value to it using the library function strcpy(). For purposes of illustration, let's assume that we want to find the number of characters in the string but prefer not to use the library function strlen() and we wish to write our own. The code for the new function is shown in Listing 2.1:

```
int mystrlen(char* str)
{
    int len = 0;

    while((*str++) != '\0') len++;
    return(len);
}
```

Listing 2.1 — mystrlen() Using a Pointer as an Iterator

Although this is a very simple function, it requires the use of an iterator. The iterator is the pointer to the string itself, `str`. This pointer has the same properties as our magic fruit iterator—it can retrieve every value in the container exactly once. Each time the `while` test is executed, `str` is dereferenced using `operator*` to obtain the character stored in that position of the array. Then, the value of `str` is incremented to move it to the next character in the string. This illustrates two of the operations that every iterator must possess—dereferencing and moving to the next object in the container.

If we try to write a function to reverse the order of the characters in a string, we find that other operations are needed for the iterator, as shown in Listing 2.2:

```
void reverse(char* str)
{
    char*    endPt;
    int      len;
    char     temp;

    len = mystrlen(str);
    if(len < 2) return;
    endPt = str + len - 1;
    while(str < endPt) {
        temp = *str;
        *str = *endPt;
        *endPt = temp;
        str++;
        endPt--;
    }
}
```

Listing 2.2 — Reversing the Order of a String

The `reverse` function requires several new operations. The initial calculation of the `endPt` requires that integer arithmetic be performed on an iterator. The goal of this operation is to advance the iterator to the last character in the string. For a character pointer, this is simple integer addition and subtraction. For pointers to types longer than a single byte, it will require a multiplication of the number to be added by the size of the type in the array. Thus, we see that when the position of an iterator is adjusted, the actual operation that is performed depends on the type that is being iterated. When we examine the iterators provided by the STL, we will see that the operation for advancing an iterator depends on the nature of the container as well.

The second new operation is operator<, performed during the while test. This compares two iterators to determine if one is less than the other. What does it mean for one iterator to be less than another? An iterator is guaranteed to visit each member of the container exactly once in a defined order. Therefore, if one iterator is less than another, it must mean that it references an element in the container that would be visited first in the normal iteration of the container.

The function also uses the dereferencing operator on the left side of an assignment. This means that the dereferencing operator must be able to both retrieve a value from the container and to store a new value into the container.

The last of the new operations is operator--, used for moving the end pointer backward. This implies a bidirectionality for the iterator. Not only can it move in the forward direction, but it can also move in the reverse direction.

From this, we can deduce that a general-purpose iterator must support the following operations:

- operator++ and operator--
- operator* as both an l-value and an r-value
- operator<, operator<=, operator>, operator>=, operator==, and operator!=
- operator+(int), operator-(int)
- operator=

Any class that supports these operations and the proper semantics can be used as an iterator. This is the basis for the iterators provided by the STL. We will not examine this idea any further at the moment, but we will return to it in our discussion of the STL iterators.

Now, let's take a look at how we can use pointers as iterators in conjunction with the STL algorithms. As an example, we write a function to find the first occurrence of a character within a string, as shown in Listing 2.3. This function will make use of the find() function provided in the STL.

```
char* MyFind(char* str, char value)
{
    char    *endPt, *result;
    int     len;

    len = mystrlen(str);
    endPt = str + len;
    result = find(str, endPt, value);
```

```
    if(result == endPt) return(NULL);
    else return(result);
}
```

Listing 2.3 — Using the STL Function <code>find()</code>

The `find()` function takes three parameters. The first two parameters are iterators that delimit the range to be searched. The first parameter references the first character to be searched, and the second parameter references the location immediately after the last character to be searched. This might seem like a strange way to indicate where the string ends, but it is the standard way of indicating ranges in the STL. Whenever an STL algorithm takes two iterators indicating a range, the first iterator will refer to the start of the range, and the second will refer to the position immediately after the end of the range. The third parameter to `find()` is the value for which it is to search.

The `find()` function returns an iterator, in this case a pointer, referencing the first occurrence of `value` in the indicated range. If the value does not occur in the range, the function returns an iterator equal to the second parameter, the past-the-end iterator for the range.

I decided that `MyFind()` would return a pointer to the `value`, if found, or NULL, if it is not present. Notice how the iterator that is returned from `find()` is compared with `endPt` to determine whether NULL should be returned.

It is also interesting to examine the calculation of `endPt`. The length of the string is added to the address of the first character, yielding the location of the string terminator one past the last character in the string. This satisfies the requirements of a past-the-end iterator for the string.

We could also sort the characters in the string by using the `sort` function from the STL. The sort function takes two parameters indicating the range of elements to be sorted. As in all STL algorithms, the first iterator refers to the first value in the range, and the second iterator refers to the location one past the end of the range. The code in Listing 2.4 demonstrates how we could sort a string:

```
char     text[32];
char*    endPt;
int      len;

strcpy(text, "abbracadabra");
```

```
len = mystrlen(text);
endPt = text + len;
sort(text, endPt);
cout << text;
```

Listing 2.4 — Using the STL Function `sort()`

The use of iterators in the `sort()` function is identical to their use in the `find()` function. In fact, all of the STL algorithms use iterators in the same way, making the library consistent and easier to learn. The `sort()` function produces an ascending sequence by default. How to get it to sort in other orders will be examined later.

Have you started to wonder what the STL functions do with the iterators passed to them? The answer is pretty much what you would expect. They perform the same operations on the iterators that we did in our functions `mystrlen()` and `reverse()`. They compare iterators, increment and decrement them, and dereference them. As long as the iterators implement these operations correctly, then the functions will be able to use the iterators and obtain correct results.

The fact that pointers satisfy all the requirements of iterators is what permits them to be used as iterators. Thus, all of the STL algorithms can be applied to arrays just as easily as the STL container classes. This extends the utility of the functions so that the same functions can be used on virtually any data structure in a program. As a result, less code has to be written, resulting is shorter development time and smaller executable programs. Once you get used to this, the idea of one sort function for arrays and another for linked lists seems like a foolish notion.

2.3 Iterator Classes

In the last section, we saw the properties that a general-purpose iterator should possess. This is the ideal type of iterator; however, not all data structures lend themselves to the efficient implementation of such iterators. Some data structures render nonsequential iterators impractical due to the lack of efficiency they would have.

To get an idea of the problem, let's take a look at how we might implement an iterator for a doubly linked list. First, we must design a doubly linked list class, as shown in Listing 2.5:

```
template <class T>
class DoubleListNode {
public:
    friend class DoubleList<T>;
    friend class DblListIterator<T>;
    DoubleListNode()
    {
        next = NULL;
        prev = NULL;
    }
private:
    T               data;
    DoubleListNode *next, *prev;
};

template <class T>
class DoubleList {
public:
    DoubleList();
    ~DoubleList();
    void insert(DblListIterator<T>& iter, T& value);
    void clear();
    void remove(DblListIterator<T>& it);
    DblListIterator<T> begin();
    DblListIterator<T> end();
private:
    DoubleListNode<T>*   head; // internal head pointer
    DoubleListNode<T>*   tail; // past-the-end node

    void _remove(DoubleListNode<T> *p);
};
```

Listing 2.5 — A Doubly Linked List Class

The list will consist of a series of DoubleListNodes chained together by pointers. Each node will contain an instance of the type T that is being stored in the list. The list will use an internal head pointer for ease of implementing the insert() and remove() operations. The iterator requires that one position past the end of the list exist, necessitating the addition of one more unused list node at the end of the list. This means that an empty list will contain two nodes—the internal head pointer and the past-the-end node. Thus, the constructor for the list would appear as in Listing 2.6:

```
template <class T>
DoubleList<T>::DoubleList()
{
    head = new DoubleListNode<T>();
    head->next = new DoubleListNode<T>();
    tail = head->next;
    tail->prev = head;
}
```

Listing 2.6 — The Constructor for a Doubly Linked List

The methods begin() and end() return iterators that reference the first member of the list and the past-the-end node, respectively. If the list is empty, begin() will return an iterator equal to that returned by end() so that an empty range is indicated. The code for these methods is shown in Listing 2.7:

```
template <class T>
DblListIterator<T> DoubleList<T>::begin()
{
    return(DblListIterator<T>(head->next));
}

template <class T>
DblListIterator<T> DoubleList<T>::end()
{
    return(DblListIterator<T>(tail));
}
```

Listing 2.7 — begin() and end() for a Doubly Linked List

The iterator must provide a constructor that can initialize an iterator given a pointer to a node in the list. It must also offer the operations expected of an iterator. The first cut at writing the iterator is shown in Listing 2.8:

```
template <class T>
class DblListIterator {
public:
    friend class DoubleList<T>;
    DblListIterator()
    {
        nodePtr = (DoubleListNode<T>*)0;
    }
    DblListIterator(DoubleListNode<T>* node);
    DblListIterator operator++(int);
    friend bool operator==(
        const DblListIterator<T>& iter1,
        const DblListIterator<T>& iter2);
    friend bool operator!=(
        const DblListIterator<T>& iter1,
        const DblListIterator<T>& iter2);
    friend bool operator<(
        const DblListIterator<T>& iter1,
        const DblListIterator<T>& iter2);
    T& operator*();
private:
    DoubleListNode<T>*    nodePtr;
};

template <class T>
DblListIterator<T>::DblListIterator(
    DoubleListNode<T>* node)
{
    nodePtr = node;
}

template <class T>
DblListIterator<T> DblListIterator<T>::operator++(int)
{
    DblListIterator<T> temp;
    temp = *this;
    nodePtr = nodePtr->next;
    return(temp);
}
```

Listing 2.8 — An Iterator for a Doubly Linked List

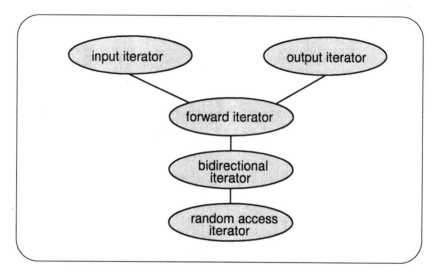

Figure 2.1 — The Iterator Hierarchy

The list iterator simply maintains a pointer to a node in the list. When we want to increment it, it follows the pointer to the next member of the list. There is no rocket science here.

The interesting question is what happens when we try to implement `opera-tor[]` to allow direct access to list nodes. The postincrement followed the pointer to the next list node, so positive subscripts could simply follow the pointer chain the required number of times. Negative subscripts require that the pointers to the previous nodes be followed. In both cases, the sequential nature of the data structure requires that subscripting must be a linear time operation.

Lists, by their nature, provide only sequential access in constant time. Do we really want to provide expensive linear-time iterators on a data structure that does not lend itself to their support? This was the question that faced the STL designers, and their answer was no. The solution they adopted was to break the iterators into a series of categories where each category offered a different set of operations. Each data structure would then support the iterator categories that it could with reasonable efficiency.

The iterators are grouped into these categories:

- input iterators

- output iterators

- forward iterators

- bidirectional iterators

- random access iterators

The iterators form a hierarchy in which iterators lower in the hierarchy have all the operations of iterators higher in the hierarchy plus additional operations. This hierarchy is depicted in Figure 2.1.

Iterators can also be constant or mutable, depending on whether dereferencing the iterator returns a constant reference or a nonconstant reference.

Not all iterators can be dereferenced. Those which can be dereferenced are termed dereferencable. It is assumed that a past-the-end iterator is never dereferencable.

An iterator is said to have a singular value if it does not reference any container. An example of this is a pointer which is declared but does not have a value assigned to it. The result of most expressions involving singular values is undefined.

An iterator j is said to be reachable from an iterator i if a finite number of applications of operator++ to i will result in j. This implies that i must be less than j and that they must both reference the same container. The notation [i, j) denotes a range of iterators beginning with i and ending with the iterator immediately before j. An iterator range [i, j) is valid only if j is reachable from i. An empty range is represented as [i, i).

2.3.1 Input Iterators

Input iterators can move only in the forward direction and can be used only to retrieve values, not to output values. Input iterators a and b of type II, referencing a type with a member m, provide these operations:

- II b(a)
- b = a
- a++
- ++a
- *a   (as an r-value only)
- a->m (as an r-value only)
- *a++
- a == b
- a != b

The expression II b(a) is a copy constructor that makes iterator b a copy of iterator a.

Input iterators have the property that if there are input iterators a and b, and a == b, then this does not imply that ++a == ++b. This is because the main purpose of input iterators is to be used as base classes for stream iterators. Stream iterators allow streams such as cin and cout to be manipulated by iterators. This is convenient for many algorithms, yet is subject to the restrictions imposed by streams.

Suppose you have two identical iterators referencing an input stream. When such an iterator is incremented, it reads a new value from the stream and stores this value within the instance of the iterator class. If two equal iterators for the same stream are each incremented, they might well read different values from the stream and become unequal, or one might reach the end of the stream. Thus, you cannot depend on two equal input iterators to remain equal after being incremented.

This limits the utility of input iterators to single pass algorithms—those that process their data in a single sequential pass. There is no operator-- since you cannot unread a value from an input stream. This ignores input stream implementations that allow a single character to be unread, since this operation can only be applied once.

2.3.2 Output Iterators

Output iterators, like input iterators, can move only in the forward direction but differ in that they can be dereferenced only to assign a value, not to retrieve a value. Output iterators a and b of class OI support the operations:

- OI b(a)
- OI b = a
- ++a
- a++
- *a   (as an l-value only)
- *a++ (as an l-value only)

Like input iterators, output iterators are provided as a base class for output stream iterators. Although you can dereference an output iterator to assign a value to it, you cannot dereference it to retrieve a value from it. This is because you cannot retrieve values from an output stream.

2.3.3 Forward Iterators

The forward iterators are designed to traverse containers to which values can be written and from which values can be retrieved. The forward iterator relaxes some of the restrictions of the input and output iterators but retains the restriction that it can only move in the forward direction. Forward iterators a and b of class FI referencing a type with a member m support these operations:

- `FI a`
- `FI b(a)`
- `FI b = a`
- `a++`
- `++a`
- `*a`

- `a->m`
- `*a++`
- `a = b`
- `a == b`
- `a != b`

Forward iterators can be dereferenced to assign a value to the referenced object or to retrieve its value. One iterator can be assigned the value of another, meaning that they refer to the same object. Iterators can also be compared for equality and inequality.

2.3.4 Bidirectional Iterators

Bidirectional iterators remove the restriction of the forward iterators that movement is possible only in the forward direction. Bidirectional iterators a and b of type BI support these operations:

- `BI a`
- `BI b(a)`
- `BI b = a`
- `a++`
- `++a`
- `*a`
- `a->m`

- `*a++`
- `a = b`
- `a == b`
- `a != b`
- `--a`
- `a--`
- `*a--`

These are the same operations supported by forward iterators, plus the decrement operators that allow the iterator to move backward as well as forward. All other properties of forward and bidirectional iterators are the same.

2.3.5 Random Access Iterators

The random access iterators remove the restriction that the iterator can be moved only to the next or previous element in the container in a single operation. Random access iterators a and b of class `RI`, plus the integer n, support these operations:

• `RI a`	• `a == b`	• `a - n`
• `RI b(a)`	• `a != b`	• `a - b`
• `RI b = a`	• `--a`	• `a[n]`
• `a++`	• `a--`	• `a != b`
• `++a`	• `*a--`	• `a < b`
• `*a`	• `a += n`	• `a > b`
• `a->m`	• `a + n`	• `a <= b`
• `*a++`	• `n + a`	• `a >= b`
• `a = b`	• `a -= n`	

This is the same set of operations supported by bidirectional iterators, plus operations that allow the iterators to be moved in a nonsequential manner. A random access iterator can be incremented or decremented by an integer value n, and this is equivalent to incrementing or decrementing the iterator by one n times. A subscript operator is defined that returns the object referenced by the iterator n positions ahead of the iterator a. This works identically to a pointer to an array when it is subscripted. The comparison operations are extended to support the relational operations.

2.4 Using Iterators

You can use iterators just like pointers to arrays with the added benefit that you can use them on all the containers defined by the STL. Virtually all of the STL algorithms employ iterators to delimit the members of a container on which they should operate. This section demonstrates the use of various iterator types in the STL algorithms and containers.

2.4.1 Stream Iterators

Stream iterators are derived from input iterators and output iterators, and they allow you to handle a stream in the same manner as any other container—using iterators. This greatly simplifies the use of streams with the STL algorithms. The restrictions on the set of available operations for input and output iterators reflect the restrictions on the streams with which they are associated.

There are two types of stream iterators—istream_iterator and ostream_iterator. These are associated with input streams and output streams, respectively. When constructed, they can be associated with any open input or output stream.

To use an iterator to read from a stream, you construct the iterator and dereference it to retrieve the first value. After that, each time the iterator is incremented with operator++, a new value is read from the stream and is stored in the iterator. This value can be retrieved by dereferencing the iterator. When the end of the stream is reached, the iterator assumes the special end-of-stream value. This end-of-stream value can be created by constructing an iterator that is not associated with any stream.

The code in Listing 2.9 shows a simple read-and-print loop that uses stream iterators to handle the input and output rather than using the streams directly:

```
#include <iterator>
#include <iostream>

using namespace std;

template <class InputIterator, class OutputIterator>
void CopyToEnd(
            InputIterator   start,
            InputIterator   end,
            OutputIterator  out)
{
    while(start != end)
    {
        *out++ = *start++;
    }
```

```
}

main()
{

    istream_iterator<int, char>    int_in(cin);
    ostream_iterator<int>          int_out(cout," ");

    CopyToEnd(int_in,
        istream_iterator<int, char>(), int_out);
    cout << endl << "EOF" << endl;
    return(0);
}
```

Listing 2.9 — Using Stream Iterators

The function CopyToEnd() is where all the action takes place. It is passed an iterator indicating the start of the stream, an iterator that is one past the end of the stream, and an iterator referring to the stream on which the output should be placed. The body of the function contains a loop that dereferences the input iterator to obtain a value and then assigns this to the dereferenced output iterator. Both iterators are then incremented, causing the current value to be printed on the output stream and a new value to be read from the input stream. The loop terminates when the input iterator becomes equal to the past-the-end iterator.

The function main() contains the declarations of the stream iterators and the call to CopyToEnd(). The templates for the stream iterators require that they be parameterized with the type of value to be input and the representation used in the input stream. In this case, the stream will take in ints, which are represented as chars in the input stream. This implies that a stream can contain only a single type of value. A stream can contain all integers, all strings, or all floating point values, but not a mixture.

The constructor for the input stream accepts a single parameter: a reference to the stream it should handle. The constructor for the output stream takes a reference to an output stream as well as a string that will be printed on the stream between every pair of values. In this case, a single space is provided that will appear as a separator between every pair of integers on the output stream.

The call to CopyToEnd() must provide an iterator that is one past the end of the input stream. This value is obtained by constructing an istream_iterator with the same template parameters as the input stream iterator but no parameters for the constructor. This produces a special iterator object that is recognized as one position past the end of the stream.

Using stream iterators in a manual fashion like this does not take advantage of their true power. Stream iterators were designed to be used in conjunction with the STL functions that expect iterators as parameters. When used in this manner, they can replace any iterator referencing a data structure stored in computer memory. Let's examine how we could use them in some common STL functions.

The STL function `accumulate()` accepts two iterators delimiting a range of elements and an initial value. It sums the elements in the range, adds the initial value, and returns the result. Getting the function to sum a series of values read from `cin` is easily accomplished, as shown in Listing 2.10, where the input is in the white box and the output is in the shaded box:

```
#include <iterator>
#include <iostream>
#include <numeric>

using namespace std;

void main()
{
    istream_iterator<int, char>    int_in(cin);
    int                            sum;

    sum = accumulate(int_in,
        istream_iterator<int, char>(), 0);
    cout << endl << "sum=" << sum << endl;
}
```

```
1 2 3
```

```
sum=6
```

Listing 2.10 — Using the STL Function `accumulate()`

The call to `accumulate()` is similar to the call to `CopyToEnd()` in the previous example. An `istream_iterator`, associated with `cin`, is constructed and passed as a reference to the first value in the sequence to be summed. The final iterator is the usual past-the-end iterator constructed by invoking the parameterless constructor. The last parameter is the initial value that will be added to the sum of the elements in the sequence.

One of the common uses of an `ostream_iterator` is to simplify the printing of a sequence. Listing 2.11 shows how the `copy()` function can be used to print out the contents of an array:

```
ostream_iterator<char*> str_out(cout,"\n");
char*           text[3] = {"hello", "and" , "goodbye"};

copy(text, text+3, str_out);
```

```
hello
and
goodbye
```

Listing 2.11 — Using the `copy()` Function with a Stream Iterator

The `copy()` function copies all of the values delimited by the first two iterators to the location referenced by the third iterator. This prints the three words (`hello`, `and`, `goodbye`) on three separate lines, since the iterator constructor tells it to print a newline character between each value. Any type of forward iterator could be used in place of the string pointer so that the same technique can be used with any type of data structure.

2.4.2 Forward Iterators

Forward iterators are used to traverse a sequence in the forward direction one element at a time. They differ from the stream iterators in that the dereference operator can be used both to set and retrieve values. As with the stream iterators, they are best suited to algorithms that make a single pass through the data. The example in Listing 2.12 shows how to use a forward iterator to increment all the values in a sequence by ten.

The use of the forward iterator is in the function `Add10()`, which compares the forward iterators for inequality and dereferences one of the iterators to both retrieve and set the value. The function `main()` calls `Add10()`, using integer pointers as forward iterators. Finally, the copy() function is passed two forward iterators, which delimit the range to be printed.

```cpp
#include <algorithm>
#include <iostream>
#include <iterator>

using namespace std;

template <class ForwardIterator>
void Add10(ForwardIterator first,
           ForwardIterator   last)
{
   while(first != last) {
      *first = *first + 10;
      first++;
   }
}

main()
{
   int                    i, data[10];
   ostream_iterator<int>  outStream(cout, " ");

   for(i=0;i<10;i++) data[i] = i;
   Add10(data, data+10);
   copy(data, data+10, outStream);
   cout << "\n";
   return(0);
}
```

```
10 11 12 13 14 15 16 17 18 19
```

Listing 2.12 — Using a Forward Iterator to Traverse a Container

Finding the beginning and end of an array is relatively easy. The job is not so easy for the STL containers, so the methods begin() and end() are provided to locate the first member of the container and the past-the-end position. These methods return iterators that can be used to traverse all the objects stored in the container. Listing 2.13 demonstrates the use of these methods on a list. The list is an STL container that implements a doubly linked list.

```
#include <list>
#include <iterator>
#include <algorithm>
#include <iostream>

using namespace std;

main()
{
    list<int>               list1;
    list<int>::iterator     list_iter;
    int                     i;
    ostream_iterator<int>   out_stream(cout, " ");

    for(i=0;i<10;i++) {
        list1.push_back(i);
    }

    copy(list1.begin(),list1.end(),out_stream);
    cout << endl;

    list_iter = list1.begin();
    while(list_iter != list1.end())
    {
        cout << *list_iter++ << ' ';
    }
    cout << endl;

    return(0);
}
```

```
0 1 2 3 4 5 6 7 8 9
0 1 2 3 4 5 6 7 8 9
```

Listing 2.13 — Using begin() and end() on a list

The program begins by declaring a list of integers and an iterator for a list of integers. Note that the template parameter for the list and its iterator must match—you cannot use a float iterator to reference a list of integers. It also declares an output stream iterator for the printing of integers. The for loop initializes the list to contain the integers from 0 to 9, in order, by adding each of the values to the tail of the list. The copy() function prints out the entire array with the methods begin() and end() used to delimit the values stored in the list. It would be impossible to find iterators referencing the beginning and end of the list without the aid of these methods.

The rest of the program uses a `while` loop to retrieve the values from the list one at a time and print them. An iterator is used for this purpose and is initialized to reference the first member of the list. Each time the loop executes, it dereferences the iterator to retrieve the value it references, prints the value, and then increments the iterator so that it will move to the next member of the list. The loop terminates when the iterator becomes equal to the past-the-end iterator.

Some STL algorithms and data structures use iterators to indicate a specific member of a container. One use of such an iterator is to allow insertion into a list before a specific member of the list. The `insert()` method of the `list` class performs this operation and requires an iterator indicating the element to insert before and the value to insert, as shown in Listing 2.14:

```
list_iter = list1.begin();
list_iter++;
list1.insert(list_iter, 100);
copy(list1.begin(),list1.end(), out_stream);
cout << endl;
```

```
0 100 1 2 3 4 5 6 7 8 9
```

Listing 2.14 — Using `insert()` on a `list`

This code obtains an iterator referencing the start of the list and then increments it until it references the element before which the value should be inserted. Since this is a forward iterator, it must be advanced one position at a time until the desired element is reached.

2.4.3 Bidirectional Iterators

A bidirectional iterator has all the properties of a forward iterator plus the ability to move the iterator backward by decrementing it. This is very useful for algorithms that require multiple passes through their data or that process the data in reverse order.

There are actually two types of bidirectional iterators: a bidirectional iterator and a reverse bidirectional iterator, the latter of which is created by applying an adaptor to a bidirectional iterator. (Adaptors are explained later.) Although they both have the capability to be moved in either direction, a bidirectional iterator is used to process the data in the forward direction from begin() to end(). A reverse bidirectional iterator is used to process the data in the reverse direction from rbegin() to rend(). The difference is how the iterators are initialized and how they determine when they are at the end of the sequence of elements stored in the container.

If you want to process the data in the forward direction, the iterator must be initialized to reference the first element in the container and terminate when it reaches the past-the-end iterator. The required values are returned by the methods begin() and end(). Processing the data in the reverse direction requires the iterator to be initialized to the last element in the container and to have a past-the-end iterator that references the element just before the first element in the sequence. These values are returned by the methods rbegin() and rend(), respectively. Accidentally initializing a bidirectional iterator with rbegin() could cause confusion and provides no way for the compiler to check that the corresponding past-the-end iterator is rbegin(). To increase the security of the iterators, the two iterator types are provided, and the initialization methods return appropriate iterator types. Thus, begin() and end() return bidirectional_iterators, and rbegin() and rend() return reverse_iterators.

Let us look at an example of how this works in practice. The list provides two iterators—iterator and reverse_iterator. Although you were led to believe that iterator was a forward iterator, both iterator and reverse_iterator are really bidirectional iterators. First we make the declarations and initialize the list, as shown in Listing 2.15:

```
#include <algorithm>
#include <list>
#include <iostream>

using namespace std;

void main()
{
    list<int>                     list1;
    list<int>::iterator           list_iter;
    int                           i;
    list<int>::reverse_iterator   rev_iter;
    ostream_iterator<int>         out_stream(
                                      cout, " ");
```

```
for(i=0;i<10;i++)
{
    list1.push_back(i);
}
copy(list1.begin(),list1.end(),out_stream);
cout << endl;
}
```

```
0 1 2 3 4 5 6 7 8 9
```

Listing 2.15 — Using a Forward Iterator to Traverse a `list`

Everything works as expected, so we try to print the list out in reverse order, as demonstrated in Listing 2.16:

```
list_iter = list1.end();
while(list_iter != list1.begin())
{
    i = *list_iter;
    cout << i << ' ';
    list_iter--;
}

cout << endl;
```

```
-842150451 9 8 7 6 5 4 3 2 1
```

Listing 2.16 — Using a Forward Iterator to Traverse a `list` in Reverse

The first attempt to print in the reverse direction produces some strange results. The first number printed is random, and the printing halts one element too soon. The problem is, as you might suspect, that we have used the methods provided for initializing forward iteration and attempted to use them for a reverse iteration. With a little reflection, we realize that the iterator was initialized to the past-the-end iterator and when it was dereferenced, it produced an unpredictable value. The `while` loop terminates when it reaches the first element of the list, before it is printed, and hence stops printing before it reaches the beginning. Obviously, we need to use `rbegin()` and `rend()`, but to use these we need to use a `reverse_iterator` since that is the type they return. Let's try again with the code in Listing 2.17:

```
rev_iter = list1.rbegin();
while(rev_iter != list1.rend())
{
    i = *rev_iter;
    cout << i << ' ';
    rev_iter++;
}

cout << endl;
```

```
9 8 7 6 5 4 3 2 1 0
```

Listing 2.17 — Using a Reverse Iterator to Traverse a `list`

Now we get the correct result. One of the interesting points to note is that when a `reverse_iterator` is incremented, it moves backward; and when it is decremented, it moves forward. This is the opposite of the behavior demonstrated by an `iterator`. This behavior means that any algorithm that accepts two iterators delimiting its range of action simply has to increment the iterator to move to the next element to be processed. If an `iterator` is passed to the algorithm, it will move in the forward direction, whereas if passed a `reverse_iterator`, it will move backward. This greatly simplifies the writing of algorithms that use iterators since the algorithm does not have to know which type of iterator it is using—the iterator itself determines the direction of movement through the sequence.

2.4.4 Random Access Iterators

Random access iterators have all the capabilities of bidirectional iterators, plus the ability to be moved in increments greater than one, the ability to be subscripted, and the ability to be compared to determine if the position of one iterator is before or after another.

The list used in the previous example supports bidirectional iterators but not random access iterators. To see how random access iterators work, we have to introduce a new container: the vector. The vector is similar to a regular array but has the added benefit that it can become larger should the storage requirements be greater than originally anticipated. The main feature we are interested in at the moment is that it supports random access iterators. A vector is constructed and initialized in the same way as a list, as in Listing 2.18:

```
vector<int>                 vect1;
vector<int>::iterator       iter1;
vector<int>::reverse_iterator rev_iter;
int                         i;
ostream_iterator<int>       out_stream(cout," ");

for(i=0;i<10;i++) vect1.push_back(i);
copy(vect1.begin(), vect1.end(), out_stream);
cout << endl;
```

```
0 1 2 3 4 5 6 7 8 9
```

Listing 2.18 — Initializing a `vector`

If we want to insert a value before the fourth element of the vector, we no longer have to obtain an iterator referencing the start of the vector and increment it three times; now we simply add three, as shown in Listing 2.19:

```
iter1 = vect1.begin();
iter1 += 3;
vect1.insert(iter1, 99);
copy(vect1.begin(), vect1.end(), out_stream);

cout << endl;
```

```
0 1 2 99 4 5 6 7 8 9
```

Listing 2.19 — Incrementing a Random Access Iterator

If we do not want to permanently modify the iterator using `operator+=`, we can simply add an integer to it to create a temporary iterator, as demonstrated in Listing 2.20:

```
iter1 = vect1.begin();
vect1.insert(iter1+3, 88);
copy(vect1.begin(), vect1.end(), out_stream);

cout << endl;
```

```
0 1 2 88 99 3 4 5 6 7 8 9
```

Listing 2.20 — Adding Three to a Random Access Iterator

Another new operation provided by random access iterators is subscripting. This works identically to subscripting an array. An iterator is provided that references a starting position and a subscript that is an offset from the starting position. The result is a reference to the element referenced by the iterator that is moved subscript positions from the starting position. Listing 2.21 uses subscripting to print the first five values in the vector:

```
iter1 = vect1.begin();
vect1.insert(iter1+3, 88);
iter1 = vect1.begin();
for(i=0;i<5;i++) cout << iter1[i] << ' ';

cout << endl;
```

```
0 1 2 88 99
```

Listing 2.21 — Subscripting a Random Access Iterator

A reverse_iterator is provided that is derived from the random_access_iterator. It behaves just like the reverse iterator provided by the list, but has the additional operations supported by random access iterators. (See Listing 2.22.)

```
rev_iter = vect1.rbegin();
while(rev_iter != vect1.rend())
{
    i = *rev_iter;
    cout << i <<    ' ';
```

```
        rev_iter++;
}

cout << endl;
```

```
9 8 7 6 5 4 3 99 88 2 1 0
```

Listing 2.22 — Using a Reverse Iterator

The final new operation provided by random access iterators is the ability to compare iterators to find if one comes before the other. This allows us to rewrite the loop to print out the first six values of the vector as shown in Listing 2.23:

```
iter2 = vect1.begin() + 5;
iter1 = vect1.begin();
while(iter1 <= iter2)
{
    i = *iter1;
    cout << i << ' ';
    iter1++;
}

cout << endl;
```

```
0 1 2 88 99 3
```

Listing 2.23 — Comparing Random Access Iterators

2.5 Iterator Functions

Only the random access iterators provide operator+ and operator-, since they can be implemented in constant time. The function advance() is provided to move input, forward, and bidirectional iterators by more than a single position at a time. This is accomplished by repeated applications of operator++ or operator--, and hence is a linear time operation. Linear time operations can slow a program considerably, and the `advance()` function should not be used indiscriminately.

The `advance()` function takes two parameters: the iterator to advance and the distance it should move. The distance can be negative only if the iterator is bidirectional or random access:

```
template <class InputIterator, class Distance>
void advance(InputIterator& i, Distance n);
```

At times a programmer will want to find the distance between two iterators. The function `distance()` is provided for this purpose:

```
template <class InputIterator>
iterator_traits<InputIterator>::difference_type
distance(InputIterator   first,
         InputIterator   last);
```

Both of these functions allow integers to be used as a distance, as shown in the following code that finds the length of a list:

```
list<int>    list1;
int          i, dist;

for(i=0;i<10;i++) list1.push_back(i);
dist = distance(list1.begin(), list1.end());
cout << "dist=" << dist << endl;
```
```
dist=10
```

Listing 2.24 — Using the STL Function `distance()`

2.6 Iterator Tags

An iterator is a member of one of the iterator categories: input iterator, output iterator, forward iterator, bidirectional iterator, and random access iterator. Some generic algorithms can take advantage of knowing the category of an iterator so that they can use a more efficient implementation using the full capabilities of the iterator passed to them.

The STL defines a series of iterator tags that correspond to the iterator categories. The tags are defined as follows:

```
namespace std {
    struct input_iterator_tag {};
    struct output_iterator_tag {};
    struct forward_iterator_tag:
      public input_iterator_tag {};
    struct bidirectional_iterator_tag:
      public forward_iterator_tag {};
    struct random_access_iterator_tag:
      public bidirectional_iterator_tag {};
}
```

These tags are simply empty structures. It is not the content of the tag that is important, but the type of the tag. Every iterator must define a member `itera-tor_category` that returns one of the five iterator tags. This can be used to provide specialized implementations of functions that take advantage of the capabilities of different iterator types.

The HP version of the STL makes use of a function `iterator_-category()` that, when passed an iterator, returns its iterator tag. Similarly, the functions `value_type()` and `distance_type()` return the type referenced by an iterator and a type to represent the difference between two iterators. These functions have been removed from the C++ standard, but you might find that some implementations still support them. If possible, you should use the replacement, `iterator_traits`, rather than these older functions.

2.7 Iterator Traits

`iterator_traits` is a structure that contains basic information on iterators that can be used by generic algorithms to determine key attributes of an iterator so that the algorithms can use the iterator effectively. `iterator_traits` provides the following:

value_type	the type referenced by the iterator,
difference_type	a type capable of representing the difference between two iterators,
pointer	the type of a pointer to the type referenced by the iterator,

```
reference              the type of a reference to the type referenced by the
                       iterator,

iterator_category    the category of the iterator.
```

This type information can be used to help a generic algorithm work with an iterator and the type referenced by the iterator. It is common for a generic algorithm to need to temporarily store a copy of the data referenced by an iterator. To do this, it needs to know the type of the data so that the temporary variable can be declared. This information is readily available from `iterator_-traits`. The iterator category can be used to pick the algorithm best suited to the capabilities of the iterator. For example, a given algorithm might be implemented differently if provided with a `random_access_iterator` than if provided with a `forward_iterator`.

The iterators themselves provide the same information as does `iterator_traits`, leaving the question of why `iterator_traits` is required. If the iterator passed to a function is a an iterator rather than a pointer, the function can get the information directly from the iterator. If a pointer is passed, there is a problem with this technique since a pointer will not have a `value_type` or any of the other attributes associated with an iterator. `iterator_traits` provides a solution to this by providing a basic definition for iterators and a special definition for pointers. The definition of `iterator_traits` for iterators is as follows:

```
template<class Iterator>
struct iterator_traits {
    typedef Iterator::difference_type
        difference_type;
    typedef Iterator::value_type          value_type;
    typedef Iterator::pointer             pointer;
    typedef Iterator::reference           reference;
    typedef Iterator::iterator_category
        iterator_category;
};
```

This takes the iterator as a template parameter and simply defines its own types in terms of the types defined by the iterator. The specialization for pointers, shown below, provides definitions that are appropriate for pointers.

```
template<class T>
struct iterator_traits<T*> {
    typedef ptrdiff_t        difference_type;
    typedef T                value_type;
    typedef T*               pointer;
    typedef T&               reference;
    typedef random_access_iterator_tag
```

```
        iterator_category;
};
```

When a generic algorithm requires type information on the iterator passed to it, it accesses the information by first creating an instance of `iterator_-traits<iterator>` and then accessing the appropriate member. This means that the same method for accessing iterator attributes can be used regardless of whether an iterator or a pointer is passed to the algorithm.

If you write your own iterator, you must either define the expected types within the iterator or provide a specialization of `iterator_traits` for your iterator. It is easier to use the first technique. Similarly, any generic algorithms you write should define all temporary variables in terms of the types returned by `iterator_traits`.

```
#include <iostream>
#include <iterator>
#include <vector>
#include <list>
#include <utility>

using namespace std;

template <class RandomIterator, class T>
RandomIterator& bsearch(
        RandomIterator          first,
        RandomIterator          last,
        T val)
{
    return _bsearch(first, last, val,
        _Iter_cat(first));
}


template <class RandomIterator, class T>
RandomIterator& _bsearch(
        RandomIterator          first,
        RandomIterator          last,
        T                       val,
        random_access_iterator_tag t)
{
    ptrdiff_t                   dist;
    RandomIterator              probe;
    RandomIterator              top;
    RandomIterator              bot;
```

```
            bot = first;
            top = last - 1;
            while(top > bot)
            {
                dist = top - bot;
                probe = bot + dist;
                if((*probe) == val)
                    return probe;
                else
                    if((*probe) < val)
                        bot = probe + 1;
                    else
                        top = probe - 1;
            }
            return last;
        }

        template <class FwdIterator, class T>
        FwdIterator& _bsearch(
                FwdIterator             first,
                FwdIterator             last,
                T val,
                forward_iterator_tag t)
        {
            while(first != last)
            {
                if((*first) == val)
                    return first;
                first++;
            }
            return last;
        }

        void main()
        {
            vector<int>     vect;
            list<int>       lst;
            int             i;

            for(i = 0; i < 10; i++)
            {
                vect.push_back(i);
                lst.push_back(i);
            }

            cout << "searching vector..." << endl;
            cout << *bsearch(vect.begin(), vect.end(), 5)
```

```
        << endl;

    cout << "searching list..." << endl;
    cout << *bsearch(lst.begin(), lst.end(), 5)
        << endl;
```

```
searching vector...
5
searching list...
5
```

```
}
```

Listing 2.25 — Specializing a Function with Iterator Tags [search1.cpp]

The program in Listing 2.25 shows how a function can be specialized to take advantage of the capabilities of the iterator it is passed. The example function searches a sequence to find the location of the first occurrence of a value. The function to perform the search is called bsearch() and does nothing but call the function _bsearch(). There are two versions of _bsearch(): the first uses a random access iterator to perform a binary search, and the second uses a forward iterator to perform a linear search. The version that is invoked is determined by the call from bsearch():

```
return _bsearch(first, last, val, _Iter_cat(first));
```

This includes one extra parameter that indicates the category of the iterator passed to the function. _Iter_cat() is a function provided in Microsoft Visual C++ 5.0 for determining the category of an iterator. It returns the iterator tag for the iterator.

Examining the signatures for _bsearch(), we see that the first requires a random_access_iterator_tag as its fourth parameter, while the second requires a forward_iterator_tag. Thus, if a random access iterator is passed to bsearch(), the binary search is used, and if a forward iterator is passed, a linear search is performed. This allows the best algorithm to be selected based on the capabilities of the iterator.

_Iter_cat() is specific to the Microsoft implementation. It performs the same function as the older function iterator_category(), which is being phased out and was removed from the implementation. This is an interim solution to the problem that iterator_traits is not fully supported. Once iterator_traits is fully implemented, the expression

```
_Iter_cat(first)
```

can be replaced by

```
typename
iterator_traits<RandomIterator>::iterator_category
```

Similarly, the declaration

```
ptrdiff_t        dist;
```

can be replaced by

```
typename
iterator_traits<RandomIterator>::difference_type dist;
```

which will allow the type of dist to be set appropriately to the iterator used.

Eventually, all compilers will conform to the standard and will use itera-
tor_traits. In the interim, you will have to check to determine the exact facilities provided by your compiler.

3
The STL Algorithms

3.1 Introduction

The Standard Template Library provides a large number of generic algorithms that can greatly simplify routine programming tasks. Although the number of algorithms might seem overwhelming at first, they can be broken into categories that make them easier to comprehend.

Several important concepts need to be introduced before you begin to explore the algorithms themselves. These include operator templates, function objects, naming conventions, and the layout of the algorithms. Each of these is explained in the following sections.

The STL defines a number of comparison operator templates that reduce the number of operators that must be implemented for the container classes in the library. The container classes implement a minimal number of comparison operators, and all other comparison operators are generated from templates. The operator templates use only the minimal operators to implement their operation.

Many functions accept a pointer to another function that they call during execution. The function pointer passed provides a method to customize the algorithm implemented by the function to which it is passed. The STL generalizes this concept to the function object, which can be used interchangeably with a pointer to a function. A function object is any object that supports `operator()`, the function call operator.

The STL provides function objects for all the common operators so that they can be passed as parameters where a function object is required. The STL also defines function adaptors that can combine functions and their parameters to yield a function object.

3.2 Operators

When we examine the STL containers in the HP implementation, we find that they implement `operator==` and `operator<` and no others. The remaining comparison operators are templates that implement their computations in terms of `operator==` and `operator<`. The C++ standard changed this so that each class implements the full set of operators. The relational templates were moved to the namespace `rel_ops` within the namespace `std`.

The following shows how we could write a template version of `operator!=` that is implemented in terms of `operator==`:

```
template <class T>
bool operator!=(const T& a, const T& b)
{
    return(!(a == b));
}
```

The other comparison operators are implemented similarly, yielding the total set:

- `operator!=`
- `operator<=`
- `operator>`
- `operator>=`

One other benefit of having these templates defined for you is that, after you include the appropriate STL header file `<utility>`, you can use the templates for any classes you define yourself. All you have to do is define `operator==` and `operator<` for your classes, and the other comparisons will be constructed from the templates when required. These operators should be implemented as nonmember functions. This is demonstrated in Listing 3.1.

```
#include <utility>
#include <string>
#include <iostream>

using namespace std;
using namespace rel_ops;

class Employee
{
private:
   string       name;
   int          id;
public:
   Employee(string nm, int eid):
      name(nm), id(eid) {}
   friend bool operator==(const Employee& e1,
                   const Employee&      e2);
   friend bool operator<(const Employee&  e1,
                   const Employee&      e2);
   friend ostream& operator<<(ostream& os,
                      Employee&   e);
};

bool operator==(const Employee&      e1,
               const Employee&      e2)
{
   return e1.id == e2.id;
}

bool operator<(const Employee&      e1,
               const Employee&      e2)
{
   return e1.id < e2.id;
}

ostream& operator<<(ostream& os,   Employee& e)
{
   os << e.id << " " << e.name;
   return os;
}

void main()
{
   Employee e1("Smith", 123);
   Employee e2("Jones", 456);

   if(e1 != e2)
```

```
    {
        cout << e1 << " not equal to "
            << e2 << endl;
    }
}
```

```
123 Smith not equal to 456 Jones
```

Listing 3.1 — Using the Relational Operators [relops.cpp]

Since the relational operators are members of the namespace `rel_ops`, this is merged with the global namespace with the `using` statement. It is also possible to qualify the relational operator if you do not want to merge all of the relational operators into the global namespace. The qualification looks like this:

```
if(rel_ops::operator!=(e1, e2)) {...}
```

3.3 Function Objects

The previous chapter demonstrated that the iterators are a generalization of the pointer. In the same way, the function object is a generalization of the function pointer. Function pointers are passed to other functions as parameters and then used to invoke the function to which they point. This invocation is accomplished by using the call operator, `operator()`, on the function pointer.

The previous chapter identified the operators that were provided by pointers and showed that any object that provided the same operators would be indistinguishable from a pointer and could be substituted for one. The same logic is applicable to function pointers. Function pointers provide `operator()`, so any other object that provides this operator can be used in place of a function pointer. A function object is an object that provides `operator()` and can be used in place of a function pointer.

A unary function object is one that requires a single parameter and returns a result. A binary function object requires two parameters and returns a result. These are represented by the classes `unary_function` and `binary_function`, respectively. These classes define some additional types describing the types of their parameter(s) and the value returned. `unary_function` defines `argument_type` and `result_type`. Similarly, `binary_function` defines `first_argument_type`, `second_argument_type`, and `result` `type`. These types might be used by algorithms to which a function object is passed and are required for function adaptors to be applied to a function object. Therefore, if you define your own function objects, you should define these types. The simplest way to do this is to derive your function object from either `unary_function` or `binary_function`.

The STL defines function objects for all the common C++ operators. It is common to want to pass one of the built-in operators to a function that is expecting a function pointer or object. Unfortunately, you cannot pass an operator, so the STL defines a series of function objects that have the same effect as the built-in operators. These are implemented as templates, have the textual name of the associated operator, and can be instantiated to work with any type for which the associated operator is implemented. The following is the definition of the binary function object `plus`:

```
template <class T>
struct plus: binary_function<T, T, T> {
   T operator()(const T& x, const T& y) const
      { return x + y; }
};
```

The other operators are implemented as function objects in the same way. The following shows the complete list of function objects defined by the STL with the operator they implement shown in parentheses after the name. Users of the HP implementation of the STL should note that `multiplies()` was called `times()` in that version.

plus (+)	negate (unary -)	greater_equal (>=)
minus (-)	equal_to (==)	less_equal (<=)
multiplies (*)	not_equal_to (!=)	logical_and (&&)
divides (/)	greater (>)	logical_or (||)
modulus (%)	less (<)	logical_not (!)

These function objects can be passed to any of the STL functions that require a binary function. One such function is `transform()`, which combines the elements in two sequences on an element-by-element basis to yield a third sequence. The function requires a binary function object that is used to combine two elements to yield a new element. This is demonstrated in Listing 3.2.

```
#include <iterator>
#include <algorithm>
#include <functional>
#include <iostream>

using namespace std;

void main()
{
   int                    in1[10], in2[10],out[10],i;
   int*                   in1_end;
   ostream_iterator<int>  out_stream(cout, " ");

   for(i=0;i<10;i++) {
      in1[i] = i;
      in2[i] = i * 3;
   }
   in1_end = in1 + 10;
   transform(in1, in1_end, in2, out, minus<int>());
   copy(out, out+10, out_stream);
   cout << endl;
}
```

```
0 -2 -4 -6 -8 -10 -12 -14 -16 -18
```

Listing 3.2 — Passing a Function Object to Transform [trnsfrm1.cpp]

The transform() function invokes the call operator on the function object passed to it, providing it with the necessary parameters drawn from the two sequences. This is typical of how function objects can be passed to a function.

Many of the STL functions expect a function object that will act as a predicate. A predicate is a function that accepts one or two parameters and returns a Boolean value indicating whether the value(s) satisfy the predicate. A typical function object that could be used as a predicate is less. This function object must be supplied with two parameters representing the values to be compared. Passing this function object to another function that works with a single sequence is insufficient since the receiving function will apply it to a member of a sequence and not have a second parameter for the predicate.

Consider the STL function replace_if(), which will traverse the members of a sequence replacing all those that satisfy a predicate with a new value. The prototype for replace_if() looks like this:

```
void replace_if(ForwardIterator    first,
      ForwardIterator              last,
      Predicate                    pred,
      const T&                     new_value);
```

If the function object less is supplied as the predicate, then it will be applied to each member of the sequence to determine if it should be replaced. The problem here is that we did not specify the second parameter required by less, and the algorithm has no idea what the sequence members should be less than. The solution is an adaptor, bind2nd, that accepts a function object and a value for its second parameter and returns a new function object that has a second parameter. Suppose you want a predicate that will be true for all values less than 10. You could create such a function object from the function object less and the parameter 10 using bind2nd:

```
bind2nd(less<int>(), 10)
```

The resulting function object can then be supplied to the replace_if() function and will allow it to determine if a sequence member is less than 10 or not:

```
replace_if(list1.begin(), list1.end(),
    bind2nd(less<int>(), 10), 50);
```

which will replace all the values less than 10 by the value 50. There is also an adaptor bind1st that binds a specific value to the first parameter of a function object. Due to the nature of the STL algorithms, this is used far less often than bind2nd. Adaptors are described in detail in Chapter 9.

3.4 The STL Algorithms

The STL provides a lot of general-purpose algorithms that computer programmers use every day. These algorithms are generic and can be applied to any data structure that provides the appropriate iterators. This includes all of the STL container classes as well as regular arrays. The wide applicability of the algorithms means that programmers will not have to rewrite these common algorithms every time they are required, consequently increasing the programmers' productivity.

There are several important points to note before beginning a study of the individual algorithms of the STL:

- When iterators are used to delimit a sequence, the first iterator usually references the first element in the sequence, and the second element usually references the element immediately after the last element in the sequence.

- Many algorithms have both an in-place version and a copying version. The in-place version performs its operation on a sequence in its original location. The copying version copies the input sequence to a new location, performing its operation during the copy, leaving the original sequence unchanged. The copying version of the function has the same name as the in-place version with the suffix _copy appended. If an operation must be performed and the result copied to another location, then it is more efficient to use the copying version of the algorithm than to use the in-place version followed by a copy. For some algorithms, such as sorts, this is not true, and copying versions of the algorithms are not provided.

- Many algorithms have an unconditional version and a predicate version. The unconditional version performs its operation on every member of a sequence, whereas the predicate version operates on only those members of the sequence for which the predicate is satisfied. The predicate versions of the functions have the suffix _if.

- You should note the type of iterator expected in the function prototype. This indicates that the function requires an iterator with at least these capabilities. You might find that some algorithms require at least a forward iterator and cannot use an input iterator, whereas others require the full capabilities of a random access iterator. If you pass an iterator with less than the required capabilities, the code will fail to compile when the function attempts to use an operator not provided by the iterator.

3.4.1 Algorithm Categories

To understand the large number of algorithms in the STL, it helps to break them into a series of categories, as depicted in Figure 3.1.

Sequence Algorithms Provide a variety of operations for manipulating sequences of elements. These include function application, rearranging elements, assigning values to multiple elements, copying sequences, searching, and element deletion. The sequence algorithms are divided into mutating sequence algorithms and nonmutating sequence algorithms. Mutating sequence algorithms modify the values in the sequence to which they are applied. Nonmutating sequence

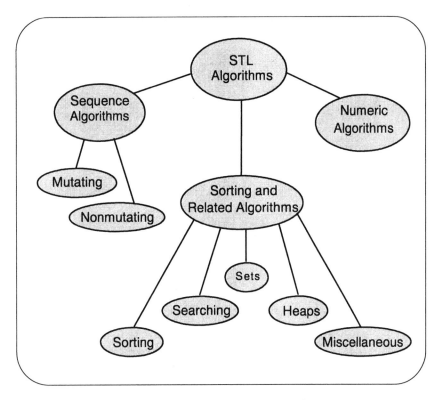

Figure 3.1 — Algorithm Categories

operations leave the contents of the container to which they are applied unchanged.

Sorting Algorithms   Include sorting, searching, merging, set operations on sorted sequences, lexicographical comparisons, and heap operations. They are generally characterized by producing or operating upon sorted sequences.

Numeric Operations   General numeric algorithms including various forms of summation and inner product. This category also includes the numeric array, `val_array`, and the operations defined on it.

The following chapters explore each of the algorithm categories in detail. If you are interested in a general overview of the algorithms read these chapters in the order presented. If you need information in a hurry, read the introductory material in each chapter and then proceed to the algorithms of interest. Although an understanding of the algorithms is not essential to using the containers, it is recommended for the general reader. If your main interest is containers, you should skim the algorithms to familiarize yourself with the operations that can be performed on containers.

4
Sequence Algorithms

4.1 Introduction

This chapter examines the sequence algorithms—those that treat their data as ordered or unordered sequences. Although there are a great number of sequence algorithms, they are divided into the subcategories of mutating sequence algorithms and nonmutating sequence algorithms. Nonmutating sequence algorithms, also called nonmodifying sequence algorithms, treat the sequence to which they are applied as read-only and leave the sequence unchanged after they terminate. Mutating sequence algorithms change the order of the sequence or the values that constitute the sequence.

4.2 Preliminaries

The Standard Template Library contains many different functions and data structures to understand. Deciding where to start the study of this mass of material is a difficult decision since you cannot understand many of the parts until you understand the parts on which they depend. You want to start with the basics, yet in order to demonstrate the basics you must resort to using more advanced features. One way to tackle this would be to start reading and, when an unfamiliar concept is encountered, skip to the appropriate section and read that before continuing. There are two reasons this approach is not workable. First, books are necessarily sequential and, no matter how well cross-indexed, a lot of page turning and book marking remains to be done. Second, the human mind does not like its train of thought interrupted. Readers struggling to understand a concept resent having to turn to a separate section, read another topic, and then return to the first, trying to remember where they were.

This book presents the material in an orderly manner, including introductory material where necessary to explain the concepts that appear in the following sections but that are not directly related to the sections. Typically, these topics are dealt with in other parts of the book, and a minimal introduction is provided to allow the reader to understand the immediate material. This is one such section.

If you skipped ahead and did not read the chapter on iterators, you should return to that chapter before continuing. Understanding iterators is crucial to understanding the material in the rest of this chapter. Virtually all algorithms use iterators, and the material will be difficult to comprehend if you don't understand iterators.

Listing 4.1 introduces several functions and data structures that are used in the examples that follow.

The program in Listing 4.1 demonstrates how an array can be used as a container, and it uses the copy() function, the list container, and a stream iterator. You will see all the objects and concepts of this simple program used repeatedly in the sections that follow.

The action of this program is simple. It declares an array and a list and inserts some values into them. It then prints them out to ensure that they are initialized correctly. The values in the array are copied to the list, which is then printed to show that they were copied properly.

```
#include <algorithm>
#include <list>
#include <iostream>

using namespace std;

main()
{
    int                     ar[10], i;
    list<int>               list1;
    ostream_iterator<int>   outStream(cout, " ");

    for(i=0;i<10;i++) {
        ar[i] = i;
        list1.push_back(0);
    }

    copy(ar, ar+10, outStream);
    cout << endl;
```

```
copy(list1.begin(), list1.end(), outStream);
cout << endl;

copy(ar, ar+10, list1.begin());
copy(list1.begin(), list1.end(), outStream);
cout << endl;

return(0);
```

```
0 1 2 3 4 5 6 7 8 9
0 0 0 0 0 0 0 0 0 0
0 1 2 3 4 5 6 7 8 9
```

```
}
```

Listing 4.1 — Example STL Functions [exfuncs.cpp]

It is assumed that you know what an array is; however, you might not understand the list as well. The term *list* refers to the linked list, a data structure commonly used in computer programs. A linked list is an example of a container data structure, since it stores other data structures. A list consists of a series of nodes joined together by pointers so that they form a chain. The list implemented in the STL is actually a doubly linked list, meaning that each node has a pointer to the node behind it as well as to the node in front of it. The nodes in a list are implemented as structures or classes, with a typical declaration looking like the following:

```
template <class T>
struct ListNode {
    T          data;
    ListNode*  next;
    ListNode*  prev;
};
```

Each list node contains an instance of the type of object being stored in the list. It also has pointers to the next node in the list and the previous node. The node at the beginning of the list has a previous pointer equal to NULL, and the node at the end of the list has a next pointer equal to NULL. These are unique pointer values that are used to mark each end of the list.

A list normally has a head pointer that references the first node in the list. A typical list is depicted in Figure 4.1.

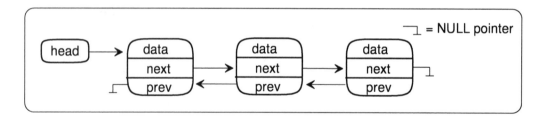

Figure 4.1 — The Structure of a Linked List

All of the functions and containers in the STL are defined as templates so that they can work with any type of data. The `list` template requires a parameter indicating the type of value to be stored in the list—in this case, a series of integer values. The method `push_back()` appends a new value as the last member of the list.

An `ostream_iterator` is a special type of iterator that is associated with an output stream. It functions just like any other iterator except that when it is dereferenced and a value assigned to it, it prints the value on the associated stream. The constructor for an `ostream_iterator` requires the name of the stream and a character string that will be printed after every value. An `ostream_iterator` can be used whenever an algorithm expects an iterator to which it will copy values. The effect will be to copy the values to an output stream rather than to an in-memory location.

The `copy()` function takes three iterators as parameters. The first two delimit the range of values to be copied, and the third indicates the position to which the values will be copied. After the function completes, a copy of the values from the first iterator up to the second has been placed at the location starting at the third iterator.

Finding the beginning and end of an array is simple: the first member is located at the start of the array, and the last member is the address of the first element plus the number of elements. Finding the endpoints of a list is more difficult since the individual nodes are not stored contiguously. The `list` class provides two methods for this purpose: `begin()`, which returns an iterator referencing the start of the list and `end()`, which returns an iterator referencing the element one past the end of the list.

One of the advantages of iterators is that they work the same regardless of the data structure to which they are applied. This allows the `copy()` function to be used to copy values from the array to an output stream as well as copying from the array to the list.

All of these STL objects and concepts are used in the examples that follow. Where others are used, they are explained as necessary. A more detailed discussion of these topics can be found by skipping ahead to the appropriate sections.

4.2.1 Pairs

Some STL algorithms return a pair of values rather than a single value. This is common in algorithms dealing with associative containers. Returning a pair of values is sufficiently common that a data structure has been created for the purpose. It is called a pair and is defined as follows:

```
template <class T1, class T2>
    struct pair {
        typedef T1    first_type;
        typedef T2    second_type;

        T1            first;
        T2            second;
    };
```

The pair is returned as a single value but allows access to the two values contained within it using the usual dot notation to access a field in a structure.

The pair has three constructors:

```
pair();

pair(const T1& a, const T2& b);

template<class U, class V>
    pair(const pair<U, V>& p);
```

The first constructor is the default constructor that initializes first to be T1() and second to be T2(). These are simply the values created by the default constructors of types T1 and T2 respectively. The second constructor is the most commonly used constructor that takes two values as arguments and constructs a pair from them. The third constructor accepts arguments of a different type and applies implicit conversions to make them the required type(s). The third constructor might not be implemented in all implementations.

Three nonmember functions are defined to work with pairs. The first two functions are operator== and operator<, allowing pairs with the same template parameters to be compared to one another. The third function is a convenience function, make_pair(), which constructs a pair from its two arguments. These are demonstrated in Listing 4.2.

```cpp
#include <utility>
#include <iostream>

using namespace std;

template<class T1, class T2>
ostream& operator<<(ostream& os,
    const pair<T1, T2>& p)
{
    os << "(" << p.first << ", " << p.second << ")";
    return os;
}

void main()
{
    pair<int, double> pid1(2, 3.14);
    pair<int, double> pid2(1, 2.4);
    pair<int, double> pid3;

    cout << pid1 << " is " <<
        ((pid1 == pid2) ? ("equal") : ("not equal"))
        << " to " << pid2 << endl;

    cout << pid2 << " is " <<
        ((pid2 < pid1) ? ("less") : ("not less"))
        << " than " << pid1 << endl;

    pid3 = make_pair(1, 5.78);
    cout << pid3 << " is " <<
        ((pid3 < pid1) ? ("less") : ("not less"))
        << " than " << pid1 << endl;

    pid3 = make_pair(5, 2.72);
    cout << pid3 << " is " <<
        ((pid3 < pid1) ? ("less") : ("not less"))
        << " than " << pid1 << endl;


    pid3 = make_pair(2, 2.72);
    cout << pid3 << " is " <<
        ((pid3 < pid1) ? ("less") : ("not less"))
        << " than " << pid1 << endl;
```

```
pid3 = make_pair(2, 6.28);
cout << pid3 << " is " <<
    ((pid3 < pid1) ? ("less") : ("not less"))
    << " than " << pid1 << endl;
}
```

```
(2, 3.14) is not equal to (1, 2.4)
(1, 2.4) is less than (2, 3.14)
(1, 5.78) is less than (2, 3.14)
(5, 2.72) is not less than (2, 3.14)
(2, 2.72) is less than (2, 3.14)
(2, 6.28) is not less than (2, 3.14)
```

Listing 4.2 — Pair Functions [pair.cpp]

The program in Listing 4.2 shows how to build a `pair` by specifying the template parameters as well as building a `pair` using `make_pair()` where the types of the parameters are deduced from the types of the arguments. The definition of `operator<` is interesting. For two pairs, *p1* and *p2*, *p1* is less than *p2* if *p1.first* is less than *p2.first*, regardless of the value of the `second` member. If the `first` member of each pair is equal, then *p1* is less than *p2* only if the *p1.second* is less than *p2.second*.

4.3 Nonmutating Sequence Algorithms

The word mutate means to change, and the nonmutating, or nonmodifying, sequence algorithms are characterized by making no changes to the sequences to which they are applied. Most of these algorithms look for one or more values in a sequence and return values indicating the result of the search they performed. These algorithms are all designed to work with unsorted sequences and make complete linear searches of the sequences to which they are applied. Algorithms that take advantage of the order in sorted sequences to yield faster search times are classified as sorting and searching algorithms and are described in Chapter 5.

4.3.1 Counting

We start our study of the sequence algorithms with a relatively simple algorithm for counting. The counting algorithm searches a sequence for values that satisfy some criterion and returns a parameter indicating the number of times a value satisfying the criterion is found in the sequence. The algorithm makes no assumptions about the order of the values in the sequence and traverses the entire sequence to perform the count. Since the algorithm makes only a single pass through the data, the complexity is *O(n)*.

As with many of the algorithms we will examine, there are two functions that implement the count algorithm: `count()` and `count_if()`. The `count()` function searches for a specific value and returns the number of times it occurs in the sequence, and the `count_if()` function counts the number of values that satisfy a predicate. Prototypes for the two functions follow:

```
template <class InputIterator, class T>
typename
iterator_traits<InputIterator>::difference_type
count(InputIterator  first,
      InputIterator  last,
      const T&       value);

template <class InputIterator, class Predicate>
typename
iterator_traits<InputIterator>::difference_type
count_if(InputIterator  first,
      InputIterator  last,
      Predicate       pred);
```

The return type of the functions is defined in terms of `iterator_traits`, which determines the type in terms of types defined by the iterator. Users of the HP implementation should note that there is a difference in the prototype for these functions.

Let's examine Listing 4.3 to count the number of fives in an array.

```
#include <algorithm>
#include <iostream>

using namespace std;

main()
{
    int                      ar[10],i,ct;
    ostream_iterator<int>    outStream(cout, " ");

    for(i=0;i<10;i++) ar[i] = i;
    ar[2] = 5;
    copy(ar, ar+10, outStream);
    ct = count(ar,ar+10,5);
    cout << "\nThere are " << ct << " fives\n";

    return(0);
}
```

```
0 1 5 3 4 5 6 7 8 9
There are 2 fives
```

Listing 4.3 — Counting Sequence Values [CountSeq.cpp]

The output of the program is straightforward as it simply presents a count of the number of fives in the array. Readers familiar with the HP implementation should note that the signature of the count() function has been changed.

Listing 4.4 uses count_if() to find the number of elements less than five.

```
#include <algorithm>
#include <iostream>
#include <functional>
#include <iterator>

using namespace std;

main()
{
    int                    ar[10],i,ct;
    ostream_iterator<int>  outStream(cout, " ");

    for(i=0;i<10;i++) ar[i] = i;
    ar[2] = 5;
    copy(ar, ar+10, outStream);
    ct = 0;
    ct = count_if(ar, ar+10, bind2nd(less<int>(), 5));
    cout << "\nThere are " << ct <<
        " less than five\n";

    return(0);
}
```

```
0 1 5 3 4 5 6 7 8 9
There are 4 less than five
```

Listing 4.4 — Conditional Counting [CondCnt.cpp]

The predicate is formed by binding the second parameter of a function object to a fixed value. When count_if() traverses the sequence, it invokes pred(*iter), where *iter is the iterator for the sequence. This call must return a Boolean value that will determine if the value returned by the dereferenced iterator is counted.

The predicate is really a function object returned by bind2nd. When the predicate is called with a single parameter, it invokes the function object to which it was bound (in this case, less) with two parameters—the first of which is a value from the sequence, and the second of which was bound by bind2nd. The result is that count_if() ends up calling less(*iter, 5), which returns true only if the first parameter is less than five.

4.3.2 Finding

The finding algorithm searches a sequence for the first occurrence of a value that satisfies some criterion. The algorithm terminates either when it finds the value for which it is searching or when it encounters the end of the sequence. The complexity is *O(n)*.

There are two functions that implement the finding algorithm: `find()` and `find_if()`:

```
template <class InputIterator, class T>
InputIterator find(InputIterator first,
                   InputIterator  last,
                   const T&       value);

template <class InputIterator, class Predicate>
InputIterator find_if(InputIterator first,
                      InputIterator  last,
                      Predicate      pred);
```

The function `find()` searches the sequence from `first` up to `last` for `value`. It returns an iterator referencing the first occurrence of `value`. If `value` does not occur in the sequence, then an iterator equal to `last` is returned.

The function `find_if()` searches the sequence for the first value that satisfies the predicate. If such a value exists, an iterator referencing it is returned; otherwise, an iterator equal to `last` is returned.

4.3.3 Finding Members

The algorithm for finding an element in a sequence that is a member of another sequence is closely related to the finding algorithm. It can be viewed as a generalization of finding that finds any one of several values rather than just a single value. It is implemented by the function `find_first_of()`:

```
template<class ForwardIterator1,
   class ForwardIterator2>
ForwardIterator1
find_first_of(ForwardIterator1    first1,
              ForwardIterator1    last1,
              ForwardIterator2    first2,
              ForwardIterator2    last2);

template<class ForwardIterator1,
```

```
      class ForwardIterator2,
      class BinaryPredicate>
ForwardIterator1
find_first_of(ForwardIterator1    first1,
              ForwardIterator1    last1,
              ForwardIterator2    first2,
              ForwardIterator2    last2,
              BinaryPredicate     pred);
```

The function `find_first_of()` locates the first occurrence of an element in a sequence that matches any element in another sequence. This is useful for applications that want to find an occurrence of any one of a series of elements. The function returns an iterator referencing the first matching element, or `last1` if there is no match.

The program in Listing 4.5 prints out all vowels that occur in a string. It begins by using `find_first_of()` to locate the first vowel. A `while` loop is used to find subsequent vowels and terminates when the past-the-end iterator for the string being searched is returned. Each time through the loop, `find_first_of()` is used to locate the next occurrence. The problem of finding the same occurrence repeatedly is circumvented by starting the search at the position immediately after the location of the last occurrence.

```
#include <algorithm>
#include <iostream>
#include <string.h>

using namespace std;

void main()
{
   char   str[16];
   char   vowels[16];
   char   *locn, *endStr, *endVowels;


   strcpy(str, "Elvis lives!");
   strcpy(vowels, "aeiouAEIOU");
   endStr = str + strlen(str);
   endVowels = vowels + strlen(vowels);

   locn = find_first_of(str, endStr, vowels,
      endVowels);
   while(locn < endStr)
   {
```

```
      cout << locn[0];
      locn = find_first_of(locn + 1, endStr, vowels,
         endVowels);
   }
   cout << endl;
```

```
Eiie
```

```
}
```

Listing 4.5 — Finding Vowels in a String [first_of.cpp]

4.3.4 Finding Adjacent Values

The algorithm for finding adjacent values searches a sequence for two adjacent values that satisfy some relationship between them. Although it is commonly used to find two adjacent values that are equal to each other, other relationships can be specified. The algorithm returns an iterator referencing the first member of the first pair of values satisfying the relationship. If no such pair of values exists, the past-the-end iterator for the sequence is returned. The complexity of the algorithm is $O(n)$.

The algorithm is implemented as a single function, adjacent_find(), that is overloaded with two signatures:

```
template <class ForwardIterator>
ForwardIterator adjacent_find(ForwardIterator   first,
                              ForwardIterator   last);


template <class ForwardIterator,
   class BinaryPredicate>
ForwardIterator adjacent_find(
                  ForwardIterator   first,
                  ForwardIterator   last,
                  BinaryPredicate   binary_pred);
```

The first form finds the first two adjacent elements in the sequence that are equal and the second finds the first two adjacent elements that satisfy the predicate. Listing 4.6 generates a sequence and then locates the first pair of elements where the first member of the pair is greater than the second.

```
#include <algorithm>
#include <iostream>
#include <iterator>
#include <functional>

using namespace std;

main()
{
    int                     ar[10], i, *iter;
    ostream_iterator<int>   outStream(cout, " ");
    greater<int>            greater_than;

    for(i=0;i<10;i++) ar[i] = i;
    ar[5] = 9;
    copy(ar, ar+10, outStream);
    cout << '\n';
    iter = adjacent_find(ar, ar+10, greater_than);
    if(iter == ar + 10) cout << "none found\n";
    else cout << "first is greater " << *iter << " "
        << *(iter+1) << '\n';
    return 0;
```

```
0 1 2 3 4 9 6 7 8 9
first is greater 9 6
```

```
}
```

Listing 4.6 — Finding Adjacent Values [adjnt1.cpp]

The program creates an instance of the binary function object greater<int>, which will be passed to adjacent_find() as the binary predicate. It then fills the array with some values, making sure that one of the pairs of values has the first member of the pair greater than the second. The call to adjacent_find() searches the entire array for a pair whose first element is greater than the second.

4.3.5 ForEach

The ForEach algorithm traverses a sequence and calls a function for every member of the sequence. The function is passed a single parameter, which is the value obtained by dereferencing the iterator used to traverse the sequence. Any value returned by the function that is called is discarded. The algorithm makes a single pass through the entire sequence and, hence, has a complexity of *O(n)*.

The forEach algorithm is implemented by the function `for_each()`:

```
template <class InputIterator, class Function>
Function for_each(InputIterator  first,
                  InputIterator  last,
                  Function       f);
```

Listing 4.7 uses the function object `multiplies` to attempt to double the values in the sequence. This will work only if `for_each()` assigns the result of the function call to a member of the sequence, as shown in the following:

```
*first = f(*first, 2).
```

`for_each()` does not make such an assignment, but simply invokes the function and discards the result, as demonstrated:

```
#include <algorithm>
#include <iostream>
#include <functional>

using namespace std;

main()
{
    int                     ar[10],i;
    ostream_iterator<int>   outStream(cout, " ");

    for(i=0;i<10;i++) ar[i] = i;
    for_each(ar, ar+10, bind2nd(multiplies<int>(),2));
    copy(ar, ar+10, outStream);
    cout << '\n';

    return 0;
}
```

```
0 1 2 3 4 5 6 7 8 9
```

Listing 4.7 — Incorrect Use of Functions with ForEach [ForEach0.cpp]

Obviously, this is not the right way to use `for_each()`. A function that does nothing other than compute a value based on its parameters and return this value as a result is called a pure function. A function is said to have a side effect when it modifies its environment by assigning to a variable in the surrounding environment or making some other change outside itself.   Since `for_each()` discards the result of the function it calls, we must use a function that has a side effect to see something actually happen. For this, we have to construct our own function object, as in Listing 4.8.

```cpp
#include <algorithm>
#include <iostream>
#include <functional>

using namespace std;

template <class T>
class PrintGt5:
    public unary_function<T, void>
{
public:
    PrintGt5(){}
    void operator()(T a) { if(a > T(5)) cout << a <<
        ' ';}
};

main()
{
    int    ar[10],i;

    for(i=0;i<10;i++) ar[i] = i;

    for_each(ar, ar+10, PrintGt5<int>());
    cout << '\n';

    return(0);
}
```

```
6 7 8 9
```

Listing 4.8 — Correct Use of Functions with ForEach [ForEach1.cpp]

This works since the function object passed to `for_each()` makes a permanent change to its environment: it prints something. Such a change is not lost when the result of the function is discarded, so the change remains after the function terminates.

It is interesting to see how the function object is created. In the definition of a function object, you saw that it was any object for which `operator()` was defined. Thus, to create a function object, all you need do is create an object that defines `operator()`. The body of `operator()` is called whenever the function object is invoked, so that is where the code to be executed is placed.

`PrintGt5` is a class template, so it can be used with many different types. The applicability of the function is restricted by the fact that `operator()` compares each value to `T(5)`, implying that there must be a conversion operator from `int` to type `T`. For special cases, it is not necessary to create a class template, although this will restrict the applicability of the class. This is demonstrated in Listing 4.9 which is only able to double the value of integers.

You are probably wondering if it is possible to write a function object that will modify the values in the sequence to which it is applied. The answer is yes—all that has to be done is to pass a reference to the value in the sequence rather than the value itself.

```
#include <algorithm>
#include <iostream>
#include <functional>

using namespace std;

class Double:
    public unary_function<int, void>
{
public:
    Double(){}
    void operator()(int& a) {a *= 2;}
};

main()
{
    int                    ar[10],i;
    ostream_iterator<int>  outStream(cout, " ");

    for(i=0;i<10;i++) ar[i] = i;

    for_each(ar, ar+10, Double());
```

```
copy(ar, ar+10, outStream);
cout << endl;

return(0);
}
```

```
0  2  4  6  8  10 12 14 16 18
```

Listing 4.9 — Modifying a Sequence with ForEach [ForEach2.cpp]

Here we see that the function modifies its environment by changing the values passed to it. Since they are passed by reference, the change affects values outside the function, and the changes remain after the function terminates.

You might be wondering whether this is a misuse of the `for_each()` function. It is supposed to be a nonmutating function, yet we were able to get it to modify the sequence to which it was applied. This is not the intended use of the function, but the STL has no way to prevent you from writing a function to modify the values to which it is applied. It is preferable to use the function `transform()`, described in the section on mutating sequence algorithms, which is provided to allow sequences to be modified.

4.3.6 Mismatching Values

The mismatch algorithm compares the corresponding values of two sequences of equal length. These pairs of values are compared by using a binary predicate, and the algorithm returns the first pair for which the predicate fails. If there are no values for which the predicate fails, the algorithm returns the past-the-end iterator for each sequence. The complexity of the algorithm is $O(n)$.

The algorithm is implemented by the function `mismatch`, which has two signatures:

```
template <class InputIterator1, class InputIterator2>
pair<InputIterator1, InputIterator2>
mismatch(InputIterator1 first1,
        InputIterator1    last1,
        InputIterator2    first2);

template <class InputIterator1, class InputIterator2,
    class BinaryPredicate>
```

```
pair<InputIterator1, InputIterator2>
mismatch(InputIterator1 first1,
         InputIterator1    last1,
         InputIterator2    first2,
         BinaryPredicate   binary_pred);
```

The first form of the function returns an iterator pair that references the first two mismatching elements in the two sequences. This form of the function uses operator== to perform the element-by-element comparison. The second form uses a user-supplied binary predicate to perform the comparison.

Listing 4.10 demonstrates how the second form of the function can be used to find the first pair of elements in two sequences where the element in the first sequence is not less than or equal to the corresponding element in the second sequence.

```
#include <algorithm>
#include <iostream>
#include <functional>

using namespace std;

main()
{
   int                     ar1[10], ar2[10], i;
   ostream_iterator<int>   outStream(cout, " ");
   pair<int*, int*>        position(0,0);

   for(i=0;i<10;i++) ar1[i] = ar2[i] = i;
   ar2[5] = 0;
   copy(ar1, ar1+10, outStream);
   cout << '\n';
   copy(ar2, ar2+10, outStream);
   cout << '\n';

   position = mismatch(ar1, ar1+10, ar2,
      less_equal<int>());
   if(position.first == ar1+10)
      cout << "None found";
   else
      cout << *(position.first) << ", " <<
         *(position.second) << '\n';
```

```
        return(0);
}
```

```
0 1 2 3 4 5 6 7 8 9
0 1 2 3 4 0 6 7 8 9
5, 0
```

Listing 4.10 — Finding Mismatching Values [mismatch.cpp]

One of the new concepts in this program is the idea of returning two iterators as a single object—the `pair`. The `pair` is a structure template that contains two members, `first` and `second`. The `pair` template is parameterized with the type of each member so that it can be used for pairs of any type. In this case, an instance of two iterators of the correct type is created. Although the `pair` does provide a parameterless constructor, `position` must be declared with the correct template parameters and initialized with two values of the correct type.

The call to `mismatch()` is fairly straightforward, and the binary predicate is generated in the usual manner. The result is assigned to the `pair` declared previously, which is then examined to determine if and where a mismatch was found.

4.3.7 Sequence Equality

Whereas the mismatch algorithm compared sequences to find the first non-matching members, the equality algorithm returns a Boolean result indicating whether two entire sequences are the same. In the general case, it determines if all element-by-element comparisons of two sequences satisfy a predicate. Since the algorithm involves a linear pass through two sequences, the complexity is $O(n)$. The implementation is the function `equal()`, which is overloaded:

```
template <class InputIterator1, class InputIterator2>
bool equal(InputIterator1  first1,
           InputIterator1 last1,
           InputIterator2 first2);

template <class InputIterator1, class InputIterator2,
    class BinaryPredicate>
bool equal(InputIterator1      first1,
           InputIterator1      last1,
```

```
              InputIterator2      first2,
              BinaryPredicate     binary_pred);
```

Both forms of the function compare the elements in the sequence from first1 up to last1 with those in the sequence beginning at first2 of the same length. The first form uses operator== to perform the comparisons, and the second allows you to specify a binary predicate. This can be used to determine if all values in the first sequence are less than those in the second, and similar operations. Listing 4.11 uses equal() to determine if all values in one sequence are less than all values in another sequence.

```
#include <algorithm>
#include <iostream>
#include <functional>

using namespace std;

main()
{
    int                    ar1[10], ar2[10], i, result;
    ostream_iterator<int>  outStream(cout, " ");

    for(i=0;i<10;i++) {
        ar2[i] = 10 + i;
        ar1[i] = i;
    }
    copy(ar1, ar1+10, outStream);
    cout << '\n';
    copy(ar2, ar2+10, outStream);
    cout << '\n';

    result = equal(ar1, ar1+10, ar2, less<int>());
    if(result) cout << "They are all less\n";
    else cout << "They are not all less\n";

    return(0);
}
```

```
0 1 2 3 4 5 6 7 8 9
10 11 12 13 14 15 16 17 18 19
They are all less
```

Listing 4.11 — Comparing Sequences [SeqCmp.cpp]

4.3.8 Searching

The find algorithm locates the first occurrence of a single value in a sequence. The search algorithm, on the other hand, locates the first occurrence of a smaller sequence within a larger sequence. This is equivalent to searching for a substring within a larger string. The algorithm returns an iterator that references the first occurrence of the subsequence within the larger sequence or an iterator equal to the past-the-end iterator for the sequence being searched if a matching subsequence is not found. A variation on the search algorithm searches for the last occurrence of a subsequence rather than the first. If a predicate other than equality is used, the algorithm will search for the subsequence whose members satisfy the predicate specified. Due to the increased number of comparisons necessary to compare sequences, the complexity of the algorithm is quadratic.

The algorithm is implemented by the overloaded functions search(), search_n(), and find_end(), each of which has two signatures. The function search() locates the first occurrence of the subsequence, and search_n() locates a subsequence of count repeated elements. find_end() locates the last occurrence of a subsequence.

```
template <class ForwardIterator1,
   class ForwardIterator2>
ForwardIterator1 search(
        ForwardIterator1   first1,
        ForwardIterator1   last1,
        ForwardIterator2   first2,
        ForwardIterator2   last2);

template <class ForwardIterator1,
   class ForwardIterator2, class BinaryPredicate>
ForwardIterator1 search(
        ForwardIterator1   first1,
        ForwardIterator1   last1,
        ForwardIterator2   first2,
        ForwardIterator2   last2,
        BinaryPredicate    binary_pred);

template <class ForwardIterator, class Size,
   class T>
ForwardIterator search_n(
        ForwardIterator   first,
        ForwardIterator   last,
        Size              count,
        const T&          val);
```

```
template <class ForwardIterator, class Size,
   class T, class BinaryPredicate>
ForwardIterator search_n(
        ForwardIterator    first,
        ForwardIterator    last,
        Size               count,
        const T&           val,
        BinaryPredicate    pred);


template <class ForwardIterator1,
    class ForwardIterator2>
ForwardIterator1 find_end(
               ForwardIterator1    first1,
               ForwardIterator1    last1,
               ForwardIterator2    first2,
               ForwardIterator2    last2);


template <class ForwardIterator1,
    class ForwardIterator2,
    class BinaryPredicate>
ForwardIterator1 find_end(
               ForwardIterator1    first1,
               ForwardIterator1    last1,
               ForwardIterator2    first2,
               ForwardIterator2    last2,
               BinaryPredicate     comp);
```

The use of the algorithm will be easier to demonstrate on character strings rather than integers as in Listing 4.12.

```
#include <algorithm>
#include <string.h>
#include <iostream>

using namespace std;

main()
{
    char                str[64], subStr[16], *iter, *iter1;
    ostream_iterator<char>  outStream(cout, "");

    strcpy(str, "John Mary Fred Sue ");
    strcpy(subStr, "Mary");

    iter = search(str, str + strlen(str), subStr,
```

```
                subStr + strlen(subStr));
        if(iter == (str + strlen(str))) cout <<
            "not found\n";
        else {
            iter1 = find(iter, iter + strlen(iter), ' ');
            copy(iter, iter1, outStream);
            cout << '\n';
        }

        return(0);
}
```

```
Mary
```

Listing 4.12 — Finding a Value in a Sequence [SeqFind.cpp]

As you can see, the STL algorithms can be combined to work with the existing string functions without problems. The function `strlen()` provides a convenient method to generate past-the-end iterators. Once the beginning of the string is located, the `find()` function is used to locate the space at the end of the substring, and the `copy()` function, in conjunction with an `ostream_iterator`, is used to print out the result.

Listing 4.13 demonstrates the use of `find_end()`.

```
#include <algorithm>
#include <iostream>
#include <string.h>

using namespace std;

void main()
{
    char    str[64];
    char    substr[8];
    char*   locn;

    strcpy(str,
        "Halloween night is the night of fright");
    strcpy(substr, "night");

    locn = find_end(str, str + strlen(str),
                    substr, substr + strlen(substr));
```

```
if(locn == (str + strlen(str)))
{
   cout << substr << " not found" << endl;
}
else
{
   cout << locn << endl;
}
```

```
night of fright
```

```
}
```

Listing 4.13 — Finding the Last Occurrence of a String [find_end.cpp]

This simple program demonstrates the use of the find_end() function. str contains an array of characters where the string "night" occurs twice. str is searched to find the last occurrence of "night". As you can see from the output, the final occurrence of the subsequence is returned.

4.4 Mutating Sequence Algorithms

The mutating sequence algorithms are characterized by changing either the order of the sequence to which they are applied or the values in the sequence. This includes functions to assign values, rearrange sequences, and apply functions to sequences.

4.4.1 Copy

The copy algorithm has been used frequently in the examples in previous sections. This demonstrates that often the simplest, most mundane operations are used more frequently than far more complex ones. The function of the copy algorithm is to copy the elements from one sequence to another. The copy algorithm is performed in linear time, $O(n)$. There are two implementations of the copy algorithm: copy() and copy_backward():

```
template <class InputIterator, class OutputIterator>
OutputIterator copy(InputIterator    first,
```

```
                          InputIterator      last,
                          OutputIterator     result);

template <class BidirectionalIterator1,
    class BidirectionalIterator2>
BidirectionalIterator2
copy_backward(BidirectionalIterator1   first,
              BidirectionalIterator1   last,
              BidirectionalIterator2   result);
```

There are several differences between these two implementations of the copy algorithm. The `copy()` function copies in the forward direction from `first` up to `last`, placing the results at successive locations starting at `result`. As a consequence, caution must be exercised if the source and destination sequences overlap. If you are careful, you can allow a partial overlap as long as `result` does not lie in the range [`first, last`), since that will not destroy the data being copied. The function returns the past-the-end iterator for the destination sequence.

`copy_backward()` copies the value `*(last - 1)` to `*result`, `*(last - 2)` to `*(result - 1)`, and so on. This means that `result` actually indicates the end of the destination sequence, not its beginning. The implementation of the algorithm implies that the source and destination sequences can overlap only if `result` does not lie in the range [`first, last`). The function returns an iterator that references the last value copied in the destination sequence, which is the start of the destination sequence.

The decision as to which function to use is usually based on whether the two sequences overlap, and if so, which ends overlap. Careful programming is required in such situations to avoid the possible destruction of data in either the source or destination sequences. Listing 4.14 demonstrates how values in a source sequence can be overwritten before they are copied, resulting in data loss. It goes on to show that the complementary function `copy_backward()` can be used to achieve a correct result where `copy()` failed.

```
#include <algorithm>
#include <iostream>

using namespace std;

main()
{
    int   i, ar[10];
    // initialize sequence
    fill(ar,ar+10,0);
```

```
for(i=0; i<5; i++) ar[i] = i + 1;

cout << "initial sequence" << endl;
copy(ar, ar+10, ostream_iterator<int>(cout, " "));
cout << endl;
copy(ar, ar+5, ar+3);
cout << "after copy(ar, ar+5, ar+3)" << endl;
copy(ar, ar+10, ostream_iterator<int>(cout, " "));
cout << endl;

// reinitialize sequence and try again
fill(ar,ar+10,0);
for(i=0; i<5; i++) ar[i] = i + 1;

copy_backward(ar, ar+5, ar+8);
cout << "after copy_backward(ar, ar+5, ar+8)\n";
copy(ar, ar+10, ostream_iterator<int>(cout, " "));
cout << endl;
return(0);
}
```

```
initial sequence
1 2 3 4 5 0 0 0 0 0
after copy(ar, ar+5, ar+3)
1 2 3 1 2 3 1 2 0 0
after copy_backward(ar, ar+5, ar+8)
1 2 3 1 2 3 4 5 0 0
```

Listing 4.14 — Using copy() and copy_backward() [CpFwdBck.cpp]

4.4.2 Swapping

The swapping algorithm exchanges two values or the contents of two sequences. Swapping of two values takes constant time, and the swapping of ranges takes linear time. Three functions are used to implement the swapping algorithm: swap(), iter_swap(), and swap_ranges():

```
template <class T>
void swap(T& a, T& b);
```

```
template <class ForwardIterator1, class
   ForwardIterator2>
void iter_swap(ForwardIterator1  a,
               ForwardIterator2  b);

template <class ForwardIterator1,
   class ForwardIterator2>
ForwardIterator2 swap_ranges(
            ForwardIterator1    first1,
            ForwardIterator1    last1,
            ForwardIterator2    first2);
```

The function swap() simply swaps two values. iter_swap() swaps two values that are referenced by iterators. swap_ranges() swaps the values stored in the range from first1 up to last1 with the values in the range of the same length beginning at first2. swap_ranges() returns a past-the-end iterator for the destination sequence.

swap() requires that the type T be assignable, and swap_ranges() requires that the two ranges do not overlap. (See Listing 4.15.)

```
#include <algorithm>
#include <iostream>

using namespace std;

main()
{
   int                      ar1[10], ar2[10], i;
   ostream_iterator<int>    outStream(cout, " ");

   for(i=0; i<10; i++) {
      ar1[i] = i;
      ar2[i] = i+10;
   }
   copy(ar1, ar1+10, outStream);
   cout << '\n';
   copy(ar2, ar2+10, outStream);
   cout << '\n';
   swap_ranges(ar1, ar1+10, ar2);
   cout << "after swap\n";
   copy(ar1, ar1+10, outStream);
   cout << '\n';
   copy(ar2, ar2+10, outStream);
   cout << '\n';
```

```
    return(0);
}
```

```
0 1 2 3 4 5 6 7 8 9
10 11 12 13 14 15 16 17 18 19
after swap
10 11 12 13 14 15 16 17 18 19
0 1 2 3 4 5 6 7 8 9
```

Listing 4.15 — Swapping Ranges [swp_rng.cpp]

4.4.3 Filling

The filling algorithm is used to fill all or part of a sequence with copies of the same value. This operation is performed in linear time. The algorithm is useful for the initialization of sequences. Two functions are used to implement the fill algorithm—`fill()` and `fill_n()`:

```
template <class ForwardIterator, class T>
void fill(ForwardIterator   first,
          ForwardIterator   last,
          const T&          value);

template <class OutputIterator, class Size, class T>
void fill_n(OutputIterator first,
            Size           n,
            const T&       value);
```

`fill()` assigns `value` to all the elements of the sequence from `first` up to `last`. `fill_n()` assigns value to the n elements of the sequence beginning at `first`.

Listing 4.16 uses `fill_n()` to assign the same value to every member in a portion of a sequence.

```
#include <algorithm>
#include <iostream>

using namespace std;

main()
{
   int                     ar[10], i;
   ostream_iterator<int>   outStream(cout, " ");

   for(i=0; i<10; i++) ar[i] = i;
   fill_n(ar+1, 5, 49);
   copy(ar, ar+10, outStream);
   cout << '\n';

   return(0);
}
```

```
0 49 49 49 49 49 6 7 8 9
```

Listing 4.16 — Filling Sequences with Identical Values [fill.cpp]

4.4.4 Generate

Like the fill algorithm, the generate algorithm fills all or part of a sequence with values. Whereas the fill algorithm used the same value all the time, the generate algorithm uses potentially different values returned from a function object that generates the values. Assuming the function object that generates the values takes constant time, the generate algorithm will take linear time. The generate algorithm is implemented by the functions generate() and generate-_n():

```
template <class ForwardIterator, class Generator>
void generate(ForwardIterator first,
          ForwardIterator   last,
          Generator         gen);

template <class OutputIterator, class Size,
     class Generator>
void generate_n(OutputIterator   first,
                Size             n,
```

```
Generator            gen);
```

The function `generate()` fills the sequence from `first` up to `last` with successive values returned from the generator, which must be a parameterless function object. The function `generate_n()` fills the next n values of the sequence beginning with `first` with the values returned by successive calls to the generator.

Once again, we are faced with the problem of providing a function object for use by a function. The function object must provide `operator()`, and it is expected to return a possibly unique value each time the generate function calls `gen.operator()`. The calculation performed by the function object and the values returned are left to the needs and discretion of the programmer. One of the simplest function objects that could be used is one that simply returns a constant value:

```cpp
class MakePi {
public:
   MakePi() {}
   float operator() () {return 3.14159;}
};
```

This satisfies the requirements of a function object but returns the same value each time it is called. The same effect could be achieved using the function `fill()`. A more useful example is shown in Listing 4.17, where the function object always returns twice the value it returned the last time it was called.

```cpp
#include <algorithm>
#include <iostream>

using namespace std;

template <class T>
class Gener {
private:
   T  value;
public:
   Gener(T& val):value(val){}
   T operator() () {
      T temp;
      temp = value;
      value *= 2;
      return(temp);
   }
};
```

```
main()
{
    int                     ar[10];
    ostream_iterator<int>   outStream(cout, " ");
    int                     initValue = 2;

    generate(ar, ar+10, Gener<int>(initValue));
    copy(ar, ar+10, outStream);
    cout << '\n';

    return(0);
}
```

```
2  4  8  16  32  64  128  256  512  1024
```

Listing 4.17 — Filling Sequences with Different Values [gen.cpp]

Here the function object `Gener` maintains a data member in which it stores the next value to be returned. Each time `operator()` is invoked, it calculates the next value and returns the current one. The `Gener` class has a constructor that initializes the value to be returned. When initialized with a value of 2, it proceeds to generate the successive powers of 2.

The version of the STL distributed by the Rensselaer Polytechnic Institute includes a function object, `IotaGen`, that works just like this. It is constructed with an initial value, and each time `operator()` is called, it returns the current value and then increments it using `operator++`. The result is a series of consecutive values similar to the ones returned by the APL function ι (iota). The SGI distribution includes a nonstandard function, `iota()`, which fills a sequence with successive values of a type that supports `operator++`.

4.4.5 Replace

The replace algorithm replaces all occurrences of values in a sequence that satisfy a predicate with a new value. The entire sequence is traversed, yielding a linear time operation. The functions `replace()` and `replace_if()` implement the replace algorithm:

```
template <class ForwardIterator, class T>
void replace(ForwardIterator  first,
             ForwardIterator  last,
```

```
                const T&              old_value,
                const T&              new_value);

template <class ForwardIterator, class Predicate,
    class T>
void replace_if(ForwardIterator    first,
                ForwardIterator     last,
                Predicate           pred,
                const T&            new_value);

template<class InputIterator, class OutputIterator,
    class T>
OutputIterator replace_copy(InputIterator first,
                            InputIterator  last,
                            OutputIterator result,
                            const T&       old_value,
                            const T&       new_value);

template<class Iterator, class OutputIterator,
    class Predicate, class T>
OutputIterator replace_copy_if(Iterator    first,
                            Iterator       last,
                            OutputIterator result,
                            Predicate      pred,
                            const T&       new_value);
```

The replace() function traverses the sequence from first up to last,
replacing all occurrences of old_value with new_value. The re-
place_if() function replaces all values in the sequence that satisfy the predicate pred with new_value. replace_copy() and replace_copy-
_if() perform the same operations but place their output at the position indi-
cated by result, leaving the original sequence unchanged. The copying versions require that the input and output ranges do not overlap.

Listing 4.18 replaces all values in a sequence that are greater than 5 with the
value -1.

```c++
#include <algorithm>
#include <iostream>
#include <functional>

using namespace std;

main()
{
    int                     ar[10], i;
```

```
ostream_iterator<int>    outStream(cout, " ");

for(i=0; i<10; i++) ar[i] = i;
replace_if(ar, ar+10, bind2nd(greater<int>(), 5),
    -1);

copy(ar, ar+10, outStream);
cout << '\n';

return(0);
}
```

```
0 1 2 3 4 5 -1 -1 -1 -1
```

Listing 4.18 — Replacing Values in a Sequence [repl.cpp]

4.4.6 Transform

The transform algorithm takes one or two sequences as input and produces a new
sequence by applying a function to them. If only one sequence is used, a unary
function must be supplied to transform each value into that which will be placed
in the result sequence. If two sequences are used, a binary function must be supplied that will be applied to corresponding members of the two input sequences
to yield a new value for the output sequence. The algorithm takes linear time,
assuming the function it calls takes constant time. The algorithm is implemented
by the transform function, which has two signatures:

```
template <class InputIterator, class OutputIterator,
    class UnaryOperation>
OutputIterator transform(InputIterator    first,
                InputIterator    last,
                OutputIterator   result,
                UnaryOperation   op);

template <class InputIterator1, class InputIterator2,
    class OutputIterator, class BinaryOperation>
OutputIterator transform(InputIterator1   first1,
                InputIterator1   last1,
                InputIterator2   first2,
                OutputIterator   result,
                BinaryOperation  binary_op);
```

The first form works on a single sequence and requires a unary function object. The resultant sequence is of the same length as the input sequence and is placed at the location referenced by `result`. The second form works with two input sequences and expects a binary function object. Both functions return a past-the-end iterator for the result sequence. Either of the input sequences can overlap the result sequence without destruction of the result sequence. If such an overlap occurs, all or part of one of the input sequences will be replaced by all or part of the result sequence, as shown in Listing 4.19.

```
#include <algorithm>
#include <iostream>
#include <functional>

using namespace std;

main()
{
    int                 ar1[10], ar2[10], result[10], i;
    ostream_iterator<int>  outStream(cout, " ");

    for(i=0; i<10; i++) ar1[i] = i;
    for(i=0; i<10; i+=2) fill_n(ar2+i, 2, i/2);
    copy(ar1, ar1+10, outStream);
    cout << '\n';
    copy(ar2, ar2+10, outStream);
    cout << '\n';
    transform(ar1, ar1+10, ar2, result,
        multiplies<int>());
    copy(result, result+10, outStream);
    cout << '\n';

    return(0);
}
```

```
0 1 2 3 4 5 6 7 8 9
0 0 1 1 2 2 3 3 4 4
0 0 2 3 8 10 18 21 32 36
```

Listing 4.19 — Transforming Two Sequences to a New Sequence [trnsfrm.cpp]

4.4.7 Remove

The remove algorithm removes all elements from a sequence that satisfy a condition. The result sequence will be shorter than the original sequence if any values were removed. This is a linear time algorithm. Four functions are used to implement the remove algorithm: `remove()`, `remove_if()`, `remove_copy()`, and `remove_copy_if()`:

```
template <class ForwardIterator, class T>
ForwardIterator remove(ForwardIterator   first,
                       ForwardIterator   last,
                       const T&          value);

template <class ForwardIterator, class Predicate>
ForwardIterator remove_if(ForwardIterator first,
                       ForwardIterator   last,
                       Predicate         pred);
template <class InputIterator, class OutputIterator,
   class T>
OutputIterator remove_copy(InputIterator  first,
                       InputIterator     last,
                       OutputIterator    result,
                       const T&          value);

template <class InputIterator, class OutputIterator,
   class Predicate>
OutputIterator remove_copy_if(InputIterator  first,
                       InputIterator     last,
                       OutputIterator    result,
                       Predicate         pred);
```

`remove()` is the most straightforward of the four functions since it searches a range for a value and removes all occurrences of it. `remove_if()` employs a predicate to identify the values that should be deleted from the sequence. All values that satisfy the predicate are removed. The two copy functions work analogously, but the original sequence is left unchanged and all values that do not satisfy the predicate are copied to the destination sequence. The result is the same—to remove the values that satisfy the predicate. `remove_copy()` eliminates all values that are equal to `value`, and `remove_copy_if()` eliminates those that satisfy its predicate. All of the functions return a past-the-end iterator for the possibly shortened sequence. As usual, the predicate must be a function object. (See Listing 4.20.)

```
#include <algorithm>
#include <list>
#include <iostream>
#include <functional>

using namespace std;

main()
{
    list<int>                list1;
    list<int>::iterator      iter;
    int                      i;
    ostream_iterator<int>    outStream(cout, " ");

    for(i=0; i<10;i++) list1.push_back(i);
    copy(list1.begin(), list1.end(), outStream);
    cout << '\n';

    iter = remove_if(list1.begin(),list1.end(),
        bind2nd(greater<int>(),6));
    copy(list1.begin(), list1.end(), outStream);
    cout << '\n';
    copy(list1.begin(), iter, outStream);
    cout << '\n';

    return(0);
}
```

```
0 1 2 3 4 5 6 7 8 9
0 1 2 3 4 5 6 7 8 9
0 1 2 3 4 5 6
```

Listing 4.20 — Removing Values from the End of a Sequence [rm_if.cpp]

Although the function removed the values from the list, it did not change the endpoint returned by end(). You can only determine the new endpoint by using the iterator returned by the function. Now what happens if values are deleted from the middle of the sequence rather than the end, as in Listing 4.21?

```
iter = remove(list1.begin(),iter, 4);
copy(list1.begin(), list1.end(), outStream);
cout << '\n';
copy(list1.begin(), iter, outStream);
cout << '\n';
```

```
0 1 2 3 5 6 6 7 8 9
0 1 2 3 5 6
```

Listing 4.21 — Removing Values from the Middle of a Sequence

If the code in Listing 4.21 is added just before the end of the previous program, we gain an insight into how the remove algorithm actually works. To remove an element, it moved all the elements down, resulting in one element being duplicated. The endpoint of the list, as returned by end(), is no longer valid, and you should be careful not to use it.

4.4.8 Unique

The unique algorithm traverses a sequence and deletes all duplicates of adjacent elements that satisfy a condition. The algorithm runs in linear time and is implemented by the functions unique and unique_copy, each of which has two signatures:

```
template <class ForwardIterator>
ForwardIterator unique(ForwardIterator    first,
                  ForwardIterator    last);

template <class ForwardIterator,
   class BinaryPredicate>
ForwardIterator unique(ForwardIterator first,
                  ForwardIterator    last,
                  BinaryPredicate    binary_pred);

template <class InputIterator, class OutputIterator>
OutputIterator unique_copy(
                  InputIterator   first,
                  InputIterator   last,
                  OutputIterator  result);

template <class InputIterator, class OutputIterator,
```

```
        class BinaryPredicate>
OutputIterator unique_copy(
            InputIterator       first,
            InputIterator       last,
            OutputIterator      result,
            BinaryPredicate     binary_pred);
```

Since the algorithm finds duplicates only if they are adjacent, it is usually applied to sequences that are sorted. This need not always be the case, and the algorithm can be applied to any sequence as long as the programmer remembers that it will remove duplicate elements only if they are adjacent.

The first form of unique removes duplicate adjacent elements that are equal. The second form of unique removes duplicate adjacent elements that satisfy the predicate supplied. unique_copy performs the same operation while making a copy of the original sequence. unique_copy removes adjacent duplicates during the copy operation, leaves the original sequence unchanged, and places the possibly shorter resulting sequence at the position referenced by result. All of the functions return a past-the-end iterator for the result sequence, which should be used in place of the value returned by end() for the result sequence. (See Listing 4.22.)

```
#include <algorithm>
#include <iostream>
#include <functional>

using namespace std;

main()
{
    int                     ar[10], i, *new_end;
    ostream_iterator<int>   outStream(cout, " ");

    for(i=0; i<10; i++) ar[i] = i;
    ar[7] = ar[8] = 6;
    ar[0] = 12;
    copy(ar, ar+10, outStream);
    cout << '\n';

    new_end = unique(ar, ar+10);
    copy(ar, new_end, outStream);
    cout << '\n';

    new_end = unique(ar, new_end, less<int>());
    copy(ar, new_end, outStream);
    cout << '\n';
```

```
    return(0);
}
```

```
12 1 2 3 4 5 6 6 6 9
12 1 2 3 4 5 6 9
12 1
```

Listing 4.22 — Deleting Duplicate Values [uniq.cpp]

The first call to unique removes all the adjacent duplicates by comparing adjacent values for equality. The second call to unique specifies a predicate equivalent to operator<, with the result that adjacent elements are considered duplicates if the first one is less than the second. The effect of this is to remove all of the sequence after the 1, since all of the elements after that are less than the element that succeeds them.

4.4.9 Reverse

The reverse algorithm, as the name implies, reverses the order of all elements in a sequence. This is a linear time algorithm that is implemented by the functions reverse() and reverse_copy():

```
template <class BidirectionalIterator>
void reverse(BidirectionalIterator   first,
             BidirectionalIterator   last);

template <class BidirectionalIterator, class
   OutputIterator>
OutputIterator reverse_copy(
             BidirectionalIterator      first,
             BidirectionalIterator      last,
             OutputIterator             result);
```

The reverse() function reverses the order of the elements in the sequence from first up to last. The reverse_copy() function copies the elements from the original sequence to the destination sequence beginning at result, reversing the order of the elements during the copy operation. reverse_copy() returns a past-the-end iterator for the destination sequence. (See Listing 4.23.)

```
#include <algorithm>
#include <string.h>
#include <iostream>

using namespace std;

main()
{
    char                    str1[16], str2[16], *iter;
    ostream_iterator<char>  outStream(cout, "");

    strcpy(str1, "i saw sue");
    reverse(str1, str1+strlen(str1));
    copy(str1, str1+strlen(str1), outStream);
    cout << '\n';

    iter = reverse_copy(str1, str1+strlen(str1), str2);
    copy(str2, iter, outStream);
    cout << '\n';

    return(0);
}
```

```
eus was i
i saw sue
```

Listing 4.23 — Reversing the Order of a Sequence [rev.cpp]

4.4.10 Rotate

The rotate algorithm moves the elements of a sequence in a circular fashion, as if the sequence formed a circle so that the beginning and ending of the sequence were connected. The input to the algorithm is the sequence to rotate and a position within the sequence indicating the amount it should be rotated. The result of the algorithm is the sequence rotated so that the element referenced within the sequence is placed at the beginning of the sequence. This is a linear time operation and is implemented by the functions rotate() and rotate_copy():

```
template <class ForwardIterator>
void rotate(ForwardIterator    first,
```

```
                    ForwardIterator    middle,
                    ForwardIterator    last);

        template <class ForwardIterator, class OutputIterator>
        OutputIterator rotate_copy(ForwardIterator    first,
                                   ForwardIterator    middle,
                                   ForwardIterator    last,
                                   OutputIterator     result);
```

The rotate() function rotates the sequence from first up to last so that the element referenced by middle, which must be in the sequence, is placed at the beginning of the sequence. The rotate_copy() function copies the sequence from first up to last to the location referenced by result, rotating the sequence during the copy operation so that the element referenced by middle is at the start of the result sequence. The input and output sequences should not overlap. The function returns a past-the-end iterator for the result sequence. (See Listing 4.24.)

```
#include <algorithm>
#include <iostream>

using namespace std;

main()
{
    int                      ar[10], i, *middle;
    ostream_iterator<int>    outStream(cout, " ");

    for(i=0; i<10; i++) ar[i] = i;
    middle = ar + 6;
    rotate(ar, middle, ar+10);
    copy(ar, ar+10, outStream);
    cout << '\n';

    return(0);
}
```

```
6 7 8 9 0 1 2 3 4 5
```

Listing 4.24 — Rotating a Sequence [rot.cpp]

The effect is to take the original sequence and rotate it so that the element in the seventh position is moved to the front of the sequence. The iterators for the beginning and end of the sequence remain valid after the operation completes.

4.4.11 Random Shuffle

The random shuffle algorithm rearranges the elements in a sequence so that their order is random. The resulting sequence will have a uniform distribution. The algorithm runs in linear time and is implemented by the `random_shuffle()` function, with two signatures:

```
template <class RandomAccessIterator>
void random_shuffle(
        RandomAccessIterator    first,
        RandomAccessIterator    last);

template <class RandomAccessIterator, class
    RandomNumberGenerator>
void random_shuffle(RandomAccessIterator   first,
                    RandomAccessIterator   last,
                    RandomNumberGenerator& rand);
```

The first form of the function uses a random number generator provided with the STL to randomly reorder the elements in the sequence. The second form allows the user to specify an alternate random number generator in the form of a function object. This function object must provide `operator()(n)`, which has to return a value of type `Distance` in the range from 0 to n-1. Listing 4.25 demonstrates the use of `random_shuffle()`.

```
#include <algorithm>
#include <iostream>

using namespace std;

main()
{
    int                     ar[10], i;
    ostream_iterator<int>   outStream(cout, " ");

    for(i=0; i<10; i++) ar[i] = i;

    for(i=0; i<4; i++) {
        random_shuffle(ar, ar+10);
        copy(ar, ar+10, outStream);
```

```
        cout << '\n';
    }

    return(0);
}
```

```
4  3  0  2  6  7  8  9  5  1
3  9  7  5  0  2  6  8  1  4
0  3  2  6  5  8  4  9  7  1
2  8  9  5  1  7  0  6  4  3
```

Listing 4.25 — Shuffling a Sequence [shuffle.cpp]

As you can see, the output from the function changes every time it is called.

4.4.12 Partitioning

Partitioning divides a sequence into two subsequences based upon whether the values satisfy a predicate. All values satisfying the predicate are placed in the first subsequence and the rest in the second subsequence.

One of the common uses of such an operation is to perform a partial sort as part of a larger sorting algorithm. For example, the quicksort selects a value in a sequence and partitions the sequence so that all members less than the value are in one subsequence, and all members greater than or equal to the value are in the other subsequence. Quicksort continues to split the sequences like this until they are small enough to be sorted conveniently with another algorithm. The resulting subsequences, each of which is sorted, are then merged to form a complete sorted sequence.

The partition algorithm runs in linear time and is implemented by the functions `partition()` and `stable_partition()`:

```
template <class BidirectionalIterator, class
    Predicate>
BidirectionalIterator partition(
            BidirectionalIterator    first,
            BidirectionalIterator    last,
            Predicate                pred);

template <class BidirectionalIterator, class
```

```
      Predicate>
BidirectionalIterator
stable_partition(BidirectionalIterator first,
              BidirectionalIterator    last,
              Predicate                pred);
```

Both of the functions have the same parameters and perform the same function. The difference is how they arrange the elements in the two subsequences. `stable_partition()` guarantees that the relative order of equal elements in each of the subsequences will be preserved, whereas `partition()` makes no such claim.

To see how partition is used, let's write the quicksort algorithm as in Listing 4.26.

```cpp
#include <algorithm>
#include <iostream>
#include <functional>

using namespace std;

void QuikSort(int* first, int* last)
{
    int    len;
    int    *pivot, *second, *splitPoint;

    len = distance(first, last);
    if(len < 2) return;
    if(len == 2) {
        second = first;
        second++;
        if(*first > *second) iter_swap(first, second);
        return;
    }
    pivot = adjacent_find(first, last,
        not_equal_to<int>());
    if(pivot == last) return;        // avoid loop
    splitPoint = partition(first, last,
        bind2nd(less<int>(),*pivot));
    if(splitPoint == first) splitPoint++;
        // avoid loop
    QuikSort(first, splitPoint);
    QuikSort(splitPoint, last);
}

main()
```

```
{
    int                     ar[10], i;
    ostream_iterator<int>   outStream(cout, " ");

    for(i=0; i<10; i++) ar[i] = i;
    random_shuffle(ar, ar+10);
    copy(ar, ar+10, outStream);
    cout << '\n';

    QuikSort(ar, ar+10);
    copy(ar, ar+10, outStream);
    cout << '\n';

    return(0);
}
```

```
4 3 0 2 6 7 8 9 5 1
0 1 2 3 4 5 6 7 8 9
```

Listing 4.26 — Using Partition to Implement Quick Sort [qsort.cpp]

The quicksort algorithm begins by checking the length of the sequence by using the function distance(). If the sequence is of length 0 or 1, it returns, since these sequences are already sorted. If the sequence is of length 2, it swaps the values if necessary to obtain a sorted sequence. If the sequence is longer, the quicksort partitions the sequence into two subsequences that will be sorted recursively.

The swapping of two out of order values is where some of the sorting occurs. The rest is performed by partitioning the sequence, which is equivalent to a partial sort. Although the partition step might not seem like much, it reduces the number of swaps that must be done and makes the algorithm quicker.

To partition the sequence, the algorithm first finds a value to use as a point to partition the sequence, called the pivot. Although many papers have been written on how a pivot should be selected, our quicksort program picks the first of two unequal adjacent values in the sequence. The function adjacent_find() is used to pick a pivot by passing a predicate of not_equal_to().

Once the pivot has been selected, the partition() function splits the sequence into one where all the values are less than the pivot, and a second where all the values are greater than or equal to the pivot. QuikSort() is then called recursively to sort each of these subsequences.

Even a short program such as quicksort can make use of several of the STL functions. As you become more familiar with the functions that are available, you will find more applications for them in your daily programming tasks.

5
Sorting and Related Algorithms

5.1 Introduction

The STL sorting and related algorithms include sorting, searching, merging, set operations, heap operations, maximum, minimum, and lexicographical comparison. These operations are either involved in sorting or manipulating sequences that are assumed to be sorted in some way. The set and heap operations actually create new data structures from existing ones by providing a set of operations to operate on the new structures. Taken together, the sorting and related algorithms form a major portion of the total STL algorithms.

5.2 Preliminaries

The algorithms in this chapter are all concerned with the ordering of elements in sequences. To perform these algorithms, it is necessary to compare elements so that an order of the elements can be established. This comparison is done in two different ways: using operator< or a function object of type Compare. A function object of type Compare must provide operator()(a, b), which returns true only if the first parameter is less than the second if it is to behave like operator<.

Most of the time the algorithms deal with sequences of classes or built-in types for which operator< is defined. A function object of type Compare can be used for those types that do not have operator< defined or when a special-purpose ordering is desired that differs from that provided by operator<. All of the algorithms that follow have an implementation using operator< and an implementation that uses a function object of type Compare.

5.3 Sorting

Sorting is one of the most common operations performed on computers with some studies reporting that 75 percent of a computer's time is spent sorting. As a result, it is important that the sorting algorithms used be as efficient as possible. The STL provides several sorting functions that run in *O(n log n)* time. These are some of the most efficient general-purpose sorting algorithms and are suitable for use in most applications. The sorting algorithm is implemented by the functions sort(), stable_sort(), partial_sort(), and part-ial- _sort_copy():

```
template <class RandomAccessIterator>
void sort(RandomAccessIterator    first,
          RandomAccessIterator    last);

template <class RandomAccessIterator, class Compare>
void sort(RandomAccessIterator    first,
          RandomAccessIterator    last,
          Compare                 comp);

template <class RandomAccessIterator>
void stable_sort(RandomAccessIterator   first,
                 RandomAccessIterator last);

template <class RandomAccessIterator, class Compare>
void stable_sort(RandomAccessIterator   first,
                 RandomAccessIterator last,
                 Compare                comp);

template <class RandomAccessIterator>
void partial_sort(
            RandomAccessIterator first,
            RandomAccessIterator middle,
            RandomAccessIterator last);

template <class RandomAccessIterator,
   class Compare>
void partial_sort(RandomAccessIterator first,
                  RandomAccessIterator middle,
                  RandomAccessIterator last,
                  Compare               comp);

template <class InputIterator,
   class RandomAccessIterator>
RandomAccessIterator partial_sort_copy(
            InputIterator           first,
```

```
        InputIterator                last,
        RandomAccessIterator         result_first,
        RandomAccessIterator         result_last);

template <class InputIterator,
    class RandomAccessIterator, class Compare>
RandomAccessIterator
partial_sort_copy(
        InputIterator                first,
        InputIterator                last,
        RandomAccessIterator         result_first,
        RandomAccessIterator         result_last,
        Compare                      comp);
```

The first form of the sort() function sorts the elements in the sequence
from first up to last in ascending order. If descending order is required,
then an appropriate compare function object can be supplied to the second form
of the function.

When sorting, there is always the question of what to do when equal elements
are encountered. There are two solutions—maintain the relative ordering of the
equal elements, or change the relative ordering. The stable_sort() function guarantees that the relative ordering of equal elements found in the initial
sequence will be preserved in the sorted sequence. The sort() function makes
no such claim and might well alter the relative ordering of equal elements. The
importance of preserving the relative ordering of equal elements depends on the
nature of the application, and the decision of which function to use is left to the
application designer.

The partial_sort() function sorts only a portion of the sequence. It
sorts the first middle - first elements of the sequence and places them at
the start of the sequence. The remaining elements are placed beginning at the
position referenced by middle and are in no particular order. par-
tial_sort_copy() sorts the number of elements equal to the minimum of
the length of the two sequences (min(last - first, result_last -
result_first)) and places them at the position referenced by re-
sult_first. It returns a past-the-end iterator for the result sequence.

Listing 5.1 demonstrates how to sort a sequence into both ascending and descending order.

```
#include <algorithm>
#include <iostream>
#include <functional>

using namespace std;

template <class T>
class DescendCmp:
    public binary_function<T, T, bool>
{
public:
bool operator()(const T a, const T b) {
        if(a < b) return false;
        return true;
    }
};

main()
{
    int                     ar[20], i;
    ostream_iterator<int>   outStream(cout, " ");

    for(i=0; i<20; i++) ar[i] = i;
    random_shuffle(ar, ar+20);
    cout << "Unsorted:    ";
    copy(ar, ar+20, outStream);
    cout << endl;

    sort(ar, ar+20);
    cout << "Ascending:   ";
    copy(ar, ar+20, outStream);
    cout << endl;

    random_shuffle(ar, ar+20);
    cout << "Unsorted:    ";
    copy(ar, ar+20, outStream);
    cout << endl;

    sort(ar, ar+20, DescendCmp<int>());
    cout << "Descending: ";
    copy(ar, ar+20, outStream);
    cout << endl;

    return(0);
```

```
}
```

```
Unsorted:     6 11  9  2 18 12 17  7  0 15  4  8 10  5  1 19 13  3 14 16
Ascending:    0  1  2  3  4  5  6  7  8  9 10 11 12 13 14 15 16 17 18 19
Unsorted:    18 15  4  5  8  3 17 13 10 16  9 11  6  1 14 19  2  0 12  7
Descending:  19 18 17 16 15 14 13 12 11 10  9  8  7  6  5  4  3  2  1  0
```

Listing 5.1 — Sorting [sort1.cpp]

An ascending sequence is obtained by using the function sort() without having to specify a comparison function. To generate a descending sequence, a function object is provided that does the exact opposite of operator<. Another reason to specify a function object to perform the comparison is when structures or classes are being sorted and you want a different comparison from that provided by operator<. Listing 5.2 shows how you could use a comparison function to sort a sequence of structures.

```cpp
#include <algorithm>
#include <iostream>
#include <functional>

using namespace std;

struct Person {
    char* name;
    int   age;
};

ostream& operator<<(ostream& os, const Person& them)
{
    os << "(" << them.name << ", " << them.age << ")";
    return os;
}

class PersonCmp:
    public binary_function<Person&, Person&, bool>
{
public:
    bool operator()(Person& p1, Person& p2)
    {
        return(p1.age < p2.age);
    }
```

```
    };

    main()
    {
        Person    folks[10] =
        {{"John",  8}, {"Sue",  12},     {"Sam",  7},
         {"Ellen", 9}, {"Cathy",  8},     {"Bobby", 9},
         {"Pete", 11}, {"Jane",  7},     {"Dick",  8},
         {"Tammy", 11}};
        ostream_iterator<Person>    outStream(cout, " ");

        sort(folks, folks+10,PersonCmp());
        copy(folks, folks+5, outStream);
        cout << endl;
        copy(folks+5, folks+10, outStream);
        cout << endl;

        return(0);
    }
```

```
(Sam, 7) (Jane, 7) (John, 8) (Cathy, 8) (Dick, 8)
(Ellen, 9) (Bobby, 9) (Pete, 11) (Tammy, 11) (Sue, 12)
```

Listing 5.2 — Sorting by Age [rec_sort.cpp]

The use of a compare function object allowed us to sort on age. We could write another compare function object or define operator< to work with the name field if we wanted to sort on name.

If you check, you will find that the relative order of the equal elements in the input sequence is preserved in the output sequence. This is misleading since we used sort(), which yields an unstable sort. It was pure chance that the order was preserved in this case. You should use stable_sort() if it is important that the relative order of equal elements be preserved.

Listing 5.3 uses partial_sort() to obtain a list of the people with the top five marks in a class.

```cpp
#include <algorithm>
#include <iostream>
#include <functional>

using namespace std;

struct Person {
    char* name;
    int    mark;
    int operator<(Person p2) { return(mark > p2.mark); }
};

ostream& operator<<(ostream& os, const Person& them)
{
    os << "(" << them.name << ", " << them.mark <<
        ")" ;
    return os;
}

class PersonCmp:
    public binary_function<Person&, Person&, bool>
{
public:
    PersonCmp() {}
    bool operator()(const Person& p1, const Person& p2)
        const
    {
        return(p1.mark > p2.mark);
    }
};

void main()
{
    Person    folks[10] =
    {{"John", 92}, {"Sue", 61},    {"Sam", 73},
     {"Ellen", 88},{"Cathy", 86},   {"Bobby", 79},
     {"Pete", 57}, {"Jane", 78},    {"Dick", 63},
     {"Tammy", 74}};
    Person*                    middle;
    ostream_iterator<Person>   outStream(cout, " ");

    middle = folks + 5;
    partial_sort(folks, middle, folks+10, PersonCmp());
    copy(folks, middle, outStream);
    cout << endl;
```

```
      }
```

```
(John, 92) (Ellen, 88) (Cathy, 86) (Bobby, 79) (Jane, 78)
```

Listing 5.3 — Partial Sort [par_sort.cpp]

5.3.1 Nth Element

The nth element algorithm places a single element from a sequence into the position in which it would lie had the entire sequence been sorted. It also ensures that all of the elements before the final position of the nth element are less than or equal to all of the elements after the nth element. This is a linear time operation and is implemented by the function nth_element():

```
template <class RandomAccessIterator>
void nth_element(
      RandomAccessIterator first,
      RandomAccessIterator nth,
      RandomAccessIterator last);
```

```
template <class RandomAccessIterator>
void nth_element(
      RandomAccessIterator      first,
      RandomAccessIterator      nth,
      RandomAccessIterator      last,
      Compare                   comp);
```

In both versions of the function, nth is an iterator that refers to the position of the element in the final sorted sequence that should be placed into its final sorted position. first and last delimit the range of the sequence in which nth lies. This algorithm is demonstrated in Listing 5.4.

```
#include <algorithm>
#include <iostream>

using namespace std;

main()
{
    int                   ar[10], i;
    ostream_iterator<int> outStream(cout, " ");

    for(i=0;i<10;i++) ar[i] = i;
    random_shuffle(ar, ar+10);
    copy(ar, ar+10, outStream);
    cout << endl;

    nth_element(ar, ar+5, ar+10);
    copy(ar, ar+10, outStream);
    cout << endl;

    return(0);
}
```

```
4 3 0 2 6 7 8 9 5 1
0 1 2 3 4 5 6 7 8 9
```

Listing 5.4 — Using nth_element() [nth_elem.cpp]

The important point to notice here is that nth_element() places the element that will lie at the sixth position (counting in origin 1) of the sorted sequence into its final position. It *does not* necessarily move the sixth element, in this case, 7, of the unsorted sequence into its final position.

5.4 Searching Algorithms

Although it might not be obvious at first, all of the searching algorithms do involve a search. The search that is used in each of the algorithms is the binary search. This is a fast search that executes in logarithmic time on sorted sequences. The use of the binary search means that all of the algorithms in this section can be used only on sorted sequences.

5.4.1 Binary Search

The binary search algorithm is a fast search algorithm for sorted sequences. It takes logarithmic time and is used as the search algorithm by all the other algorithms in this section. The binary search algorithm itself is used to find a specific value in the sequence. The algorithm is implemented by the function binary_search():

```
template <class ForwardIterator, class T>
bool binary_search(ForwardIterator  first,
                   ForwardIterator  last,
                   const T&         value);

template <class ForwardIterator, class T,
    class Compare>
bool binary_search(ForwardIterator  first,
                   ForwardIterator  last,
                   const T&         value,
                   Compare          comp);
```

Both versions of binary_search() search the sequence from first up to last for value. The second form allows the use of a comparison function other than operator<. This is useful if the sequence is in descending rather than ascending order. The function returns a Boolean result indicating if the value is in the sequence.

The binary search makes repeated probes into the sequence to find the value for which it is looking. The first probe is halfway through the sequence. It examines this value and, if it is the value for which it is searching, the algorithm returns the result and terminates. If the probe is not the value for which it is searching, the algorithm determines if the probe is less than or greater than the search value and cuts the search range in half. It then repeats the process until it either finds the value, or the search range becomes an empty sequence.

Figure 5.1 shows the steps performed by the binary search when looking for the value 9. The binary search utilizes three iterators to reference positions in the sequence. The iterators bot and top indicate the lower and upper end of the search range, respectively. The iterator probe refers to the element in the sequence that will be tested to see if it is equal to the value being sought.

The algorithm begins at the top left of the diagram with bot and top referencing the ends of the sequence being searched. probe is set to reference the element halfway through the search range. The element referenced by probe is less than 9, so the bottom of the search range is set to be one greater than the

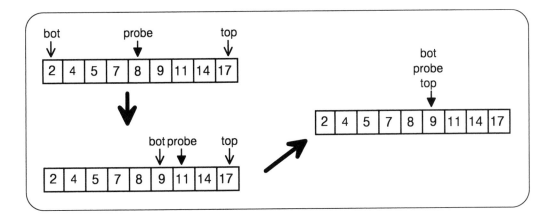

Figure 5.1 — Binary Search for the Value 9

`probe` position. The probe position is then recalculated, and 11 is probed. This is depicted in the lower left of the diagram.

Since 11 is greater than 9, `top` is set to one less than the probe position, and the probe position is recalculated. This causes all three iterators to align, and the value is found. Had there been no occurrence of 9 in the sequence, the algorithm would have terminated when `top` became less than `bot`.

Each time the binary search makes an unsuccessful probe, it divides the search range in half. A finite search range can be cut in half only so many times before there is nothing left. In fact, a search range of size n can be cut in half approximately $\log_2 n$ times, which means that the binary search will terminate after this many probes or less. Thus, the binary search is $O(\log n)$.

Listing 5.5 demonstrates the use of `binary_search()` on a sequence in ascending order.

```
#include <algorithm>
#include <iostream>

using namespace std;

void main()
{
    int   ar[10] = {1, 3, 4, 5, 7, 8, 9, 11, 14, 15};
    int   found = 0;

    found = binary_search(ar, ar+10, 4);
    if(found) cout << "4 is present"  << endl;
    else cout << "4 is absent" << endl;

    found = binary_search(ar, ar+10, 6);
    if(found) cout << "6 is present" << endl;
    else cout << "6 is absent" << endl;
}
```

```
4 is present
6 is absent
```

Listing 5.5 — Binary Search [bin_srch.cpp]

5.4.2 Lower Bound

The lower bound algorithm searches a sorted sequence for the first element that is greater than or equal to a specified value. This is the first position into which the value can be inserted without violating the sequence order. It returns an iterator that references this element or a past-the-end iterator if such an element does not exist. The algorithm runs in logarithmic time and is implemented by the function lower_bound():

```
template <class ForwardIterator, class T>
ForwardIterator lower_bound(
        ForwardIterator   first,
        ForwardIterator   last,
        const T&          value);

template <class ForwardIterator, class T, class
    Compare>
```

```
ForwardIterator lower_bound(
        ForwardIterator    first,
        ForwardIterator    last,
        const T&           value,
        Compare            comp);
```

Listing 5.6 searches a sorted sequence to find the lower bound of the subsequence of values greater than or equal to 5.

```
#include <algorithm>
#include <iostream>

using namespace std;

void main()
{
    int                    ar[10], i, *iter;
    ostream_iterator<int>  outStream(cout, " ");

    for(i=0;i<10;i++) ar[i] = i;
    iter = lower_bound(ar, ar + 10, 5);
    if(iter == ar + 10) cout << "Not found";
    else copy(iter, ar+10, outStream);
    cout << endl;
}
```

```
5 6 7 8 9
```

Listing 5.6 — Lower Bound [lbound.cpp]

Although this works fine with a sequence in ascending order, a variation is needed if the sequence is in descending order. Since the order of the sequence has been reversed, all logic used to process the sequence must also be reversed, meaning that the lower_bound() function must use operator> rather than operator<. This is shown in Listing 5.7, where the lower_bound() function finds the lower bound on a sequence in descending order.

```
#include <algorithm>
#include <functional>
#include <iostream>

using namespace std;

void main()
{
    int                     ar[10], i, *iter;
    ostream_iterator<int>   outStream(cout, " ");

    for(i=0;i<10;i++) ar[i] = 9 - i;
    iter = lower_bound(ar, ar + 10, 5,greater<int>());
    if(iter == ar + 10) cout << "Not found";
    else copy(iter, ar+10, outStream);
    cout << endl;
}
```

```
5 4 3 2 1 0
```

Listing 5.7 — Lower Bound of a Sequence in Descending Order [plbound.cpp]

In the sorting functions, a special-purpose function object was created to perform the comparisons. This is not always necessary, particularly if one is dealing with the built-in types. The function object greater can be used as long as the type to which it is applied defines operator<. This is because greater is implemented as a template, so that it can work with any type, and its operation is expressed in terms of operator<.

5.4.3 Upper Bound

The upper bound algorithm finds the first value in a sorted sequence that is greater than a specified value. This can also be viewed as the last position into which the value can be inserted without violating the ordering of the sequence. The algorithm is implemented by the function upper_bound():

```
template <class ForwardIterator, class T>
ForwardIterator upper_bound(
        ForwardIterator   first,
        ForwardIterator   last,
```

```
          const T&              value);

template <class ForwardIterator, class T,
    class Compare>
ForwardIterator upper_bound(
          ForwardIterator    first,
          ForwardIterator    last,
          const T&           value,
          Compare            comp);
```

Listing 5.8 uses `upper_bound()` to find the position into which a new value can be inserted into a sorted sequence so as to maintain the order of the sequence.

```
#include <algorithm>
#include <list>
#include <iostream>

using namespace std;

void main()
{
    int                     i;
    list<int>               list1;
    list<int>::iterator     iter;
    ostream_iterator<int>   outStream(cout, " ");

    for(i=0;i<5;i++) list1.push_back(i);
    for(i=10;i<15;i++) list1.push_back(i);
    copy(list1.begin(), list1.end(), outStream);
    cout << endl;
    iter = upper_bound(list1.begin(), list1.end(), 7);
    copy(iter, list1.end(), outStream);
    cout << endl;

    list1.insert(iter, 1, 7);
    copy(list1.begin(), list1.end(), outStream);
    cout << endl;
```

```
}
```

```
0 1 2 3 4 10 11 12 13 14
10 11 12 13 14
0 1 2 3 4 7 10 11 12 13 14
```

Listing 5.8 — Upper Bound [ubound.cpp]

Although the list is created in sorted order, a gap has been left in the middle to allow for the insertion of one or more values. The call to `upper_bound()` returns a reference to the element in front of which a 7 can be inserted without disrupting the overall order of the sequence. It does not matter whether the value that `upper_bound()` is looking for is actually in the sequence, since it only has to find the first value greater than it. The iterator returned by `upper_bound()` is used directly in the `insert()` function and results in the proper insertion of the value 7 into the list.

The algorithm also works correctly if it is asked to find the upper bound on a value that is beyond the limits of the existing sequence. For example, if you tried to find the upper bound of 20 in a sequence from 0 … 14, the past-the-end iterator would be returned. Using this as the position to insert the value into the list would insert the value at the end of the list, the correct position.

5.4.4 Equal Range

The equal range algorithm searches a sorted sequence for a range of values that are all equal to a specified value. This implies that the specified value could be inserted at any point in the resulting range. The algorithm is implemented by the function `equal_range()`:

```
template <class ForwardIterator, class T>
pair<ForwardIterator, ForwardIterator>
equal_range(ForwardIterator    first,
            ForwardIterator    last,
            const T&           value);

template <class ForwardIterator, class T,
    class Compare>
pair<ForwardIterator, ForwardIterator>
equal_range(ForwardIterator    first,
```

```
ForwardIterator     last,
const T&            value,
Compare             comp);
```

equal_range() searches the sorted sequence from first up to last for a range of elements equal to value. If such a range exists, it returns a pair of iterators delimiting the range. If no such range exists, it returns a pair of iterators, both of which are equal to first.

The pair of iterators is returned as a structure designed for this purpose, called pair. A pair consists of two values called first and second. The rationale for using such a data structure is that it allows two values to be moved around as easily as a single value. The declaration for the structure looks like this:

```
template <class T1, class T2>
struct pair {
    T1 first;
    T2 second;
    pair();
    pair(const T1& a, const T2& b);
    template<class R, class S>
        pair(const pair<R, S>& p);
};
```

This is implemented as a template so that it can be used to represent a pair of any two values, not just two iterators. In fact, the two values stored in the pair do not even have to be of the same type. A constructor is provided that will create a pair from the two values passed to it. There is also a nonmember convenience function, make_pair(), that accepts two values and returns a pair representing its parameters. The use of a pair in conjunction with equal-_range() is shown in Listing 5.9.

```
#include <algorithm>
#include <list>
#include <iostream>

using namespace std;

void main()
{
    list<int>       list1;
    int             i;
    ostream_iterator<int>   outStream(cout, " ");
    pair<list<int>::iterator, list<int>::iterator>
        range;
```

```
        for(i=0; i<10; i+=2) {
            list1.push_back(i);
            list1.push_back(i);
        }
        copy(list1.begin(), list1.end(), outStream);
        cout << endl;

        range = equal_range(list1.begin(), list1.end(), 6);
        copy(range.first, range.second, outStream);
        cout << endl;
}
```

```
0  0  2  2  4  4  6  6  8  8
6  6
```

Listing 5.9 — Equal Range [eq_range.cpp]

One point to keep in mind is that the second member of the pair returned is a past-the-end iterator for the subsequence, not a reference to the last member of the subsequence. It is also worth noting how the pair range is declared.

5.4.5 Merge

The merge algorithm merges two sorted sequences to yield a third sorted sequence that contains all of the elements from the first two sequences. This algorithm usually runs in linear time but might be $O(n \log n)$ if memory is not available. The algorithm is stable—that is, the relative order of equal elements in the two input sequences is maintained in the final sequence. The algorithm is implemented by the functions merge() and inplace_merge():

```
template <class InputIterator1, class InputIterator2,
    class OutputIterator>
OutputIterator merge(InputIterator1 first1,
                     InputIterator1 last1,
                     InputIterator2 first2,
                     InputIterator2 last2,
                     OutputIterator result);

template <class InputIterator1, class InputIterator2,
    class OutputIterator, class Compare>
```

```
OutputIterator merge(InputIterator1 first1,
                     InputIterator1 last1,
                     InputIterator2 first2,
                     InputIterator2 last2,
                     OutputIterator result,
                     Compare        comp);

template <class BidirectionalIterator>
void inplace_merge(
        BidirectionalIterator   first,
        BidirectionalIterator   middle,
        BidirectionalIterator   last);

template <class BidirectionalIterator, class Compare>
void inplace_merge(
        BidirectionalIterator   first,
        BidirectionalIterator   middle,
        BidirectionalIterator   last,
        Compare                 comp);
```

The merge() function merges the sequence from first1 up to last1 with the sequence from first2 up to last2 and places the resulting sequence at the location referenced by result. The function returns a past-the-end iterator for the result sequence. The result sequence should not overlap with either of the input sequences. The merge() function always runs in linear time.

inplace_merge() merges two contiguous subsequences from first up to middle and from middle up to last into a single sorted sequence that replaces the two original subsequences. If sufficient memory is available to make a copy of the result sequence, the function will run in linear time; otherwise, it will be $O(n \log n)$.

The use of the merge functions is demonstrated in Listing 5.10.

```
#include <algorithm>
#include <iostream>

using namespace std;

void main()
{
    int                     in1[10], in2[10],
                            result[20], *end, i;
    ostream_iterator<int>   outStream(cout, " ");

    for(i=0; i<10; i++) {
```

```
        in1[i] = i * 3;
        in2[i] = i * 2;
}
copy(in1, in1+10, outStream);
cout << endl;
copy(in2, in2+10, outStream);
cout << endl;
end = merge(in1, in1+10, in2, in2+10, result);
copy(result, end, outStream);
cout << endl << "--- inplace ---" << endl;

copy(in1, in1+10, result);
copy(in2, in2+10, result+10);
copy(result, result+20, outStream);
cout << endl;
inplace_merge(result, result+10, result+20);
copy(result, result+20, outStream);
cout << endl;
}
```

```
0 3 6 9 12 15 18 21 24 27
0 2 4 6 8 10 12 14 16 18
0 0 2 3 4 6 6 8 9 10 12 12 14 15 16 18 18 21 24 27
--- inplace ---
0 3 6 9 12 15 18 21 24 27 0 2 4 6 8 10 12 14 16 18
0 0 2 3 4 6 6 8 9 10 12 12 14 15 16 18 18 21 24 27
```

Listing 5.10 — Merge [merge.cpp]

5.5 Set Algorithms

The algorithms in this section treat a sorted sequence as a set and implement a basic collection of set operations. The algorithms also work with multisets — sets that allow multiple copies of a single value. The multiset operations are a generalization of the set operations so that set union includes the total number of occurrences of each element, and set intersection removes duplicate elements.

Many implementations of sets impose a restriction on the cardinality of the type stored in the set. Such implementations typically use bitmaps to represent sets and restrict the cardinality to the number of bits in a word on the architecture on which they are implemented. Such implementations also preclude the storage of duplicate values in sets. The STL implementation has neither of these restrictions, although it will not have the performance of a bitmap implementation.

There is a possibility of confusing terms when using sets, since the STL provides two associative containers called the set and multiset. These are designed for the fast storage and retrieval of objects and have little to do with the implementation of mathematical sets as described in this section. Mathematical sets are created by using the set algorithms, not by using a particular container.

5.5.1 Includes

The includes algorithm determines if all the members of one set are contained in a second set and returns a Boolean result. One set is defined to be a subset of another if the number of occurrences of each element in the first set is less than or equal to the number of occurrences in the second set. The algorithm runs in linear time and is implemented by the function includes():

```
template <class InputIterator1, class InputIterator2>
bool includes(InputIterator1    first1,
              InputIterator1    last1,
              InputIterator2    first2,
              InputIterator2    last2);

template <class InputIterator1, class InputIterator2,
    class Compare>
bool includes(InputIterator1    first1,
              InputIterator1    last1,
              InputIterator2    first2,
              InputIterator2    last2,
              Compare           comp);
```

The includes() function returns true if the set or multiset represented by the sequence from first1 up to last1 contains all of the set or multiset represented by the sequence from first2 up to last2. The second form of the function allows the use of a comparison operation other than operator< for complex types or sequences that are not in ascending order. Listing 5.11 demonstrates the use of the includes() function.

```
#include <algorithm>
#include <iostream>

using namespace std;

void main()
{
    int    set1[5] = {1, 2, 3, 4, 5};
    int    set2[5] = {2, 3, 3, 4, 5};
    int    set3[6] = {2, 3, 3, 3, 4, 5};
    int    set4[2] = {2, 5};

    if(includes(set1, set1+5, set2, set2+5))
        cout << "set2 is subset of set1" << endl;
    else cout << "set2 is not subset of set1" << endl;

    if(includes(set2, set2+5, set3, set3+6))
        cout << "set3 is subset of set2" << endl;
    else cout << "set3 is not subset of set2" << endl;

    if(includes(set3, set3+6, set2, set2+5))
        cout << "set2 is subset of set3" << endl;
    else cout << "set2 is not subset of set3" << endl;

    if(includes(set1, set1+5, set4, set4+2))
        cout << "set4 is subset of set1" << endl;
    else cout << "set4 is not subset of set1" << endl;
}
```

```
set2 is not subset of set1
set3 is not subset of set2
set2 is subset of set3
set4 is subset of set1
```

Listing 5.11 — Set Inclusion [set_in.cpp]

set2 is not a subset of set1 since the repeated value 3 occurs more times in set2 than it does in set1. For the same reason, set3 is not a subset of set2, but set2 is a subset of set3 since set2 has only two 3's, whereas set3 has three 3's. Finally, set4 is a subset of set1 since all of the values in set4 occur in set1.

5.5.2 Set Union

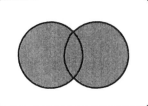

The set union algorithm performs the union of two sets or multisets represented as sorted sequences. If duplicate values occur in either of the input sequences, then the result sequence will contain the duplicate value the maximum of the number of times the value is duplicated in either of the input sequences. For example, if the first sequence contains one 3 and the second sequence contains three 3s, then the result will contain three 3s. If the same value occurs in the two input sets, then the value from the first input set will be copied to the result. The algorithm takes linear time and is implemented by the function set_union():

```
template <class InputIterator1, class InputIterator2,
   class OutputIterator>
OutputIterator set_union(InputIterator1    first1,
                         InputIterator1    last1,
                         InputIterator2    first2,
                         InputIterator2    last2,
                         OutputIterator    result);

template <class InputIterator1, class InputIterator2,
   class OutputIterator, class Compare>
OutputIterator set_union(InputIterator1    first1,
                         InputIterator1    last1,
                         InputIterator2    first2,
                         InputIterator2    last2,
                         OutputIterator    result,
                         Compare           comp);
```

set_union() forms the union of the sets represented by the sorted sequences from first1 up to last1 and first2 up to last2, placing the result at the location referenced by result. The function returns the past-the-end iterator for the result sequence. The result sequence should not overlap with either of the input sequences. Listing 5.12 demonstrates the use of set_union().

```
#include <algorithm>
#include <iostream>

using namespace std;

void main()
{
    int                 set1[5] = {2, 3, 3, 4, 5};
    int                 set2[6] = {2, 3, 3, 3, 4, 5};
    int                 result[15], *end;
    ostream_iterator<int>   outStream(cout, " ");

    end = set_union(set1, set1 + 5, set2, set2 + 6,
        result);
    copy(result, end, outStream);
    cout << endl;
}
```

```
2 3 3 3 4 5
```

Listing 5.12 — Set Union [set_un.cpp]

Because the value 3 is duplicated in one of the input sequences, the result sequence contains a total of three 3's since that was the maximum number of times it was duplicated in either of the input sequences. This is the definition applied to multisets. If set_union() is applied to sets as opposed to multisets, it will perform a normal set union operation.

To get a better idea of how duplicates are handled, we need to create a set containing instances of either structures or classes. (SeeListing 5.13.) This will allow us to differentiate between records that have the same key so that we can see which values end up in the result.

```
#include <algorithm>
#include <iostream>

using namespace std;

struct Person {
   char   name[16];
   int    age;
};

bool operator<(const Person& p1, const Person& p2)
{
   return(p1.age < p2.age);
}

ostream& operator<<(ostream& os, const Person& p)
{
   os << p.name << ", " << p.age ;
   return(os);
}

void main()
{
   Person   set1[3] = {{"George", 19}, {"Sam", 20},
      {"Marty", 23}};
   Person   set2[4] = {{"Mary", 18}, {"Susan", 20},
      {"Sonya", 20}, {"Gail", 21}};
   Person   result[10], *end;

   end = set_union(set1, set1+3, set2, set2+4,
      result);
   copy(result, end,
      ostream_iterator<Person>(cout, "\n"));
   cout << "----------------------" << endl;
   end = set_union(set2, set2+4, set1, set1+3,
      result);
   copy(result, end,
      ostream_iterator<Person>(cout, "\n"));
```

```
}
```

```
Mary, 18
George, 19
Sam, 20
Sonya, 20
Gail, 21
Marty, 23
------------------------
Mary, 18
George, 19
Susan, 20
Sonya, 20
Gail, 21
Marty, 23
```

Listing 5.13 — Set Union with Structures [s_rec_un.cpp]

The two input sets contain a total of three people of age twenty—one in the first set and two in the second. The definition of a union of sets containing duplicates states that the result will repeat the duplicated element the maximum number of times it occurs in either input set. This is two, so obviously one of the input values has to be dropped.

The set union algorithm works by comparing a value from the first set with a value from the second set. If these two values are the same, only one of them needs to appear in the result, and the algorithm copies the one from the first input set. The previous example performs the union of set1 and set2 followed by the union of set2 and set1. In the first case, it compares Sam to Susan and copies Sam, whereas in the second union, it compares Susan to Sam and copies Susan.

5.5.3 Set Intersection

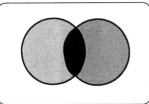

The set intersection algorithm computes the intersection of two sets represented as sorted sequences. If multisets are used, then for each element duplicated in the input sets, the result will duplicate the element the minimum number of times it is duplicated in either of the input sets. If a value occurs in both input sets, then the value from the first input set will be copied to the resultant set. The algorithm runs in linear time and is implemented by the function set_intersection():

```
template <class InputIterator1, class InputIterator2,
   class OutputIterator>
OutputIterator set_intersection(
                InputIterator1 first1,
                InputIterator1 last1,
                InputIterator2 first2,
                InputIterator2 last2,
                OutputIterator result);

template <class InputIterator1, class InputIterator2,
   class OutputIterator, class Compare>
OutputIterator set_intersection(
                InputIterator1 first1,
                InputIterator1 last1,
                InputIterator2 first2,
                InputIterator2 last2,
                OutputIterator result,
                Compare        comp);
```

The functions intersect the set from first1 up to last1 with the set from first2 up to last2, placing the result at the location referenced by result. A past-the-end iterator for the result sequence is returned. The result sequence should not overlap either of the input sequences. (See Listing 5.14.)

```
#include <algorithm>
#include <iostream>

using namespace std;

void main()
{
    int           set1[6] = {2, 3, 3, 4, 5, 9};
    int           set2[6] = {2, 3, 3, 3, 4, 5};
    int           result[15], *end;
```

```
ostream_iterator<int>   outStream(cout, " ");

end = set_intersection(set1, set1 + 6, set2,
    set2 + 6, result);
copy(result, end, outStream);
cout << endl;
}
```

> 2 3 3 4 5

Listing 5.14 — Set Intersection [set_int.cpp]

The important point to notice here is that the value 3 occurs twice in the result—the minimum number of times it occurs in either of the input sets.

5.5.4 Set Difference

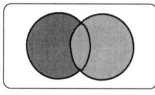 The set difference algorithm computes the difference between two sets where set difference is defined as all the values in the first set with all the values that occur in the second set removed. This is a linear time algorithm that is implemented by the function set-_difference():

```
template <class InputIterator1, class InputIterator2,
    class OutputIterator>
OutputIterator set_difference(
    InputIterator1 first1, InputIterator1 last1,
    InputIterator2 first2, InputIterator2 last2,
    OutputIterator result);

template <class InputIterator1, class InputIterator2,
    class OutputIterator, class Compare>
OutputIterator set_difference(
    InputIterator1 first1,  InputIterator1 last1,
    InputIterator2 first2,  InputIterator2 last2,
    OutputIterator result,  Compare         comp);
```

The functions calculate the set difference as the values in the first sequence minus the values in the second sequence. The result is placed at the location referenced by result, and a past-the-end iterator for the result sequence is returned. The result sequence should not overlap either of the input sequences, as shown in Listing 5.15.

```cpp
#include <algorithm>
#include <iostream>

using namespace std;

void main()
{
    int            set1[6] = {2, 3, 3, 4, 5, 9};
    int            set2[6] = {2, 3, 3, 3, 4, 5};
    int            result[15], *end;
    ostream_iterator<int>  outStream(cout, " ");

    end = set_difference(set1, set1 + 6, set2,
        set2 + 6, result);
    copy(result, end, outStream);
    cout << endl;

    end = set_difference(set2, set2 + 6, set1,
        set1 + 6, result);
    copy(result, end, outStream);
    cout << endl;
}
```

```
9
3
```

Listing 5.15 — Set Difference [set_diff.cpp]

The interesting point in this example is that `set2` - `set1` returns a 3, and `set1` - `set2` does not. Since 3 is a duplicate value, a 3 is removed from the first sequence every time one is encountered in the second sequence. Thus, `set2` - `set1` leaves one 3, whereas the reverse deletes all 3's.

5.5.5 Set Symmetric Difference

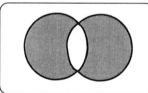

The set symmetric difference algorithm calculates the symmetric difference of two input sets represented as sorted sequences. It is defined as all the values in both sets that are not in the intersection set. Although this operation is commutative when applied to sets, it is not commutative when applied to multisets. It is a linear time algorithm that is implemented by the function set_symmetric_difference():

```
template <class InputIterator1, class InputIterator2,
    class OutputIterator>
OutputIterator set_symmetric_difference(
     InputIterator1 first1, InputIterator1 last1,
     InputIterator2 first2, InputIterator2 last2,
     OutputIterator result);

template <class InputIterator1, class InputIterator2,
    class OutputIterator, class Compare>
OutputIterator set_symmetric_difference(
     InputIterator1 first1, InputIterator1 last1,
     InputIterator2 first2, InputIterator2 last2,
     OutputIterator result, Compare comp);
```

As with the other set functions, the input and output sequences cannot overlap. Listing 5.16 demonstrates the use of the functions.

```
#include <algorithm>
#include <iostream>

using namespace std;

void main()
{
    int             set1[6] = {2, 3, 3, 4, 5, 9};
    int             set2[6] = {2, 3, 3, 3, 4, 5};
    int             result[15], *end;
    ostream_iterator<int>   outStream(cout, " ");

    end = set_difference(set1, set1 + 6, set2,
        set2 + 6, result);
    copy(result, end, outStream);
    cout << endl;
    end = set_symmetric_difference(set2, set2 + 6,
        set1, set1 + 6, result);
```

```
        copy(result, end, outStream);
        cout << endl;
}
```

```
9
3 9
```

Listing 5.16 — Symmetric Set Difference [sym_diff.cpp]

5.6 Heap Algorithms

Not only can sorted sequences be used to represent sets, but they can also be used to represent a more complex data structure—the heap. Heaps are normally represented as trees, and they are introduced using the tree notation.

A heap, shown in Figure 5.2, is a binary tree with the property that the value of any node in the tree is greater than or equal to the value of any of its children. This differs from the definition of a binary search tree which states that the value of any node is greater than its left child but less than or equal to its right child. Since the heap is not as ordered as a binary search tree, it is referred to as a partially ordered tree.

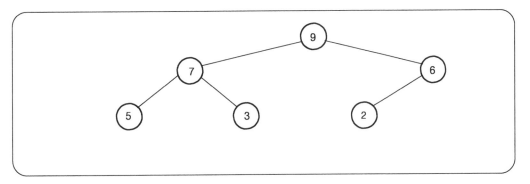

Figure 5.2 — A Simple Heap

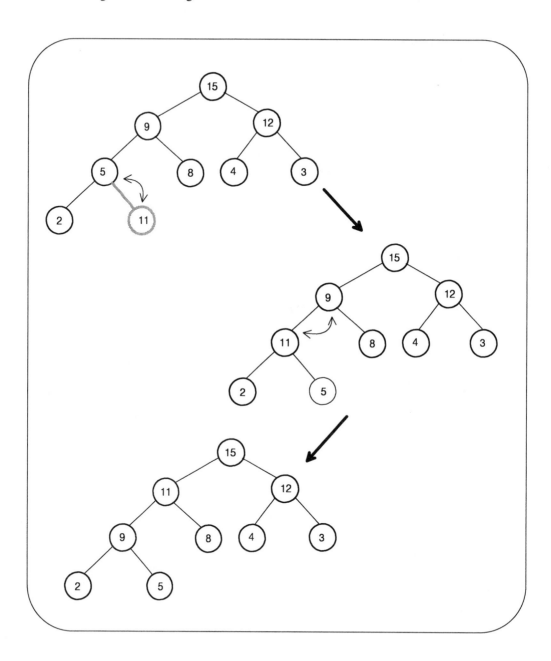

Figure 5.3 — Insertion into a Heap

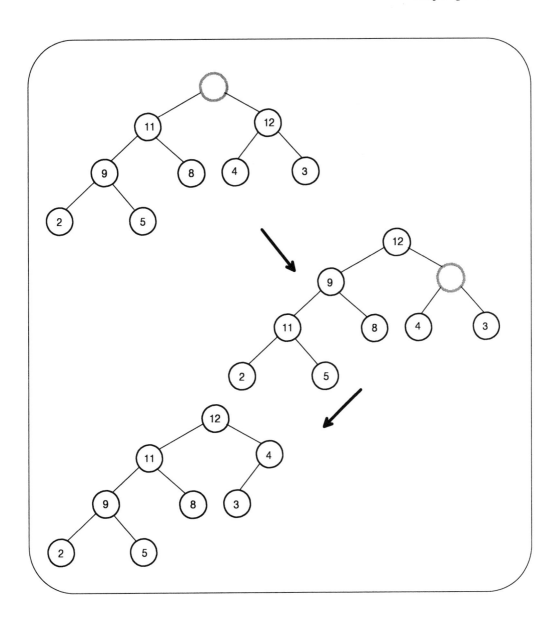

Figure 5.4 — Deletion from a Heap

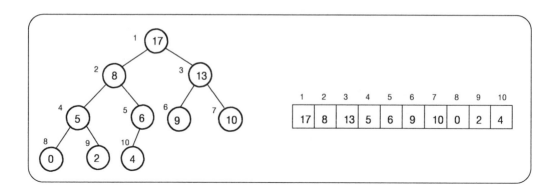

Figure 5.5 — Representing a Tree as a Sequence

Several properties make the heap a useful data structure. Since each node is greater than either of its children, the largest value in the heap must be at the root. This makes it convenient for applications that frequently want to access the greatest value in a set of values. Further, since it is a tree, if the root is removed, a heap can be remade into a tree by moving values up from lower levels in $O(\log n)$ time. A new value can also be inserted in $O(\log n)$ time. This not only makes it convenient for many applications, but efficient as well.

Insertion into a heap is accomplished by placing the new node as the leftmost child of the lowest level of the tree. Since this is rarely the correct position for the node in the heap, it must be moved to the correct position. To do this, the node is repeatedly exchanged with its parent until either its parent is greater than it, or it reaches the root.

This procedure is illustrated in Figure 5.3, where the value 11 is inserted into an existing heap. The tree at the top left shows the new value being inserted as the leftmost child at the lowest level. Since it is greater than its parent, it is exchanged with its parent, as shown in the tree at the top right. It is still greater than its parent, so it is exchanged once again to yield the tree in the lower portion of the diagram. At this point, the tree has been restored to have the properties of a heap, and the insertion is complete.

Deletion from a heap is performed by removing the root and reforming the resulting two trees into a heap. It makes sense to remove the root since that is the value of interest in most applications of heaps. The two trees are reformed into a heap by selecting a new root as the larger of the roots of the two subtrees. This leaves one of the subtrees without a root so the larger of its two children is promoted to the position of root. This process continues until a leaf is promoted to become the root of a subtree.

Deletion from a heap is shown in Figure 5.4, where the root is removed from the final heap of the previous diagram. Once the root is removed, node 12 is promoted to be the new root, leaving its subtree without a root. Node 4 is promoted to this position and one leaf is lost from the tree.

This is all well and fine for dealing with trees, but the STL algorithms deal with sequences. This anomaly can be cured if we can represent a tree as a sequence. Fortunately, such a technique exists for a class of trees called almost complete binary trees.

An almost complete binary tree is one where every node is either a leaf or has two children except the rightmost node at the level one above the bottom, which is allowed to have a single child. Any tree with these properties can have its nodes numbered sequentially from the root downward in left-to-right order. The values in the nodes can then be stored in a sequence based on the numbering of the nodes.

A sequence such as this has one very interesting property: to find the position of the left child of any node, you simply double the value of its position in the sequence. For example, in Figure 5.5, the left child of node 17 in position 1 must be in position 2, and the left child of node 5 in position 4 must be in position 8. The right child of any node can be found by multiplying the node's position by 2 and adding 1. To find the parent of a node, divide its position by 2 and round down the result.

This technique allows an almost complete binary tree to be stored in a sequence. Fortunately, a heap can always be maintained as an almost complete binary tree and can thus always be stored in a sequence. This allows the STL to treat any sequence as a heap as long as the appropriate algorithms are used.

Several functions are provided to create and manipulate heaps represented as sequences. The most basic of these functions is make_heap(), which creates a heap from an unsorted sequence:

```
template <class RandomAccessIterator>
void make_heap(
    RandomAccessIterator    first,
    RandomAccessIterator    last);

template <class RandomAccessIterator, class Compare>
void make_heap(
    RandomAccessIterator first,
    RandomAccessIterator last,
```

```
Compare                    comp);
```

make_heap() rearranges the elements in the range from first up to last so that they form a heap. This is an $O(n)$ operation that must be performed before any of the subsequent heap operations can be used. Once a heap has been created, elements can be inserted into the heap using push_heap() and removed from the heap using pop_heap():

```
template <class RandomAccessIterator>
void push_heap(
    RandomAccessIterator first,
    RandomAccessIterator last);

template <class RandomAccessIterator, class Compare>
void push_heap(
    RandomAccessIterator first,
    RandomAccessIterator last,
    Compare              comp);

template <class RandomAccessIterator>
void pop_heap(
    RandomAccessIterator first,
    RandomAccessIterator last);

template <class RandomAccessIterator, class Compare>
void pop_heap(
    RandomAccessIterator first,
    RandomAccessIterator last,
    Compare              comp);
```

pop_heap() removes the value from the top of the heap and places it at the end of the sequence. The resulting sequence is one element shorter than the original, and you must remember to adjust the past-the-end iterator for the sequence appropriately. The resulting sequence is also a heap, and the operations necessary to reform the heap after the top element has been removed require $O(\log n)$ time.

push_heap() allows a new element to be inserted into a heap. The new element is placed at the end of the sequence, and push_heap() is called with a past-the-end iterator that includes the new element at the end. This incorporates the new element into the existing heap in $O(\log n)$ time.

Once data are represented as a heap, it is a simple matter to use pop_heap() to create a reasonably efficient sort. Since the heap has the highest value at the top of the heap, it can be removed and placed at the end of the sequence, resulting in a shortening of the sequence. If this is done repeatedly until there are no more values in the heap, a sequence is obtained that is sorted into ascending order. Since the pop_heap() operation is of order $O(\log n)$ and it is invoked n times, the resulting sort is of order $O(n \log n)$. This is called the heap sort and is of the same order as the fastest sort known, the quicksort. The STL provides the function sort_heap(), which performs a heap sort on a heap represented as a sequence. The function destroys the heap, but leaves a sorted sequence in its place.

```
template <class RandomAccessIterator>
void sort_heap(RandomAccessIterator first,
               RandomAccessIterator last);

template <class RandomAccessIterator, class Compare>
void sort_heap(RandomAccessIterator first,
               RandomAccessIterator last,
               Compare             comp);
```

One of the common applications of heaps is to implement a priority queue: an abstract data structure that is like a queue but which is sorted so that the greatest element is always at the top of the queue. This has numerous applications including the queuing of tasks in an operating system that are waiting for the CPU. Most operating systems associate a priority with each task so that the CPU will be dispatched to the task of highest priority. The scheduler is continuously starting tasks and removing them from the ready queue. Tasks are added to the end of the queue when new tasks are created and when tasks waiting for some event become ready to run. The queue must be sorted by the priority of each task, and the heap provides the perfect vehicle to model this situation. Tasks can be added to the queue using push_heap(), and tasks can be removed using pop_heap().

Another application could be maintaining a list of workers in a labor union. In many unions, the labor hall receives requests for workers from prospective employers. The union maintains a list of members who are currently seeking employment and gives jobs to workers, removing them from the available list. Normally, the job is given to the most senior member on the current list. Therefore, the list must be sorted based on seniority, with the most senior member at the top. Once again, this can be modelled perfectly using a heap to maintain a priority queue.

5.7 Miscellaneous Algorithms

This section contains a collection of algorithms that do not fit into any other category. This includes algorithms to find maxima and minima, perform comparisons similar to alphabetical ordering, and generate permutations.

5.7.1 Maximum and Minimum

The STL provides functions to find the maximum and minimum of two elements as well as functions to find the maximum and minimum values in a sequence. The functions that work with two elements run in constant time, whereas those that handle sequences run in linear time. The functions for two elements are `max()` and `min()`, and those for sequences are `max_element()` and `min_element()`:

```
template <class T>
const T& min(const T& a, const T& b);

template <class T, class Compare>
const T& min(const T&     a,
             const T&     b,
             Compare      comp);

template <class T>
const T& max(const T& a, const T& b);

template <class T, class Compare>
const T& max(const T&     a,
             const T&     b,
             Compare      comp);

template <class ForwardIterator>
ForwardIterator max_element(ForwardIterator   first,
                            ForwardIterator   last);

template <class ForwardIterator, class Compare>
ForwardIterator max_element(ForwardIterator   first,
                            ForwardIterator   last,
                            Compare           comp);

template <class ForwardIterator>
ForwardIterator min_element(ForwardIterator   first,
                            ForwardIterator   last);
```

```
template <class ForwardIterator, class Compare>
ForwardIterator min_element(ForwardIterator  first,
                            ForwardIterator  last,
                            Compare          comp);
```

The functions `max()` and `min()` return the largest and smallest of two elements, respectively. The functions `max_element()` and `min_element()` return iterators that reference the largest and smallest elements in a sequence.

Listing 5.17 shows how `min_element()` can be used to implement a horribly inefficient $O(n^2)$ sort. Take this as an example of how *not* to write a sort.

```
#include <algorithm>
#include <iostream>

using namespace std;

void main()
{
   int    ar[10] = {8, 3, 5, 2, 0, 9, 1, 7, 6, 4};
   int    i, *iter;

   for(i=10; i>0; i--) {
      iter = min_element(ar, ar+i);
      cout << *iter << ' ';
      remove(ar, ar+i, *iter);
   }

   cout << endl;
}
```

```
0 1 2 3 4 5 6 7 8 9
```

Listing 5.17 — Finding the Minimum of a Sequence [min.cpp]

This is actually one of the simplest sorting algorithms. The `for` loop is performed once for every element in the sequence and finds and removes the minimum element each time. Since the sequence is shortened by one element each time an element is removed, it guarantees that the correct range is searched as the values are removed.

5.7.2 Lexicographical Comparison

The lexicographical comparison algorithm compares two sequences similar to the way two words are compared to determine which comes first in alphabetical order. The easiest way to understand this is to begin by considering how we sort words into alphabetical order.

A word beginning with A is placed before a word beginning with B since A comes before B in the ordered sequence we call the alphabet. Similarly, a word beginning with AB is lexicographically less than one that begins with AC since the first letters are equal and the second letter of the first word is less than the second letter of the second word. There are two important points to note here. First, the entire process depends on the existence of an ordered sequence of the elements that constitute the sequence. In this example it is the alphabet, whereas for integers it is the natural ordering of the integers. For other types, the ordering is defined by the action of operator<, which can be defined appropriately for user-defined types. The second point to note is that the closer a letter is to the start of the word, the greater its importance in the sorting of the words.

The STL algorithms are generalized, and lexicographical comparison can be applied to sequences of any type, not just characters. Consider a sequence of integers (3 6 2). Is this less than or greater than the sequence (3 5)? It is greater since the first elements in the two sequences are equal, and the second element of the first sequence is greater than the second element of the second sequence.

The lexicographical comparison algorithm is implemented by the function lexicographical_compare(), which executes in linear time, proportional to the shorter of the two sequences being compared:

```
template <class InputIterator1, class InputIterator2>
bool lexicographical_compare(
            InputIterator1    first1,
            InputIterator1    last1,
            InputIterator2    first2,
            InputIterator2    last2);

template <class InputIterator1, class InputIterator2,
    class Compare>
bool lexicographical_compare(
            InputIterator1    first1,
            InputIterator1    last1,
            InputIterator2    first2,
            InputIterator2    last2,
            Compare           comp);
```

The function returns a Boolean value of `true` if the sequence from `first1` up to `last1` is lexicographically less than the sequence from `first2` up to `last2`. If this is not the case, then `false` is returned. The second form of the function permits the specification of a comparison function other than `operator<`. This is useful for defining another order for the comparison or when user-defined types are involved. (See Listing 5.18.)

```cpp
#include <algorithm>
#include <iostream>

using namespace std;

void main()
{
    char   serial[2][7] = {"03963A", "03963D"};
    bool   result;

    result = lexicographical_compare(serial[0],
        serial[0] +  6, serial[1], serial[1] + 6);
    cout << serial[0] << " is ";
    if(result) cout << "less ";
    else cout << "greater ";
    cout << "than " << serial[1] << endl;
}
```

```
03963A is less than 03963D
```

Listing 5.18 — Lexicographical Comparison [lex_cmp.cpp]

5.7.3 Permutations

A permutation is an ordering of the elements in a sequence. For any given sequence, there are many possible permutations of the elements. The STL permutation algorithms are designed to generate all permutations of a given sequence. This is done by assuming that the set of all possible permutations forms a lexicographically ordered set of sequences. The algorithms require that the original sequence be lexicographically sorted. For example, the sequence of integers (0 1 2) would have the following permutations:

0 1 2

```
0 2 1
1 0 2
1 2 0
2 0 1
2 1 0
```

As you can see, these sequences are all different permutations of the original. Further, they are lexicographically sorted to form an ordered set of sequences. The STL permutation functions assume that any sequence passed to them is a member of the sorted set and can generate either the next or previous member of the set.

The number of possible permutations for a sequence of length n is $n!$, where the exclamation point indicates the *factorial* function. The factorial of an integer n is defined as $n \times (n-1) \times (n-2) \ldots \times 1$, so the factorial of 3, denoted as $3!$, is defined as $3 \times 2 \times 1 = 6$. This explains the six permutations of the three elements in the previous example. Be aware that factorials increase very quickly, as shown in Table 5.1.

One of the uses of permutations is in generating all possible arrangements of elements in a brute force algorithm. Such algorithms solve a problem by trying all possible permutations of a sequence until they find one that works. Although this approach is not elegant, it is the only known solution for some problems. Such algorithms should be avoided whenever possible due to the rapid explosion in the number of permutations as the length of the sequence increases.

0!	1
1!	1
2!	2
3!	6
4!	24
5!	120
6!	720
7!	5,040
10!	3,628,800
15!	1,307,674,368,000

Table 5.1 — Sample Factorials

The permutation algorithms are implemented by the functions next-_permutation() and prev_permutation(). These functions each run in linear time and generate the next permutation in the lexicographically ordered sequence and the previous one, respectively:

```
template <class BidirectionalIterator>
bool next_permutation(BidirectionalIterator   first,
                      BidirectionalIterator   last);

template <class BidirectionalIterator, class Compare>
bool next_permutation(BidirectionalIterator   first,
                      BidirectionalIterator   last,
                      Compare                 comp);

template <class BidirectionalIterator>
bool prev_permutation(BidirectionalIterator   first,
                      BidirectionalIterator   last);

template <class BidirectionalIterator, class Compare>
bool prev_permutation(BidirectionalIterator   first,
                      BidirectionalIterator   last,
                      Compare                 comp);
```

The functions return a Boolean value indicating whether the next permutation exists. When the end of the sorted set of permutations is reached, the algorithms return false indicating that the next permutation does not exist, and restore the original order of the sequence. This means that if an ordered sequence is passed to the permutation algorithms, they can be called repetitively to generate all possible permutations. This is demonstrated in Listing 5.19.

```
#include <algorithm>
#include <iostream>

using namespace std;

void main()
{
    int                     ar[4], i;
    bool                    exists;
    ostream_iterator<int>   outStream(cout, " ");

    for(i=0;i<4;i++) ar[i] = i;
    copy(ar, ar+3, outStream);
    cout << endl;

    exists = next_permutation(ar, ar+3);
```

```
while(exists) {
   copy(ar, ar+3, outStream);
   cout << endl;
   exists = next_permutation(ar, ar+3);
}
cout << "after last permutation" << endl;
copy(ar, ar+3, outStream);
cout << endl;
}
```

```
0 1 2
0 2 1
1 0 2
1 2 0
2 0 1
2 1 0
after last permutation
0 1 2
```

Listing 5.19 — Generating Permutations [perm.cpp]

The program begins with a sorted sequence and then repeatedly calls next-_permutation() until it returns false, indicating that no further permutations exist. The final call to next_permutation() returns false and reverses the order of the elements in the sequence, yielding the original permutation.

6
Generalized Numeric Algorithms

6.1 Introduction

This chapter describes algorithms for common numeric operations on sequences including calculating running sums, inner products, and the difference between adjacent elements. It also describes the numeric array—an array that permits operations on all members of an array at once and provides sophisticated subscripting methods. Although there are fewer members of this category of algorithms, their common usage makes them an important component of the STL.

6.2 Accumulation

The accumulate algorithm is similar to the APL reduction operator. It takes a sequence of values and an operator, places the operator between every pair of values in the sequence, and evaluates the resulting expression. The result is what is returned from evaluating the expression. This is a linear time algorithm and is implemented by the function accumulate():

```
template <class InputIterator, class T>
T accumulate(InputIterator first,
             InputIterator  last,
             T              init);

template <class InputIterator, class T,
    class BinaryOperation>
T accumulate(InputIterator first,
        InputIterator    last,
        T                init,
        BinaryOperation  binary_op);
```

Both forms of the function require an initial value, which will be placed at the start of the sequence before the operator is inserted. In the case where a sequence of zero length is passed to the functions, they will return the initial value, `init`. The first form of the function inserts `operator+` between the elements, and the second form inserts `binary_op` between the elements, as in Listing 6.1.

```cpp
#include <numeric>
#include <functional>
#include <iostream>

using namespace std;

void main()
{
    int                     ar[5], i, sum;
    ostream_iterator<int>   outStream(cout, " ");

    for(i=0;i<5;i++) ar[i] = i + 1;
    copy(ar, ar+5, outStream);
    cout << endl;

    sum = accumulate(ar, ar+5, 0);
    cout << "+: " << sum << endl;

    sum = accumulate(ar, ar+5, 0, minus<int>());
    cout << "-: " << sum << endl;

    sum = accumulate(ar, ar+5, 1, multiplies<int>());
    cout << "*: " << sum << endl;
}
```

```
1 2 3 4 5
+: 15
-: -15
*: 120
```

Listing 6.1 — Accumulating Sequences [accum.cpp]

This demonstrates how the `accumulate()` function works with different operators. The default, `operator+`, produces the sum of the values in the sequence, `operator-` yields the negative sum, and `operator*` the product. The actual expressions that are evaluated are as follows:

```
0 + 1 + 2 + 3 + 4 + 5 =   15
0 - 1 - 2 - 3 - 4 - 5 = -15
1 * 1 * 2 * 3 * 4 * 5 = 120
```

The use of `operator*` requires an initial value of 1 rather than zero; otherwise, the result would always be zero.

6.3 Inner Product

The inner product algorithm calculates the inner product of two sequences of the same length. An inner product is calculated by using two operators to combine the elements of the two sequences to yield a single value. This is done by applying one operator to each pair of corresponding elements from the two sequences to yield a sequence of intermediate values of the same length as the original sequences. This intermediate sequence is then accumulated using the other operator to yield a single value as the result. Normally, the elements are combined with `operator*` and the accumulation performed with `operator+`. This is demonstrated with the following sequences:

```
sequence 1:    2     4     6     8
               *     *     *     *
sequence 2:    3     4     5     6
               ⇓     ⇓     ⇓     ⇓
intermediate:  6 + 16 + 30 + 48 = 100
```

These sequences yield a final result of `100`. Other operators can be substituted for `operator*` and `operator+`, yielding different results, but the basic algorithm remains the same. The algorithm runs in linear time and is implemented by the function `inner_product()`:

```
template <class InputIterator1,
   class InputIterator2, class T>
T inner_product(InputIterator1   first1,
                InputIterator1   last1,
                InputIterator2   first2,
                T                init);

template <class InputIterator1,
   class InputIterator2, class T,
   class BinaryOperation1, class BinaryOperation2>
T inner_product(InputIterator1   first1,
```

```
InputIterator1    last1,
InputIterator2    first2,
T                 init,
BinaryOperation1  binary_op1,
BinaryOperation2  binary_op2);
```

Both forms of the function allow an initial value to be specified that is prepended to the start of the intermediate sequence before the accumulation is performed. If an initial value of 10 had been used with the preceding example, the following accumulation would have been performed:

```
10 + 6 + 16 + 30 + 48 = 110
```

The second form of the function allows the specification of operators other than operator* and operator+, as are used by the first form of the function. binary_op2 is used to perform the element-by-element operation, and binary_op1 is used to perform the accumulation. This is demonstrated in Listing 6.2.

```
#include <numeric>
#include <functional>
#include <iostream>

using namespace std;

void main()
{
    int                   ar1[5], ar2[5], i, prod;
    ostream_iterator<int> outStream(cout, " ");

    for(i=0;i<5;i++) {
        ar1[i] = i;
        ar2[i] = i + 2;
    }
    copy(ar1, ar1+5, outStream);
    cout << endl;
    copy(ar2, ar2+5, outStream);
    cout << endl;

    prod = inner_product(ar1, ar1+5, ar2, 0);
    cout << "*+: " << prod << endl;

    prod = inner_product(ar1, ar1+5, ar2, 15,
        plus<int>(), minus<int>());
    cout << "-+: " << prod << endl;
```

```
}
```

```
0  1  2  3  4
2  3  4  5  6
x+:  50
-+:  5
```

Listing 6.2 — Inner Product [in_prod.cpp]

The second calculation is performed as follows:

```
sequence 1:        0     1     2     3     4
                   -     -     -     -     -
sequence 2:        2     3     4     5     6
                   ⇓     ⇓     ⇓     ⇓     ⇓
intermediate:  15 + -2 + -2 + -2 + -2 + -2 = 5
```

The initial value is prepended to the intermediate sequence before the accumulation is performed.

6.4 Partial Sum

The partial sum algorithm calculates a running total of all the elements in a sequence. The result is a sequence of the same length as the original sequence. Operators other than `operator+` can be specified to perform analogous operations. The algorithm is implemented by the function `partial_sum()`, which runs in linear time:

```
template <class InputIterator, class OutputIterator>
OutputIterator partial_sum(InputIterator  first,
                           InputIterator  last,
                           OutputIterator result);

template <class InputIterator, class OutputIterator,
    class BinaryOperation>
OutputIterator partial_sum(InputIterator  first,
                           InputIterator  last,
                           OutputIterator result,
                           BinaryOperation binary_op);
```

The function calculates a running total of the elements in the sequence from `first` up to `last` and places the resultant sequence at the location referenced by `result`. The past-the-end iterator for the result sequence is returned, as shown in Listing 6.3.

```cpp
#include <numeric>
#include <functional>
#include <iostream>

using namespace std;

void main()
{
    int                ar[10], result[10], i, *end;
    ostream_iterator<int>   outStream(cout, " ");

    for(i=0;i<10;i++) ar[i] = i *i + 1;

    end = partial_sum(ar, ar+10, result);
    copy(ar, ar+10, outStream);
    cout << endl;
    copy(result, end, outStream);
    cout << endl;
    end = partial_sum(ar, ar+10, result, minus<int>());
    copy(result, end, outStream);
    cout << endl;
}
```
```
1 2 5 10 17 26 37 50 65 82
1 3 8 18 35 61 98 148 213 295
1 -1 -6 -16 -33 -59 -96 -146 -211 -293
```

Listing 6.3 — Partial Sum [par_sum.cpp]

6.5 Adjacent Difference

The adjacent difference algorithm calculates the difference between adjacent elements in a sequence by subtracting (or using an alternate operator) the second member of each pair of adjacent elements from the first. The result is another sequence of the same length as the original. This linear time algorithm is implemented by the function adjacent- _difference():

```
template <class InputIterator, class OutputIterator>
OutputIterator adjacent_difference(
                InputIterator   first,
                InputIterator   last,
                OutputIterator  result);

template <class InputIterator, class OutputIterator,
   class BinaryOperation>
OutputIterator adjacent_difference(
                InputIterator      first,
                InputIterator      last,
                OutputIterator     result,
                BinaryOperation    binary_op);
```

The functions calculate the difference between every pair of elements in the range from first up to last and place the resultant sequence of the same length at the location referenced by result. Since the number of differences is one less than the number of elements, the first element of the result sequence is a copy of the first element of the original sequence. The second form allows an operator other than operator- to be used. adjacent_difference() is demonstrated in Listing 6.4.

```
#include <numeric>
#include <functional>
#include <iostream>

using namespace std;

void main()
{
    int                   ar[10], result[10], i, *end;
    ostream_iterator<int>   outStream(cout, " ");

    for(i=0;i<10;i++) ar[i] = i *i + 1;

    end = adjacent_difference(ar, ar+10, result);
    copy(ar, ar+10, outStream);
    cout << endl << "-: ";
    copy(result, end, outStream);
    cout << endl << "+: ";
    end = adjacent_difference(ar, ar+10, result,
        plus<int>());
    copy(result, end, outStream);
```

```
        cout << endl;
}
```

```
1  2  5  10  17  26  37  50  65  82
-:  1  1  3  5  7  9  11  13  15  17
+:  1  3  7  15  27  43  63  87  115  147
```

Listing 6.4 — Adjacent Difference [adj_diff.cpp]

6.6 Numeric Arrays

The numeric array is provided to simplify operations on arrays of numbers and is implemented by the class valarray. The valarray is a container for objects that is similar to the array. It defines numerous functions to perform operations on the entire array. These array operations permit a single value to be used as a function argument and used to modify every value in the array. They also allow two valarrays of the same size to be operated upon in an element-by-element fashion. Listing 6.5 shows an example.

```
#include <valarray>
#include <iostream>

using namespace std;

void main()
{
    int             ar1[] = {1, 2, 3};
    int             ar2[] = {2, 5, 6};
    const size_t    AR_SIZE = 3;
    size_t          i;
    valarray<int>   v1(ar1, AR_SIZE);
    valarray<int>   v2(ar2, AR_SIZE);

    v1 += 2;
    for(i = 0; i < AR_SIZE; i++)
        cout << v1[i] << " ";
    cout << endl;

    v1 += v2;
```

```
    for(i = 0; i < AR_SIZE; i++)
        cout << v1[i] << " ";
    cout << endl;
}
```

```
3 4 5
5 9 11
```

Listing 6.5 — `valarray` Operations [valar1.cpp]

`valarray` also defines several different ways the array can be subscripted. These include subscripting a single element, a group of arbitrary elements, and a group of elements spaced a fixed distance apart.

While `valarray` can contain any type, most of the operations defined on it are only applicable to numeric types. If the operation performed on a `valarray` is to succeed, the operation must be defined for the type stored in the `valarray`.

Although `valarray` is a container, it is not a container in the same sense as the other STL containers. While you might think it is a sequence container, it does not satisfy the requirements of a sequence container. It does not provide an iterator or the methods `begin()` and `end()`. The `valarray` is best thought of as a special type of array rather than as one of the STL containers.

6.6.1 Subscripting

The `valarray` provides some interesting subscripting capabilities by overloading `operator[]`. Some of these subscripting capabilities use helper classes to represent the subscripts and to return the result of the subscript operation.

The simplest form of subscripting uses a single value of type `size_t` to indicate the member of the `valarray` to return. This works the same as subscripting an ordinary array. Valid subscripts extend from zero up to one less than the number of elements in the `valarray`. Subscripting a nonexistent element does not extend the array—it causes an error.

Another `valarray` can also be used as an argument for `operator[]`, returning a result array of the same length as the array used to hold the subscripts. The `valarray` used as a subscript is constructed in the usual manner and must contain valid subscripts. The exact type returned depends on whether the result of operator[] is used as an l-value or an r-value.

When the result of operator[] is used as an r-value, a valarray of the expected length is returned. If the result of operator[] is used as an l-value, an instance of indirect_array is returned. indirect_array is a class that contains a reference to the array that was subscripted as well as the valarray used as an argument to operator[].

The class indirect_array defines the same operators as does valarray. As a result, the indirect_array behaves identically to a valarray, except only the elements specified by the subscript are affected. To see how this works, consider Listing 6.6:

```cpp
#include <valarray>
#include <iostream>

using namespace std;

void main()
{
    size_t              i, sub_ar[] = {1, 3, 5};
    int                 data_ar[] = {1, 2, 3, 4, 5, 6,
7};
    int                 add_ar[] = {1, 2, 3};
    valarray<size_t>    sub_val(sub_ar, 3);
    valarray<int>       data_val(data_ar, 7);
    valarray<int>       add_val(add_ar, 3);

    data_val[sub_val] += add_val;

    for(i = 0; i < 7; i++)
    {
        cout << data_val[i] << " ";
    }
    cout << endl;
}
```

```
1 3 3 6 5 9 7
```

Listing 6.6 — Simple Subscripting [valar2.cpp]

The `valarrays` are created from the corresponding regular arrays. Subscripting `data_val` with `sub_val` returns an instance of `indirect_array`, which references `data_val` and has the subscripts `sub_val`. The member `operator+=` of `indirect_array` is then used to perform the addition so that only the members specified by the subscripts are affected. This same technique is used with the `slice_array`, `gslice_array`, and `mask_array` described below. None of these classes can be instantiated directly—they are only created as a result of subscripting.

`valarray` is a one-dimensional array. This poses a problem for applications that require higher-dimensional arrays. Fortunately, it is a simple matter to use a one-dimensional array to represent a multi-dimensional array. Mapping a multi-dimensional array onto a one-dimensional array is made even simpler by using the class `slice`.

The class `slice` has this constructor:

```
slice(size_t start, size_t len, size_t stride);
```

`start` is the starting subscript, `len` is the number of subscripts, and `stride` is the increment to add to the starting subscript to generate a total of `len` subscripts. If this class is constructed properly, it can represent a slice through a multi-dimensional array. To see how this works, we will begin by examining how to store a two-dimensional array as a `valarray`.

Figure 6.1 shows how a one-dimensional array can be used to represent a two-dimensional array stored in row major order. Common operations on two-dimensional arrays include operations on all the members of a row or column. This requires that the subscripts for all members of a row or column be generated. The `slice` class provides the necessary functionality to do this.

To generate the subscripts for all members of a column, we would use the following constructor:

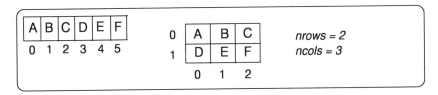

Figure 6.1 — Mapping a 2-Dimensional Array to a 1-Dimensional Array

```
slice(colNum, nrows, ncols);
```

`colNum` is the index of the desired column. The starting value is `colNum`, a value from 0 to 2, which is the first subscript to be generated. The second parameter is `nrows`, which will generate a subscript for each row. The third parameter is the distance between the elements in each row that are in the same column, which is the number of columns. If we want all values for column 1 and substitute numeric values for variables, we get the following:

```
slice(1, 2, 3);
```

which will generate these subscripts:

```
1, 4
```

Examining the one-dimensional array in Figure 6.1, we see that these are indeed the correct subscripts of all members of column 1.

The same idea can be used to generate the subscripts for all members of a row in a two-dimensional array. The slice to generate the subscripts for all members of row `rowNum` is constructed as follows:

```
slice(rowNum * ncols, ncols, 1);
```

The starting index is the number of columns multiplied by the desired row, since each row contains `ncols` members. The number of subscripts to generate is `ncols`, the number of members of a row. The stride is set to 1 since each member of a row is adjacent to the next.

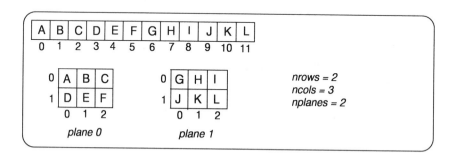

Figure 6.2 — Mapping a 3-D Array onto a 1-D Array

The same technique can be extended to three dimensions at a cost of slightly more complicated arithmetic. Figure 6.2 depicts the mapping of a three-dimensional array onto a one-dimensional array in row major order by plane.

The three-dimensional array has two rows, three columns, and two planes. The `slice` to access all members of `colNum` in all planes is this:

```
slice(colNum, nrows * nplanes, ncols);
```

`colNum` is the start of each column in plane 0. The total number of rows in all planes is `nrows * nplanes`, which is the number of subscripts that must be generated. The stride is `ncols`, since that is the separation of one column from the next.

Accessing all elements of a column in a single plane requires slightly more complicated arithmetic:

```
slice(colNum + planeNum * nrows * ncols, nrows,
  ncols);
```

The expression `planeNum * nrows * ncols` calculates the number of elements in the one-dimensional array before the start of the desired plane. The number of subscripts has been reduced to `nrows` since that is the number of elements in a column of a single plane. This technique can be extended to arrays of higher dimensions so that the fact that the `valarray` is only one-dimensional is not really a restriction.

The result of subscripting with a `slice` depends on whether the expression is used as an r-value or an l-value. If used as an r-value, a `valarray` is returned. If used as an l-value, an instance of a `slice_array` is returned. This contains a reference to the array being subscripted and the `slice` to generate the subscripts. Other than that, it behaves the same as the `indirect_array` described previously. A `slice_array` cannot be instantiated directly—it can only be created as a result of subscripting a `valarray` with a `slice`.

Boolean subscripting of a `valarray` is permitted using `valarray<bool>` as the subscript. This has the effect of returning all of the members of the `valarray` that correspond to `true` in the subscripts. If the result of the subscript operation is used as an r-value, a `valarray` containing the results is returned. If the result is used as an l-value, a `mask_array` is returned. The `mask_array` is a helper class, similar to the `indirect_array`, and is transparent to the user.

Listing 6.7 demonstrates how to subscript a `valarray`.

```cpp
#include <valarray>
#include <iostream>
#include <cctype>

using namespace std;

void main()
{
    const int          nrows = 3;
    const int          ncols = 4;
    valarray<int>      ar(nrows * ncols);
    valarray<size_t>   val_subscr(3);
    valarray<int>      result3(3);
    slice              slice_subscr(1,nrows, ncols);
    bool               bool_vect[]
                       = {false, false, false, true,
                          false, false, true, false,
                          false, true, false, false};
    valarray<bool>     bool_subscr(bool_vect, 12);
    int                i;

    for(i = 0; i < (nrows * ncols); i++)
{
        ar[i] = i;
    }

    val_subscr[0] = 2;
    val_subscr[1] = 7;
    val_subscr[2] = 10;

    // subscript with a valarray
    result3 = ar[val_subscr];
    cout << "ar[2, 7, 10] = ";
    for(i = 0; i < 3; i++)
    {
        cout << result3[i] << " ";
    }

    // use a valarray subscript for assignment
    ar[val_subscr] = 42;
    cout << endl << "ar [2, 7, 10] = 42 -> ";
    for(i = 0; i < (nrows * ncols); i++)
    {
        cout << ar[i] << " ";
    }

    // assign using a slice array
```

```
    ar[slice_subscr] = 84;
    cout << endl << "ar [*, 1] = 84 -> ";
    for(i = 0; i < (nrows * ncols); i++)
    {
        cout << ar[i] << " ";
    }

    // select elements using a bool valarray
    result3 = ar[bool_subscr];
    cout << endl << "ar[bool_subscr] = ";
    for(i = 0; i < 3; i++)
    {
        cout << result3[i] << " ";
    }

    cout << endl;
}
```

```
ar[2, 7, 10] = 2 7 10
ar [2, 7, 10] = 42 -> 0 1 42 3 4 5 6 42 8 9 42 11
ar [*, 1] = 84 -> 0 84 42 3 4 84 6 42 8 84 42 11
ar[bool_subscr] = 3 6 84
```

Listing 6.7 — Subscripting `valarray` [subscr.cpp]

The program in Listing 6.7 declares `ar` as a `valarray` of length 12. `val_subscr`, `slice_subscr`, and `bool_subscr` are used to hold integer subscripts, a `slice` subscript, and Boolean subscripts, respectively. The first subscripting operation uses `val_subscr` to assign three members of `ar` to `result3`. The second subscript operation uses `val_subscr` to generate an `indirect_array` to assign 42 to the members indicated by the subscripts. The third subscript operation treats the array as a 3×4 matrix and uses a `slice` to assign 84 to all members of column 1. The final subscript operation uses a `valarray<bool>` to extract elements in specific positions.

6.6.2 Methods and Functions

Numerous methods and functions are defined for use with `valarray`. The program in Listing 6.8 demonstrates the use of some of these.

```
#include <valarray>
#include <iostream>
#include <algorithm>
#include <cmath>

using namespace std;

int fn(int n)
{
    return (n - 7) * 2;
}

void main()
{
    valarray<int>        ar(10);
    valarray<int>        ar1(10);
    valarray<int>        result(10);
    int              i;

    for(i = 0; i < 10; i++)
    {
        ar[i] = i;
        ar1[i] = 9 - i;
    }

    result = ar * 2;

    cout << "ar   = ";
    for(i = 0; i < 10; i++)
    {
        cout << ar[i] << " ";
    }

    cout << endl << "ar1   = ";
    for(i = 0; i < 10; i++)
    {
        cout << ar1[i] << " ";
    }

    cout << endl << "ar * 2 = ";
    for(i = 0; i < 10; i++)
    {
        cout << result[i] << " ";
    }

    result = ar + ar1;
    cout << endl << "ar + ar1 = ";
```

```
for(i = 0;  i < 10;  i++)
{
    cout << result[i] << " ";
}

cout << endl << "ar.max() = " << ar.max() << endl;
cout << "ar.sum() = " << ar.sum() << endl;

result = ar.shift(3);
cout << "ar.shift(3) = ";
for(i = 0;  i < 10;  i++)
{
    cout << result[i] << " ";
}

result = ar.shift(-2);
cout << endl << "ar.shift(-2) = ";
for(i = 0;  i < 10;  i++)
{
    cout << result[i] << " ";
}

result = ar.cshift(3);
cout << endl << "ar.cshift(3) = ";
for(i = 0;  i < 10;  i++)
{
    cout << result[i] << " ";
}

result = ar.apply(fn);
cout << endl << "ar.apply(fn) = ";
for(i = 0;  i < 10;  i++)
{
    cout << result[i] << " ";
}

result = pow(ar, 2);
cout << endl << "pow(ar, 2) = ";
for(i = 0;  i < 10;  i++)
{
    cout << result[i] << " ";
}

result = pow(ar, ar1);
cout << endl << "pow(ar, ar1) = ";
for(i = 0;  i < 10;  i++)
{
```

```
        cout << result[i] << " ";
    }

    result += ar;
    cout << endl << "result += ar = ";
    for(i = 0; i < 10; i++)
    {
        cout << result[i] << " ";
    }
    cout << endl;
}
```

```
ar       = 0 1 2 3 4 5 6 7 8 9
ar1      = 9 8 7 6 5 4 3 2 1 0
ar * 2   = 0 2 4 6 8 10 12 14 16 18
ar + ar1 = 9 9 9 9 9 9 9 9 9 9
ar.max() = 9
ar.sum() = 45
ar.shift(3) = 3 4 5 6 7 8 9 0 0 0
ar.shift(-2) = 0 0 0 1 2 3 4 5 6 7
ar.cshift(3) = 3 4 5 6 7 8 9 0 1 2
ar.apply(fn) = -14 -12 -10 -8 -6 -4 -2 0 2 4
pow(ar, 2) = 0 1 4 9 16 25 36 49 64 81
pow(ar, ar1) = 0 1 128 729 1024 625 216 49 8 1
result += ar = 0 2 130 732 1028 630 222 56 16 10
```

Listing 6.8 — valarray Functions [ar_func.cpp]

The program begins by declaring three integer valarrays of ten members each. It then initializes ar and ar1 and prints their contents. Next, ar is multiplied by the constant 2 and assigned to result, which is then printed. ar is added to ar1 and assigned to result, showing that arrays of the same length can be used with an operator. The methods max() and sum() are used to find the maximum and sum of the values in ar, respectively. The shift() method can shift the values in either direction, with zeroes added to fill the vacated positions. The cshift() method performs a circular shift so that the elements that spill off one end of the array reappear at the other end. apply() applies a function, in this case, fn, to every member of the array.

7
Sequence Containers

7.1 Introduction

This is the first of two chapters discussing containers. A container is a data structure that contains or stores instances of other data structures or objects. Containers make it much easier to move groups of objects around, since several objects can be referred to by a single name and manipulated as a group. Containers do more than just store a group of objects—they determine how objects are stored and how they can be accessed and retrieved.

Containers are divided into two broad categories—sequence containers and associative containers. The sequence containers store objects in a sequential manner. Objects in sequence containers can be accessed either sequentially or randomly, depending on the nature of the container. Associative containers associate a key value with every object stored in the container. A key is like a name and can be used to retrieve a value from an associative container. Normally, associative containers arrange the keys so that they form an index for the objects stored in the container. This results in much faster retrieval of an object than is possible with a sequence container.

Some of the associative containers separate the data being stored from the index. The index only contains the key that identifies the data object and is arranged so that it can be searched as quickly as possible. Each key in the index has a reference to the data object associated with it so that once the key is found, the data object can be retrieved by following the reference.

Sequence containers are much simpler, as they store only the data objects and arrange them in a linear fashion. Data objects are referenced in a straightforward manner without the use of an index. Although this dispenses with the need for additional memory to store the index, it can dramatically increase retrieval times for some applications.

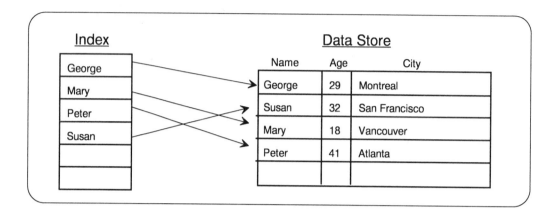

Figure 7.1 — An Index for an Associative Container

To make effective use of container data structures, you need to understand what each container is, how it works, how to use it, and when to use one container in preference to another.

Each container implements what is called an abstract data type. An abstract data type consists of the following.

- A conceptual model of what the data type is and how it works.

- An implementation of the data type.

- A series of operations that can be performed on the data type to manipulate the data stored within it. This takes the form of a series of functions or methods that work on the data type. These methods are called the application program interface (API) for the data type.

Each container models some common, real-world situation. The task of the software architect or programmer is to identify the container that most closely models the problem being solved. Selecting the wrong container will make programming more difficult, as it will not model the problem easily. Once a model is selected, the architect must consider efficiency. This involves determining how the data in the container will be accessed, how frequently, and so on. This is a crucial aspect of program design since an incorrect choice can cause a program to execute several orders of magnitude more slowly.

For example, a list stores its data in a sequential fashion. To retrieve a specific item, the program must search for it from the beginning of the list. If data are to be stored once and retrieved frequently in no particular order, the list would not be a good choice of container. Retrieving from a list in random order will, on average, require that half the list be searched each time an element is retrieved. If the list contains a million objects, this will result in a program that runs *very* slowly. In this case, one of the associative containers that has an index would be a more appropriate choice.

The STL also provides container adaptors. These alter the interface of a container to create a new container. The container adaptors include the `stack`, `queue`, and `priority_queue`. These are discussed in Chapter 9.

7.2 Container Operations

Although many containers support operations specific to their own functional requirements, they all share a core set of operations. These are detailed in Table 7.1, where it is assumed that x and y are instances of a container type and r is a reference to the same container type. The declarations for a hypothetical container type C would be the following:

```
C x, y, &r;
```

In addition to these operations, every container provides `typedefs` for an iterator, constant iterator, reference, constant reference, difference type, size type, and value type. These provide type definitions for the use of programs using the containers.

The iterator allows the container to be traversed in an organized fashion. If a container is empty, then `x.begin() == x.end()`.

Expression	Explanation
`C::value_type`	The type stored in the container.
`C::reference`	A reference to the type stored in the container.
`C::const_reference`	A constant reference to the type stored in the container.
`C::iterator`	An iterator for the container.
`C::const_iterator`	A constant iterator for the container.
`C::difference_type`	A signed integral type that can represent the difference in two iterators.
`C::size_type`	An unsigned integral type that can represent any valid number of container members.
`C x`	Creates an empty container.
`C()`	Creates an empty container.
`C(y)`	Creates a copy of y.
`C x(y)`	Creates x as a copy of y.
`C x = y`	Creates x and initializes it to have the value of y.
`x.~C()`	The destructor is applied to every element in the container and all memory is deallocated..
`x.begin()`	Returns an iterator referencing the first element in the container.
`x.end()`	Returns a past-the-end iterator for the elements in the container.
`x.size()`	Returns the current number of elements stored in the container.
`x.max_size()`	Returns the largest possible number of elements that can be stored in the container.
`x.empty()`	True if no elements are in the container.
`x == y`	True if all elements in the two containers are equal.
`x != y`	True if not all the elements in the two containers are equal.
`x = y`	Assigns the value of the container y to the container x by performing a deep copy.
`x < y`	True if the elements of x are lexicographically less than those of y.
`x > y`	True if the elements of x are lexicographically greater than those of y.
`x <= y`	True if the elements of x are lexicographically less than or equal to those of y.

Expression	Explanation
`x >= y`	True if the elements of x are lexicographically greater than or equal to those of y.
`x.swap(y)`	Swaps all the elements of x with those of y.

Table 7.1 — Requirements Common to all Containers

A reversible container is just like a container but supports a reverse iterator in addition to the forward iterator. The reverse iterator allows the elements in the container to be retrieved in the reverse of the order in which they are stored. Such iterators cannot be initialized with `begin()` and `end()` like forward iterators are. To function properly, reverse iterators must be initialized with `rbegin()` and `rend()`.

Should any of the insert operations for a reversible container throw an exception, it is guaranteed that they have not modified the container. The additional requirements supported by reversible containers are summarized in Table 7.2.

A sequence container stores the elements within it in a strictly linear fashion. This means that one element is stored after another, and the arrangement of elements will not change unless the programmer invokes methods to change the order of the elements. This differs from the associative containers where the programmer accesses the elements through an index and is unaware of the physical arrangement of the elements, and where the container can rearrange the physical storage without affecting the program using the container. Sequence

Expression	Explanation
`C::reverse_iterator`	A reverse iterator for the container.
`C::const_reverse_iterator`	A constant reverse iterator for the container.
`x.rbegin()`	Returns a reverse iterator that references the last element in the sequence.
`x.rend()`	Returns a past-the-end reverse iterator for the beginning of the sequence.

Table 7.2 — Additional Reversible Container Requirements

Expression	Explanation
C x(n, elem)	Constructs a new sequence that is initialized to contain n copies of the element elem.
C x(iter1, iter2)	Constructs a new sequence whose elements are copies of those referenced by the iterators from iter1 up to iter2 in an existing container.
x.insert(iter, elem)	Inserts a copy of elem directly before the element referenced by iter.
x.insert(iter, n, elem)	Inserts n copies of elem directly before the element referenced by iter.
x.insert(iter, first, last)	Inserts copies of the elements referenced by the iterators first up to last immediately before the element referenced by iter.
x.erase(iter)	Deletes the element referenced by iter from the sequence.
x.erase(first, last)	Deletes all the elements in the range of the iterators first up to last.
x.clear()	Deletes all elements from the container.

Table 7.3 — Additional Requirements of Sequence Containers

containers provide the additional operations, shown in Table 7.3, for convenience in dealing with sequences.

In addition to the requirements of all sequence containers, the operations shown in Table 7.4 can be provided. Whether these operations are provided for a given container is determined by efficiency. They are provided only for containers for which they can be implemented to run in constant time.

The push_back() and push_front() methods allow easy appending of new elements to either end of the sequence. pop_front() and pop_back() provide the same convenience for deleting elements from either end, and front() and back() allow direct access to the first and last elements without using iterators. Finally, a subscript operation can be defined to provide true random access to any element in the container.

Expression	Container	Explanation
`x.front()`	vector, list, deque	Returns a reference to the first element in the container.
`x.back()`	vector, list, deque	Returns a reference to the last element in the container.
`x.push_back(elem)`	vector, list, deque	Appends `elem` to the end of the sequence.
`x.push_front(elem)`	list, deque	Inserts `elem` before the first element in the container.
`x.pop_front()`	list, deque	Deletes the first element in the container.
`x.pop_back()`	vector, list, deque	Deletes the last element in the container.
`x[n]`	vector, deque	Returns a reference to the nth element in the container.
`x.at(n)`	vector, deque	Returns a reference to the nth element in the container.

Table 7.4 — Optional Requirements of Sequence Containers

7.3 Vectors

The vector is probably the simplest of the sequence containers. It is implemented as a contiguous block of memory similar to an array. The features of a vector include the following:

- amortized constant time insertions and deletions at the end,

- linear time insertions and deletions at interior positions,

- automatic storage management, and

- satisfies all the requirements of a reversible container and a sequence.

The easiest way to think of a vector is as an array that can grow if it is not large enough. This is done for you via the automatic storage management feature of the vector. When a vector is created, a finite amount of storage is allocated to hold the elements. If elements are inserted and exceed this storage space, a larger block of memory is allocated, the old elements are copied to the newly allocated memory, and the old memory is freed.

This operation is convenient, but it is computationally very expensive. It also means that the constant and linear time operations are only average speeds. If an operation requires new memory to be allocated, it will take much longer. This performance difference makes the vector unsuitable for applications where additional memory will have to be allocated frequently. The average operation speeds are valid only if additional memory allocation is done infrequently, as was intended by the designers.

The vector makes efficient use of memory, since very little information other than the actual data in the vector is stored. This is in contrast to a container such as the list, discussed later in this chapter, which requires two extra pointers to be associated with every element in the list. The list has the advantage that it supports constant time insertions and deletions at any point in the list. Unfortunately, this extra speed can be attained only by consuming extra memory. One way to look at this is that you can either store information that will reduce the calculations you will have to perform, consuming space, or you can recalculate something every time, consuming time. This is called the space-time tradeoff, and program designers are faced with it constantly.

As we examine the containers, we will continually face the space-time trade-off, and it will become one of the principal contributing factors in the decision to use one container in preference to another. Since it is expensive for a vector to obtain additional space, you should create it with enough space for its application. In the unlikely event that additional space is required, you can obtain it at the cost of decreased performance. This is preferable to having the program fail due to insufficient memory. On the other hand, if too much storage is preallocated and not used, memory is being wasted. Therefore, the vector is best suited to those applications where an accurate estimate of the storage requirements can be obtained before the application begins to execute. Otherwise, you should consider another container.

Let us begin our study of how to use the vector by examining Listing 7.1—a simple program to sum the values stored in a vector of integers.

```
#include <vector>
#include <algorithm>
#include <iostream>

using namespace std;

void main()
{
    vector<int>               vect(10,0);
    vector<int>::iterator     iter;
    int                       i, sum = 0;
    ostream_iterator<int>     outStream(cout, " ");

    for(i=0;i<10;i++) vect[i] = i;
    copy(vect.begin(), vect.end(), outStream);
    cout << endl;

    for(iter = vect.begin(); iter != vect.end();
        iter++) sum += *iter;
    cout << sum << endl;
}
```

```
0 1 2 3 4 5 6 7 8 9
45
```

Listing 7.1 — Summing a Vector [vect_sum.cpp]

Despite the shortness of this program, it illustrates several important points about vectors. The program begins by declaring a vector of integers that contains ten elements, all initialized to zero. This constructor is obtained from the list of sequence container operations in Table 7.3. Once the vector is created, it is filled with the values from 0 to 9 by a for loop that uses the subscript operation to assign a value to each element. The entire vector is then printed out using the copy() function.

The copy() function requires two iterators to delimit the range of values to be printed. These are obtained from the methods begin() and end(), which are defined for every container.

Finally, the values in the vector are summed by a second for loop. This accesses the values in the vector via an iterator rather than by subscripting, demonstrating that it can be done either way. The iterator is defined by the vector class and is declared as vector<int>::iterator. We will find that every container defines its own iterators and that they are all declared in this manner.

The limits of a vector can be altered only by using one of the methods provided for that purpose: insert(), erase(), push_front(), push-_back(), pop_front(), or pop_back(). Attempting to subscript outside the range of allocated space is not permitted and will result in anomalous values or might cause the program to crash. The preceding methods automatically update the iterators returned by begin() and end() whenever the size of the vector changes, as demonstrated in Listing 7.2.

```cpp
#include <vector>
#include <algorithm>
#include <iostream>

using namespace std;

void main()
{
    vector<int>             vect(15,0);
    ostream_iterator<int>   outStream(cout, " ");

    copy(vect.begin(), vect.end(), outStream);
    cout << endl;
    cout << "size = " << vect.size() << endl ;
    cout << "max size = " << vect.max_size() << endl;
    cout << "capacity = " << vect.capacity() << endl;

    vect.push_back(98);
    copy(vect.begin(), vect.end(), outStream);
    cout << endl;
    cout << "size = " << vect.size() << endl ;
    cout << "max size = " << vect.max_size() << endl;
    cout << "capacity = " << vect.capacity() << endl;

    vect.erase(vect.begin());
    copy(vect.begin(), vect.end(), outStream);
    cout << endl;
    cout << "size = " << vect.size() << endl ;
    cout << "max size = " << vect.max_size() << endl;
```

```
    cout << "capacity = " << vect.capacity() << endl;
}
```

```
0 0 0 0 0 0 0 0 0 0 0 0 0 0 0
size = 15
max size = 1073741823
capacity = 15
0 0 0 0 0 0 0 0 0 0 0 0 0 0 0 98
size = 16
max size = 1073741823
capacity = 30
0 0 0 0 0 0 0 0 0 0 0 0 0 0 98
size = 15
max size = 1073741823
capacity = 30
```

Listing 7.2 — Vector Size and Capacity [vect_sz.cpp]

The vector is created with fifteen elements, as is shown by the printout of the vector, and confirmed by the value returned from `size()`. The value of `max_size()` is the total number of elements that can be stored in the vector and remains unchanged despite insertions and deletions. The value returned by `capacity()` is the amount of memory currently allocated for the vector expressed as the number of elements it can contain. `push_back()` increases the length of the vector by one, and `erase()` decreases it by one. When `push_back()` requires extra storage, the amount of memory allocated to the vector is doubled so that it will have space to grow without having to constantly perform memory allocations.

In some cases, you will be able to predict the amount of space required by the vector when it is created, yet wants to be able to use a vector of a variable length less than this maximum size. The method `reserve()` is provided to deal with this problem. `reserve()` accepts a single parameter that is the maximum number of elements for which memory should be allocated. If this is less than the amount of memory currently allocated, no action is taken. If it is greater than the currently allocated memory, then new memory is allocated and the values from the old memory copied. This reallocation invalidates any iterators, references, or pointers to the vector, since they would now point to the deallocated storage. This same problem occurs when storage is reallocated by methods such as `push_back()` and you must be very careful to avoid using such pointers or iterators after they have been invalidated. Fortunately, the iterators returned by methods such as `begin()` and `end()` are updated when storage is reallocated and they can be used safely. This is shown in the Listing 7.3.

```cpp
#include <vector>
#include <algorithm>
#include <iostream>

using namespace std;

void main()
{
    vector<int>             vect;
    ostream_iterator<int>   outStream(cout, " ");

    cout << "size = " << vect.size() << endl;
    cout << "capacity = " << vect.capacity() << endl;

    vect.reserve(50);
    cout << "size = " << vect.size() << endl;
    cout << "capacity = " << vect.capacity() << endl;

    vect.push_back(5);
    vect.push_back(34);
    copy(vect.begin(), vect.end(), outStream);
    cout << endl << "size = " << vect.size() << endl;
    cout << "capacity = " << vect.capacity() << endl;

}
```

```
size = 0
capacity = 0
size = 0
capacity = 50
5 34
size = 2
capacity = 50
```

Listing 7.3 — Reserving Space in a Vector [vect_res.cpp]

When the vector is created by the parameterless constructor, no storage is allocated and the capacity is zero. Invoking the `reserve()` method allocates sufficient storage for fifty elements, yet the size remains zero since none of these elements is being used. As elements are inserted with `push_back()`, the size increases while the capacity remains the same. We could continue to insert elements until all fifty positions were full, and then storage would automatically be reallocated. The values returned by `size()` and `capacity()` can be used to predict when storage will be reallocated and when pointers will be invalidated.

Insertion and deletion require that all elements after the insertion or deletion point be moved physically to create or delete space in the vector. This is an expensive operation that requires linear time and should be used infrequently. All iterators, references, and pointers to elements after the deletion point are invalidated by these operations and should not be used.

The vector supports a random access iterator that can have integer values added and subtracted. This can be implemented in constant time due to the array-like nature of the storage. Listing 7.4 demonstrates this by implementing the bubble sort algorithm to sort the elements in a vector. The bubble sort is an inefficient $O(n^2)$ sort that makes repeated passes through the vector, swapping pairs of elements that are out of order. This process continues until it makes an entire pass without switching any values, indicating that the vector is sorted.

```cpp
#include <vector.>
#include <algorithm>
#include <iostream>

using namespace std;

void main()
{
    vector<int>             vect(10, 0);
    vector<int>::iterator   iter;
    int                     i, sorted = 0;
    ostream_iterator<int>   outStream(cout, " ");

    for(iter=vect.begin(), i=1; iter != vect.end();
        iter++, i++) {
        if((i%2) == 0) *iter = i;
        else *iter = -1 * i;
    }
    copy(vect.begin(), vect.end(), outStream);
    cout << endl;

    while(!sorted) {
```

```
            sorted = 1;
            for(iter=vect.begin(); iter != (vect.end() - 1);
                iter++) {
                if(*iter > *(iter + 1)) {
                    iter_swap(iter, iter+1);
                    sorted = 0;
                }
            }
        }

        copy(vect.begin(), vect.end(), outStream);
        cout << endl;
}
```

```
-1 2 -3 4 -5 6 -7 8 -9 10
-9 -7 -5 -3 -1 2 4 6 8 10
```

Listing 7.4 — Using Bubble Sort on a Vector [bsort.cpp]

Since the bubble sort algorithm requires that each element be compared with the one adjacent to it, *iter must be compared to *(iter + 1). This only works because the iterator provided by the vector is a random access iterator that permits this operation.

7.3.1 Bit Vectors

Vectors of bits are represented in the latest C++ compilers as vector<bool>. This is an efficient representation that is superior to using shorts to hold Boolean values. Older compilers do not support the type bool, so the C++ standard provides the bitset for use with those compilers. bitset replaces the class bit_vector that was supplied with the HP distribution. The bitset provides several operations specifically for working with Boolean values. The program in Listing 7.5 demonstrates how to use vector<bool>.


```
#include <vector>
#include <algorithm>
#include <iostream>

using namespace std;
```

```
main()
{
    vector<bool>              bv;
    vector<bool>::iterator    iter;

    bv.push_back(true);
    bv.push_back(true);
    bv.push_back(true);
    bv.push_back(false);
    bv.push_back(true);
    copy(bv.begin(), bv.end(),
        ostream_iterator<bool>(cout,""));
    cout << endl;

    iter = bv.begin() ;
    bv.insert(iter, false);
    copy(bv.begin(), bv.end(),
        ostream_iterator<bool>(cout,""));
    cout << endl;

    bv.erase(iter);

    copy(bv.begin(), bv.end(),
        ostream_iterator<bool>(cout,""));
    cout << endl;

    return(0);
}
```

```
11101
011101
11101
```

Listing 7.5 — Using vector<bool>. [boolvect.cpp]

Although the latest C++ standard calls for the implementation of the type bool, few of the previous generations of compilers actually provided it. As a result, you could not declare a container as vector<bool>. The STL designers recognized this problem and implemented a special class called the bit_vector to address the shortcomings in older compilers. It provides a set of operations identical to the vector and can be used interchangeably with a vector. Listing 7.6

illustrates how to create and use a `bit_vector`. This code was compiled with the HP implementation of the STL.

```cpp
#include <bvector.h>
#include <algo.h>

main()
{
    bit_vector            bv;
    bit_vector::iterator iter;

    bv.push_back(1);
    bv.push_back(1);
    bv.push_back(1);
    bv.push_back(0);
    bv.push_back(1);
    copy(bv.begin(), bv.end(),
        ostream_iterator<bool>(cout,""));
    cout << "\n";

    iter = bv.begin() ;
    bv.insert(iter, 0);
    copy(bv.begin(), bv.end(),
        ostream_iterator<bool>(cout,""));
    cout << '\n';

    bv.erase(iter);

    copy(bv.begin(), bv.end(),
        ostream_iterator<bool>(cout,""));
    cout << "\n";

    return(0);
}
```

```
11101
011101
11101
```

Listing 7.6 — Using a `bit_vector` [bit_vect.cpp]

7.4 Lists

The vector has several limitations on the speed of insertions and deletions since they can be performed in constant time only if they are at the end of the vector. The list overcomes these limitations and provides constant time insertions and deletions at any point in the list. This is accomplished by using noncontiguous storage to hold the elements that comprise the list.

As is usual in the world of data structures, every gain in efficiency must be traded off against a cost in storage or a loss in other capabilities. Although the list provides fast insertions and deletions, it consumes slightly more storage and no longer provides fast random access to the elements. However, bidirectional iterators are provided that can traverse the list in either the forward or reverse directions even though this must be done in a sequential fashion.

A list consists of a series of nodes, each of which contains an instance of some other data type. (See Figure 7.2) Each node augments the data type stored within it by adding a pointer to the next node in the list and the previous node. This arrangement allows the list to be traversed in either the forward or reverse direction, although this must be done one node at a time in a linear fashion. This linear arrangement makes the list suitable for applications that need to traverse the data sequentially rather than accessing elements in random order.

The forward and reverse pointers must be added to every node stored in the list, and this can consume a considerable amount of storage in a large list. On many machines, a pointer occupies 4 bytes, resulting in an overhead of 8 bytes per node to store data in a list. If the size of the data stored in the list nodes is large, say 100 bytes or more, the storage overhead required by the pointers will be relatively small. On the other hand, should you create a list of 4-byte integers, the storage required by the pointers is greater than the size of the data! This additional space required by the pointers must be considered before deciding to adopt the list as a container.

You might be wondering how insertion and deletion of list nodes can be performed in constant time when the list can be traversed only in linear time. The answer is that it is all done by the manipulation of pointers. Consider a list with a node to be deleted. The node to be deleted is pointed to by the nodes directly before and after it and can be reached only by following one of those pointers. For ease of discussion we'll call the node to be deleted B, the node before it A, and the node following it C. Node B can be deleted by making the next pointer of A point to C and the previous pointer of C point to A. This is illustrated in Figure 7.3, where the original pointers to node B are shown as dashed lines and the pointers after its deletion as solid lines.

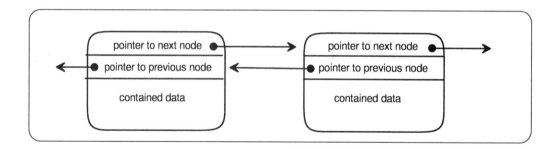

Figure 7.2 — Next and Previous Pointers of List Nodes

Since the node being deleted will no longer be used, and no program will follow the pointers in the node, it is not necessary to change its pointers. The entire deletion process was accomplished by changing only two pointers, and the time required for this is constant regardless of the position of the node being deleted.

Insertion is likewise accomplished via pointer manipulation. In this case, we assume that we are trying to insert a new node B between two existing nodes A and C. The next pointer of A must be made to point to the new node, as must the previous pointer of C. The process is completed by having the previous pointer of B point to A and the next pointer of B point to C. This is illustrated in Figure 7.4, where the original pointers are shown as dashed lines.

Once again, this operation can be accomplished in constant time since only four pointers need to be manipulated. The operation is the same regardless of the position of the insertion point in the list.

The storage for a list is managed very differently from that of a vector. Whereas the storage for the vector is allocated as a single, contiguous block, the storage for the list is allocated in discrete chunks. This means that adding and deleting nodes to and from a list will never require the storage reallocation performed by a vector.

Another difference between the vector and the list is that pointers and references to the nodes in a list are not invalidated by insertion and deletion. In the vector, insertion and deletion require the physical movement of data to accommodate the new element or to occupy the space vacated by a deleted element. As a result, references to memory locations are no longer valid since different data occupy the memory. In the list, only the pointers in the nodes are changed, while the node itself continues to occupy the same memory location. Pointers or

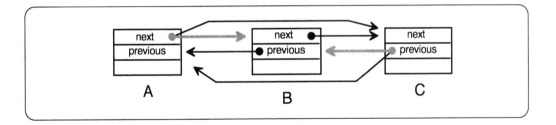

Figure 7.3 — Rearranging Pointers to Delete a Node

references to a deleted node should not be used, since the memory might well have been reused by your own or another application.

7.4.1 List Implementation

The HP implementation of the STL list uses its own memory management scheme where a block of memory is preallocated and managed directly by the list. This was done because implementations of the operators new and delete are notoriously inefficient. Each time they are invoked, they call the operating system or the runtime support provided by the C++ compiler. These use a complex, general-purpose memory management scheme that must deal with variable-sized chunks of memory being allocated and freed. It is possible to write a

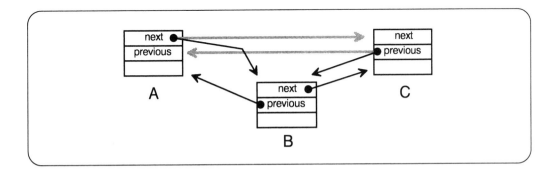

Figure 7.4 — Inserting Node B into a List

memory management routine that offers better performance if fixed-sized chunks of memory are used.

STL implementations conforming to the latest standard make use of allocators to encapsulate the memory management scheme. The standard allocator uses the standard memory management facilities of the operating system or compiler and is not the most efficient. It is possible to replace the allocator with a custom allocator that does the same thing as was done in the HP list implementation. There is an example of how to write an allocator in Chapter 10.

7.4.2 List Examples

As an initial example of a list, we look at how we might maintain a list of names in alphabetical order. The names in Listing 7.7 are inserted into the list one at a time, with a search before each insertion to determine the position at which the name should be inserted.

```
#include <string>
#include <iterator>

using namespace std;

void main()
{
    list<string>             nameList;
    list<string>::iterator   iter;
    string                   *temp;
    int                      i;
    ostream_iterator<string>  outStream(cout, "\n");
    char*        sourceList[9] = {
        "Sam",      "Mary",      "Sue",
        "Allen",    "Chris",     "Delores",
        "Melissa",  "Patricia",  "Donald"};

    for(i=0;i<9;i++) {
        temp = new string(sourceList[i]);
        for(iter=nameList.begin(); iter !=
            nameList.end(); iter++) {
            if(*temp < *iter) break;
        }
        nameList.insert(iter, *temp);
        delete temp;
    }
```

```
        copy(nameList.begin(), nameList.end(), outStream);
}
```

```
Allen
Chris
Delores
Donald
Mary
Melissa
Patricia
Sam
Sue
```

Listing 7.7 — An Ordered List of Names [ord_list.cpp]

The names are stored in a list whose template parameter is the class string. A for loop is used to insert each of the names into the list. Each time through the loop, a linear search is performed to find the position at which the name should be inserted. In some cases, such as the initial insertion, the insertion point is after the last element in the list. In this case, the search sets the iterator indicating the insertion point to be the past-the-end iterator for the list. The insertion is then performed by inserting before the past-the-end iterator so that the inserted element becomes the last in the list. The actual insertion is done by the method insert, which requires an iterator indicating the element to insert before and the element to be inserted. Note that the element that was inserted is deleted immediately after its insertion and that this has no effect on the value stored in the list. This is because the insert method copies the value of the element into storage allocated by the list itself.

This example demonstrates how to maintain a list in sorted order by hand. In practice, it would make more sense to use the function lower_bound() to determine the insertion position, as it would use a binary search rather than a linear search.

7.4.3 List Operations

Since the list is designed to provide fast insertions and deletions from the middle of the list, it provides several operations to aid in performing such manipulations. These operations can be applied only to list containers and no others. In addition to the list-specific operations, some of the general STL algorithms are duplicated as methods of the list class. Although the general STL algorithms can be applied to a list, the class-specific methods usually offer an advantage, such as increased performance, and should be used in preference to the more general algorithm.

The list class defines several versions of the `splice` method, which destructively moves elements from one list and inserts them into a second list. The term *destructive move* means that the element is removed from the first list after being inserted into the second. All of the `splice()` methods operate in linear time. The three signatures are:

```
void splice(iterator position, list<T>& x);

void splice(iterator position,
      list<T>& x,
      iterator i);

void splice(iterator position,
      list<T>& x,
      iterator first,
      iterator last);
```

The first form of the method inserts the entire list x into the target list immediately before `position`. `position` must be an iterator that references a location in the target list. After the method terminates, the list x is left empty. The list x and the target list *cannot* be the same.

The second form moves the single element referenced by the iterator i from the list x to the target list in constant time. The third form moves all the elements in the range from `first` up to `last` from the list x to the target list. If x and the target list are the same, then the move takes constant time; otherwise, it takes linear time. Exercise care when the two lists are the same to ensure that `position` is not in the range `first` up to `last`; otherwise, unpredictable results will occur.

Whereas the `erase()` method accepts one or two iterators to indicate the elements to delete from the list, the `remove()` method accepts a single value and then traverses the list removing all elements that are equal to this value. This is useful if an iterator for the element(s) to be deleted is not available. Be aware, however, that the entire list will be searched for the value, requiring linear time:

```
void remove(const T& value);
```

The method `unique()` works the same as the STL function of the same name. It removes duplicate adjacent values from a sorted list in linear time:

```
void unique();
```

The method `merge()` performs a destructive merge of two sorted lists. The elements from the argument list are merged into the target list, and the argument list is empty when the method terminates. If two equal elements are merged, the element from the target list will precede the element from the argument list. The method requires linear time:

```
void merge(list<T>& x);
```

The `reverse()` method is similar to the STL function of the same name and reverses the order of the entire list in linear time:

```
void reverse();
```

The `sort()` method sorts the entire list and is stable, since it preserves the relative order of equal elements. This method requires approximately $O(n \log n)$ time:

```
void sort();
```

A more extensive example of the application of lists involves keeping track of the inventory at a wine store. The store stocks numerous wines that are identified by the name of the wine, the winery that produced it, the country of origin, the color, year of production, and price. Queries are allowed that permit various attributes to be specified, and all wines matching those attributes will be retrieved. The format of a query is a series of attribute name and value pairs. In the case of the year, one of the operators (=, !=, <, >, <=, >=) must be used between the attribute name and its value to specify the desired relationship. The query to find all red French wines bottled before 1994 would look like this:

```
color red country france year < 1994
```

The query is evaluated by AND'ing all the red wines with all the French wines, then AND'ing this with the wines bottled before 1994. Although it is possible to make a linear pass through the data to identify all the wines that have these properties, it is more efficient to build inverted indices. An inverted index is a list of all wines that have the same value for a given attribute. An inverted index is constructed for each value of every attribute of interest so that when all the red wines are needed there is a list of them readily available.

As an example of inverted lists, consider a list of people indexed by sex and hair color. Lists are maintained for every value of the attributes sex and color.

Name	Sex	Color	ID
Ann	F	brown	1
George	M	red	2
Betty	F	blonde	3
Susan	F	black	4
Jim	M	brown	5
Frank	M	black	6
Jennifer	F	blonde	7
Willis	M	blonde	8

Inverted Indices

Sex	
M	F
2	1
5	3
6	4
8	7

Color			
black	blonde	brown	red
4	3	1	2
6	7	5	
	8		

Figure 7.5 — Inverted Indices for Sex and Hair Color

These lists contain the identifiers of the people whose attributes have these values. These inverted lists are shown in Figure 7.5.

To find all the males with black hair, you have to find the IDs that are on both the male inverted list and the black hair inverted list. If the two lists are maintained in sorted order, then the balance line algorithm can be used to find the elements common to the two lists in linear time. The balance line algorithm initializes two iterators, one referring to the start of each list. If the two elements are equal, one of them is output to the result list, and both iterators are advanced. When one element is less than the other, the iterator for the lesser element is advanced, but no value is copied to the output list. This continues until the end of one of the lists is reached, when the algorithm terminates.

This implementation stores the wine inventory information in an ASCII file that is read into memory and inverted every time the program is started. A typical inventory file appears in Listing 7.8.

Candelabra	Gallo	USA	pinotnoir	1992	red	9.95
PrinceVert	B&G	France	burgundy	1990	white	12.00
VinePrinz	Mueller	Germany	mosel	1993	white	8.50
ColdDuck	ChateGai	Canada	zinfandel	1995	white	7.25
Challenge	Jordan	Canada	zinfandel	1994	rose	6.75
Exuberance	Niagara	Canada	mosel	1993	white	8.95
Outback	Hardys	Astlia	burgundy	1992	red	9.50

Listing 7.8 — Wine Inventory File [stock.dat]

Listing 7.8 contains the wine name, winery, country, grape variety, year of production, color, and price. Internally, the wines are stored as instances of the class `Wine` in a list. The class `Wine` as well as classes to represent queries and tokens produced during the scanning of queries are defined in the header file `wine.h`, shown in Listing 7.9.

```
#ifndef WINE_H
#define WINE_H

#include <string.h>
#include <iostream>
#include <list>

using namespace std;

#define NAME_LEN    16

enum Fruit {
    unknown1,
    apple,
    blueberry,
    burgundy,
    pinotNoir,
    mosel,
    zinfadel
};

enum Color {
    unknown2,
    white,
    rose,
    red
};
```

```
enum Country {
   unknown3,
   france,
   germany,
   spain,
   italy,
   canada,
   usa,
   chile,
   safrica,
   australia
};

/////////////////////////////
// the representation of a wine
/////////////////////////////
class Wine {
public:
   Wine();
   friend bool operator==(const Wine&  w1,
                          const Wine&  w2);
   friend bool operator==(const Wine&  w,
                          const int&   i);
   friend bool operator<(const Wine&   w1,
                          const Wine&   w2);
   friend ostream& operator<<(ostream&    os,
                              const Wine& w);
   friend istream& operator>>(istream& is,
                              Wine&    w);

   char       name[NAME_LEN];
   char       winery[NAME_LEN];
   Country    country;
   Fruit      variety;
   int        year;
   Color      color;
   float      price;
   int        sequenceNumber;
};

//////////////////////////////////////////////////////
// a list that has a textual or numeric
// identifier associated with it
//////////////////////////////////////////////////////
class IdList {
public:
```

```
        IdList();
        void sort();

        list<int>    contents;
    };

class NamedList: public IdList {
public:
        NamedList();
        NamedList(const char*);
        friend bool operator==(const NamedList&    n1,
                                const char*        str);
        friend bool operator==(const NamedList&    n1,
                            const NamedList&       n2);
        friend bool operator<(const NamedList& n1,
                            const NamedList&   n2);
private:
        char                     id[NAME_LEN];
    };

class IntList: public IdList {
public:
        IntList();
        IntList(int);
        friend bool operator==(const IntList&    l1,
                            const IntList&       l2);
        friend bool operator<(const IntList&    l1,
                            const IntList&       l2);

        int    id;
    };

/////////////////////////////////////////////////
// the representation of a token as returned
// by the scanner
/////////////////////////////////////////////////
class Token {
public:
        Token();
        enum TokenType {
            overflow,    // token too long for buffer
            ident,       // a string value
            nameW,       // keyword "name"
            countryW,    // keyword "country"
            wineryW,     // keyword "winery"
            yearW,       // keyword "year"
            colorW,      // keyword "color"
```

```
        fruitW,        // keyword "fruit"
        eq,            // =
        neq,           // !=
        lt,            // <
        gt,            // >
        leq,           // <=
        geq,           // >=
        intval,        // an integer value
        floatval       // a float value
    };
    TokenType      type;
    char           strVal[NAME_LEN];
    int            intVal;
    float          floatVal;
};

/////////////////////////////////
// the representation of a query
/////////////////////////////////
class Query {
public:
    Query();
    void       Clear();
    char       wineName[NAME_LEN];
    char       wineryName[NAME_LEN];
    Color      wineColor;
    Country    countryName;
    Fruit      fruitName;
    int        year;
    Token::TokenType   yearOper;
};

/////////////////////
// global functions
/////////////////////
ostream& CountryPrint(ostream&, Country);
ostream& FruitPrint(ostream& os, Fruit);
ostream& ColorPrint(ostream& os, Color);
Country CountryRead(istream&);
Fruit FruitRead(istream&);
Color ColorRead(istream&);

/////////////////////
// global variables
/////////////////////
extern int      wineSeqNum;
```

```
#endif
```

Listing 7.9 — The Header File [wine.h]

Although there are an unlimited number of wine names, wineries, and years of production, there are a finite number of grape varieties, countries, and wine colors. As a result, enumerations are defined for fruit type, country, and color. The definition of the class `Wine` provides data members to store all the information from the inventory file as well as the methods necessary to handle the data.

Since there can be an unlimited number of wine names, wineries, and years of production, these are inverted as lists of inverted lists. The classes `Named-List` and `IntList` are used to represent an inverted list that has a textual or integral identifier associated with it. For example, an instance of a `NamedList` would be used to store references to all of the wines that have that particular name. The actual name is stored in the class `NamedList`, and the references to all wines with that name are stored in the list contained within the class. The instances of the class `NamedList` are themselves stored in a list that can then be searched to find the references to a particular wine.

The `Token` class is used to return tokens from the query scanner to the query parser. The `Query` class stores the query specifications after they have been parsed. The query parsing process is not involved in the list processing of this example and is not examined in detail. The scanner, `GetToken()`, breaks the query into a series of tokens representing keywords, identifiers, and operators in the query. The token is then passed to the query parser, `ParseQuery()`, which checks to see that the tokens conform to the definition of a query and constructs an instance of the class `Query` to represent the textual query.

The implementation of the classes and functions declared in `wine.h` is in the file `wine.cpp`.

```
#include <wine.h>

Wine::Wine()
{
    name[0] = winery[0] = '\0';
    country = france;
    variety = burgundy;
    year = 0;
    color = white;
    price = 0.0;
```

```
      sequenceNumber = 0;
}

bool operator==(const Wine& w1, const Wine& w2)
{
   if(0 != strcmp(w1.winery, w2.winery))
      return(false);
   if(0 != strcmp(w1.name, w2.name)) return(false);
   if(w1.country != w2.country) return(false);
   if(w1.variety != w2.variety) return(false);
   if(w1.year != w2.year) return(false);
   if(w1.color != w2.color) return(false);
   return(true);
}

bool operator==(const Wine& w, const int& i)
{
   if(w.sequenceNumber == i) return(true);
   return(false);
}

ostream& operator<<(ostream& os, const Wine& w)
{
   os << w.name << ", " << w.winery << ", ";
   CountryPrint(os, w.country);
   os << ", " ;
   FruitPrint(os, w.variety);
   os << ", " << w.year << ", " ;
   ColorPrint(os, w.color);
   os << ", " << w.price ;
   return(os);
}

bool operator<(const Wine& w1, const Wine& w2)
{
   return w1.sequenceNumber < w2.sequenceNumber ;
}


ostream& CountryPrint(ostream& os, Country c)
{
   switch(c) {
      case  france:
         os << "France";
         break;
      case  germany:
         os << "Germany";
```

```cpp
            break;
        case  spain:
           os << "Spain";
           break;
        case  italy:
           os << "Italy";
           break;
        case  canada:
           os << "Canada";
           break;
        case  usa:
           os << "USA";
           break;
        case  chile:
           os << "Chile";
           break;
        case  safrica:
           os << "SAfrica";
           break;
        case  australia:
           os << "Australia";
           break;
        default:
           os << "unknown";
           break;
    }
    return(os);
}

ostream& ColorPrint(ostream& os, Color c)
{
    switch(c) {
        case white:
           os << "white";
           break;
        case rose:
           os << "rose";
           break;
        case red:
           os << "red";
           break;
        default:
           os << "unknown";
           break;
    }
    return(os);
}
```

```
ostream& FruitPrint(ostream& os, Fruit f)
{
    switch(f) {
        case apple:
            os << "apple";
            break;
        case blueberry:
            os << "blueberry";
            break;
        case burgundy:
            os << "burgundy";
            break;
        case pinotNoir:
            os << "pinot noir";
            break;
        case mosel:
            os << "mosel";
            break;
        case zinfadel:
            os << "zinfadel";
            break;
        default:
            os << "unknown";
            break;
    }
    return(os);
}

istream& operator>>(istream& is, Wine& w)
{
    is >> w.name;
    is >> w.winery;
    w.country = CountryRead(is);
    w.variety = FruitRead(is);
    is >> w.year;
    w.color = ColorRead(is);
    is >> w.price;
    w.sequenceNumber = wineSeqNum++;
    return(is);
}

Fruit FruitRead(istream& is)
{
    char  input[32];

    is >> input;
```

```
    strlwr(input);
    if(0 == strcmp(input, "apple")) return(apple);
    if(0 == strcmp(input, "blueberry"))
        return(blueberry);
    if(0 == strcmp(input, "burgundy"))
        return(burgundy);
    if(0 == strcmp(input, "pinotnoir"))
        return(pinotNoir);
    if(0 == strcmp(input, "mosel")) return(mosel);
    if(0 == strcmp(input, "zinfadel"))
        return(zinfadel);
    return(unknown1);
}


Color ColorRead(istream& is)
{
    char  input[32];

    is >> input;
    strlwr(input);
    if(0 == strcmp(input, "white")) return(white);
    if(0 == strcmp(input, "rose")) return(rose);
    if(0 == strcmp(input, "red")) return(red);
    return(unknown2);
}

Country CountryRead(istream& is)
{
    char  input[32];

    is >> input;
    strlwr(input);
    if(0 == strcmp(input, "france")) return(france);
    if(0 == strcmp(input, "germany")) return(germany);
    if(0 == strcmp(input, "spain")) return(spain);
    if(0 == strcmp(input, "italy")) return(italy);
    if(0 == strcmp(input, "canada")) return(canada);
    if(0 == strcmp(input, "usa")) return(usa);
    if(0 == strcmp(input, "chile")) return(chile);
    if(0 == strcmp(input, "safrica")) return(safrica);
    if(0 == strcmp(input, "australia"))
        return(australia);
    return(unknown3);
}

IdList::IdList()
```

```
{
}

NamedList::NamedList()
{
    id[0] = '\0';
}

NamedList::NamedList(const char* str)
{
    strcpy(id, str);
}

bool operator==(const NamedList& n1, const char* str)
{
    return (0 == strcmp(n1.id, str));
}

bool operator==(const NamedList& n1,
                const NamedList& n2)
{
    return (0 == strcmp(n1.id, n2.id));
}

bool operator<(const NamedList& n1,
               const NamedList& n2)
{
    return (0 > strcmp(n1.id, n2.id));
}

IntList::IntList()
{
    id = -1;
}

IntList::IntList(int i)
{
    id = i;
}

bool operator==(const IntList& l1, const IntList& l2)
{
    return (l1.id == l2.id);
}

bool operator<(const IntList& l1, const IntList& l2)
{
```

```
      return(l1.id < l2.id);
}

Token::Token()
{
   type = overflow;
   strVal[0] = '\0';
   intVal = 0;
   floatVal = 0.0;
}

Query::Query()
{
   Clear();
}

void Query::Clear()
{
   wineName[0] = wineryName[0] = '\0';
   wineColor = unknown2;
   countryName = unknown3;
   fruitName = unknown1;
   year = -1;
}
```

Listing 7.10 — Implementation File [wine.cpp]

Notice in this file the definition of operator== for many of the classes. This operator is required by the STL algorithms in the functions unique() and remove(). In general, the use of any STL function that performs a search requires that operator== be defined on the class that is being searched. Similarly, functions that copy values will want operator= defined, and functions that sort or compare values will want operator<.

Functions such as ColorRead() and ColorPrint() are used to convert enumerations between text and the internal representation and vice versa. These functions work directly with streams so they can be used either with cin and cout or string streams.

Most of the logic for the query system is in the file wines.cpp, shown in Listing 7.11.

```
#include "wine.h"
```

```
#include <fstream>
#include <strstream>
#include <cctype>

void ProcessQueries();
list<int>* EvalQuery(Query& qry);
void MakeIndices(Wine& w, int);
template<class T>
int EvalOp(T& a, Token::TokenType op, T& b);
int ParseQuery(char* line, Query& qry);
char* GetToken(char* line, Token& tok);
void ListMerge(list<int>& result, list<int> adder);

list<Wine>    stock;          // wine inventory list
list<int>     wineColor[4];   // inverted lists on color
list<int>     wineVariety[7]; // inverted lists on type
list<int>     wineCountry[10];  // inverted countries
list<NamedList>    wineName;      // inverted names
list<NamedList>    wineryName;    // inverted wineries
list<IntList>      wineYear;      // inverted years
int                wineSeqNum = 0;

class WinePrinter {
public:
   void operator()(Wine& w){cout << w;}
};

main()
{

    ifstream        stockFile("stock.dat", ios::in);
    int                          stockSize = 0;
    Wine                         temp;
    list<Wine>::iterator         iter;

    if(!stockFile) {
       cerr << "cannot open stock file\n";
       return(1);
    }


/////////////////////////////////////////////////
// Read stock list from file and build
// inverted indices.
/////////////////////////////////////////////////
    stockFile >> temp;
    while(stockFile) {
```

```
         iter = stock.insert(stock.end(),temp);
         MakeIndices(temp, temp.sequenceNumber);
         stockSize++;
         stockFile >> temp;
      }

   ProcessQueries();
   return(0);
}

//////////////////////////////////////////////////////
// Take a single instance of a wine and add
// its iterator in the stock list to all the
// inverted indices to which it belongs.
//////////////////////////////////////////////////////
void MakeIndices(Wine& w, int seqNum)
{
   list<NamedList>::iterator          nameIter;
   list<IntList>::iterator            intIter;
   char                               done;

   for(nameIter=wineName.begin(), done=0;
      nameIter != wineName.end(); nameIter++) {
      if(*nameIter == w.name) {
         (*nameIter).contents.push_back(seqNum);
         done = 1;
         break;
      }
   }
   if(!done) {
      nameIter = wineName.insert(wineName.end(),
         NamedList(strlwr(w.name)));
      (*nameIter).contents.push_back(seqNum);
   }

   for(nameIter=wineryName.begin(), done=0;
      nameIter != wineryName.end(); nameIter++) {
      if(*nameIter == w.winery) {
         (*nameIter).contents.push_back(seqNum);
         done = 1;
         break;
      }
   }
   if(!done) {
      nameIter = wineryName.insert(wineryName.end(),
         NamedList(strlwr(w.winery)));
      (*nameIter).contents.push_back(seqNum);
```

```
          }

          for(intIter=wineYear.begin(), done=0;
             intIter != wineYear.end(); intIter++) {
             if(*intIter == w.year) {
                 (*intIter).contents.push_back(seqNum);
                 done = 1;
                 break;
             }
          }
          if(!done) {
             intIter = wineYear.insert(wineYear.end(),
                 IntList(w.year));
             (*intIter).contents.push_back(seqNum);
          }

          wineColor[w.color].push_back(seqNum);
          wineVariety[w.variety].push_back(seqNum);
          wineCountry[w.country].push_back(seqNum);
    }

    /////////////////////////////////////////////
    // Repeatedly read query lines, parse them,
    // evaluate the query, and print the result.
    /////////////////////////////////////////////
    void ProcessQueries()
    {
        char                     queryLine[256];
        Query                    query;
        int                      posn;
        list<int>*               result;
        list<Wine>::iterator     wineIter;
        list<int>::iterator      intIter;
        ostream_iterator<int>    outStream(cout,"\n");

        while(cin.getline(queryLine, 256)) {
           if(!(posn = ParseQuery(queryLine, query))) {
              result = EvalQuery(query);
              wineIter = stock.begin();
              intIter = result->begin();
              while(intIter != result->end()) {
                  if(*wineIter == *intIter) {
                      cout << *wineIter << '\n';
                      intIter++;
                  }
                  wineIter++;
              }
```

```
            delete result;
        }
        else cerr << "parse error at position "
            << posn << '\n';
        query.Clear();
    }

}

///////////////////////////////////////////////////
// Evaluate a query by merging all the inverted lists
// that contain elements that match the query.
///////////////////////////////////////////////////
list<int>* EvalQuery(Query& qry)
{
    list<int>*                       result;
    list<int>                        tempResult;
    char                             first = 1, found;
    list<NamedList>::iterator        nameIter;
    list<IntList>::iterator          intIter;
    ostream_iterator<int>            outStream(cout, " ");

    result = new list<int>;

    found = 0;
    if(qry.wineName[0] != '\0') {
        for(nameIter=wineName.begin(); nameIter !=
            wineName.end()  && (! found); nameIter++) {
            if(*nameIter == qry.wineName) {
                if(first) {
                    first = 0;
                    result->insert(result->end(),
                        (*nameIter).contents.begin(),
                        (*nameIter).contents.end());
                }
                else
                    ListMerge(*result,
                        (*nameIter).contents);
                found = 1;
            }
        }
    }
    found = 0;
    if(qry.wineryName[0] != '\0') {
        for(nameIter=wineryName.begin(); nameIter !=
            wineryName.end()  && (! found); nameIter++) {
            if(*nameIter == qry.wineryName) {
```

```
                     if(first) {
                        first = 0;
                        result->insert(result->end(),
                           (*nameIter).contents.begin(),
                           (*nameIter).contents.end());
                     }
                     else
                        ListMerge(*result,
                           (*nameIter).contents);
                     found = 1;
                  }
            }
         }

         if(qry.fruitName != unknown1) {
            if(first) {
               first = 0;
               result->insert(result->end(),
                  wineVariety[qry.fruitName].begin(),
                  wineVariety[qry.fruitName].end());
            }
            else
               ListMerge(*result,
                  wineVariety[qry.fruitName]);
         }

         if(qry.wineColor != unknown2) {
            if(first) {
               first = 0;
               result->insert(result->end(),
                  wineColor[qry.wineColor].begin(),
                  wineColor[qry.wineColor].end());
            }
            else
               ListMerge(*result, wineColor[qry.wineColor]);
         }

         if(qry.countryName != unknown3) {
            if(first) {
               first = 0;
               result->insert(result->end(),
                  wineCountry[qry.countryName].begin(),
                  wineCountry[qry.countryName].end());
            }
            else
               ListMerge(*result,
                  wineCountry[qry.countryName]);
```

```
        }

    if(qry.year > 0) {
        for(intIter=wineYear.begin();intIter !=
            wineYear.end(); intIter++) {
            if(EvalOp((*intIter).id, qry.yearOper,
                qry.year)) {
                tempResult.insert(tempResult.end(),
                    (*intIter).contents.begin(),
                    (*intIter).contents.end());
                tempResult.sort();
            }
        }
        if(first) {
            first = 0;
            result->insert(result->end(),
                tempResult.begin(), tempResult.end());
        }
        else
            ListMerge(*result, tempResult);
    }

    return(result);
}

//////////////////////////////////////////////////////
// Use a modified balance line algorithm to merge
// the adder list into the result list so that only
// the common elements remain in the result.
//////////////////////////////////////////////////////
void ListMerge(list<int>& result, list<int> adder)
{
    list<int>::iterator     resIter, addIter, temp;
    ostream_iterator<int>   outStream(cout," ");

    resIter = result.begin();
    addIter = adder.begin();

    while(resIter != result.end() && addIter !=
        adder.end()) {
        if(*resIter < *addIter) {
            temp = resIter;
            resIter++;
            result.erase(temp);
        }
        else if(*resIter > *addIter) {
            addIter++;
```

```
        }
        else {
           addIter++;
           resIter++;
        }
     }
     result.erase(resIter, result.end());
}

//////////////////////////////////////////////////
// Evaluate the result of a boolean operator
// on two operands.
//////////////////////////////////////////////////
template<class T>
int EvalOp(T& a, Token::TokenType op, T& b)
{
   switch(op) {
      case Token::eq:
         return( a == b );
         cout << "EvalOp: " << a << "=" << b << '\n';
         break;
      case Token::gt:
         return( a > b );
         cout << "EvalOp: " << a << ">" << b << '\n';
         break;
      case Token::lt:
         return( a < b );
         cout << "EvalOp: " << a << "<" << b << '\n';
         break;
      case Token::geq:
         return( a >= b );
         cout << "EvalOp: " << a << ">=" << b << '\n';
         break;
      case Token::leq:
         return( a <= b );
         cout << "EvalOp: " << a << "<=" << b << '\n';
         break;
      case Token::neq:
         return( a != b );
         cout << "EvalOp: " << a << "!=" << b << '\n';
         break;
   }
   return(0);
}
```

```
/////////////////////////////////////////////////
// Parse a textual query and transform it into
// an instance of the Query class.  If an error
// occurs, it will return the position in the
// line at which the error was found;
// otherwise it will return 0.
/////////////////////////////////////////////////
int ParseQuery(char* line, Query& qry)
{
    Token       tok;
    char*       lp;
    istrstream* bufstream;

    lp = line;
    while(lp = GetToken(lp, tok)) {
        switch(tok.type) {
        case Token::nameW:
            lp = GetToken(lp, tok);
            if(tok.type != Token::ident)
                return(lp - line);
            strcpy(qry.wineName, tok.strVal);
            break;
        case Token::wineryW:
            lp = GetToken(lp, tok);
            if(tok.type != Token::ident)
                return(lp - line);
            strcpy(qry.wineryName, tok.strVal);
            break;
        case Token::colorW:
            lp = GetToken(lp, tok);
            if(tok.type != Token::ident)
                return(lp - line);
            bufstream = new istrstream(
                tok.strVal, NAME_LEN);
            qry.wineColor = ColorRead(*bufstream);
            delete bufstream;
            break;
        case Token::countryW:
            lp = GetToken(lp, tok);
            if(tok.type != Token::ident)
                return(lp - line);
            bufstream = new istrstream(
                tok.strVal, NAME_LEN);
            qry.countryName = CountryRead(*bufstream);
            delete bufstream;
            break;
        case Token::fruitW:
```

```
              lp = GetToken(lp, tok);
              if(tok.type != Token::ident)
                  return(lp - line);
              bufstream = new istrstream(
                  tok.strVal, NAME_LEN);
              qry.fruitName = FruitRead(*bufstream);
              delete bufstream;
              break;
          case Token::yearW:
              if(!(lp = GetToken(lp, tok)))
                  return(lp - line);
              if(tok.type != Token::eq &&
                  tok.type != Token::leq &&
                  tok.type != Token::geq &&
                  tok.type != Token::lt &&
                  tok.type != Token::gt)
                  return(lp - line);
              qry.yearOper = tok.type;
              if(!(lp = GetToken(lp, tok)))
                  return(lp - line);
              if(tok.type != Token::intval)
                  return(lp - line);
              qry.year = tok.intVal;
              break;
          }
      }
      return(0);
}


////////////////////////////////////////////////////
// Scan the input line to find and return the
// next token.  On error, the token type is
// Token::overflow.  The function returns a
// pointer to where scanning stopped or NULL
// when there are no more tokens on the line.
////////////////////////////////////////////////////
char* GetToken(char* line, Token& tok)
{
    char  buf[32], *pt, done = 0, identified = 0;

    pt = buf;
    while((*line == ' ') || (*line == '\t')) line++;

    switch(*line) {
      case '=':
```

```
            tok.type = Token::eq;
            done = identified = 1;
            break;
        case '<':
            if(*(line+1) == '=') {
                tok.type = Token::leq;
                line++;
            }
            else tok.type = Token::lt;
            done = identified = 1;
            break;
        case '>':
            if(*(line+1) == '=') {
                tok.type = Token::geq;
                line++;
            }
            else tok.type = Token::gt;
            done = identified = 1;
            break;
        case '!':
            if(*(line+1) == '=') {
                tok.type = Token::neq;
                line++;
            }
            else tok.type = Token::overflow;
            done = identified = 1;
            break;
        case '\0':
            return(NULL);
            break;
        default:
            *pt++ = *line++;
            while((! strchr(" \t<>=!", *line)) &&
                *line != '\0')
                *pt++ = *line++;
            *pt = '\0';
            line--;
            break;
    }
    line++;

    if(identified) return(line);
    if(isdigit(buf[0])) {
        if(strchr(buf, '.')) {
            tok.floatVal = atof(buf);
            tok.type = Token::floatval;
        }
```

```
        else {
            tok.intVal = atoi(buf);
            tok.type = Token::intval;
        }
        return(line);
    }
    if(0 == strcmp(buf, "country")) {
        tok.type = Token::countryW;
        return(line);
    }
    if(0 == strcmp(buf, "color")) {
        tok.type = Token::colorW;
        return(line);
    }
    if(0 == strcmp(buf, "name")) {
        tok.type = Token::nameW;
        return(line);
    }
    if(0 == strcmp(buf, "winery")) {
        tok.type = Token::wineryW;
        return(line);
    }
    if(0 == strcmp(buf, "year")) {
        tok.type = Token::yearW;
        return(line);
    }
    if(strlen(buf) > NAME_LEN) {
        tok.type = Token::overflow;
        return(line);
    }
    tok.type = Token::ident;
    strcpy(tok.strVal, buf);
    return(line);
}
```

Listing 7.11 — Implementation File [wines.cpp]

Looking at wines.cpp, we see that several lists are declared at the start of the file. These are the inverted lists that will hold the numeric identifiers associated with instances of Wine that have particular properties. Some of these, such as wineColor, are used to index a finite number of values. Such inverted lists are stored as an array of lists of integers. Other attributes, such as wineName, can have an unpredictable number of values and are stored as a list of Named-List or IntList so that each inverted list has an identifier associated with it.

The function `main()` is fairly simple. It reads the inventory data from the file, calls `MakeIndices()` to build the inverted lists, and then starts to process the queries.

The first list processing is encountered in the function `MakeIndices()`. It is passed the newly read wine information and the instance identifier. It then adds the identifier to each of the inverted lists to which it pertains. You might wonder why an integral identifier is used rather than the iterator for the instance. The reason for this is that the merge algorithm to be used in query evaluation requires that the lists be sorted and that the bidirectional iterator supported by the list does not define `operator<` and, hence, cannot be sorted. The method `push_back()` is used to append the identifier to the ends of the lists. Since these identifiers are assigned in ascending order, the resulting inverted lists will also be in ascending order.

The function `ProcessQuery()` reads in the query line and calls `EvalQuery()` to have the query parsed and evaluated. The result is returned as a list of wine identifiers and is processed against the main inventory list, printing out all wine instances that match the identifiers on the result list.

The function `EvalQuery()` accepts a query and creates a list of wine identifiers that satisfy the query. This is done by examining each field in the query and, if it has a non-null value, inserting the appropriate inverted list into the result list. The first inverted list inserted into the empty result is simply appended to the end, and subsequent inverted lists are merged using the function `List-Merge()` that uses a modified balance line algorithm to produce a result that is the and of the two lists. The output of this merge function is always a sorted list. In the case of a query involving a year, special processing must be performed. Since year query operators such as < or > might cause it to match several inverted lists, the result is accumulated in a temporary list by appending each list onto the end. The temporary list is then sorted before being merged with the rest of the result list.

You might wonder why the `insert()` method is always used to append one list onto the end of the other. Although it might seem more natural to use `copy()`, this will not work since `copy()` assumes that the space to receive the data has already been allocated. In the case of a list this is not so, and the `copy()` function overwrites the end of the list, resulting in data loss or a program crash. You might consider `splice()` as an alternative, but it has the undesirable property that it deletes the elements from the source list. This destroys the inverted list so that it cannot be used in subsequent queries. The combining of several inverted year lists would best be accomplished by merging the two lists so that a sorted list would result. Unfortunately, the `merge()` method destroys the source list. Thus, the new list is appended to the end of the temporary result, which is sorted before being merged with the result.

The function `ListMerge()` merges two lists so that the result is the and of the two lists. The result of the merge is placed in the list represented by the first parameter. It compares the two lists on an element-by-element basis, and if it finds an element in the first list that is not in the second, it deletes it. Elements on the second list that are not on the first are also removed from the result. Only elements common to both lists remain in the result.

The remaining functions are concerned with low-level query processing and evaluation, and you can examine the details to determine how they function.

The SGI implementation of the STL also provides the class `slist`, which is a singly linked list. This class is not in the C++ standard and is only available in the SGI implementation. It has only forward pointers between nodes, resulting in less storage overhead. This implies that `slist` can provide only a forward iterator rather than the bidirectional iterator provided by the `list` class. `slist` can be more space-efficient for applications that require only a forward iterator and will never be ported to environments in which the SGI implementation is not available.

7.5 Deques

The deque is a sequential container similar to the vector. It provides a random access iterator and is subscriptable in constant time. The difference is that the vector provides constant time insertions and deletions only at the end, and the deque provides constant time insertions and deletions at either the front or the end of the sequence. Insertions and deletions at other positions in the deque require linear time.

The properties of a deque make it well suited to applications that require frequent additions and deletions at either end of the sequence. A common use of such a data structure is in the modelling of queues. A queue is a sequence in which additions are performed at one end and deletions at the other. It works the same as a queue of customers waiting for a bank teller. Customers leave the front of the queue to go to the first available teller, and new customers entering the bank join the end of the queue.

Although the list can offer the same functionality in the same time, it extracts a price in additional memory usage that the deque does not require. Therefore, applications that require insertions and deletions at either end with infrequent insertions and deletions in the middle should use a deque in preference to a vector or a list.

Insertions and deletions at internal positions invalidate iterators, pointers, and references to the deque, and these should not be used after an insertion or deletion at an internal position.

7.5.1 Deque Implementation

The capability of a deque that permits insertions and deletions at either end in constant time requires a special implementation that can support these operations. The vector has to grow only at one end, so a block of contiguous memory is allocated and new values are added to empty space at the end of the memory block. In the deque, the same basic strategy is used except that rather than inserting the first value at the beginning of the memory block, it is inserted in the middle of the block. This leaves empty space before and after the elements of the deque so that it can grow in both directions, as shown in Figure 7.6.

This solution does not handle the problem of what happens when the block of memory becomes full. The vector handles this problem by allocating a larger block and then copying the data from the old block to the new one. The deque takes a different approach and allocates a new block without deleting the original one. New elements are then stored in the additional memory block. This creates the problem of locating the block that contains a particular element. This is solved by providing a storage map that points to all the blocks in the deque.

When the first element of the deque is inserted, only memory block 0 is allocated, and the new element is inserted in the middle of this block. As more elements are added to the end of the deque, the first block becomes full and a second block is allocated. The map contains pointers to each block and, like the blocks themselves, is filled from the middle so that blocks can be added to either end. This process can continue until the map becomes full, when a new, larger map is allocated and the pointers from the old map are copied to the middle of the new map. The old map is then deleted.

One other difference between the vector and the deque is that as more elements are added, they can both grow, but only the deque can shrink when elements are deleted. When enough elements are deleted from a deque so that one of the blocks becomes empty, the empty block is deleted and the map updated to reflect the new arrangement of blocks. As a result, the deque can make more efficient use of memory than the vector. Of course, the difference will only be apparent in applications that delete a lot of elements.

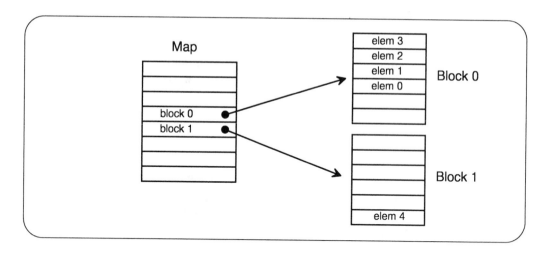

Figure 7.6 — Implementation of the Deque

The drawback of the deque implementation is in the efficiency of subscripting. In a computer, all subscripts must be resolved into machine addresses before the storage can actually be accessed. In the case of the vector, this is easily done by multiplying the number of elements that come before the element being sought by the number of bytes in each element and adding this onto the address of the first element in the vector:

```
addr(vect[n]) = addr(vect[0]) + bytesPerElement *
                (n - 1).
```

In the case of the deque, the calculation is complicated by the fact that the deque can be spread over several physical memory blocks. The first step is to determine the block in which the element resides and then the offset of the element within that block. This is then added to the starting address of the block to yield the final memory location of the element. This calculation would look like this:

```
offsetFromStart = indexOf(deque[0]) + n
blockNumber = offsetFromStart / elementsPerBlock
offsetInBlock = offsetFromStart - (blockNumber *
    elementsPerBlock)
addr(deque[n]) = addr(blockNumber) + offsetInBlock *
    bytesPerElement.
```

As you can see, this calculation is far more complicated than that used by the vector. The additional computations take time, rendering subscripting of a deque slower than subscripting of a vector. This is summarized in the following:

Container	additions	subtractions	multiplications	divisions
vector	1	1	1	0
deque	2	1	2	1

So subscripting of a deque requires one addition, one multiplication, and one division more than subscripting a vector. At the speed of modern CPUs, these additional operations take very little time. However, even a small time penalty, if repeated often enough, can add up to a significant amount of time. If you have a small amount of data or subscript infrequently, the difference might not be noticeable in your application.

7.6 Choosing a Sequence Container

One of the tricks to using the STL is to be able to decide which container is right for a particular application. This decision is usually based on the required functionality as well as efficiency considerations. Table 7.5 summarizes the capabilities of the various containers.

Since the vector and deque are subscriptable and provide random access iterators, they are suitable for applications that require access to the elements in nonsequential order. The list is best suited to algorithms that make a linear pass through the contents in either the forward or reverse directions. The vector allows storage to be preallocated so that storage requirements can be anticipated and met efficiently.

Table 7.6 shows the results of performing 10,000 insertions at three different positions in the three containers. The middle position chosen was just in front of the second element in the sequence. In some cases this might yield better speeds than could be expected with other insertion positions. The speeds are in hundredths of seconds as measured on a 66 MHz Intel 80486.

Although the vector offers excellent speed for insertions at the end, performance drops precipitously if the insertion is at any other position. The deque offers excellent speed for insertions at either end, with slightly worse performance for an insertion in the middle. You should expect the performance for interior

Container	Subscriptable	Iterator	Storage Management	Access	Special Ops
vector	✓	random	auto or pre-allocated	random	reserve
deque	✓	random	auto	random	
list	✗	bidirectional	auto	sequential	splice

Table 7.5 — Capabilities of Sequence Containers

insertions to drop further if the insertion point is farther from one of the ends. The list provides the same insertion time regardless of position.

These factors make vectors suited for applications where all insertions occur at the end, whereas deques can be used for applications requiring insertions at either end, and lists can be used for applications that make insertions at any position.

In terms of space, the deque requires the additional space for the map of the allocated blocks. This is a small fraction of the space occupied by the data and can usually be ignored. The list, on the other hand, maintains forward and reverse pointers for each node in the list. If the data stored in the nodes are small, the size of the pointers can actually be larger than the data. In any case, these pointers occupy a significant amount of memory and must be taken into account.

To illustrate the process involved in deciding on a particular container, we will consider the problem of calculating the marks for a group of students. The input to the program consists of a series of lines of data, each containing a student's name followed by a list of integer marks. These data are presented to the program in unsorted order, and the program must calculate the average mark for each student and print out the names and averages sorted alphabetically.

Let us consider the requirements for a container to store the sequence of students. There is no way to determine the exact number of students, although an approximate upper bound can be found. The requirement that the output be sorted means that the results cannot simply be calculated on the fly and printed, but must be stored so that they can be sorted. Since the printing process makes a single linear pass through the data, only sequential access is required. The best way to sort the data is to use the STL sort() function, which sorts by

Container	Beginning	Middle	End
vector	3,828	3,845	0
deque	5	72	6
list	6	6	5

Table 7.6 — Speed (sec. / 100) for 10,000 Insertions

swapping out-of-order values. The data themselves will consist of a character string representing the student's name and a float representing the average mark. The average can be calculated as the marks are read and the original marks discarded, since only the average need be printed.

Since we tend to think of this as a list of students, it would seem natural to use a list to store the student data. This is a possibility, but the memory management scheme employed by the list means that more memory than necessary will be allocated. To reduce memory usage, the vector could be used since it allows us to preallocate sufficient storage for the largest number of students expected. Should this maximum be exceeded, the vector is capable of enlarging itself so that the program will not crash.

The vector can provide linear access at about the same cost as the list. The reason for this is that a vector increments its iterator by simply adding the element size onto a pointer. The list follows a real pointer, which involves calculating its offset in the list node and retrieving the value. The speed difference between these two operations is minimal.

The vector uses contiguous storage so that there is no overhead associated with the storage of each element. The list requires two extra pointers per node. If we assume that we will have on the order of a few hundred students or less, then the overhead required by the list is on the order of a couple of thousand bytes.

The last point to consider is the swapping of elements during sorting. The vector will physically copy one element to the other. If we assume that each element contains 32 bytes for the name and average, then each swap will require three copy operations since the use of a third temporary variable is required for the swapping of two values. This means that 96 bytes will be copied in every swap! The list can swap values by simply rearranging pointers, and a swap will require that eight pointer copies be performed (including the use of temporary variables). If we assume that each pointer is 4 bytes, then this amounts to 32 bytes being copied each time a swap is performed. Thus, it will be quicker to sort a list than to sort a vector, given that they contain the same type of data.

Now, it is time for our decision. We can use a vector and save space, while taking longer, or we can use a list and save time while wasting memory. This is the famous space-time tradeoff and must be decided based on the nature of the application, its requirements, and environment. If the application is run on a PC, then memory is probably not the limiting factor, and getting quick results is of greater importance. On the other hand, in a time-sharing environment, memory might be available but you will have to wait in a queue based on the amount of time the program will consume. In this case, it makes sense to waste some memory to save time, since this could dramatically lower the turnaround time to get the results.

Although this analysis might seem long and involved, it is the process that every programmer must follow when deciding on the data structures in a program. Poor choices can lead to abysmally slow programs, bloated memory hogs, or both.

7.7 Strings

The STL provides a string class implemented as a reversible sequence container. This container has been generalized so that it can not only contain characters, but it can contain any type that is similar to a character and treat it the same way as a C character string is treated. While the utility of treating other types as strings might not be immediately obvious, there are indeed situations that require other types to be treated in a manner similar to strings. The main reason for the generalization is to allow the class to be used with different representations of characters such as ASCII, Unicode, etc.

The string class provides numerous functions for manipulating strings. Since the string class is a sequence container, it provides all the operations you would expect of a sequence container. These include the iterators and the familiar be-gin() and end() functions for retrieving iterators to the beginning and end of the string. The class also provides all of the familiar string-handling operations including assignment, concatenation, insertion, deletion, substring, comparison, and string length.

Most of the class methods are overloaded so that they are interoperable with arrays of the type stored in the container. This makes it convenient to use strings in conjunction with regular arrays. Methods providing access to individual members of the string are also overloaded so that you can access the members either using iterators or subscripts.

The string is implemented by the class `basic_string`. A template is provided so that this class can be used to contain different types. For convenience, `typedefs` are provided defining the specializations `string`, which can be used for regular characters and the class `wstring` for wide characters.

A summary of the commonly used string methods is shown in Table 7.7. The methods that require a parameter are overloaded to work with an instance of `basic_string` or with a zero-terminated array. Refer to the STL Reference in the appendices for the complete list of methods and precise prototypes.

```cpp
#include <string>
#include <iostream>
#include <string.h>

using namespace std;

void main()
{
    string      s1 = "The";
    string      s2 = "dog";
    char        cstr1[16];
    const char* output;
    char        space[2];

    strcpy(cstr1, "brown");
    strcpy(space, " ");

    s1 += space;
    s1 += s2;
    s1.insert(4, string(cstr1) + space);

    output = s1.c_str();

    cout << output << endl;
```

Method	Explanation
`at(posn)`	Returns a reference to the member at `posn`.
`c_str()`	Returns a pointer to a zero-terminated array of the string contents.
`length()`	Returns the number of members in the string.
`append(str)`	Appends `str` to the string.
`assign(str)`	Assigns `str` to the string.
`insert(posn, str)`	Inserts `str` before `posn` in the string.
`erase(posn, len)`	Removes `len` members starting at `posn`.
`replace(posn, len, str)`	Replaces the `len` members starting at `posn` with `str`.
`find(str)`	Returns the location of the first occurrence of `str`.
`find_first_of(str)`	Returns the location of the first member of the string that is in `str`.
`compare(str)`	Lexicographically compares the string to `str`. Returns a negative value if the string is less than `str`, zero if they are equal, and a positive value if the string is greater than `str`.
`operator+=(str)`	Appends `str` to the string.
`operator=(str)`	Assigns `str` to the string.
`operator== (string, str)`	Returns `true` if `string` equals `str`.
`operator< (string, str)`	Returns `true` if `string` is less than `str`.

Table 7.7 — Summary of Common String Operations

```
}
```

```
The brown dog
```

Listing 7.12 — Using Arrays as Strings [str_chr.cpp]

Listing 7.12 demonstrates how ordinary character arrays can be used in conjunction with the `basic_string` class. Two instances of `string` are declared and assigned values that are zero-terminated character arrays. `string` is a specialization of `basic_string` to store type `char` and is the common substitute for a character array. `operator=` for the class `basic_string` is overloaded so that zero-terminated arrays can be assigned directly. The zero-terminated arrays `cstr1` and `space` are assigned the values "brown" and " ", respectively. The string `s1` has `space` and `s2` concatenated onto it, showing that `operator+=` is defined as concatenation and that it is overloaded to work with both strings and arrays.

The next line inserts a string into the string `s1` just before position 4. An iterator could have been used to indicate the insertion position instead of a numeric position. The string that is inserted is built from two zero-terminated arrays. The first array is converted to a string using a constructor. The second array is appended to the new string using an overloaded version of `operator+`, which appends the array onto the string and returns the result as a string.

The final assignment uses the method `c_str()` to retrieve a pointer to a zero-terminated array from the instance of the string class. This array is then printed.

Listing 7.13 demonstrates the use of some of the string-searching methods.

```
#include <string>
#include <iostream>

using namespace std;

void main()
{
    string            s1 = "the name of the game";
    string            s2 = "the";
    string            vowels = "aeiouAEIOU";
    string::size_type posn;
    string::size_type startPos;
```

```
cout << "s1 = \"" << s1 << "\" of length " <<
   s1.length() << endl;
cout << "s2 = \"" << s2 << "\" of length " <<
   s2.length() << endl;

posn = s1.find(s2);
if(posn == string::npos)
{
   cout << "s1 does not contain \"" << s2 << "\""
      << endl;
}
else
{
   cout << "the first \"" << s2 <<
      "\" is in position " << posn << endl;
}

startPos = 5;
posn = s1.find(s2, startPos);
if(posn == string::npos)
{
   cout << "s1 does not contain \"" << s2 <<
      "\" after posn " << startPos << endl;
}
else
{
   cout << "the first \"" << s2 <<
      "\" after position " << startPos <<
      " is in position " << posn << endl;
}

posn = s1.rfind(s2);
if(posn == string::npos)
{
   cout << "s1 does not contain \"" << s2 <<
      "\"" << endl;
}
else
{
   cout << "the last \"" << s2 <<
      "\" is in position " << posn << endl;
}

startPos = 10;
posn = s1.rfind(s2, startPos);
if(posn == string::npos)
```

```cpp
{
    cout << "s1 does not contain \"" << s2 <<
        "\"" << endl;
}
else
{
    cout << "the last \"" << s2 <<
        "\" before position " << startPos <<
        " is in position " << posn << endl;
}

posn = s1.find_first_of(vowels);
if(posn == string::npos)
{
    cout << "s1 contains no chars in vowels" <<
        endl;
}
else
{
    cout << "the first char in the sequence \"" <<
        vowels << "\" is in position " <<
        posn << endl;
}

posn = s1.find_first_not_of(s2);
if(posn == string::npos)
{
    cout << "s1 only contains chars in s2" << endl;
}
else
{
    cout << "the first char not in the sequence \""
        << s2 << "\" is in position " << posn <<
        endl;
}
```

```
}
```

```
s1 = "the name of the game" of length 20
s2 = "the" of length 3
the first "the" is in position 0
the first "the" after position 5 is in position 12
the last "the" is in position 12
the last "the" before position 10 is in position 0
the first char in the sequence "aeiouAEIOU" is in
position 2
the first char not in the sequence "the" is in
position 3
```

Listing 7.13 — The Find Methods of basic_string [str_find.cpp]

The program in Listing 7.13 begins by using the method find() to locate the first occurrence of "the" in the string "the name of the game". This either returns the position of the occurrence, if there is one, or returns string::npos, if there is no such occurrence. string::npos is a special value that is guaranteed not to be a valid position in the string and is used to indicate that the string being sought was not found.

The next call to find() shows that the search need not begin at the start of the string but can start at some position later in the string. This position must be specified numerically since an iterator cannot be used for this purpose.

The method rfind() performs the same operation as find() but starts searching from the end of the string rather than the beginning. The second call to rfind() shows that the search can being before the end of the string. In this case, the offset is measured from the end of the string rather than the beginning.

Listings 7.14 and 7.15 use the methods find_first_of() and find_-first_not_of() to find the first element in the string that occurs in the parameter string or is absent from the parameter string, respectively.

```
#include <string>
#include <iostream>

using namespace std;

void main()
```

```
{
    string   s1 = "abc";
    string   s2 = "def";
    string   s3 = "abc";
    string   t  = "true";
    string   f  = "false";

    cout << "s1 = " << s1 << endl;
    cout << "s2 = " << s2 << endl;
    cout << "s3 = " << s3 << endl;

    cout << "s1.compare(s2) = " << s1.compare(s2)
        << endl;
    cout << "s1.compare(s3) = " << s1.compare(s3)
        << endl;

    cout << "s1 < s2 = " << ((s1 < s2) ? t : f)
        << endl;
    cout << "s1 <= s2 = " << ((s1 <= s2) ? t : f)
        << endl;
    cout << "s1 > s2 = " << ((s1 > s2) ? t : f)
        << endl;
    cout << "s1 >= s2 = " << ((s1 >= s2) ? t : f)
        << endl;
    cout << "s1 == s2 = " << ((s1 == s2) ? t : f)
        << endl;
    cout << "s1 != s2 = " << ((s1 != s2) ? t : f)
        << endl;
}
```

```
s1 = abc
s2 = def
s3 = abc
s1.compare(s2) = -1
s1.compare(s3) = 0
s1 < s2 = true
s1 <= s2 = true
s1 > s2 = false
s1 >= s2 = false
s1 == s2 = false
s1 != s2 = true
```

Listing 7.14 — Comparing Strings [str_cmp.cpp]

Listing 7.14 shows the methods and operators for comparing strings. The method `compare()` lexicographically compares one string to another and returns a negative `int` if the first string is less than the second, zero if they are equal, and a positive `int` if the first is greater. All of the comparison operators are defined on strings and perform as you would expect. Both the `compare()` method and the operators are overloaded to work with arrays as well as instances of `basic_string`.

```
#include <string>
#include <iostream>

using namespace std;

void main()
{
    int                      i1[] = {1, 2, 4, 8, 0 };
    int                      i2[] = {16, 32, 64, 0 };
    int                      look_for[] = {8, 16, 0};
    const int*               int_ptr;
    basic_string<int>::iterator   iter;
    basic_string<int>        s1 = i1;
    basic_string<int>::size_type  posn;

    cout << "original = ";
    for(iter = s1.begin(); iter != s1.end(); iter++)
    {
        cout << *iter << " ";
    }
    cout << endl;

    cout << "s1.length() = " << s1.length() << endl;

    s1.append(i2);
    cout << "after append = ";
    for(iter = s1.begin(); iter != s1.end(); iter++)
    {
        cout << *iter << " ";
    }
    cout << endl;

    posn = s1.find(look_for);
    if(posn == basic_string<int>::npos)
    {
        cout << "substring not found" << endl;
    }
```

```
    else
    {
        cout << "substring in position " << posn <<
            endl;
    }

    int_ptr = s1.c_str();
    cout << "final array = ";
    while(*int_ptr)
    {
        cout << *int_ptr++ << " ";
    }
    cout << endl;
}
```

```
original = 1 2 4 8
s1.length() = 4
after append = 1 2 4 8 16 32 64
substring in position 3
final array = 1 2 4 8 16 32 64
```

Listing 7.15 — Using basic_string to Store ints [int_str.cpp]

The program in Listing 7.15 demonstrates how the class basic_string can be used to store integers rather than characters. The code in this example works just as if characters had been used rather than integers. Note that each of the integer arrays is terminated by a zero—just as is done with character arrays. This implies that the integer arrays cannot contain zero as a value, since it will be interpreted as the array terminator whenever it is encountered.

An implementation of the basic_string class might or might not use reference counts. It is usual for a program to have several copies of the same string. Since these are the same, there is no reason to actually duplicate them in memory, as this simply wastes space. Reference-counted string implementations allow several instances of the same string to reference the same memory location holding the string. While this will save memory, it has to be implemented so that it is invisible to the user. For example, the following code must work as expected.

```
string        s1("alpha");
string        s2(s1);
string::iterator  iter = s1.begin();
```

```
*iter = 'X';
cout << s1 << endl;
cout << s2 << endl;
```

```
X1pha
alpha
```

Thus, when one of the strings is altered, the other remains unchanged, as it should. This must be true whether a reference-counted implementation is used or not.

The use of reference counts can also have implications for multithreaded applications since several instances of a string might share data. In such cases, you will have to implement locking on the string primitives to ensure mutual exclusion.

7.7.1 Character Traits

As mentioned previously, `basic_string` is a generalized string class that can actually hold many different types of data. One of the reasons for this is that there is no longer a single character set in use. It used to be that ASCII characters were used and you could depend on a character to occupy a single byte. As internationalization has increased in importance, so has the need to represent characters from non-European languages. As a result, several character sets are in common usage.

These character sets differ in the amount of memory occupied by a character and the number of characters that can be represented. This implies that the properties and basic operations that can be performed might differ from one character set to another. The STL deals with these differences by abstracting the differing properties and operations and encapsulating them in the class `char_traits`. Different character sets can have specializations of the `char_traits` class that are appropriate to their definitions of characters. The appropriate version of `char_traits` is passed as a template parameter to the string class. The methods in the string class perform basic character operations by calling the methods in `char_traits`, thus isolating the string class from differences in character sets.

The operations defined in `char_traits` include the following:

- assignment
- comparison

- copying

- finding a character in an array of characters

- determining the number of characters in a zero terminated array

- converting characters to an integer representation and

- converting integers to a character representation

All of the methods and functions that work with strings use the methods of `char_traits` to manipulate the underlying representation of a character. Any methods or functions you write to work with strings should use the `char_traits` methods as well.

8
Associative Containers

8.1 Introduction

Although the sequence containers can certainly hold any data you wish to store, they are limited in how the data can be retrieved. There are two ways to find a value stored in a sequential container—subscripting and searching. If the container is subscriptable and you remember the position where a particular piece of data was stored, you can use the subscript to efficiently retrieve the data. If the container is not subscriptable or you do not remember the position in which it was stored, the only option is to perform a search. This could be a binary search for sorted subscriptable containers or a linear search for other containers.

The associative containers store data so that they can be retrieved using an identifier known as a key. The key is a group of one or more attributes of an object that can be used to identify it. For example, a student might be identified by a student number, which is unique to that student. Each member of the container is associated with a key when it is placed in the container. The member can be retrieved at a later time by simply specifying the key.

Some associative containers allow for the use of duplicate keys. This would be useful if you wanted to store your student information in an associative container and use the surname as the key. This means that several objects might be returned in answer to a query for a single key.

The associative containers maintain an association between a key and a member of the container similar to the way our minds associate a name with a face. When we are given someone's name, it is a simple matter to recall his or her face. The indexing techniques used by the mind are vastly different from those of a computer; however, the resulting functionality is the same.

How the data are stored by an associative container should not concern the user of such a class. An associative container guarantees that the data can be stored by key and retrieved. It says nothing about the physical order in which the data elements will be stored. If you need to process the data in a specific order using an iterator, then one of the sequence containers might be more appropriate. Applications that use associative containers usually store data and retrieve them in random order, without worrying about the order in which they are physically stored. While these statements are true of associative containers in general, the STL associative containers are implemented so that iterators can return the elements in sorted order.

The STL requires that iterators for associative containers return the elements in non-descending order, where the order is determined by comparing the key associated with each element. This implies that iterators for associative containers which do not contain duplicates will return the elements in ascending order.

The STL provides four types of associative containers. Two of these store only the keys themselves without any data being associated with the key. The other two store data that are associated with keys. Each of these categories is further divided into a class that stores only unique keys and one that allows duplicate keys. These classes are shown in Table 8.1.

The sets store only the keys—not any values associated with the keys. This makes sets suitable for applications where the key itself is the datum and you are primarily concerned with determining if a particular key is in the container. In this way, the STL set is similar to the mathematical concept of a set and can be considered a generalization of it. Although some computer languages provide a set type, they are usually limited in their cardinality (the number of unique keys that can be stored in the set) and the types that can be stored in the set. The STL set is not limited in these ways and can store any number of values of any type.

The map stores data that have a key associated with them. The keys are not limited to just integers or enumeration types but can be any type. Maps implement a storage model similar to the associative memory of our own minds, making them suitable for retrieval of data that can be identified by a key. It is well-suited to the implementation of associative arrays—arrays whose subscripts need not be simple integers or enumerations.

8.2 Associative Container Operations

Just as with the sequential containers, the associative containers have many operations in common. These can be broken into groups depending on the nature of the containers to which they apply. Many of these operations will be familiar to you since they duplicate the functionality of some of the general-purpose STL

	Key Only	**Key and Data**
Unique Keys	set	map
Duplicate Keys	multiset	multimap

Table 8.1 — The Associative Containers

algorithms. The associative containers support all of the operations that can be performed on a container and Table 8.2 shows only the requirements specific to associative containers.

In addition to these common operations, there are two different versions of the `insert()` method for containers that support unique keys and duplicate keys.

Most of these operations, such as `insert()` and `erase()`, will be familiar to you from working with the sequence containers. Others, such as `find()` and `count()`, are specific to the associative containers, although they do have analogues in the general STL algorithms that can be used on sequence containers. The `insert()` and `erase()` operations are similar to the `include()` and `exclude()` set operations provided by some programming languages that support sets.

Note that some of the operations will perform differently if used on a container that supports duplicate keys than if used on one that supports unique keys. `count()` is an example of one such operation. Although it will perform as expected on containers with either key type, the results are limited to 0 or 1 for containers that support unique keys.

The `insert()` operation is more interesting, since the return type is entirely different when the container supports duplicate keys than when unique keys are supported. When duplicate keys are allowed, the familiar iterator referring to the newly inserted element is returned. Containers supporting unique keys actually return two results in the form of a `pair<iterator, bool>`.

Expression	Explanation
`C::key_type`	The type of the key for the container.
`C::key_compare`	The type of the key comparison function that defaults to `less<key_type>`.
`C::value_compare`	The same as `key_compare` for sets and multisets. For maps and multimaps, it is an ordering function on the first member of a pair, where the first member is the key.
`C()`	Creates an empty container using `Compare()`, a template parameter, as a comparison function.
`C(cmp)`	Creates an empty container using `cmp` as a comparison function.
`C(iter1, iter2, cmp)`	Creates a container and inserts the elements from `iter1` up to `iter2` using the comparison function `cmp`.
`C(iter1, iter2)`	Creates a container and inserts the elements from `iter1` up to `iter2` using the comparison function `Compare()`.
`C::key_comp()`	Ceturns the key comparison object.
`C::value_comp()`	Returns the value comparison object constructed from the key comparison object.
`x.insert(val)`	For containers with unique keys, inserts `val` provided it is not already in the container. It returns a `pair<iter, bool>` where the second member indicates if the insertion was successful and the first refers to the inserted value. For containers supporting duplicate keys, it returns an iterator referencing the inserted value.
`x.insert(iter, val)`	Behaves the same as `x.insert(val)` but uses `iter` as a hint as to where to insert the value.
`x.insert(iter1, iter2)`	Inserts the values from `iter1` up to `iter2`.
`x.erase(key)`	Deletes all members whose key is `key`. It returns the number of elements deleted.
`x.erase(iter)`	Deletes the element referenced by `iter`. No result is returned.

Expression	Explanation
x.erase(iter1, iter2)	Deletes all elements in the range from iter1 up to iter2. No result is returned.
x.clear()	Deletes all elements in the container. No result is returned.
x.find(key)	Returns an iterator referencing an element with a key of key or end() if there is no such element.
x.count(key)	Returns the number of elements whose key equals key.
x.lower_bound(key)	Returns an iterator referencing the first element whose key is not less than key.
x.upper_bound(key)	Returns an iterator referencing the first element whose key is greater than key.
x.equal_range(key)	Returns a pair or iterators delimiting a range of elements with the key, key.

Table 8.2 — Requirements Common to all Associative Containers

Since only unique keys are supported, it is possible that an insertion might fail due to an attempt to insert a value that is already in the container. The success of the insertion is conveyed to the invoking program as the Boolean value in the second member of the pair. The first member of the pair is always an iterator referring to the element being inserted in the container, whether this was the first time it was inserted or not.

Unlike some of the sequence containers, insertion and deletion to and from an associative container do not invalidate iterators, pointers, or references to members of the container not directly involved in the operation. In this respect, the associative containers behave just like the list for exactly the same reason. The memory for each element in the container is allocated as a discrete unit that is not subject to relocation when other elements in the container are rearranged.

The template for an associative container requires three parameters—the type of the elements being stored in the container, a comparison function object that can be used to compare the elements in the container, and an allocator. This comparison object is used both for ordering the elements within the container and determining the equality of elements. As such, it must behave the same as operator< would on the elements. In most cases, less<type> is a good choice, and that is the default value for the parameter. Similarly, the allocator defaults to the default allocator so that, often, only a single template parameter is needed. (See Listing 8.1.)

```
#include <set>
#include <iostream>

using namespace std;

void main()
{
    set<int>             set1;
    set<int>::iterator   iter;
    int                  i;

    set1.insert(3);
    set1.insert(6);
    set1.insert(8);

    for(i=0; i< 10; i++) {
        iter = set1.find(i);
        if(iter != set1.end())
            cout << i << " is in the set\n" ;
    }
}
```

```
3 is in the set
6 is in the set
8 is in the set
```

Listing 8.1 — Creating a Set of Integers [set1.cpp]

Since nothing special needs to be done to compare two integers, less<int> is suitable as a comparison object. The method find() is used to determine if a value is in the set.

When a user-defined type is stored in a set, there are a couple of ways of defining a comparison object. One of the simplest ways is to define operator<

for the data type. This can then be used by the definition of `less`, shown in the following:

```
template <class T>
struct less : binary_function<T, T, bool> {
   bool operator()(const T& x, const T& y) const
   {
      return x < y;
   }
};
```

Thus, the function object `less` invokes `operator<` if it is defined on the class. This technique is used in the following example, which uses a set to store the hobbies of a group of people.

8.3 Sets

The set is an ordered associative container that supports unique keys. The multiset, discussed in the next section, is the same as the set but allows duplicate keys. The set stores only keys rather than a key and data associated with it, as do the map and multimap. This, combined with the fact that it is sorted, makes the set perfect for implementing the mathematical concept of a set. Listing 8.2 demonstrates the use of sets.

The stipulation that a set can only store keys is not as restrictive as it seems at first. A key is some sort of value that identifies a record so that it can be differentiated from other records. There is no requirement that the key be the entire record, however. It is common to create a class `Employee` to store the information on the employees in a company:

```
class Employee {
public:
   Employee(int id, const char* nam, int ag,
      float pa);
   friend bool operator<(const Employee&  e1,
                         const Employee&  e2);
   friend ostream& operator<<(ostream& os,
      Employee& e);
private:
   int    employeeId;
   char   name[32];
   int    age;
   int    pay;
};
```

In a case like this, the actual key that identifies each employee is `employ-eeId`. This member of the class is only a portion of the class, yet it meets the requirements of a key in that it uniquely identifies a particular employee. Instances of this class can be stored in a set, but it is not immediately obvious how we store *just the key*. In truth, the entire instance is stored in the set, but the comparison function object that determines the equality of two `Employee` instances is written so that it only compares the `employeeId` member. One way to do this is to write `operator<` for the class so that it compares the `employ-eeId` members:

```
bool operator<(const Employee&    e1,
               const Employee&    e2)
{
    return(e1.employeeId < e2.employeeId);
}
```

This operator can then be transformed into a comparison function object using `less<Employee>`. Since this is the only function used by the set to compare elements, we are in effect storing and retrieving keys, as that is all that is ever compared. In reality, the keys carry some extra baggage with them, but this is invisible to the comparison function used for insertion and deletion.

```
#include <set>
#include <algorithm>
#include <iostream>
#include <iterator>
#include <string>

using namespace std;

void main()
{
    set<string>    supperVeggies;
    set<string>    lunchVeggies;
    set<string>    allVeggies;

    supperVeggies.insert(string("broccoli"));
    supperVeggies.insert(string("corn"));
    supperVeggies.insert(string("cauliflower"));
    supperVeggies.insert(string("kale"));
    supperVeggies.insert(string("lettuce"));
    supperVeggies.insert(string("potato"));
    supperVeggies.insert(string("squash"));
    supperVeggies.insert(string("turnip"));

    lunchVeggies.insert(string("avocado"));
```

```
lunchVeggies.insert(string("arugula"));
lunchVeggies.insert(string("beet"));
lunchVeggies.insert(string("corn"));
lunchVeggies.insert(string("capsicum"));
lunchVeggies.insert(string("aubergine"));

cout << "vegetable for both lunch and supper are:"
   << endl;
set_intersection(supperVeggies.begin(),
   supperVeggies.end(), lunchVeggies.begin(),
   lunchVeggies.end(),
   ostream_iterator<string>(cout, " "));

set_union(supperVeggies.begin(),
   supperVeggies.end(), lunchVeggies.begin(),
   lunchVeggies.end(),
   inserter<set<string> >
   (allVeggies,allVeggies.begin()));

cout << endl << "all vegetables are:" <<endl;
copy(allVeggies.begin(), allVeggies.end(),
```

```
vegetable for both lunch and supper are:
corn
all vegetables are:
arugula aubergine avocado beet broccoli capsicum
cauliflower corn kale lettuce potato squash turnip
```

```
   ostream_iterator<string>(cout, " "));
cout << endl;
}
```

Listing 8.2 — Using Set Operations [vegset.cpp]

In the program in Listing 8.2, the call to set_intersection() appears
to function as expected. The call to set_union(), however, has an inserter as its final parameter. The inserter is an adaptor that uses the in-
sert() method to insert values into the container. You might expect that
allVeggies.begin() would be used as the third parameter, but this does
not work since the begin() method, in most implementations, returns a constant iterator. This means that you cannot assign a value to the iterator and must
use the insert() method. This is different from the C++ standard, which says

that begin() should return an iterator rather than a constant iterator. Check your implementation for the exact definition of begin().

Listing 8.3 shows how sets can be used with user-defined classes.

```cpp
#include <algorithm>
#include <set>
#include <stdarg.h>
#include <string>
#include <vector>
#include <iostream>

using namespace std;

enum HobbyType {
    // zero reserved for var arg usage
    unknownHobby = 1,
    knitting,
    sewing,
    reading,
    stampCollecting,
    coinCollecting,
    cardCollecting,
    birdWatching,
    photography
};

class HobbyInfo {
public:
    HobbyInfo();
    HobbyInfo(HobbyType typ);
    friend bool operator<(const HobbyInfo& l,
        const HobbyInfo& r);
    friend ostream& operator<<(ostream& os,
        const HobbyInfo& h);
    HobbyType    hobbyName;
};

ostream& operator<<(ostream& os, const HobbyInfo& h)
{
    switch(h.hobbyName) {
    case knitting: os << "knitting";
        break;
    case sewing: os << "sewing";
        break;
    case reading: os << "reading";
        break;
```

```
         case stampCollecting: os << "stamp collecting";
            break;
         case coinCollecting: os << "coin collecting";
            break;
         case cardCollecting: os << "card collecting";
            break;
         case birdWatching: os << "bird watching";
            break;
         case photography: os << "photography";
            break;
      }
      return(os);
}


HobbyInfo::HobbyInfo()
{
      hobbyName = unknownHobby;
}

HobbyInfo::HobbyInfo(HobbyType typ)
{
      hobbyName = typ;
}

bool operator<(const HobbyInfo& l, const HobbyInfo& r)
{
      return(l.hobbyName < r.hobbyName);
}


class Person {
public:
      Person();
      Person(const char* nam, int ag, ...);
      string                 name;
      int                    age;
      set<HobbyInfo >        hobbies;
      friend bool operator<(const Person& l,
         const Person& r);
      friend bool operator==(const Person& l,
         const Person& r);
};

Person::Person(const char* nam, int ag, ...)
{
      va_list     ap;
```

```
      HobbyInfo    hobby;
      int          tmp;

      name = nam;
      age = ag;
      va_start(ap, ag);
      while((tmp = va_arg(ap, int)) != 0) {
         hobbies.insert(HobbyInfo((HobbyType)tmp));
      }
      va_end(ap);
}

bool operator<(const Person& l, const Person& r)
{
   return l.name < r.name;
}

bool operator==(const Person& l, const Person& r)
{
   return l.name == r.name;
}

ostream& operator<<(ostream& os, const Person& p)
{
   set<HobbyInfo >::iterator   iter;

   os << p.name << ", " << p.age ;
   for(iter=p.hobbies.begin(); iter !=
      p.hobbies.end(); iter++) {
      os << ", " << *iter;
   }
   return(os);
}

main()
{
   vector<Person>              people;
   vector<Person>::iterator    iter;
   ostream_iterator<Person>    outStream(cout, "\n");

   people.push_back(Person("Jean Anne", 18,
      sewing, reading, 0));
   people.push_back(Person("Billy Bob", 22,
      cardCollecting, 0));
   people.push_back(Person("Jimmy Joe", 48,
      photography, coinCollecting, 0));
   people.push_back(Person("Sue Ellen", 35,
```

```
      knitting, stampCollecting, 0));

    copy(people.begin(), people.end(), outStream);
    return(0);
}
```

```
Jean Anne, 18, sewing, reading
Billy Bob, 22, card collecting
Jimmy Joe, 48, coin collecting, photography
Sue Ellen, 35, knitting, stamp collecting
```

Listing 8.3 — Using a Set to Represent Hobbies [hobby.cpp]

Listing 8.3 shows how sets can be used to store the hobbies of a group of people. The class `Person` stores the information on a person including his or her name, age, and the hobbies in which he or she has an interest. Since a person can be interested in each hobby only once, the `set` is an ideal data structure for representing a person's hobbies. All the instances of `Person` in the program are stored in a `vector` for easy retrieval.

If we look more closely at the class `Person`, we see that the set of hobbies is declared as follows:

```
set<HobbyInfo> hobbies;
```

rather than this more direct declaration:

```
set<HobbyType> hobbies;
```

The reason for introducing a seemingly superfluous class `HobbyInfo` is that it is necessary to make the program compile. When a `set` is destroyed, it first invokes the destructor for all of the objects contained within it. This works fine for a user-defined class for which a, possibly default, destructor is provided. It also works for the built-in types since the STL header files define special destructor-like functions for them that do nothing. It does not work for a user-defined enumeration since the STL attempts to call `~HobbyType()`, which does not exist. Thus, the enumeration is wrapped in a class for which a destructor can be provided.

The constructor for the class `Person` uses a variable-length argument list since it cannot be predicted how many hobbies must be passed. These hobbies are then added to the set using the `insert()` method.

At times, you will find that you want the set comparison to behave differently than operator<. In this case, you must define your own function object to perform the comparison. The declaration for a comparison object for the class HobbyInfo would look like this:

```
class HobbyCompare {
public:
    int operator()(HobbyInfo& a, HobbyInfo& b)
    {
        return(a.hobbyName < b.hobbyName);
    }
};
```

This defines operator() to do the real work of the comparison, and the programmer is free to make it behave differently than operator<. To use this comparison object, the declaration of the set in the class Person would have to be changed to the following:

```
set<HobbyInfo, HobbyCompare>      hobbies;
```

Another interesting point about this program is the order in which the hobbies are printed. Examining the program, we see that the hobbies are printed by using an iterator to traverse the set and print out all the values stored in the set. When the data for Jimmy Joe was inserted, photography was placed before coin collecting, but in the output the order was reversed. This is easily explained by noting that the associative containers store their contents in sorted order. Referring to the definition of the enumeration, we see that coin collecting does indeed come before photography, and hence is printed first. You can always depend on an iterator for a sorted container to traverse the contents in an order determined by the comparison object for the container.

If you think this example is somewhat contrived, you are correct. For this particular application, a sequence container could be used just as well as a set. The use of a set would make more sense if the application had to answer queries of the form "list all people with an interest in photography." Even then, a sequence container could still be used and, assuming it was sorted, yield comparable efficiency. The set begins to make sense if it is implemented with a hash table, which would be more efficient in most cases. The advantages and disadvantages of hash tables are discussed later in this chapter.

8.4 Multisets

The multiset is just a set that can contain duplicate values. The programmer will notice only a small difference in the APIs of the set and the multiset. As mentioned previously, the insert() method for the multiset returns a single iterator indicating the position of the newly inserted element rather than the pair returned by the set. Of course, the count() method might return a value greater than one. This was impossible for the set, which did not allow duplicates.

When working with multisets, the possibility always exists that there is more than a single copy of each value in the container. The find() method will return an iterator referencing the first element in the container that matches the key provided to find(). To find all of the elements that match a certain key, the method equal_range() should be used. This will return an iterator pair, indicating the range of elements that match the key. This range will be contiguous, since all of the elements in the container are sorted.

8.5 Maps

The map differs from the set in that it stores a key and an associated value rather than just a key. Although this might not seem like a major difference, it makes the map suitable for use in a different range of applications. One of the main applications of the map is in the implementation of associative arrays.

The associative array is similar to a regular array, except that the key can be of any type, not just an integer. This greatly extends the usefulness of the array. Consider the case where you are running a charity campaign with several canvassers knocking on doors to collect money for a worthy cause. Each day the canvassers report their names and the amounts of money they collected. It is expected that each canvasser will make several reports, and new canvassers will join the campaign and others quit as time goes by. The information from the canvassers is collected into a file such as Listing 8.4.

```
Ted     66
Alice   98
Bob     78
Alice   45
Ted     23
Joan    64
Fred    28
```

```
Joan   96
Alice  21
Bob    36
Alice  32
Ted    83
Joan   55
Fred   70
```

Listing 8.4 — Sample Canvasser Data [canvas.dat]

What is needed is a program like Listing 8.5 to read the information on the canvassers and generate a report showing the total amount collected by each canvasser. To do this, we have to associate an accumulator with the name of each canvasser. When each line of data is read, the program will look up the canvasser's name in the map, retrieve the associated accumulator, and increment it.

```cpp
#include <map>
#include <fstream>
#include <iostream>
#include <string>

using namespace std;

class Total {
public:
    int    totalValue;
    Total(): totalValue(0) {}
    Total operator+=(int a)
    {
       totalValue += a;
       return(*this);
    }
};
ostream& operator<<(ostream& os, const Total& t)
{
    os << t.totalValue;
    return(os);
}

main()
{
    ifstream         dataFile("canvas.dat", ios::in);
    char             name[16];
    int              dollars;
```

```
map<string, Total, less<string> >   canvassers;
map<string, Total, less<string> >::iterator
   iter;

if(!dataFile) {
   cerr << "cannot open data file\n";
   exit(1);
}

while((dataFile >> name >> dollars)) {
   canvassers[name] += dollars;
}

for(iter=canvassers.begin(); iter !=
   canvassers.end(); iter++) {
   cout << (*iter).first << ", " <<
      (*iter).second << '\n';
}

return(0);
}
```

```
Alice, 196
Bob, 145
Fred, 98
Joan, 272
Ted, 172
```

Listing 8.5 — The Canvasser Program [canvas.cpp]

After reading what the program had to do, you are probably surprised that it is so short. This is due, in large part, to the convenience offered by the map class. Let us begin by looking at the representation of the accumulator.

The accumulator is represented by the class Total, consisting of a single integer value. Operators are defined to increment the accumulator value and to print the value onto a stream. This class is used in preference to an integer since it can initialize itself when it is constructed. Since these accumulators will be created by the map itself, and not our program, this is an important capability.

The map to store the accumulators is declared as follows:

```
map<string, Total, less<string> >   canvassers;
```

This is read as stating that the `map` will have a key of type `string`, a value of type `Total` associated with each key, and a comparison function `less<string>` that can be used to compare keys. The comparison parameter could have been left to the default value since that is `less<keyType>`, which would be the same thing.

Data are read from the input stream and inserted into the `map` by this statement:

```
canvassers[name] += dollars;
```

The first thing you notice here is that the `map` is subscriptable with the key used as a subscript. The type returned by the subscript operator is a reference to the instance of the class `Total` associated with the key. Once a reference to the accumulator is found, `operator+=` is used to add the new value onto it. When the end of the stream is reached, all the calculations have been done and the results stored.

The next question is, "How do you subscript a value that does not exist?" The first time the subscript operator is used with a name, the name will not be in the `map` and you would expect the operation to fail. The subscript operation succeeds due to the clever implementation of the subscript operator, shown in the following:

```
Allocator<T>::reference operator[](const key_type& k)
{
    return (*((insert(value_type(
        k, T())))).first)).second;
}
```

As you can see, the subscript operator really performs an insertion. If the object being inserted is already in the container, it returns a reference to it. If it is not in the container, it inserts it and then returns a reference to the newly inserted element. Regardless of whether the key is in the container, it returns a reference to a valid object of the correct type. The result is a subscript operator that is much easier for the programmer to use.

The final step is to use an iterator to print all the values onto a stream. Pay particular attention to how the dereference operator works in conjunction with a `map`. The trouble with a `map` is that there are two pieces of information associated with each element referenced by an iterator—the data stored there and the key for the data. The usual way the STL represents two things is with the class `pair`. The same technique is used here with the key stored in the first member of the pair and the data associated with the key stored in the second member of the pair. Thus, the line

```
cout << (*iter).first << ", " <<
```

```
(*iter).second << '\n';
```

is used to print out both the key and the accumulator associated with each key.

Some applications will want to insert a value into a map using the `insert()` method directly rather than the subscript operator. As you can see from the body of the subscript operator shown previously, the `insert()` method takes a parameter of type `value_type`. This is a `typedef`, and the actual type is `pair<const key_type, value_type>`. The construction of such a pair for the preceding subscript operator would look like this:

```
insert(pair<const key_type, value_type>(k, T()))
```

The examples in Chapter 11 demonstrate the use of the `insert()` method for `maps`.

8.5.1 Multimaps

The multimap is just like the map but supports duplicate keys. This difference necessitates a change in the `insert()` method, which returns an iterator referencing the newly inserted member rather than a `pair` as returned by the `insert()` method for the map. The methods `count()` and `equal_range()` can also indicate that more than a single element matches a given key. Otherwise, the multimap behaves just like the map.

Multimaps are useful in applications where it is normal to have several values associated with a single key. One such case would be storing information about people where the surname is used as a key.

8.6 Associative Container Implementation

The associative containers are designed to be searched frequently and efficiently. There are many data structures suitable for efficient searching, including various types of trees and hash tables. The implementation selected is a variation of the binary tree called a red-black tree. Although this is slower than a hash table in the average case, the worst-case performance of a hash table is far slower than the worst case performance of a red-black tree. To understand how the associative containers are implemented and to see why I made the implementation decisions I did, it is necessary to understand how both trees and hash tables work. For a more thorough discussion of these topics, refer to [MUS95a].

8.6.1 Trees

A tree is a nonlinear data structure that can be much faster to search than a sequential data structure such as a list. The simplest, most common type of tree is the binary tree. A binary tree consists of a collection of nodes joined by branches. Each node has either one or two children and is an internal node, or has no children and is a leaf. Figure 8.1 shows a typical binary tree and some of the terminology associated with trees.

The terminology used with binary trees is a combination of terms used for real trees and the terms used in connection with family trees. In Figure 8.1, B and C are said to be the children or offspring of A, which is said to be their parent. A is a grandparent of D and E, whereas B, C, D, E, and F are all descendants of A. B and C are siblings since they share a common parent. B is the root of a subtree consisting of the nodes B, D, and E.

One of the most common uses of the binary tree is as a data structure that can be searched rapidly. A binary tree can be searched if the nodes are arranged so that the left child of any node is less than the parent and the right child is greater than or equal to the parent. A tree that has this property is called a binary search tree and is depicted in Figure 8.2.

To understand why it is faster to search for a value in a binary search tree rather than a list, note that at each node, you decide whether the value for which you are looking is to the left or right of the current node. Each time such a decision is made, the number of nodes remaining to be searched is cut approximately in half. This means that the number of nodes that must be compared to find a value is less than or equal to the number of times the number of nodes in the tree can be halved. As mentioned before, the number of times a value n can be

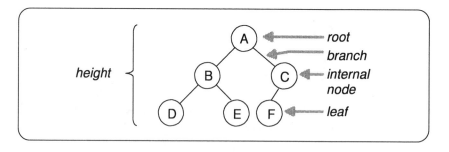

Figure 8.1 — Parts of a Binary Tree

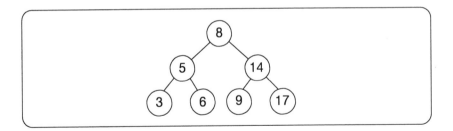

Figure 8.2 — A Binary Search Tree

halved is $\log_2 n$. This is the same as the height of the tree, which is the number of nodes from the root to the lowermost leaf.

Insertion into a binary search tree is performed by first searching for the value in the tree. When the leaf level is reached and the value is not found, the new value is added as the left or right child of the leaf. When a node is deleted, the greater of its children is promoted to its place. This node now has one extra child that must be inserted into one of the subtrees of its parent. For example, if node 8 were deleted from the tree in Figure 8.2, node 14 would move up to take its place. Node 9 would now be an extra child that must be inserted into the subtree rooted at node 5. In the general case, node 9 might be the root of a subtree, all of whose values would have to be inserted into the subtree rooted at node 5.

The optimal search performance for a binary tree can be attained only when the tree is balanced, as shown in Figure 8.3. A binary tree is said to be balanced if the difference in the heights of any two subtrees with a common parent is less than or equal to 1. If a tree is unbalanced, then less than half of the tree might be discarded when a node is examined, resulting in longer search times. In the extreme case, all nodes are left children or right children, and the search becomes a linear one.

To guarantee optimal search times, binary trees must be kept balanced. This is done by recursively balancing every subtree in the tree. When an unbalanced subtree is found, it can be balanced by rotating it about the root.

The tree in Figure 8.4 must be rotated clockwise to balance it. This places node 5 at the root and makes node 8 its right child. The problem is what to do with node 7, which used to be the right child of node 5. It is passed to node 8, the old root, and becomes its new left child. Of course, you can rotate a tree in the counter-clockwise direction, and all of the foregoing procedures are reversed.

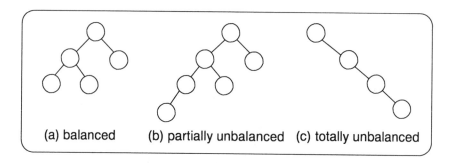

Figure 8.3 — Balanced and Unbalanced Trees

In a binary tree, the worst-case search time will be the time to search from the root to a leaf. If the tree is balanced, the worst-case search time will be approximately the same for any value at the leaf level. The average performance is less that the worst case, since the datum might be located above the leaf level. In a large tree, this can make a significant difference in how long it takes to find individual values.

For some applications, it is important that the time to retrieve a value be the same regardless of the value. This can be guaranteed only if all of the nodes are the same distance from the root. One tree that has this property is a 2-4 tree [VWY90].

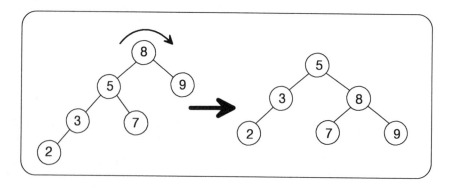

Figure 8.4 — Balancing a Tree

In a 2-4 tree, every node has between two and four children. The actual data are stored at the leaf level, and all leaves are the same distance from the root. The internal nodes contain index information making it possible to locate a value at the leaf level. Each internal node contains three pieces of information—the value of the largest descendants of the first, second, and third children. A typical 2-4 tree is shown in Figure 8.5.

Finding a value is as simple as starting at the root and looking at the index information to determine the subtree that might contain the value being sought. This process continues down the tree until the leaf level is reached. At that point, a linear search is performed on the sibling leaves, which are sorted from left to right. If an internal node has only two children, the third index value is not used and is represented as a hyphen in the diagram.

Insertion into a 2-4 tree is accomplished by searching for the value from the root downward. When the leaf level is reached, it is inserted as a new child of the parent. At this point, several situations can arise. If the parent has two or three children, the new node is added and everything is fine. If the parent already has four children, then the new node is added as a temporary fifth child, and the children must be redistributed to other nodes.

Redistributing the children of a node that has a temporary fifth child is the most complicated phase of insertion into a 2-4 tree. If the parent has a sibling that has less than four children, then the children can be shared amongst the siblings at the parent level so that each parent has four or less children. In the case where the siblings of the parent are all full, there is no choice but to create a new

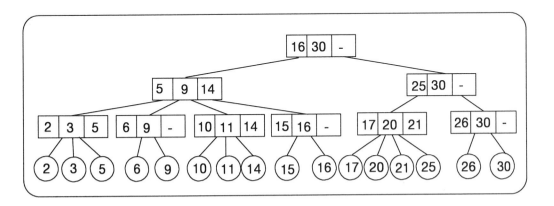

Figure 8.5 — A 2-4 Tree

node at the parent level. When this is done, the five children are split between the two parent nodes, with one parent receiving two children and the other three.

It is possible that the creation of a new node at the parent level caused its parent to have a fifth child. When this happens, the same technique is used to redistribute the children or to create a new node at the parent level. This series of changes ripples up the tree and can, in some cases, cause a new root to be created. Thus, 2-4 trees are said to grow in height from the root.

Figure 8.6 shows the steps in the insertion of node 18 into the tree from Figure 8.5.

Here we see that the insertion of node 18 creates a parent with five children. Since the parent has a sibling with two children, the extra child can be shared among the siblings at the parent level. Inserting the value of 22 causes no problems since it can be added as the fourth child of a parent node, as shown in Figure 8.7.

If we continue this process and insert node 23 into the tree, we find that once again, we have a parent with a fifth child. This time, all the parent's siblings have a full complement of children, and there is no choice but to split the parent. This process is depicted in Figure 8.8.

The deletion of nodes is the opposite of the insertion process. If node 26 were to be deleted from the preceding tree, it would leave the parent with only a single child. This violates the rule that a node must have between two and four children, so the situation must be rectified by attempting to share the children among the parent's siblings. Since the internal node to the left has only three children, the parent can be deleted and its lone child adopted by the parent with three children. The resulting tree is shown in Figure 8.9.

The 2-4 tree is not the only member of this family. 2-3 trees and trees of other sizes are well known. In the general case, an n-m tree has between m and $\lceil m/2 \rceil$ children of each internal node. These trees are perfect as indices for information stored on disks. The leaf level is stored in a series of physical disk allocation units (sectors or tracks), and the internal nodes are stored in other disk allocation units and act as an index to the physical allocation units storing the data.

The actual tree used to implement the STL associative containers is a variation of the 2-4 tree called the red-black tree. The red-black tree is really a 2-4 tree mapped onto a binary search tree. It differs from a binary search tree in that the branches connecting the nodes are colored either red or black. Black branches represent the regular downward branches of the 2-4 tree, and red branches connect the index values of the internal nodes. Figure 8.10 shows a 2-4 tree and the corresponding red-black tree.

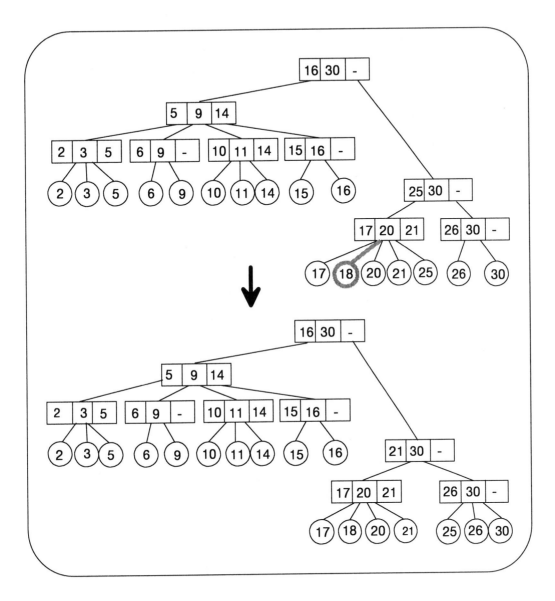

Figure 8.6 — Insertion of Node 18 into a 2-4 Tree

Each node in the 2-4 tree containing *n* index entries generates *n-1* nodes in the red-black tree. Thus, the root of the 2-4 tree creates node 8 at the root of the

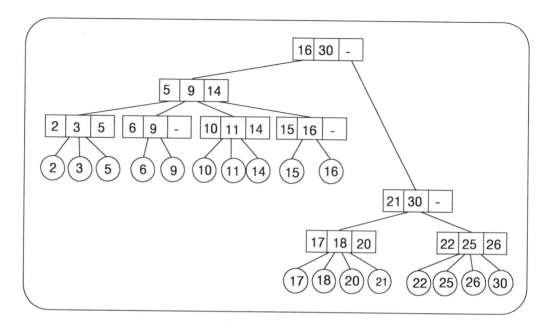

Figure 8.7 — Insertion of Node 22 into a 2-4 Tree

red-black tree. The two downward branches from the root of the 2-4 tree generate the downward black branches from the root of the red-black tree. The left child of the root of the 2-4 tree has three index values and will generate two nodes in the red-black tree. It creates node 5 in the red-black tree, which is placed as a right child of node 3 and joined by a red branch to show that it is part of the index information. The right child of the 2-4 root contains two values and generates node 9 in the red-black tree. Node 12 is then shown as a regular child of node 9. The actual data at the root level are not repeated in the red-black tree if they were already included from the index information.

A red-black tree can be searched just like a binary search tree and can retrieve a value in $O(\log n)$ time. Insertion into a red-black tree is complex and is not discussed here.

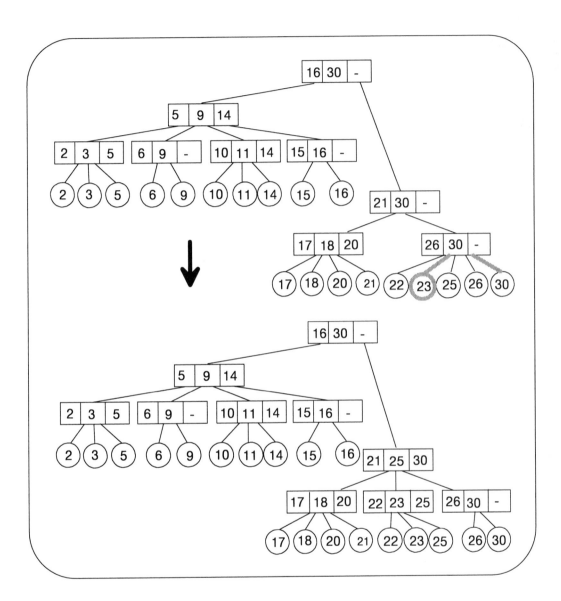

Figure 8.8 — Inserting Node 23 into a 2-4 Tree

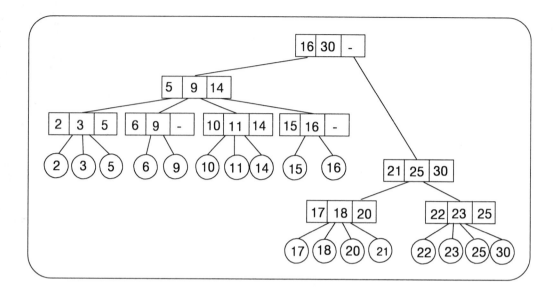

Figure 8.9 — Deletion of Node 26 from a 2-4 Tree

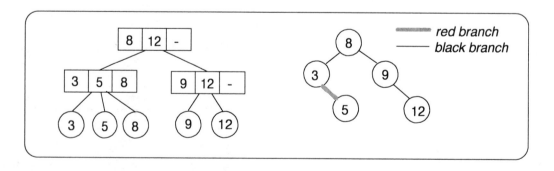

Figure 8.10 — A 2-4 Tree and Corresponding Red-Black Tree

8.6.2 Hash Tables

The other way of implementing an associative container is by using a hash table. Hash tables have two main uses: mapping keys from a large key space to a smaller one and fast retrieval of values. Often we are faced with a problem where the keys are drawn from a very large number of possible keys such as social security numbers. Although it is convenient to use identification numbers to uniquely identify people, many applications store information only on a very small fraction of the population. This makes it impractical to allocate an array big enough to store the millions of possible keys and then use only a few hundred or thousand locations in the array. Hashing provides a solution to this problem by transforming the millions of possible keys into a few hundred or thousand. As you might suspect, this cannot be done perfectly since there is no way to turn millions of keys into thousands of keys uniquely. When two or more keys hash to the same value, a collision is said to occur. These collisions are the biggest problem associated with hashing, and the way they you handle them determines the overall efficiency of the technique.

The other use of hashing is to take advantage of its fast retrieval to create a container that also has fast retrieval. To understand how this works, we need to examine some simple hashing algorithms.

Suppose you have keys in the range from 1 ... 1000 but plan to store only about 100 pieces of data identified by these keys. One of the simplest ways to do this is to take the last two digits of the key, which will be a number in the range 0 ... 99. This can be calculated by dividing the key by 100 and taking the remainder. This is called a modulo operation and is directly supported by the % operator in the C family of languages. Many other hashing techniques exist such as breaking the key into smaller parts and then OR'ing them together to yield a smaller value.

Hash tables are often implemented as simple arrays, and the hash value is used as an index into the array. The calculation of the hash value is a simple operation that is independent of the number of values stored in the hash table. This means that if all goes well, a value can be retrieved from a hash table in $O(1)$ time. This is considerably faster than a tree and makes the hash table very attractive.

Unfortunately, things do not always go well. Sometimes two or more keys hash to the same value. When this happens, the data must be stored in another location. There are two main approaches to handling these collisions—closed addressing and chaining.

In the closed-addressing technique, a collision is resolved by storing the data in another free location in the array. The simplest technique to find a free location is to perform a linear search, which greatly increases the time to perform an insertion. On retrieval, the key being sought is compared to the one stored at the location indicated by the hash value. If the right key is not found, a linear search is performed to find it. In the case where the key is not present in the hash table, the entire array must be searched to verify that the key is not present. At this point our very fast $O(1)$ retrieval technique has degenerated into a less-than-exciting $O(n)$ linear search. This means that the time to retrieve a value is not constant and that the worst-case performance is far worse than that provided by a tree.

This technique is illustrated in Figure 8.11, where various keys are inserted in the order shown. A simplified hashing algorithm is employed that uses the last digit of the key as the hash value. Insertions proceed normally until the attempt to insert 53, which generates the first collision. The hashing algorithm dictates that this should be stored in position 3 in the array, but this position is already occupied. At this point, a linear search is begun in the forward direction for the first unoccupied space. If a space is found, the new element is inserted. The search algorithm uses wraparound logic so that when the end of the array is reached, it simply wraps around to the beginning and continues searching.

The other collision-resolution technique is chaining. In this technique, each entry in the hash table is really the head of a linked list. Every key that hashes to

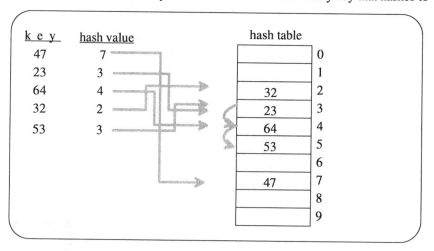

Figure 8.11 — Collision Resolution by Closed Addressing

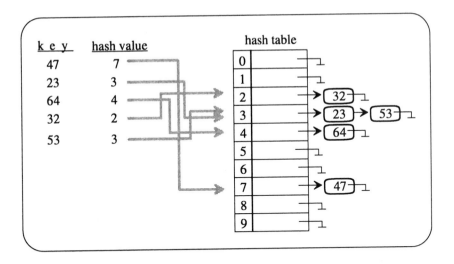

Figure 8.12 — Collision Resolution by Chaining

the same value is simply stored in the linked list rooted there. This is an improvement over the previous technique, since only the keys that collide have to be searched to determine if a key is absent. Still, this is a linear search and should be avoided if at all possible.

In Figure 8.12, the same values are inserted into the hash table, but no values are stored in the hash table itself—they are all in a linked list whose head is stored in the hash table. When a collision occurs during the insertion of node 53, the new value is simply appended to the linked list. Since there is no particular order to the elements in this list, new values can be placed at either end of the list, whichever is more convenient.

The likelihood of a collision can be reduced by increasing the size of the hash table. The problem with this is that the probability of collision drops to zero only when the array becomes as large as the number of keys, and every time we increase the size of the table, more memory is wasted. Once again, we are faced with a space-time tradeoff.

Since uniform retrieval times cannot be guaranteed for a hash table and the worst case performance can be considerably worse than a tree, the designers of the STL decided to use a tree as the underlying data structure for associative containers. It is possible that a hash table might be better suited to specific applications but would have undesirable performance characteristics for many applications. Thus, a lower average performance data structure was used to guarantee better worst-case performance so that the generality of the associative containers would not be compromised. Another reason to use a tree implementation is that it renders the associative containers sorted. This allows algorithms that depend on a sorted sequence, such as the set algorithms, to be used.

8.7 Hash Table Implementations

Despite the concerns over the worst-case performance of hash tables, their average case performance makes them very attractive for many applications. The requirements for hashed associative containers can be found in [BFM95]. There are hash table implementations in the HP and SGI distributions of the STL.

Since the hash table implementation is not yet part of the STL, I will provide only a minimal amount of detail and a short example. If you are interested in exploring this further, see the references at the end of the book and the implementations included with the HP and SGI distributions of the STL. The HP distribution provides two separate hash table implementations, both using chaining as the method of collision resolution. The difference in the two implementations is the way resizing of the hash table is handled when the number of collisions rises to the point where performance begins to degrade.

One way to handle this problem is to wait until the hash table is too small and then allocate a new, larger hash table and rehash all the values to insert them into the new table. This is called intermittent resizing and can cause long waits while the hash table is being rebuilt. The alternate technique is one called gradual resizing, where the size of the hash table is increased a few positions at a time but more frequently, so that the time to do the resizing is spread over many insertions and does not result in periodic long response times.

The subdirectory bfhash in the HP STL distribution contains a hash table implementation that uses intermittent resizing, whereas the subdirectory dmhash contains an implementation that uses gradual resizing. Both of these experimental implementations have yet to be adopted as part of the STL and carry a warning that they have not been thoroughly tested. I recommended that you use them only on an experimental basis to gain an appreciation of the kind of performance that can be obtained using an associative container implemented with a hash table. The SGI implementation has no warnings and is believed to be stable.

The key difference between the tree implementation of an associative container and the hash table implementation is that the tree implementation is ordered and the hash table implementation is not. This causes a change in the constructor for the associative containers. Whereas the tree implementation requires a comparison function that induces an ordering on the values in the container (i.e., operator<), the hash table implementation needs a function that determines if two values are the same (i.e., operator==). This also has consequences for the class iterators. Iterators for tree implementations return the values in sorted order, while the iterators for hash tables return the values in a seemingly random order determined by the hash function and order of insertion of the data.

Listing 8.6 uses the bfhash implementation to demonstrate an associative container's use of a hash table implementation and to give you an idea of the performance you can expect. This program was compiled by Borland C++ 4.5.

```
#include <hash.h>
// bfhash implementation of associative containers
#include <iostream.h>
#include <dos.h>
#include <set.h>

#define NUM_INSERTS   10000

//////////////////////////////////////////////////////////
// simple minded function to calculate the
// difference between two times.  This will fail if
// run when the hour changes!!!
//////////////////////////////////////////////////////////
long TimeDiff(struct time& start, struct time& finish)
{
    long  s = 0, f = 0;

    s = start.ti_hund + (100 * start.ti_sec) +
        (6000 * start.ti_min);
    f = finish.ti_hund + (100 * finish.ti_sec) +
        (6000 * finish.ti_min);
    return(f - s);
}

main()
{
    set<int, less<int> >        set0;
    hash_set<int, hasher<int>, equal_to<int> >
                                set1;
    int                         i;
    struct time                 start, finish;
```

```
    for(i=0; i< NUM_INSERTS; i++)
        set0.insert(i);

    gettime(&start);
    for(i=0; i< NUM_INSERTS; i++)
        set0.find(i);
    gettime(&finish);
    cout << NUM_INSERTS <<
        " retrievals from tree = " <<
        TimeDiff(start, finish) << '\n';

    for(i=0; i< NUM_INSERTS; i++)
        set1.insert(i);

    gettime(&start);
    for(i=0; i< NUM_INSERTS; i++)
        set1.find(i);
    gettime(&finish);
    cout << NUM_INSERTS <<
        " retrievals from hash table = " <<
        TimeDiff(start, finish) << '\n';
    cout << "size=" << set1.size() <<
        ", max size=" << set1.max_size()
        << ", buckets=" << set1.bucket_count() << '\n';

    return(0);
}
```

```
10000 retrievals from tree = 11
10000 retrievals from hash table = 6
size=10000, max size=5461, buckets=8073
```

Listing 8.6 — Timing a Tree Versus a Hash Table [hash_tim.cpp]

The header file contains declarations for the classes hash_set, hash_multiset, hash_map, and hash_multimap. You will notice a couple of differences in the declaration of a hash_set as opposed to a set:

```
hash_set<int, hasher<int>, equal_to<int> >
    set1;
```

An extra template parameter is required that specifies the hash function. A hash function, implemented by the class hasher, is provided in the header file and is used here. This hash function breaks the key into bytes and then OR's the bytes together to yield the hash value. If you don't like this, you can provide your own hash algorithm by declaring a class, as demonstrated in the following:

```
template <class T>
class MyHasher {
public:
    int operator()(T key);
};

template <class T>
int MyHasher::operator()(T key)
{
    ... // a better hash algorithm
}
```

The second difference is in the comparison function passed as the third template parameter. In the case of a set, less<int> was used to order the data. Hash tables do not order the data, so we use a function that can determine if two data items are equal.

Many parameters can be passed to the constructor for the class hash_set to tune the performance of the hash table. The preceding program has let all these values default so that all choices will be made by the class itself. The output shows the time for the two methods in hundredths of seconds as measured on a 90 MHz Intel Pentium. In this case, the hash table is about twice as fast as the tree.

The number of buckets is the number of entries in the hash table, and we see that it is just slightly smaller than the number of values stored in the table. This implies that collisions are relatively rare and, when they do occur, probably only a list of length two has to be searched. A hash table that is organized this way will give very near its optimal performance.

The implementation of a hash table using gradual resizing is found in the subdirectory dmhash and is organized somewhat differently than that of bfhash. A different header file is provided for each of the containers, and you must include the header for the container(s) you want. A collection of hash functions is provided in the header hashfun.h, and you can use the one that suits your needs or define your own.

8.8 Container Selection

The set is useful as a container to hold one or more copies of objects and is sufficient to implement any associative container you might want; however, it is not the most convenient container for some applications. For many applications, it is more convenient to view the key and data as associated, but separate, entities. This is especially convenient for applications that use the associative-memory model.

Many associative-memory applications take advantage of the fact that they can implement efficient random access data structures whose keys need not be simple integers. Use of a map to support string keys is among the most common applications of this data structure.

Deciding whether unique or multiple keys should be supported depends entirely on the requirements of the application. You must make this choice on the basis of the capabilities required and not on questions of efficiency.

9
Adaptors

9.1 Introduction

We have all seen adaptors—those little things that go on the ends of hoses so that they will connect properly with a fitting of a different size. The adaptors provided by the STL are not much different. They connect onto an existing object on one side and make it appear differently on the other side. They do not really change the object to which they are applied; they simply alter its appearance.

In Chapter 3, we looked at function adaptors. These adaptors are able to take a function object as a parameter and transform it into a new function object that does something different. They do not change the way the function object passed to them works, but modify the environment in which it is invoked. To the programmer using the function adaptor, it appears that a new function object has been created that might have different parameters from the original function object.

Now we'll look at two more classes of adaptors. One type is used on iterators and is able to alter their behavior. The other is applied to containers and generates new containers from existing ones.

All of the adaptors share one trait: they change the way something looks and, in doing so, create something similar to, yet different from, the original. This technique often saves a lot of implementation effort since it is usually easier to adapt an existing object to a new purpose than it is to build a new object from scratch.

9.2 Container Adaptors

Container adaptors change one container into a new container. This is accomplished by changing the interface (set of public methods and data members) to the class. In most cases, the new class requires a subset of the capabilities of the original class. All the container has to do is to hide some of the existing methods, possibly change some, and sometimes add a few new methods. The result is what appears to be a new container, but most of the implementation effort has been avoided.

The implementation of container adaptors is really quite simple. The adaptor contains an instance of the container on which it is based. It provides its own set of methods that invoke the methods of the container within it to perform the necessary actions. A typical container adaptor is declared as follows:

```
template <class Container>
class ContainerAdaptor {
protected:
   Container    cont;
public:
   // public methods for ContainerAdaptor
};
```

This is the simplest way of creating a new container. The restriction is that the class being created must have a lot in common with the class from which it is adapted. Although this might seem unlikely, there are in fact some common containers that are very similar to the containers we have already built.

9.3 The Stack

A stack is a list with the restriction that insertions and deletions can occur only at one end. This is sometimes referred to as a Last In First Out (LIFO) list and is depicted in Figure 9.1. You can think of a stack as being just like the stack of trays at a cafeteria. Clean trays are placed at the top of the stack and disappear on a spring mechanism under the counter. When a customer wants a tray, only the top one is accessible, and it is removed from the top of the stack. Stacks have the interesting property that when values are removed from a stack, they emerge in the opposite of the order in which they were placed on the stack. This makes them useful for many applications.

The stack does not provide all the operations of a general list. In fact, everything that can be done with a stack can be done with only four operations:

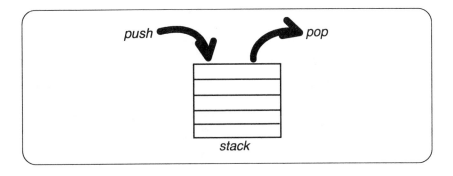

Figure 9.1 — Basic Stack Operations

push(value)	Pushes a new value onto a stack.
pop()	Removes the value from the top of the stack.
top()	Returns the value at the top of the stack without removing it.
empty()	Returns a Boolean value indicating if the stack is empty.

Since the stack is just a special type of list, it seems natural that it should be implemented by adapting one of the existing containers capable of representing a list. This includes all of the sequence containers—the vector, deque, and list. The STL implementation of the stack is limited to being based on one of the sequence containers. Table 9.1 presents a list of the most important operations defined for the stack adaptor.

Expression	Explanation
`push(v)`	Pushes the value v onto the stack.
`pop()`	Removes the value at the top of the stack *without returning it.*
`top()`	Returns the value at the top of the stack *without removing it.*
`empty()`	Returns a Boolean indicating if the stack is empty.
`size()`	Returns the number of values in the stack.
`operator<()`	Compares two stacks.
`operator==()`	Compares two stacks.

Table 9.1 — Stack Operations

Most of these methods are implemented by simply calling the method of the same name in the underlying container. For example, `stack::push()` calls `container::push_back()`, `stack::pop()` calls `container::pop_back()`, and `stack::operator<()` invokes `container:: operator<()`. This limits the containers on which the adaptor can be based to those that provide the required methods. It also means that the comparison of two stacks is defined by the comparison operator of the underlying container.

The following example shows how a stack can be used to convert an expression from infix to postfix. Infix is the way we usually write arithmetic expressions—for example, $a \times (b + c)$. This is called infix because the operators are placed between the operands. Expressions such as this are evaluated using a series of rules. The rules are that subexpressions in parentheses should be evaluated before those not in parentheses, multiplication and division should be performed before addition and subtraction, and the expression should be evaluated from left to right unless one of the previous rules dictates otherwise.

Postfix expressions place the operators after the operands to which they apply. The postfix version of the preceding expression is $abc + \times$. Such an expression is evaluated by looking from left to right until the first operator is found. This operator is then applied to the previous two operands and the result replaces the operator and its operands. This process continues until the end of the string is reached. In this case, you read from left to right until you encounter the first operator, $+$. This is applied to the previous two operands b and c, and the result of this calculation is used to replace the subexpression $bc+$. We scan ahead and find another operator, $\times$, which is applied to a and the result of the previous calculation.

One of the things you should note about the postfix expression is that the parentheses have disappeared. Unlike infix expressions, postfix expressions are unambiguous and do not need parentheses to clarify the order of evaluation. Using the rules of evaluation, there is only one way they can be interpreted. Therefore, the priority of operators and use of parentheses that is required with infix expressions are eliminated. This lack of ambiguity makes them very useful in programming languages where complex expressions have to be evaluated. Usually one of the first steps performed by a compiler is to convert infix expressions to postfix.

One way to convert an infix expression to postfix is to use a stack and the following set of rules.

1. Scan the infix expression from left to right.

2. If the input is an operand, copy it to the output string.

3. If it is an operator and it is of higher priority than the operator at the top of the stack, then push it onto the stack.

4. If it is of lower priority than the top of the stack, then pop the stack and copy the operators to the output string until an operator of higher priority is at the top of the stack. Then push the operator that was read.

5. If an open parenthesis is found, then push it.

6. If a closing parenthesis is found, then pop the stack, copying the operators to the output string, until an opening parenthesis is found. Then discard both of the parentheses.

We simplify the problem by stating that an operand may be only a single character, no spaces are permitted in the expression, and the expression is terminated by the special character "$". The use of the special terminating character makes it easier to recognize the end of the string and simplifies the coding. The operators have the following priorities, from high to low:

1. *, /

2. +, -

3. $

4. (,)

Listing 9.1 shows a program which uses this algorithm to convert infix expressions to postfix.

```
#include <vector>
#include <stack>
#include <algorithm>
#include <iostream>

using namespace std;

vector<char>                        inString, outString;
stack<char, vector<char> > stk;

int Priority(char c)
{
    switch(c) {
        case '/':
        case '*':
            return(3);
            break;
        case '+':
        case '-':
            return(2);
            break;
        case '$':
            return(1);
            break;
        case '(':
            case ')':
            return(-1);
            break;
        default:
            return(0);
            break;
    }
}

void ProcessChar(char c)
{
    if(Priority(c) == 0) {
        // operand
        outString.push_back(c);
        return;
    }
    if(stk.empty() || c == '(') {
        // stack is empty or char is (
        stk.push(c);
        return;
    }
    if(c == ')') {
```

```
        // pop and copy to output until (,
        // then discard parentheses
        while(stk.top() != '(') {
            outString.push_back(stk.top());
            stk.pop();
        }
        stk.pop();
        return;
    }
    if(Priority(c) > Priority(stk.top())) {
        // priority of char > than stack top, so push
        stk.push(c);
        return;
    }
    while((! stk.empty()) && (Priority(c) <=
        Priority(stk.top()))) {
        // char is < priority of stack top,
        // so pop until greater, then push
        outString.push_back(stk.top());
        stk.pop();
    }
    stk.push(c);
}

main()
{

    istream_iterator<char, char>  inStream(cin);
    ostream_iterator<char>        outStream(cout, "");


    for(; inStream !=
        istream_iterator<char, char>(); inStream++)
        inString.push_back(*inStream);

    for_each(inString.begin(),inString.end(),
        ProcessChar);
    copy(outString.begin(), outString.end(),
        outStream);
    cout << '\n';

    return(0);
```

```
a*((b+c)/(d-e)+f)/g$
abc+de-/f+*g/
```

}

Listing 9.1 — Using a Stack to Convert Infix to Postfix [postfix.cpp]

Two functions are used—`Priority()`, which returns a numeric priority for each character passed to it, and `ProcessChar()`, which embodies the rules listed previously. The main program reads the input into a vector, uses `for_each()` to apply `ProcessChar()` to each of the characters in the input, and then copies the result to `cout`. All the real work occurs in `ProcessChar()`, which handles the stack and copies the characters to the output vector.

The `stack` used in this example is declared as follows:

```
stack<char, vector<char> > stk;
```

This is read as "create a stack from a vector of characters." The second template parameter is optional. If it is not specified, `deque<T>` will be used, where `T` is the first parameter. Thus, the first template parameter is the type to be stored in the stack, and the second is the type of the container to be adapted to a stack. These template parameters have been changed from those in the HP implementation. The result is a stack that can hold a series of characters.

Although the examples so far have created a stack from a `vector`, this need not always be the case, and the stack could be created from a deque or list as well. The decision should be based on questions of efficiency of time and space. Since all of the sequence containers allow constant time insertions and deletions at the end, there is no clear choice to be made on the basis of time. In terms of space, both the `deque` and `list` require more space than the `vector`. Although this would seem to argue against their usage, remember that the `deque` can actually free space once it has been allocated and is no longer used. This means that if you expect a stack to grow very large and then shrink down to almost nothing, the `deque` will make the most efficient use of storage. The use of a `list` will, of course, incur the overhead of two pointers for every element in the list. In the general case for small stacks, the `vector` is probably a good choice. The default container, the `deque`, is a good choice for larger stacks or for those whose size cannot be predicted.

9.4 Queues

The queue, like the stack, is another form of specialized list, and its operations are a subset of the general operations supported by sequence containers. A queue is characterized by having elements placed onto one end of the queue and removed from the other end. This is exactly the behavior exhibited by a queue of customers waiting for a teller at a bank. Queues are sometimes referred to as First In First Out (FIFO) lists. Queues are often used when data have to be saved and processed later in the same order in which they were placed on the queue. The operations defined on a queue are summarized in Table 9.2.

These methods are not much different than those provided by the stack, although it is now possible to access both the value at the front and back of the queue. The difference lies in the implementation of `push()` and `pop()`, in that they now operate on opposite ends of the underlying container using `container::push_back()` and `container::pop_front()`. As with the stack, the container on which the queue is based must provide the methods invoked by the adaptor.

A queue must add values at one end of the container and remove them from the other. A `vector` cannot do this in constant time and does not provide all of the required methods, so it is ruled out as a choice for an underlying container. As new values are added to the end of a queue and removed from the front, it tends to *creep* through memory. This behavior means that it is best implemented using a container that can handle the queue style of memory usage. Both the

Expression	Explanation
`push(v)`	append the value v to the end of the queue
`pop()`	remove a value from the front of the queue without returning it
`front()`	return the value at the front of the queue without removing it
`back()`	return the value at the back of the queue without removing it
`empty()`	return a Boolean indicating if the queue is empty
`size()`	return the number of values stored in the queue
`operator==()`	compare two queues
`operator<()`	compare two queues

Table 9.2 — Queue Operations

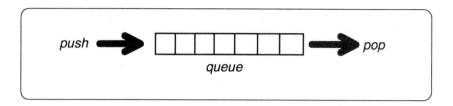

Figure 9.2 — Basic Queue Operations

deque and list satisfy these requirements and offer addition and deletion at either end in constant time. The deque and list can, with some overhead, delete memory once it is no longer used. The deque does not incur the overhead of the pointers required by the list and is the default container if one is not specified.

The following shows an example that pushes some values onto a queue and then pops them off. Users of the HP implementation should note that the template parameters as well as the file containing the class have changed in the C++ standard. Also note that the values come out of the queue in the same order in which they were inserted. Queues, unlike stacks, do not change the order in which the values are returned. (See Listing 9.2.)

```cpp
#include <deque>
#include <queue>
#include <iostream>

using namespace std;

void main()
{
    queue<int>  q1;
    int         i;

    for(i=0;i<10;i++) q1.push(i);

    while(! q1.empty()) {
       cout << q1.front() << ' ';
       q1.pop();
    }
    cout << endl;
```

```
0 1 2 3 4 5 6 7 8 9
```
}

Listing 9.2 — A Simple Queue [queue1.cpp]

9.5 Priority Queues

In an ordinary queue, values are retrieved from the queue in the same order in which they were inserted. When a value is removed from a priority queue, it is the highest (or lowest) value currently in the queue. This is true regardless of the order in which the data were inserted into the queue. You can think of a priority queue as a queue that sorts its values so that the one of greatest priority is always returned.

Priority queues have many uses. Imagine a situation where people could be placed on a queue in any order, but the oldest person on the queue should be the next one removed from the queue. Priority queues are often used inside operating systems to select the next task to receive the services of the CPU. Each task is assigned a priority, and the one with the highest priority is removed from the queue and starts to execute.

Priority queues are implemented using heaps. The heap was discussed in detail in Section 5.6, so only a brief discussion is presented here. The heap is a special form of binary tree that is partially sorted so that the value of each child node in the tree is less than the value of its parent. This is sufficient to guarantee that the greatest value in the heap is stored at the root. Heaps have properties that allow them to be stored in a regular sequence container. This means that the root of the tree will be stored in the first physical location of the container—a position that is readily accessible.

Heaps are also a good choice for the implementation of priority queues due to their efficiency. Since the heap is a variant of the tree, it allows insertion in $O(\log n)$ time. This is far faster than implementing the priority queue as a list and re-sorting it every time a value is inserted or deleted.

Table 9.3 shows the operations provided by the priority queue. One of the first things you will note is that the priority queue provides constructors similar to those of other containers. The priority queue template requires three

Expression	Explanation
`priority_queue(cmp=Compare())`	Constructs an empty queue using `cmp` as a comparison function.
`priority_queue(iter1, iter2, cmp=Compare())`	Constructs a queue and initializes it with the values from `iter1` up to `iter2`, using `cmp` for comparison.
`push(v)`	Adds the value `v` onto the queue.
`pop()`	Removes the value at the top of the queue.
`top()`	Returns the value at the top of the queue.
`empty()`	Returns a Boolean indicating if the queue is empty.
`size()`	Returns the number of values in the queue.

Table 9.3 — Priority Queue Operations

parameters—the type to store in the priority queue, the type of container it will use to store the values, and a comparison function object that will be used to compare the values in the container so that they can be sorted. The last two parameters default to a `vector` and `less`, respectively. The comparison function object should perform the same way as `operator<()`. The constructor allows you to specify an alternate comparison object or to use the default comparison object provided as a parameter to the template.

Listing 9.3 shows how values can be inserted into a priority queue in random order and retrieved in sorted order.

```
#include <vector>
#include <stack>
#include <iostream>
#include <string>
#include <algorithm>
#include <queue>
#include <functional>

using namespace std;
```

```
class Person {
public:
   string   name;
   int    age;
   Person(){age = 0;}
   Person(char* nam, int ag):age(ag)
      {name = nam;}
   friend bool operator<(const Person& p1,
      const Person& p2);
   friend bool operator==(const Person& p1,
      const Person& p2);
};

bool operator<(const Person& p1, const Person& p2)
{
   return(p1.age < p2.age);
}

bool operator==(const Person& p1, const Person& p2)
{
   return p1.name == p2.name;
}

main()
{
   priority_queue<Person>
      pq;

   pq.push(Person("Fred", 14));
   pq.push(Person("Sally", 7));
   pq.push(Person("Jennifer", 9));
   pq.push(Person("Elizabeth", 15));
   pq.push(Person("James", 8));

   while(! pq.empty()) {
      cout << (pq.top()).name << ", " <<
         (pq.top()).age << '\n';
      pq.pop();
   }
   return(0);
```

```
Elizabeth, 15
Fred, 14
Jennifer, 9
James, 8
Sally, 7
```

}

Listing 9.3 — Using a Priority Queue [pri_que.cpp]

Notice that you can have the comparison based on one member of the `Person` class by supplying an appropriate comparison function. In this case, the default `less` is used, and `operator<` is defined appropriately. If you want the item of least priority at the top of the stack, you could use `greater<Person>` as a comparison function.

Priority queues call `begin()` and `end()` and, hence, cannot be used with ordinary arrays. If you really want to use an array as a priority queue, you can use the underlying heap functions directly. Priority queues do not invoke `pop_front()`, so a `vector` can be used as the underlying container. A `list` is ruled out, since the heap is designed to work with contiguous storage that offers an efficient implementation of `operator[]`, which heaps use. A `deque` could be used, but in the general case, the storage overhead required for this implementation would not be warranted. For most purposes, the `vector` is the best choice.

9.6 Iterator Adaptors

We have seen how the use of adaptors can simplify the creation of new containers from existing ones. Now we see how the same principle can be applied to iterators to yield new iterators. Three adaptors are defined for use with iterators:

reverse iterators   Alter the behavior of bidirectional or random access iterators so that they traverse the container from back to front.

insert iterators   When these iterators are assigned a value, instead of overwriting the previous value in the location, they insert a new value into the container.

raw storage iterators   Allow algorithms and containers to write to uninitialized memory by applying the appropriate constructor to the memory before the write is permitted to proceed.

As with all adaptors, iterator adaptors extend the functionality of existing components with very little additional implementation effort.

9.6.1 Reverse Iterators

The purpose of the reverse iterators is to allow a container to be traversed from back to front as well as from front to back. The containers themselves provide reverse iterators as `typedefs` created by applying the reverse iterator adaptor to their existing iterators. Similarly, the methods `rbegin()` and `rend()` are created by applying reverse iterator adaptors to the results of the existing methods `begin()` and `end()`. This means that the reverse iterator adaptors have constructors that can transform an existing forward iterator into a reverse iterator.

The implementation of the reverse iterators is fairly simple. They provide their own version of `operator++` that decrements the pointer to the storage for the container rather than incrementing it. For example, the `reverse_iterator` class defines `operator++` as

```
self& operator++()
{
    --current;
    return *this;
}
```

where `current` is the value of the forward iterator that is used to represent the position in the container, and `self` is `typedefed` to be a reverse iterator.

Reverse iterators also provide constructors that perform the arithmetic necessary to convert a forward iterator into a reverse iterator. The result of a few arithmetic reversals is an iterator that really does go in the opposite direction of a forward iterator.

An example of the usage of reverse iterators can be found in Chapter 2, where iterators in general are discussed.

9.6.2 Insert Iterators

Normally, when you assign a value to the dereferenced value of an iterator, it overwrites the value referenced by the iterator. The insert operators behave differently in that rather than replacing values in the container, they insert new values into the container. Three different insert iterators are provided:

back_insert_iterator   An iterator that is used to append values onto the end of a container. It does this by invoking the container's `push_back()` method. This limits its applicability to the `vector`, `list`, and `deque`.

front_insert_iterator   Always inserts values at the start of the container by invoking `push_front()` on the underlying container. Thus, it can be used only with `lists` and `deques`.

insert_iterator   Can be used to insert a value at any point in a container. The insertion point is determined by an iterator passed to the `insert_iterator` constructor. It can be used with any container supporting the method `insert()`.

Let's begin by looking at the example of a `back_insert_iterator` in Listing 9.4:

```
#include <vector>
#include <algorithm>
#include <iostream>

using namespace std;

main()
{
    vector<int>                              v1;
    back_insert_iterator<vector<int> >       append(v1);
    int                                      i;

    v1.reserve(50);
    for(i=0; i<10; i++) *append = i;
    copy(v1.rbegin(), v1.rend(), append);
    copy(v1.begin(), v1.end(),
        ostream_iterator<int>(cout, " "));
```

```
return(0);
```

```
0 1 2 3 4 5 6 7 8 9 9 8 7 6 5 4 3 2 1 0
```

```
}
```

Listing 9.4 — Using a `back_insert_iterator` [bck_ins.cpp]

The constructor for the `back_insert_iterator` requires that the container on which it is to operate be passed as a parameter. Once this connection is made, any assignments to the iterator will be appended to the end of the container. This is demonstrated in the `for` loop, where the values from 1 ... 10 are appended to the vector. Then the values already in the container are copied in reverse order to the back insert iterator. The result is the integers from 0 ... 9 followed by the integers from 9 ... 0.

One important note is that fifty spaces are reserved in the vector before it is used. Without this, the vector would grow as each integer was added, resulting in the reallocation of a larger amount of memory and copying of the values from the old memory. This would invalidate the iterators in the statement

```
copy(v1.rbegin(), v1.rend(), append);
```

since memory would be reallocated during the copy. The result would be that corrupt values could be placed into the vector or that the program would crash.

This illustrates the true utility of the insert iterators—using them in conjunction with one of the STL algorithms. The insert iterators are derived from the class `output_iterator` and can be used whenever an output iterator is expected.

When we try to use a `front_insert_iterator`, we find that the results are slightly different, as shown in Listing 9.5.

```
#include <deque>
#include <algorithm>
#include <iostream>

using namespace std;

main()
{
    deque<int>                            d1;
    front_insert_iterator<deque<int> >  prepend(d1);
```

```
    int                                        i;

    for(i=0; i<10; i++) *prepend = i;
    copy(d1.begin(), d1.end(), prepend);
    copy(d1.begin(), d1.end(),
       ostream_iterator<int>(cout, " "));
    return(0);
```

```
0 1 2 3 4 5 6 7 8 9 9 8 7 6 5 4 3 2 1 0
```

```
}
```

Listing 9.5 — Using a front_insert_iterator [fro_ins.cpp]

The program begins by inserting the numbers from 0 ...9, but after insertion, they are in the order 9 ...0. The reason for this is that once the first number, 0, is inserted, it becomes the front of the deque and the next number is inserted in front of it. This has the effect of seeming to reverse the order in which the numbers are inserted. The copy() function also uses a front_insert_iterator with the result that the order of the sequence is reversed again. Thus, the final result has the sequence in both the forward and reverse orders.

Insert iterators work similarly to back insert iterators in that they insert the values in the order in which they are assigned to the iterator. The insert iterator constructor requires both the container into which it should insert and an iterator indicating the position in front of which it should insert the values. (See Listing 9.6.)

```
#include <list>
#include <algorithm>
#include <iostream>

using namespace std;

main()
{
    list<int>              l1;
    list<int>::iterator    iter;
    int                    i;

    for(i=0; i<10; i++) l1.push_back(i);
    iter = l1.begin();
```

```
    advance(iter, 5);
    copy(iter, ll.end(),
        insert_iterator<list<int> >(ll, iter));
    copy(ll.begin(), ll.end(),
        ostream_iterator<int>(cout, " "));

    return(0);
}
```

```
0 1 2 3 4 5 6 7 8 9 5 6 7 8 9
```

Listing 9.6 — Using an `insert_iterator` [ins_iter.cpp]

The program begins by inserting the numbers 0 ...9 into the list and positioning an iterator at the position of the 5 in the list. It then copies the values from the 5 to the end of the list to the position just before the 5. Be careful not to write an expression like the following:

```
    copy(ll.begin(), ll.end(),
        insert_iterator<list<int> >(ll, iter));
```

This will create an infinite loop since the iterator indicating the beginning of the range to be copied is before the insertion point. Each time a value is copied, a value is inserted, with the result that it never reaches the end of the list. This causes the list to grow to the point where it eventually exhausts the memory of the computer.

9.7 Function Adaptors

The function adaptors exist to adapt functions, methods, and function objects. They can convert a function or method into a function object, alter the result of a function, or assign a constant value to a function parameter.

9.7.1 Not1

not1 is a function adaptor that takes a function object that returns a Boolean result and logically negates the result. This is a convenience adaptor that uses the adaptor unary_negate to actually do the work. It is rarely necessary to call unary_negate directly. The function that is negated must satisfy the requirements of a unary_function and return a Boolean result. (See Listing 9.7.)

```cpp
#include <functional>
#include <iostream>
#include <algorithm>

using namespace std;

void main()
{
    int      ar[10];
    int      i;

    for(i = 0; i < 10; i++)
    {
        ar[i] = i;
    }

    cout << "there are " <<
        count_if(ar, ar + 10,
            not1(bind2nd(less<int>(), 3)))
        <<  " not less than 3" << endl;
}
```

```
there are 7 not less than 3
```

Listing 9.7 — Using not1   [not1.cpp]

The program in Listing 9.7 uses not1 to negate the result of the function object less. The result is that instead of producing a count of the number of values in the array that are less than 3, it produces a count of the values that are greater than or equal to 3.

9.7.2 Not2

not2 is a function adaptor that, like not1, negates the result of a function object. Rather than negating the result of a unary_function, not2 negates the result of a binary_function. This is demonstrated in the program in Listing 9.8.

```cpp
#include <functional>
#include <iostream>
#include <algorithm>

using namespace std;

void main()
{
    int       ar1[5], ar2[5];
    bool      result[5];
    int       i;

    for(i = 0; i < 5; i++)
    {
        ar1[i] = i;
        ar2[i] = 4 - i;
    }

    cout << "ar1 = ";
    for(i = 0; i < 5; i++)
    {
        cout << ar1[i] << ' ';
    }
    cout << endl << "ar2 = ";
    for(i = 0; i < 5; i++)
    {
        cout << ar2[i] << ' ';
    }

    transform(ar1, ar1 + 5, ar2, result,
        not2(equal_to<int>()));

    cout << endl << "result = ";
    for(i = 0; i < 5; i++)
    {
        cout << result[i] << ' ';
    }
    cout << endl;
```

```
}
```

```
ar1 = 0 1 2 3 4
ar2 = 4 3 2 1 0
result = 1 1 0 1 1
```

Listing 9.8 — Using not2 [not2.cpp]

9.7.3 Pointers to Functions and Methods

There are times, such as when providing an argument for an adaptor, when a function object is required. While you can certainly write your own function objects by defining operator() for a class, you will often have a function that implements the required operation and wish to turn it into a function object. The adaptors for pointers to functions and methods can quickly transform a function or member into a function object.

9.7.4 ptr_fun

ptr_fun is a function that takes a pointer to a function and returns a function object. ptr_fun has two signatures—one for unary functions and one for binary functions. It returns an instance of either pointer_to_unary-_function or pointer_to_binary_function. These are both function objects and can be adapted themselves. These function objects are demonstrated in Listing 9.9.

```
template <class Arg1, class Result>
   pointer_to_unary_function<Arg1, Result>
   ptr_fun(Result (*f)(Arg1));

template <class Arg1, class Arg2, class Result>
   pointer_to_binary_function<Arg1,Arg2,Result>
   ptr_fun(Result (*f)(Arg1, Arg2));
```

```
#include <functional>
#include <algorithm>
#include <iostream>
#include <string.h>
```

```cpp
using namespace std;

void main()
{
    char* names[] =
        {
            "John",   "Sue",    "Alice", "Bob", "Ted",
            "George", "Taylor", "Gayle", "Cindy", "Rita"
        };
    char  **result, nm[10];

    strcpy(nm, "Taylor");

    result = find_if(names,
        names + 10,
        not1(bind2nd(ptr_fun(strcmp), nm)));
    if(result == (names + 10))
    {
        cout << "not found" << endl;
    }
    else
    {
        cout << *result << endl;
    }
}
```

```
Taylor
```

Listing 9.9 — Using `ptr_fun` [ptr_fun.cpp]

The program in Listing 9.9 shows how `ptr_fun()` can be used to transform a function, `strcmp()`, into a function object. The result is a `pointer_to_binary_function` that is then adapted using `bind2nd()` to set the second parameter to "Taylor". `strcmp()` returns zero if two strings are equal and nonzero if they are unequal. This is the opposite of what is needed, so `not1()` is used to negate the result.

The convenience functions `mem_fun()` and `mem_fun1()` do for methods what `ptr_fun()` does for functions. The `mem_fun()` function takes a pointer to a class method and returns an adaptor that can invoke the method on an object. The adaptor is an instance of `mem_fun_t`, which is a subclass of `unary_function`. It is important to understand how the `mem_fun_t` adaptor invokes the method before attempting to use either the adaptor or its convenience function.

mem_fun() requires a pointer to a method *M*, which has no parameters and returns a result of type *R*. This method pointer is passed to the constructor for the adaptor mem_fun_t. When an algorithm invokes the method, it does so by calling operator() on the adaptor with the usual syntax for a function call. operator() of mem_fun_t requires a single parameter—a pointer, *P*—to the object on which it should invoke the method. Thus, operator() invokes the function as (P->*M)(). The implication of this is that the parameter an algorithm passes to operator() must be a pointer to an object on which the method can be invoked.

mem_fun1() is the same as mem_fun() but works with a method, *M*, which takes a single parameter, *A*, and returns a result, *R*. mem_fun1() returns an instance of the adaptor class mem_fun1_t whose operator() requires two parameters. The first parameter is a pointer to the object on which the method should be invoked, and the second is the argument to the method. Thus, if it is invoked as operator()(P, A), it invokes the method as (P->*M)(A).

This is demonstrated in Listing 9.10, which uses transform() to invoke a method on an array of objects.

```
#include <functional>
#include <iostream>
#include <algorithm>

using namespace std;

class Counter
{
private:
    int        value;
public:
    Counter(){ value = 0; }
    int increment(int n)
    {
        value += n;
        return value;
    }
    int getValue(){return value;}
};

void main()
```

```
{
    Counter      *cntr[5];
    int          inc[5];
    int          result[5];
    int          i;

    for(i = 0; i < 5; i++)
    {
        cntr[i] = new Counter();
        inc[i] = 10 + i;
    }

    transform(cntr, cntr + 5, inc, result,
        mem_fun1(Counter::increment));

    for(i = 0; i < 5; i++)
    {
        cout << cntr[i]->getValue() << ' ';
    }
    cout << endl;
}
```

```
10 11 12 13 14
```

Listing 9.10 — Using mem_fun1 [mem_fun1.cpp]

There are two important points to notice about this program. First, the array cntr is an array of Counter*, not an array of Counter. The values in the array will be passed as the first argument to operator() of mem_fun1_t. We must make the array object pointers rather than objects because operator() requires a pointer to an object, not an object. The second point is how the pointer to the method is generated. The expression Counter::increment generates a pointer to the method increment() of the class Counter.

If you have a container of objects rather than a container of pointers to objects, you should use the convenience functions mem_fun_ref() and mem_fun1_ref(). These are analogous to mem_fun() and mem_fun1() but work with references to objects rather than pointers to objects. They return the adaptors mem_fun_ref_t and mem_fun1_ref_t, respectively. The program in Listing 9.11 is identical to the program in Listing 9.10 except it has been altered to work with object references rather than object pointers.

```cpp
#include <functional>
#include <iostream>
#include <algorithm>

using namespace std;

class Counter
{
private:
    int        value;
public:
    Counter(){ value = 0;}
    int increment(int n)
    {
        value += n;
        return value;
    }
    int getValue(){return value;}
};

void main()
{
    Counter        cntr[5];
    int            inc[5];
    int            result[5];
    int            i;

    for(i = 0; i < 5; i++)
    {
        inc[i] = 10 + i;
    }

    transform(cntr, cntr + 5, inc, result,
        mem_fun1_ref(Counter::increment));

    for(i = 0; i < 5; i++)
    {
        cout << cntr[i].getValue() << ' ';
    }
    cout << endl;
```

```
10  11  12  13  14
}
```

Listing 9.11 — Using `mem_fun1_ref` [mem_ref.cpp]

10
Memory Management

10.1 Introduction

The STL provides facilities for memory management. These include the allocator class, the raw storage iterator, temporary buffers, the `auto_ptr`, and some utility functions. The allocator class is a general-purpose allocator that is the default allocator used by all the STL containers. The raw storage iterator is an object that can write values to uninitialized memory by first constructing the required object and then assigning a value. `auto_ptr` is a smart pointer that can be wrapped around a pointer to dynamically allocated memory so that the dynamically allocated memory is freed when the scope in which the `auto_ptr` is allocated is destroyed.

10.2 Allocators

All STL containers have an associated allocator that is used to perform all memory-management functions. The Standard C++ Library defines a single memory model that is used by the containers to perform all dynamic memory management. An alternate allocator can be provided to implement a different memory model or allocation strategy.

Implementing an allocator is necessary if you are using a 16-bit memory model or a larger model not supported by the default allocator. The default allocator uses a general-purpose allocator accessed via `operator new`. General-purpose allocators must be able to manage variable-sized blocks of memory. This causes them to have poor performance relative to an allocator that manages fixed-sized memory blocks. Thus, you can dramatically improve performance by writing your own allocator.

The HP implementation of the STL provides several allocator classes to deal with different memory models. This scheme did not work well, as it lacked portability between compilers.

In the HP implementation, some of the containers, such as the list, pre-allocate blocks of memory that are managed by the containers themselves. This allows several lists holding instances of the same type to share a single memory pool. This increases the likelihood that when one container releases memory, another will allocate it. Thus, memory is passed between containers by the rapid memory management of the list, with far fewer requests to the system memory manager.

Although most implementations of the STL no longer use this memory-sharing model, it can be built relatively easily and be used in applications where there will be a direct benefit from such a management scheme.

Note that allocators separate the allocation operation from that of construction. Allocators provide the methods `allocate()` and `de-allocate()` for allocating and freeing memory. They also provide the methods `construct()` and `destroy()` for the construction and destruction of objects, as shown in Listing 10.1.

```
#ifndef OBJ_ALLOCATOR_H
#define OBJ_ALLOCATOR_H

#include <cctype>
#include <stddef.h>

template <class T>
class ObjAllocator
{
    public:
        typedef size_t      size_type;
        typedef ptrdiff_t   difference_type;
        typedef T*          pointer;
        typedef const T*    const_pointer;
        typedef T&          reference;
        typedef const T&    const_reference;
        typedef T           value_type;

    private:
        struct FreeRecord
        {
            char* begin;
            size_t    size;
```

```
    };

    union AlignRecord
    {
        long      n1;
        long double n2;
    };

    size_t          storageSize ;
    size_t          objSize;
    size_t          numAllocated;
    char*           storageArea ;
    size_t          nextToAlloc ;
    FreeRecord*     freeList;
    size_t          freeListSize;

protected:
    int align(size_t n)
    {
        return ( n == sizeof(AlignRecord)) ?
            (n) :
            (1 + (n / sizeof(AlignRecord))) *
                sizeof(AlignRecord);
    }

    pointer getFreeSpace(size_t n)
    {
        if(freeListSize == 0)
        {
            return (pointer)0;
        }
        if(freeList[freeListSize - 1].size < n)
        {
            return (pointer)0;
        }
        freeListSize--;
        return (pointer)freeList[freeListSize].begin;
    }

public:

    ObjAllocator() throw()
    {
        storageSize = 100;
        numAllocated = 0;
        objSize = align(sizeof(T));
        storageArea = (char*)::operator new (objSize
```

```
              * storageSize);
         nextToAlloc = 0;
         freeList = new FreeRecord[storageSize];
         freeListSize = 0;
      };

      ObjAllocator(const ObjAllocator& alloc) throw()
      {
         if(storageArea != (char*)0)
         {
            delete [] storageArea;
         }
         if(freeList != (FreeRecord*)0)
         {
            delete [] freeList;
         }
         storageSize = alloc.storageSize;
         numAllocated = alloc.numAllocated;
         nextToAlloc = alloc.nextToAlloc;
         freeListSize = alloc.freeListSize;
         objSize = alloc.objSize;
         storageArea = (char*)::operator new (objSize
            * storageSize);
         freeList = new FreeRecord[storageSize];
      };

      ~ObjAllocator()
         throw()
      {
         if(storageArea != (char*)0)
         {
            delete [] storageArea;
         }
         if(freeList != (FreeRecord*)0)
         {
            delete [] freeList;
         }
      }

      pointer address(reference x) const
      {
         return &x;
      }

      const_pointer address(const_reference x) const
      {
         return &x;
```

```
    }

pointer allocate(
    size_type      n,
    const_pointer  hint = 0)
{
    pointer p;

    if((storageSize - numAllocated) < n)
    {
        p = getFreeSpace(n);

        if( p == 0)
        {
            return (pointer)0;
        }
        else
        {
            return p;
        }
    }
    p = (pointer)(storageArea + numAllocated *
        objSize);
    numAllocated += n;
    return p;
}

void deallocate(void *p, size_type n)
{
    freeList[freeListSize].begin = (char*)p;
    freeList[freeListSize].size = n;
    freeListSize++;
}

size_type max_size() const
    throw()
{
    return storageSize - numAllocated;
}

void construct(pointer p, const T& val)
{
    ::new (p) T(val);
}

void destroy(pointer p)
{
```

```
                p->T::~T();
        }
    };

#endif
```

Listing 10.1 — Sample Allocator [objalloc.h]

Listing 10.1 shows an example of what an allocator might look like. Not all compilers implement all of the capabilities of the latest C++ standard; therefore, an allocator that works with a particular compiler and implementation might well be different.

This is a simple-minded allocator that preallocates storage for a limited number of objects. The constructor begins by computing the size of the storage required for each object so that each object will be aligned properly. It then allocates the space.

When space is deallocated, it is added onto a list of free space that is maintained as a simple array of FreeRecords. The FreeRecord contains the address of the start of the free space and an indication of its length. When the allocated space is exhausted, the allocator examines the most recent entry on the free list to see if it can satisfy the request. If it can, the storage is removed from the free list and returned. The simplistic array implementation of a free list does not lend itself to more complex searches for free space.

The allocation of space is performed by allocate(), which attempts to get the space from the unallocated area of the storageArea. If there is insufficient space, it resorts to the free list.

This program is not meant to demonstrate how to manage memory effectively—there are obvious improvements to be made to the allocator. It does serve to show how a custom allocator might be written. Should an allocator for a different memory model be required, the typedefs would have to be modified to reflect the memory model.

Listing 10.2 shows how you can use the allocator.

```
#include "objalloc.h"
#include <iostream>
#include <list>
#include <iterator>

using namespace std;

class MyClass
{
private:
   int      n;
public:
   MyClass()
   {
      n = 55;
   }
   void setN(int nn) { n = nn; }
   int getN() {return n;}
};

void main()
{
   ObjAllocator<MyClass>        alloc;
   ObjAllocator<int>        intAlloc;
   MyClass                  *p, temp;

   p = alloc.allocate(1, (MyClass*)0);
   cout << "uninitialized = " << p->getN() << endl;
   alloc.construct(p, temp);
   cout << "initialized = " << p->getN() << endl;
}
```

```
uninitialized = -842150451
initialized = 55
```

Listing 10.2 — Testing the Allocator [alloctst.cpp]

10.3 Uninitialized Memory Operations

This section describes one iterator and several functions that deal with uninitialized memory. This is memory that has not had an object instantiated in it. These facilities typically combine the operations of construction and assignment into a single operation. These capabilities are used by the STL algorithms, but can be used directly in applications as well.

10.3.1 Raw Storage Iterators

The raw storage iterator is another output iterator that is distinguished by being able to write into uninitialized memory. This means that the memory to which it assigns values does not have to be initialized by the constructor for the class that will be stored there. The raw storage iterator accomplishes this by invoking the class constructor on the memory to which it is writing just before performing the assignment. This initialization is illustrated in Listing 10.3.

```
#include <iterator.h>
#include <string.h>
#include <malloc.h>
#include <iostream.h>
#include <defalloc.h>

class Person {
public:
    Person();
    Person(char* nam);
    Person(const Person& p);
private:
    int    age;
    char   name[32];
    friend ostream& operator<<(ostream& os, Person& p);
};

Person::Person()
{
    age = 999;
    strcpy(name, "noName");
    cout << "default called\n";
}

Person::Person(char* nam)
{
```

```
      strcpy(name, nam);
      cout << "named called\n";
}

Person::Person(const Person& p)
{
      strcpy(name, p.name);
      age = 50;
}

ostream& operator<<(ostream& os, Person& p)
{
      os << p.name << " ," << p.age;
      return(os);
}

main()
{
      char* ar;

      ar = (char*)malloc(sizeof(Person));
      *raw_storage_iterator<Person*, Person>
         ((Person*)ar) = Person("George");
      cout << *((Person*)ar) << "\n";

      return(0);
}
```

Listing 10.3 — Using a `raw_storage_iterator` [raw_iter.cpp]

The template for the `raw_storage_iterator` takes two parameters—the type of the iterator for the class stored in the uninitialized memory
and the type of the class itself. The constructor takes a pointer to the start of the
uninitialized memory. The raw storage iterator overloads `operator=` so that it
calls the function `construct()`, which then invokes `operator new` to call
the copy constructor for the class with the placement syntax. The con-
`struct()` function is defined as follows:

```
template <class T1, class T2>
inline void construct(T1* p, const T2& value)
{
      new (p) T1(value);
}
```

In Listing 10.3, `Person("George")` invokes the constructor that accepts a character pointer. `operator=` for the `raw_storage_iterator` invokes `construct(ar, Person("George))`, which then invokes the copy constructor using `operator new`. You can see that this is true since only the copy constructor assigns `age` the value 50.

Raw storage iterators are used mainly by the STL algorithms, but you could use them in your own programs. This could be useful for overlaying one data structure on top of another and similar but not recommended applications.

10.3.2 Other Uninitialized Memory Operations

The `raw_storage_iterator` provides a way for algorithms using iterators to write to uninitialized memory. The functions described in this section also write to uninitialized memory. Each of these functions implements an algorithm in its own right, whereas the `raw_storage_iterator` has to be used in concert with an algorithm.

```
template <class InputIterator, class ForwardIterator>
ForwardIterator
uninitialized_copy(InputIterator    first,
                   InputIterator    last,
                   ForwardIterator  result);

template <class ForwardIterator, class T>
void uninitialized_fill(ForwardIterator    first,
                        ForwardIterator    last,
                        const T&           x);

template <class ForwardIterator, class Size, class T>
void uninitialized_fill_n(ForwardIterator first,
                          Size            n,
                          const T&        x);
```

The function `uninitialized_copy()` copies the values from `first` up to `last` to the series of location(s) beginning at `result`. It does this by using `operator new` with the placement syntax to write the value into memory. The value to be written is constructed as `T(*first)` and `first` is incremented repeatedly until it is equal to `last`. This means that the class `T` must be copy constructible.

`uninitialized_fill()` fills the sequence from `first` up to `last` with the value x. The value to be assigned is constructed using `T(x)`, meaning that class `T` must be copy-constructible.

uninitialized_fill_n() also fills memory with a single value but uses a count to determine the amount of memory to be filled rather than a past-the-end iterator. Thus, it fills the n locations beginning at first with the value constructed by T(x). Once again, the class T must be copy-constructible as in Listing 10.4.

```cpp
#include <memory>
#include <iostream>
#include <vector>
#include <algorithm>

using namespace std;

class InitClass
{
private:
   int       n;
public:
   InitClass()
   {
      n = 99;
      cout << "InitClass constructed" << endl;
   }
   ~InitClass(){}
   void setN(int nn) { n = nn;}
   int getN() {return n;}
   friend ostream& operator<<(ostream& os,
      const InitClass& ic);
};

ostream& operator<<(ostream& os, const InitClass& ic)
{
   os << ic.n;
   return os;
}

void main()
{
   vector<InitClass>              vect1;
   InitClass                      init;
   int                            i;
   const int                      VECT_SIZE = 3;
   ostream_iterator<InitClass>    ostr(cout, " ");

   for(i = 0; i < VECT_SIZE; i++)
   {
```

```
        vect1.push_back(*(new InitClass()));
    }
    copy(vect1.begin(), vect1.end(), ostr);
    cout << endl;

    init.setN(50);
    uninitialized_fill(vect1.begin(), vect1.end(),
        init);
    copy(vect1.begin(), vect1.end(), ostr);
    cout << endl;
}
```

Listing 10.4 — Using uninitialized_fill(). [unfill.cpp]

10.4 Temporary Buffers

Some algorithms require the use of additional memory to perform their tasks. Containers could obtain temporary storage from their allocator, but that might not be the best source. If a custom allocator is used, it might have limited amounts of storage, or allocating storage for temporaries might adversely affect the performance of the allocator or layout of the container. get_temporary_buffer() can provide temporary memory for both containers and algorithms. Where this memory is obtained is not specified, but most implementations would likely use the standard heap.

10.5 auto_ptr

An auto_ptr is a smart wrapper around a regular pointer that aids in the partial automation of memory management. When an auto_ptr is created, it is associated with a pointer to an object that has been dynamically allocated. When the auto_ptr leaves the scope in which it was created, it is destroyed, and the destructor of the auto_ptr invokes the destructor of the pointer with which it is associated. Thus, the programmer no longer has to call delete on dynamically allocated objects, since they can be destroyed at the end of scope by wrapping them in an auto_ptr. Careful placement of auto_ptrs in the correct scope is a significant step towards the elimination of memory leaks.

The auto_ptr class defines operator*() and operator->() so that an instance of auto_ptr can be used just as the encapsulated pointer would be used. Several auto_ptrs can encapsulate the same pointer, but only one of them owns the pointer at any time. The object referenced by the pointer will be destroyed when the auto_ptr that owns it is destroyed. Ownership is established when an auto_ptr is created and associated with a pointer. When the value of an auto_ptr is assigned to another auto_ptr or is used as the parameter to the copy constructor of another auto_ptr, ownership is transferred. Thus, only the destruction of the auto_ptr that was assigned the value of the original auto_ptr will trigger the destruction of the object referenced by the encapsulated pointer. The method release() is provided if the programmer wants to force an auto_ptr to relinquish its ownership of a pointer. If two auto_ptrs are constructed to encapsulate the same pointer, the behavior is undefined, so this situation must be avoided. (See Listing 10.5.)

```cpp
#include <memory>
#include <iostream>

using namespace std;

class MyClass
{
    private:
        int      n;
    public:
        MyClass(){n = 2;}
        ~MyClass()
        {
            cout << "Destroying MyClass" << endl;
        }
        void setN(int nn) { n = nn;}
        int getN() {return n;}
};

void ptrMaker()
{
    MyClass      *myClassPtr;
    {
        cout << "entering outer scope" << endl;
        myClassPtr = new MyClass();
        auto_ptr<MyClass> aptr1(myClassPtr);
        aptr1->setN(5);
        cout << "n=" << (*aptr1).getN() << endl;
        {
```

```
            cout << "entering inner scope" << endl;
            auto_ptr<MyClass>      aptr2(aptr1);
            aptr2->setN(7);
            cout << "aptr2 says n=" << aptr2->getN()
                << endl;
            cout << "aptr1 says n=" << aptr1->getN()
                << endl;
            cout << "leaving inner scope" << endl;
        }
        cout << "leaving outer scope" << endl;
    }
}

void main()
{
    ptrMaker();
}
```

```
entering outer scope
n=5
entering inner scope
aptr2 says n=7
aptr1 says n=7
leaving inner scope
Destroying MyClass
leaving outer scope
```

Listing 10.5 — Using `auto_ptr` [aptr1.cpp]

The program in Listing 10.5 demonstrates some of the capabilities of the `auto_ptr`. `MyClass` is a simple class containing an integer value and provides methods to get and set this value. The class destructor prints a message so that its destruction will be apparent. The function `ptrMaker()` contains two nested scopes to show when an `auto_ptr` triggers destruction of the object it owns.

The code in the outer scope allocates an instance of `MyClass` and then constructs an `auto_ptr`, `aptr1` to encapsulate it. The value of `*myClassPtr` is set to 5 using `aptr1` to indirectly reference the object. The value is then printed by dereferencing `aptr1` to access the object. Within the inner scope, `aptr2` is constructed to reference the pointer within `aptr1` and assume ownership of the pointer. The value of the object is set, and both `auto_ptrs` are shown capable of accessing the object. The important point to notice is that the object is destroyed when exiting the inner scope, since that is when `aptr2`, the owner of the pointer, is destroyed.

Note that an instance of `auto_ptr` cannot be dynamically allocated. If an `auto_ptr` were dynamically allocated, it would not reside in the run time stack frame for its scope and would not be automatically destroyed when the scope was exited. This would defeat the reason for using an `auto_ptr` in the first place.

11
Putting the STL to Work

11.1 Introduction

The preceding chapters introduced the concepts of the STL and showed examples of how you can use it. The purpose of this chapter is to show how you can use the STL for larger problems. Although this book does not address problems on an industrial scale, it does describe the solution of many problems encountered in an industrial setting.

The first example is a banking system that demonstrates the use of several of the container classes and illustrates how object pointers can be stored in containers. The second example shows how to build a hierarchical symbol table using a map of maps. It discusses what is required to create your own container classes, how to provide iterators for them, and how to make them operate in the same manner as the containers provided by the STL.

11.2 A Banking Problem

We begin by examining a problem that might be encountered in a modern banking system. The input is a series of transactions that might originate from tellers or automatic teller machines. The transactions have been designed more to demonstrate how to solve problems with the STL rather than being a faithful representation of a banking system. The transactions follow:

open	Open a new account and assign an initial balance to it.
close	Close an existing account, withdrawing any money left in the account.
deposit	Deposit a sum of money into an account.

withdraw	Withdraw a sum of money from an account.
transfer	Transfer a sum of money from one account to another.
newcust	Create a new customer.
joincustact	Add a new customer to an account. Each account can have several owners, and each customer can have several accounts.
findcust	Find all customers with a given last name.
print	Print a list of deposit/withdrawal transactions that have been made to an account since the last time such a list was printed.
balance	Print a balance for an account.

Examining this list of transactions, we can define a series of classes to represent the entities in the banking system. A bank account is represented as in Listing 11.1.

```
class Account {
public:
   Account(int ID, float bal = 0.0):
     accountID(ID), balance(bal) {}
   Account(vector<Customer*> custs);
   float GetBalance() {return balance;}
   float MakeDeposit(float amt);
   float MakeWithdrawl(float amt);
   void PrintTransactionList();
   virtual void AddInterest(Date& today) {}
   void EraseTransactionList();
   void AddTransaction(Transaction* t);
   void  AddCustomer(Customer& cust);
   void DelCustomer(Customer& cust);
   void DeleteAccountFromCustomers();
   friend ostream& operator<<(
      ostream& os, Account& a);
   friend bool operator<(
      const Account& a, const Account& b);
   friend bool operator==(
      const Account& a, const Account& b);
   static void setDailyRate(float r)
      {dailyInterestRate = r;}
   static void setSavingsRate(float r)
      {savingsInterestRate = r;}
protected:
```

```
    vector<Customer*>     customers;
    vector<Transaction*>  transactionList;
    float                 balance;
    static float          dailyInterestRate;
    static float          savingsInterestRate;
    int                   accountID;
};
```

Listing 11.1 — The Class `Account`

The interesting point about this class is the way it stores customers and transactions. The customer is a permanent entity in any banking system and we can
assume that we will maintain a container of customers somewhere in the system
that will hold every customer. It is not safe to store the customer objects themselves in the account class since deleting an account would delete the customer
who owned it. In many cases, this might not be desirable. Therefore, the account class maintains the list of customers owning the account as a vector of
pointers to instances of the class `Customer`, which are actually stored in another data structure. (See Listing 11.2.)

```
class Customer {
private:
    string              firstName;
    string              lastName;
    int                 customerID;
    vector<Account*>    accountList;
public:
    Customer(string first, string last, int id):
       firstName(first), lastName(last), customerID(id)
       {}
    Customer(): customerID(0) {}
    string GetFirst(){ return firstName;}
    string GetLast(){ return lastName; }
    int    GetCustomerID(){ return customerID; }
    void   AddAccount(Account& act);
    void   DelAccount(Account& act);
    friend ostream& operator<<(
       ostream& os, Customer& a);
    friend bool operator<(
       const Customer& a, const Customer& b);
```

```
friend bool operator==(
     const Customer& a, const Customer& b);
};
```

Listing 11.2 — The Class `Customer`

There is no real problem with storing pointers in a container; you just have to be aware that the default comparison operators will compare the pointers themselves, not the objects to which they point. Thus, if your application or container requires the comparison of objects whose pointers are stored in a container, you must define a comparison operator to correctly compare object pointers. For the class `Customer`, such a comparison operator would look like this:

```
int operator<(Customer* a, Customer* b)
{
    return((*a) < (*b));
}
```

In this example, the vector of customers is traversed to print the owners of each account but is never searched, so there is no need for such a comparison operator.

The storage of transactions is a different matter. Although customers must have persistence for the duration of the execution, transactions are much more transient. The purpose of the transaction class is to represent the information obtained from the input stream of transactions until the internal data structures can be updated. The only reason to save transactions after this point is so that a list of deposits and withdrawals for each account can be produced. The obvious place to store such a list is with the account itself. Thus, the transaction list is a vector of objects rather than object pointers, since the transactions will not be stored elsewhere.

The transactions are represented by an abstract base class and a subclass for each transaction type as shown in Listing 11.3.

```
class Transaction {
public:
   Transaction(): accountID(0), date(Date(0,0,0)),
      transactionValue(0.0) {}
   Transaction(int actID, Date dte, float transVal):
      accountID(actID), date(dte),
      transactionValue(transVal) {}
   virtual ostream& Print(ostream& os);
```

```
   virtual void Process() {}
protected:
   int   accountID;
   Date  date;
   float transactionValue;
};
```

Listing 11.3 — The Abstract Base Class Transaction

The base class includes information common to most transactions such as the account number, transaction date, and amount of money involved in the transaction. The subclasses contain additional attributes and/or specialized methods to handle specific transaction types. One such subclass, Deposit, is shown in Listing 11.4.

```
class Deposit: public Transaction {
public:
   Deposit(): Transaction(0, Date(0,0,0), 0.0) {}
   Deposit(int actID, Date dte, float transVal):
      Transaction(actID, dte, transVal){}
   ostream& Print(ostream& os);
   virtual void Process();
};
```

Listing 11.4 — The Class Deposit

This class adds no new attributes; however, it does redefine the virtual methods Print() and Process() to perform the functions appropriate to a deposit transaction. The code for these methods is typical of the code for the same methods in all the classes derived from Transaction. (See Listing 11.5.)

```
ostream& Deposit::Print(ostream& os)
{
   os << "Deposit: ";
   Transaction::Print(os);
   return os;
}

void Deposit::Process()
```

```
{
    accountMapType::iterator        iter;

    iter = accountByNumber.find(accountID);
    if(iter == accountByNumber.end())
    {
        throw BadAccount(accountID);
    }
    (*iter).second.MakeDeposit(transactionValue);
}
```

Listing 11.5 — Virtual Methods for the Class Deposit

The Process() method of each transaction class is responsible for performing whatever operations are necessary to process the transaction. In the case of a deposit, this involves updating the account balance and adding the transaction to the list of transactions for the account. This requires that we understand how the accounts are stored so that we can retrieve the account that needs to be updated.

Account information must be stored for the duration of the program. Furthermore, it must be stored in such a way that the accounts can be retrieved easily and quickly based on a unique key, the account number. The STL container that meets these criteria is the map, which lets us store the accounts keyed by integer account numbers:

```
map<int, Account, less<int> > accountByNumber;
```

Many of the transaction processing functions require an account number to retrieve an account, so the function FindAccountByNumber() is provided to reduce the repetition of code. This function invokes the find() method on the map and returns the iterator from the find() method. When dereferenced, the iterator yields a pair, the first member of which is a reference to the key and the second a reference to the object. In the method Deposit ::Process(), the second member of the pair (the account) is updated to reflect the deposit transaction.

Customer instances are also stored in a map, keyed on a unique customer number assigned to each customer:

```
map<int, Customer, less<int> >    customerById;
```

The requirement that the program be able to list all customers with a particular last name forces us to provide some sort of access to customer information keyed on last name. We could traverse the map containing all the customers looking for those with a particular last name, but this would involve a slow linear search since the data would be organized by customer number, not name. If we assume that this will be a fairly frequent operation, then it makes sense to speed it up by providing a secondary index into the container of customers.

Last names are not unique, so a secondary index keyed on last names must be able to handle duplicate keys. The customer objects are already stored in the map `customerById`, so there is no need to replicate them, and pointers to the objects can be stored in the secondary index. The solution is to use a `multimap`:

```
multimap<string, Customer*, less<string> >
   customerByName;
```

Enough preamble. Let's take a look at the entire program, as shown in Listing 11.6.

```
#ifndef BANK_H
#define BANK_H

#include <vector>
#include <string>
#include <map>
#include <utility>
#include <functional>
#include <iostream>
#include <algorithm>

using namespace std;

class Account;
class SavingsAccount;
class DailyInterestAccount;
class Customer;
class Transaction;
class Deposit;
class Withdrawl;
class Transfer;
class OpenAccount;
class CloseAccount;
class Balance;
class PrintTransactions;
class CreateCustomer;
class JoinCustAccount;
```

```
class Date {
public:
   Date(): day(0), month(0), year(0) {}
   Date(int da, int mo, int yr): day(da),
      month(mo), year(yr) {}
   enum DateFormat{MDY, DMY, YMD, YDM};
   int GetDay(){ return day;}
   int GetMonth() { return month;}
   int GetYear() { return year;}
   friend ostream& operator<<(ostream& os, Date& d);
   friend istream& operator>>(istream& is, Date& d);
private:
   static DateFormat dateFormat;
   static char       dateSeparator;
   int               day, month, year;
};

class Transaction {
public:
   Transaction(): accountID(0), date(Date(0,0,0)),
      transactionValue(0.0) {}
   Transaction(int actID, Date dte, float transVal):
      accountID(actID), date(dte),
      transactionValue(transVal) {}
   virtual ostream& Print(ostream& os);
   virtual void Process() {}

protected:
   int    accountID;
   Date   date;
   float  transactionValue;
};

class Deposit: public Transaction {
public:
   Deposit(): Transaction(0, Date(0,0,0), 0.0) {}
   Deposit(int actID, Date dte, float transVal):
      Transaction(actID, dte, transVal)
   {
   }
   virtual ostream& Print(ostream& os);
   virtual void Process();
};

class Withdrawl: public Transaction {
public:
   Withdrawl(): Transaction(0, Date(0,0,0), 0.0) {}
```

```cpp
   Withdrawl(int actID, Date dte, float transVal):
      Transaction(actID, dte, transVal)
   {
   }
   virtual ostream& Print(ostream& os);
   virtual void Process();
};

class Transfer: public Transaction {
public:
   Transfer(): Transaction(0, Date(0,0,0), 0.0) {}
   Transfer(int actID, Date dte, float transVal,
      int fromAcct):
      Transaction(actID, dte, transVal)
   {
   }
   virtual ostream& Print(ostream& os);
   virtual void Process();
private:
   int   fromAccount;
};

class OpenAccount: public Transaction {
public:
   OpenAccount(): Transaction(0, Date(0,0,0), 0.0) {}
   OpenAccount(int actID, Date dte, float transVal):
      Transaction(actID, dte, transVal)
   {
   }
   virtual ostream& Print(ostream& os);
   virtual void Process();
};

class CloseAccount: public Transaction {
public:
   CloseAccount(): Transaction(0, Date(0,0,0), 0.0) {}
   CloseAccount(int actID, Date dte, float transVal):
      Transaction(actID, dte, transVal)
   {
   }
   virtual ostream& Print(ostream& os);
   virtual void Process();
};

class Balance: public Transaction {
public:
   Balance(): Transaction(0, Date(0,0,0), 0.0) {}
```

```
      Balance(int actID, Date dte):
         Transaction(actID, dte, 0.0)
      {
      }
      virtual ostream& Print(ostream& os);
      virtual void Process();
};

class PrintTransactions: public Transaction {
public:
   PrintTransactions(): Transaction(0, Date(0,0,0),
      0.0) {}
   PrintTransactions(int actID, Date dte):
      Transaction(actID, dte, 0.0)
   {
   }
   virtual ostream& Print(ostream& os);
   virtual void Process();
};

class CreateCustomer: public Transaction {
public:
   CreateCustomer(): Transaction(0, Date(0,0,0), 0.0)
      {}
   CreateCustomer(Date dte, string first,
      string last, int idNum):
      Transaction(idNum, dte, 0.0), lastName(last),
      firstName(first), customerID(idNum)
   {
   }
   virtual ostream& Print(ostream& os);
   virtual void Process();
private:
   string    lastName;
   string    firstName;
   int       customerID;
};

class JoinCustAccount: public Transaction {
public:
   JoinCustAccount(): Transaction(0, Date(0,0,0), 0.0)
      {}
   JoinCustAccount(int actID, Date dte, int custNum):
      Transaction(actID, dte, 0.0), custID(custNum)
   {
   }
   virtual ostream& Print(ostream& os);
```

```cpp
      virtual void Process();
private:
   int       custID;
};

class FindCustomer: public Transaction {
public:
   FindCustomer(): Transaction(0, Date(0,0,0), 0.0) {}
   FindCustomer(string last):
      Transaction(0, Date(0,0,0), 0.0), lastName(last)
   {
   }
   virtual ostream& Print(ostream& os);
   virtual void Process();
private:
   string   lastName;
};

class Account {
public:
   Account(int ID, float bal = 0.0):
     accountID(ID), balance(bal) {}
   Account(vector<Customer*> custs);
   float GetBalance() {return balance;}
   float MakeDeposit(float amt);
   float MakeWithdrawl(float amt);
   void PrintTransactionList();
   virtual void AddInterest(Date& today) {}
   void EraseTransactionList();
   void AddTransaction(Transaction* t);
   void  AddCustomer(Customer& cust);
   void DelCustomer(Customer& cust);
   void DeleteAccountFromCustomers();
   friend ostream& operator<<(ostream& os,
      Account& a);
   friend bool operator<(const Account& a,
      const Account& b);
   friend bool operator==(const Account& a,
      const Account& b);
   static void setDailyRate(float r)
      {dailyInterestRate = r;}
   static void setSavingsRate(float r)
      {savingsInterestRate = r;}
protected:
   vector<Customer*>    customers;
   vector<Transaction*> transactionList;
   float                balance;
```

```
      static float          dailyInterestRate;
      static float          savingsInterestRate;
      int                   accountID;
};

class SavingsAccount: public Account {
public:
   SavingsAccount(vector<Customer*> custs):
      Account(custs) {}
   virtual void AddInterest(Date& today);
};

class DailyInterestAccount: public Account {
public:
   DailyInterestAccount(vector<Customer*> custs):
      Account(custs) {}
   virtual void AddInterest(Date& today);
};

class Customer {
private:
   string             firstName;
   string             lastName;
   int                customerID;
   vector<Account*>   accountList;
public:
   Customer(string first, string last, int id):
      firstName(first), lastName(last), customerID(id)
      {}
   Customer(): customerID(0) {}
   string GetFirst(){ return firstName;}
   string GetLast(){ return lastName; }
   int    GetCustomerID(){ return customerID; }
   void   AddAccount(Account& act);
   void   DelAccount(Account& act);
   friend ostream& operator<<(ostream& os,
      Customer& a);
   friend bool operator<(const Customer& a,
      const Customer& b);
   friend bool operator==(
      const Customer& a, const Customer& b);
};

class BankException {
public:
   BankException(){}
};
```

```cpp
class NSF: public BankException {
public:
   NSF(){}
};

class AccountException: public BankException {
public:
   int accountNumber;
   AccountException(int n): accountNumber(n) {}
};

class BadAccount: public AccountException {
private:
public:
   BadAccount(int n): AccountException(n) {}
};

class DuplicateAccount: public AccountException {
private:
public:
   DuplicateAccount(int n): AccountException(n) {}
};

class BadCustomer: public AccountException {
private:
public:
   BadCustomer(int n): AccountException(n) {}
};

//////////////////////////////////////////////////
//                    GLOBALS
//////////////////////////////////////////////////

typedef map<int, Account, less<int> >  accountMapType;
typedef map<int, Customer, less<int> >
   customerIDMapType;
typedef multimap<string, Customer*, less<string> >
   customerNameMapType;
```

```
extern accountMapType        accountByNumber;
extern customerIDMapType     customerById;
extern customerNameMapType   customerByName;

#endif
```

Listing 11.6 — Header File bank.h

The details to note are the definition of the type Date, the subclasses of the Account class, and the various exceptions that can be thrown when errors are encountered.

11.3 Symbol Tables

A symbol table is a data structure used by most compilers to keep track of information on the objects defined in the program being compiled. The symbol table is accessed frequently during compilation and must offer efficient insertion and retrieval times based on a key. This requirement makes the map the obvious choice for implementing a symbol table.

The structure of the symbol table depends on the structure of the language being compiled. Some languages have a single global scope and can employ a symbol table consisting of a single map. Other languages have scopes nested within one another and require a symbol table that can model this situation.

We begin our exploration of symbol tables by examining a cross-reference generator that stores all object names in a single scope. The symbol table for this is implemented as a single map in which all the object names are stored. Then, we examine how to build a more complex symbol table that can provide support for nested scopes.

11.3.1 A Cross-Reference Generator

A cross-reference generator is a simple programming tool that was popular in the earlier days of computing. Its input is the source code of a computer program, and its output is a listing of all the objects (types, variables, etc.) used in the program with the line number(s) on which each object is found. This was a useful tool in the days when programmers worked on punched cards and read their programs from paper listings. It has fallen into disuse since the introduction of CRT terminals and full-screen text editors.

The cross-reference generator introduced here is designed to work with C and C++ and assumes that all object names are unique throughout the program. In other words, it cannot tell the difference between a variable declared in a function and a variable of the same name declared in the global scope. To differentiate the two, the program would have to parse the language—a task beyond the scope of this simple example. It is also limited in that it will process strings in quotes and inside comments. Both of these limitations can be removed with a little extra effort.

Let us begin by examining the code in Listing 11.7 and then discuss how it works.

```cpp
#include <map>
#include <functional>
#include <vector>
#include <iostream>
#include <string>
#include <algorithm>

using namespace std;

class Token {
public:
    string      tokenText;
    long        lineNum;

    Token(): lineNum(0L) {}
    Token(string text, long line): tokenText(text),
        lineNum(line) {}
};

class Scanner {
public:
    Scanner(istream& is);
    int operator()(Token& t);
private:
    long     currentLine;
    istream* inputStream;
};

class XrefList {
public:
    XrefList(){}
```

```
      void append(long ref);
      friend ostream& operator<<(ostream& os,
         XrefList& l);
private:
   vector<long>        references;
};

void XrefList::append(long ref)
{
   references.push_back(ref);
}

ostream& operator<<(ostream& os, XrefList& l)
{
   copy(l.references.begin(),
      unique(l.references.begin(),
      l.references.end()),
      ostream_iterator<long>(cout,", "));
   return(os);
}

int KeyWord(const string& wrd)
{
   if(wrd == "for")        return(1);
   if(wrd == "while")      return(1);
   if(wrd == "continue")   return(1);
   if(wrd == "return")     return(1);
   if(wrd == "break")      return(1);
   if(wrd == "if")         return(1);
   if(wrd == "else")       return(1);
   if(wrd == "do")         return(1);
   if(wrd == "int")        return(1);
   if(wrd == "long")       return(1);
   if(wrd == "short")      return(1);
   if(wrd == "char")       return(1);
   if(wrd == "double")     return(1);
   if(wrd ==  "signed")    return(1);
   if(wrd == "unsigned")   return(1);
   if(wrd == "void")       return(1);
   if(wrd == "extern")     return(1);
   if(wrd ==  "operator")  return(1);
   if(wrd == "virtual")    return(1);
   if(wrd == "overload")   return(1);
   if(wrd == "inline")     return(1);
   if(wrd == "public")     return(1);
   if(wrd == "private")    return(1);
   if(wrd == "protected")  return(1);
```

```
        return(0);
}

Scanner::Scanner(istream& is)
{
    inputStream = &is;
    currentLine = 1L;
}

int Scanner::operator()(Token& t)
{
    char   ch, buf[64];
    int    pt = 0;

    inputStream->get(ch);
    if(!(*inputStream)) return(0);

    while(!isalpha(ch)) {
        if(ch == '\n') currentLine++;
        inputStream->get(ch);
        if(!(*inputStream)) return(0);
    }
    t.lineNum = currentLine;
    while(isalpha(ch)) {
        buf[pt++] = ch;
        inputStream->get(ch);
        if(!(*inputStream)) {
            buf[pt] = '\0';
            t.tokenText = string(buf);
            return(1);
        }
    }
    buf[pt] = '\0';
    if(ch == '\n') currentLine++;
    t.tokenText = string(buf);
    return(1);
}

void main()
{
    Scanner                          scanner(cin);
    map<string, XrefList, less<string> >
                                     symtab;
    map<string, XrefList, less<string> >::iterator
                                     iter;
    Token                            toke;
    pair<map<string, XrefList,
```

```
                less<string> >::iterator, bool>
                                        symPair(iter, 1);

    while(scanner(toke)) {
      if(!KeyWord(toke.tokenText)) {
        symPair = symtab.insert(
          pair<const string, XrefList>
          (toke.tokenText, XrefList()));
        ((*symPair.first).second).
          append(toke.lineNum);
      }
    }
    for(iter=symtab.begin(); iter != symtab.end();
      iter++) {
      cout << (*iter).first << ", " <<
        (*iter).second << '\n';
    }
}
```

Listing 11.7 — A Cross-Reference Generator [xref.cpp]

The key to how the program works is in the class XrefList. This class has
a single attribute

```
vector<long>    references;
```

that is used to store a list of the line numbers on which any single identifier occurs. The symbol table itself is defined as a map in the function main.

```
map<string, XrefList, less<string> >    symtab;
```

It uses a string as its key and stores values of type XrefList. The function main obtains tokens from the scanner and inserts them into the map used as
a symbol table. Since the map supports only unique keys, it does not insert the
same name twice, but returns an iterator referencing the current occurrence of
the key. If the key is not in the map, it is inserted, and a reference to it is returned. Either way, a reference to the key and the object associated with the key
is returned.

It is interesting to examine how an object must be constructed before being
inserted into the map. The value to be inserted must be a pair whose first
member is the key and whose second member is the value associated with the
key. This is built using a pair constructor that specifies the types the pair is to
contain. Note that the key type must be declared to be a constant:

```
pair<const string, XrefList>(toke.tokenText,
    XrefList())
```

The object associated with the key is of type `XrefList`, and the `main()` function appends the line number—on which the identifier was found—onto the list of line numbers encapsulated within the `XrefList` object.

The identifiers are represented by the class `Token`, which contains two attributes—the text of the token, represented as a `string`, and the line number on which it was found. The `Token` attributes are filled in by `operator()` of the class `Scanner`. This is a simple-minded scanner that gathers up all contiguous strings of alphabetic characters and returns them as a single token. This technique will also return keywords in the language as if they were identifiers. To get around this problem, the function `KeyWord()` is called to determine that a token is not a keyword before it is inserted into the symbol table.

The class `XrefList` provides its own insertion operator, which ensures that duplicate line numbers are removed before they are printed. Duplicate line numbers will occur if an identifier occurs more than once on the same line. They are removed using the function `unique()`, which returns a past-the-end iterator for the possibly shorter sequence. This iterator is then used to delimit the vector copied to the output stream:

```
ostream& operator<<(ostream& os, XrefList& l)
{
    copy(l.references.begin(),
        unique(l.references.begin(),
        l.references.end()),
        ostream_iterator<long>(cout,", "));
    return(os);
}
```

11.3.2 Hierarchical Symbol Tables

Using a map directly as a symbol table imposes the limitation that there can only be a single scope. When we deal with real programming languages, we find that they have nested scopes and allow identifiers to be duplicated in different scopes. This implies that the symbol table itself must be hierarchical in nature to reflect the structure of the programming language. Such a symbol table can be built using a series of maps where each map corresponds to one of the scopes in the program being parsed.

The fact that a scope can contain another scope means that the maps in the symbol table must be able to hold other maps. Of course, they must also be able to hold the types and variables declared in the scope. This requires a more complex data structure to represent two different types of objects in a single map. Furthermore, since we do not know beforehand what type of data will be stored in the symbol table, we must write a series of class templates to allow for the storage of different types.

The header file in Listing 11.8 presents a solution to this problem in the form of a series of class templates.

```
#ifndef SYMTAB_H
#define SYMTAB_H

#include <map>
#include <string>
#include <iterator>
#include <vector>

using namespace std;

template <class ContentType>
class SymTabScope;

/////////////////////////////////
// EXCEPTIONS
/////////////////////////////////
class SymTabError {
public:
   SymTabError(){}
};

class SymTabBadOp: SymTabError {
public:
   SymTabBadOp(){}
};

class SymTabNotFound: SymTabError {
public:
   SymTabNotFound(){}
};

class SymTabDuplicate: SymTabError {
public:
   SymTabDuplicate(){}
};

/////////////////////////////////////////////
// PATH - represents a path through the sym tab
// hierarchy as a vector of strings
/////////////////////////////////////////////
class SymTabPath {
protected:
   vector<string>    path;
public:
   // public classes
   typedef vector<string>::iterator iterator;
```

```
        // public methods
        SymTabPath() {}
        void append(string name){path.push_back(name);}
        void clear() {path.erase(path.begin(),path.end());}
        iterator begin(){return path.begin();}
        iterator end() { return path.end();}
    };


    ////////////////////////////////////////////
    // convenience functions to make paths
    ////////////////////////////////////////////
    SymTabPath mkPath(string s1)
    {
        SymTabPath p;
        p.append(s1);
        return p;
    }


    SymTabPath mkPath(string s1, string s2)
    {
        SymTabPath p;
        p.append(s1);
        p.append(s2);
        return p;
    }


    SymTabPath mkPath(string s1, string s2, string s3)
    {
        SymTabPath p;
        p.append(s1);
        p.append(s2);
        p.append(s3);
        return p;
    }


    ////////////////////////////////////////////
    // abstract base class for symbol table entries
    ////////////////////////////////////////////
    template <class ContentType>
    class SymTabEntry {

    public:
        SymTabEntry(){}
        virtual void insert(string key, ContentType& entry)
            {}
        virtual void insert(string key) {}
        virtual void insert(SymTabEntry& scope) {}
```

```
    virtual void remove(string key) {}
    virtual int IsScope()
        {cout << "entry called\n";return 0;}
    virtual SymTabScope<ContentType>* GetScope()
    {
        throw SymTabBadOp();
        return 0;
    }
    virtual ContentType GetData() {
        ContentType x;
        throw SymTabBadOp();
        return x;
    }
    virtual SymTabEntry<ContentType>*
        Find(string name){
            throw SymTabBadOp();
            return 0;
    }
};

//////////////////////////////////
// SYMBOL TABLE SCOPE
//////////////////////////////////
template <class ContentType>
class SymTabData;

template <class ContentType>
class SymTabScope: public SymTabEntry<ContentType> {
private:
    map<string, SymTabEntry<ContentType>*,
        less<string> > subScope;
public:
    typedef ContentType          value_type;
    typedef value_type*          pointer;
    typedef const value_type*    const_pointer;
    typedef value_type&          reference;
    typedef const value_type&    const_reference;
    typedef size_t               size_type;
    typedef ptrdiff_t            difference_type;
    typedef map<string, SymTabEntry<ContentType>*,
        less<string> >::iterator iterator;
    typedef map<string, SymTabEntry<ContentType>*,
        less<string> >::const_iterator const_iterator;
    iterator begin(){return subScope.begin();}
    iterator end(){return subScope.end();}
    SymTabScope() {}
    void insert(string key, ContentType& entry)
```

```
      {
        SymTabData<ContentType>*   tmp;
        tmp = new SymTabData<ContentType>(entry);
        subScope.insert(pair<const string,
           SymTabEntry<ContentType>* >   (key, tmp));
      }
      void insert(string key);
      void insert(string key,
        SymTabScope<ContentType>& scope);
      void remove(string key);
      virtual int IsScope(){return 1;}
      SymTabEntry<ContentType>* Find(string name);
      SymTabScope<ContentType>* GetScope()
        {return this;}
};

/////////////////////////////////
// SYMBOL TABLE DATA
/////////////////////////////////
template <class ContentType>
class SymTabData: public SymTabEntry<ContentType> {
private:
   ContentType    data;
public:
   SymTabData();
   SymTabData(ContentType& entry): data(entry) {}
   virtual ContentType GetData(){return data;}
   ContentType operator*(){return data;}
   virtual int IsScope(){return 0;}
};

/////////////////////////////////////
// USER-LEVEL SYMBOL TABLE
/////////////////////////////////////
template <class ContentType>
class SymbolTable {
private:
   SymTabScope<ContentType>    subScope;
   SymTabScope<ContentType>*   currentScope;
public:
   typedef SymTabScope<ContentType>::iterator
      iterator;
   iterator begin(){return subScope.begin();}
   iterator end(){return subScope.end();}
   SymbolTable(){currentScope = &subScope;}
   SymTabScope<ContentType> GetScope()
      {
```

```
          return subScope;
       }
       void CdRel(SymTabPath& path);
       void CdAbs(SymTabPath& path);
       SymTabEntry<ContentType>* FindRel(
          SymTabPath& path);
       SymTabEntry<ContentType>* FindAbs(
          SymTabPath& path);
       void InsertRel(SymTabPath& path, string name,
          ContentType& entry);
       void InsertAbs(SymTabPath& path, string name,
          ContentType& entry);
       void InsertRel(SymTabPath& path, string name,
          SymTabScope<ContentType>& scope);
       void InsertAbs(SymTabPath& path, string name,
          SymTabScope<ContentType>& scope);
       void DeleteRel(SymTabPath& path, string name);
       void DeleteAbs(SymTabPath& path, string name);

};

template <class ContentType>
void SymTabScope<ContentType>::insert(string key)
{
    SymTabScope<ContentType>*  tmp;

    tmp = new SymTabScope<ContentType>();
    if(! (subScope.insert(pair<const string,
       SymTabEntry<ContentType>* >
       (key, tmp))).second)
       throw SymTabDuplicate();
}

template <class ContentType>
void SymTabScope<ContentType>::insert(string key,
    SymTabScope<ContentType>& scope)
{
    if(! (subScope.insert(pair<const string,
       SymTabEntry<ContentType>* >(key,
       (SymTabEntry<ContentType>*)&scope))).second)
       throw SymTabDuplicate();
}

template <class ContentType>
void SymTabScope<ContentType>::remove(string name)
{
    map<string, SymTabEntry<ContentType>*,
```

```
            less<string> >::iterator    iter;

    iter = subScope.find(name);
    if(iter == subScope.end()) throw SymTabNotFound();
    subScope.erase(iter);
}

template <class ContentType>
SymTabEntry<ContentType>*
SymTabScope<ContentType>::Find(string name)
{
    map<string, SymTabEntry<ContentType>*,
        less<string> >::iterator    iter;

    iter = subScope.find(name);
    if(iter == subScope.end()) throw SymTabNotFound();
    return (*iter).second;
}

template <class ContentType>
void SymbolTable<ContentType>::CdRel(SymTabPath& path)
{
    SymTabPath::iterator        pathIter;
    SymTabEntry<ContentType>*   scope;

    for(pathIter=path.begin();
        pathIter != path.end(); pathIter++) {
        scope = currentScope->Find(*pathIter);
        if(!scope->IsScope()) throw SymTabNotFound();
        currentScope = (SymTabScope<ContentType>*)
            &scope;
    }
}

template <class ContentType>
void SymbolTable<ContentType>::CdAbs(SymTabPath& path)
{
    SymTabPath::iterator        pathIter;
    SymTabEntry<ContentType>*   scope;

    currentScope = &subScope;
    for(pathIter=path.begin(); pathIter != path.end();
        pathIter++) {
        scope = currentScope->Find(*pathIter);
        if(!scope->IsScope()) throw SymTabNotFound();
        currentScope =
            (SymTabScope<ContentType>*)&scope;
```

```
    }
}

template <class ContentType>
SymTabEntry<ContentType>*
SymbolTable<ContentType>::FindRel(SymTabPath& path)
{
    SymTabPath::iterator        pathIter;
    SymTabEntry<ContentType>*   scope;
    int                         lastWasScope = 1;

    scope = currentScope;
    for(pathIter=path.begin(); pathIter != path.end();
        pathIter++) {
        if(!lastWasScope) throw SymTabNotFound();
        scope = scope->Find(*pathIter);
        lastWasScope = scope->IsScope();
    }
    return (scope);
}

template <class ContentType>
SymTabEntry<ContentType>*
SymbolTable<ContentType>::FindAbs(SymTabPath& path)
{
    SymTabPath::iterator        pathIter;
    SymTabEntry<ContentType>*   scope;
    int                         lastWasScope = 1;
    scope = &subScope;
    for(pathIter=path.begin(); pathIter != path.end();
        pathIter++) {
        if(!lastWasScope) throw SymTabNotFound();
        scope = scope->Find(*pathIter);
        lastWasScope = scope->IsScope();
    }
    return (scope);
}

template <class ContentType>
void SymbolTable<ContentType>::InsertRel(
        SymTabPath&     path,
        string          name,
        ContentType&    entry)
{
    SymTabPath::iterator        pathIter;
    SymTabEntry<ContentType>*   scope;
    SymTabData<ContentType>     newData(entry);
```

```
      scope = currentScope;
      for(pathIter=path.begin(); pathIter != path.end();
         pathIter++) {
         scope = (scope->Find(*pathIter));
         if(!scope->IsScope() ) throw SymTabNotFound();
      }
      ((SymTabScope<ContentType>*)scope)->insert(
         name, entry);
   }

   template <class ContentType>
   void SymbolTable<ContentType>::InsertAbs(
                     SymTabPath&    path,
                     string         name,
                     ContentType&   entry)
   {
      SymTabPath::iterator       pathIter;
      SymTabEntry<ContentType>*  scope;

      scope = &subScope;
      for(pathIter=path.begin(); pathIter != path.end();
         pathIter++) {
         scope = (scope->Find(*pathIter));
         if(!scope->IsScope() ) throw SymTabNotFound();
      }
      ((SymTabScope<ContentType>*)scope)->insert(
         name, entry);
   }

   template <class ContentType>
   void SymbolTable<ContentType>::InsertRel(
                     SymTabPath&                 path,
                     string                      name,
                     SymTabScope<ContentType>&   newScope)
   {
      SymTabPath::iterator       pathIter;
      SymTabEntry<ContentType>*  scope;

      scope = currentScope;
      for(pathIter=path.begin(); pathIter != path.end();
         pathIter++) {
         scope = (scope->Find(*pathIter));
         if(!scope->IsScope() ) throw SymTabNotFound();
      }
      ((SymTabScope<ContentType>*)scope)->insert(
         name, newScope);
```

```
}

template <class ContentType>
void SymbolTable<ContentType>::InsertAbs(
                SymTabPath&                 path,
                string                      name,
                SymTabScope<ContentType>&   newScope)
{
   SymTabPath::iterator       pathIter;
   SymTabEntry<ContentType>*  scope;

   scope = &subScope;
   for(pathIter=path.begin(); pathIter != path.end();
      pathIter++) {
      scope = (scope->Find(*pathIter));
      if(!scope->IsScope() ) throw SymTabNotFound();
   }
   ((SymTabScope<ContentType>*)scope)->insert(
      name, newScope);
}

template <class ContentType>
void SymbolTable<ContentType>::DeleteRel(
      SymTabPath& path,
      string      name)
{
   SymTabPath::iterator       pathIter;
   SymTabEntry<ContentType>*  scope;

   scope = currentScope;
   for(pathIter=path.begin(); pathIter != path.end();
      pathIter++) {
      scope = (scope->Find(*pathIter));
      if(!scope->IsScope() ) throw SymTabNotFound();
   }
   scope->remove(name);
}

template <class ContentType>
void SymbolTable<ContentType>::DeleteAbs(
      SymTabPath& path,
      string      name)
{
   SymTabPath::iterator       pathIter;
   SymTabEntry<ContentType>*  scope;

   scope = &subScope;
```

```
    for(pathIter=path.begin(); pathIter != path.end();
      pathIter++) {
      scope = (scope->Find(*pathIter));
      if(!scope->IsScope() ) throw SymTabNotFound();
    }
    scope->remove(name);
}

#endif
```

Listing 11.8 — Header File symtab.h

Let us begin by examining the class SymTabEntry. This is an abstract superclass for the nodes that will comprise the symbol table. It represents a single entry in the symbol table, and its subclasses, SymTabScope and SymTab-Data, represent subscopes and entries in the symbol table, respectively. The superclass contains no data itself but declares virtual functions that will be redefined by the subclasses. All of these classes are templates that have a parameter, ContentType, that specifies the type of data to be stored in the symbol table.

The class SymTabData has a single data member of type ContentType. This is where the information on the symbol table entries is stored. The class SymTabScope contains a map that has a string as a key and stores other SymTabEntrys that can be either subscopes or symbol table data entries. It is this structure that allows the hierarchical nesting of scopes in the same way programming languages do it. The string used as a key is the identifier that can be used to name a type, variable, or scope that is found within the source program.

The class SymbolTable is used by the application program to create a symbol table. It has two data members—a SymTabScope representing the top-level scope in the program, and a scope pointer. The structure of the symbol table is similar to that of a directory tree, and it is convenient to treat it in the same way. The symbol table uses the scope pointer to keep track of the current scope just as a shell keeps track of the working directory. All the methods have two versions—one that uses an absolute path from the top-level scope to specify a scope (ending in Abs), and one that uses a relative path from the current scope (ending in Rel). The functions CdRel() and CdAbs() are used to change the current scope.

A path is simply a vector of strings, each of which is the name of a scope. It is followed from either the top-level scope or the current scope to find the scope being referenced. The path is represented by the class SymTabPath, which provides methods to append a new scope onto the end of the path and to erase the entire path. These methods invoke the methods `push_back()` and `erase()` on the underlying `vector` to perform their tasks.

The classes `SymTabPath`, `SymTabScope`, and `SymbolTable` all provide iterators for accessing their contents. Since each of these enclose an STL class that has its own iterator, we can use the iterators of the STL classes rather than writing our own from scratch. This is done by using a `typedef` to define the iterator for the symbol table classes to be the same as the iterator for the underlying STL classes. The methods `begin()` and `end()` simply return the results of the methods of the same name belonging to the STL container.

A symbol table such as this is usually used as part of a compiler in conjunction with a parser. A compiler is normally broken into several components:

- A lexical analyzer (or scanner) that reads the input text and returns a stream of tokens. The tokens represent the important objects in the text stream such as keywords, operators, identifiers, parentheses, and the like.

- A parser that reads the stream of tokens from the lexical analyzer, checks that the token stream adheres to the rules of the language, and recognizes higher-level constructs such as expressions, statements, scopes, functions, and the like.

- A symbol table used to store information on objects seen previously during the compilation process. This is how the parser can determine that objects are of the right type when they are used after being declared.

- A code generator that can generate machine code corresponding to the operations recognized by the parser.

Parsers are very complex pieces of software and often recognize language constructs in what we would consider a strange order. Consider the case of recognizing a scope in the C family of languages:

```
main()
{
    statement-1;
    statement-2;
    ...
    statement-n;
}
```

The identifier `main` will be found followed by parentheses and recognized to be some sort of function. At this point it could be a function definition, function invocation, or forward declaration. Most parsers will encounter the opening curly bracket and then encounter a series of statements that will be recognized as a statement list. It is only when the closing curly bracket is encountered that the parser will recognize that an opening curly bracket followed by a statement list and a closing curly bracket is a compound statement that forms its own scope. Finally, it will realize that the compound statement was preceded by a function header and conclude that a function is being defined.

If any of the statements in the compound statement are declarations, the identifiers will have to be placed in a scope. The problem is that the scope has not been recognized at this point. Furthermore, it is only when the compound statement is recognized that it can be connected with the function name on the first line and the name of the function associated with the scope. Declarations within the compound statement must be stored somewhere, so our program must be able to create temporary scopes without a name until additional information becomes available.

The solution to this problem is to have the parser create a nameless scope by creating an instance of `SymTabScope`. Objects declared within the scope can be placed into the symbol table scope, which can then be inserted into the larger symbol table using these methods:

```
SymbolTable::InsertRel(SymTabPath& path, string name,
    ContentType& entry) or
SymbolTable::InsertAbs(SymTabPath& path, string name,
    ContentType& entry)
```

These methods allow a scope to be prepared outside the symbol table and then inserted and named at the same time.

Examining the iterator for the symbol table, we see that it is the same as the iterator for the `SymTabScope`, which is really a `map` iterator. This will return pointers to all of the `SymTabEntrys` in the map. The fact that some of these happen to be scopes in their own right makes no difference to the iterator—it does not have the ability to traverse a subscope. As a result, the iterator as defined will only traverse the topmost scope in the symbol table.

To correct this problem, we have to write our own iterator from scratch that has the ability to traverse subscopes. The STL defines some basic iterator types that are recognized by all the STL algorithms. Many of these algorithms are specialized to take advantage of the capabilities of the iterator they are passed. For example, if the `sort()` function is passed a bidirectional iterator, it cannot use `operator[]()` and will employ a different algorithm than if it is passed a random access iterator where it can use `operator[]()`. Naturally, we want our own iterators to behave just like, and be indistinguishable from, the iterators defined by the STL.

To ensure that our own iterators are indistinguishable from the STL iterators, we must do the following:

- Derive them from one of the STL iterator types (input, output, forward, bidirectional, or random access).

- Provide all the methods required by the iterator type from which it is derived.

The code in Listing 11.9 is an iterator for the SymbolTable class that is derived from the class forward_iterator, provides all the methods required of a forward iterator, and is able to traverse subscopes.

```
#ifndef SYMTAB_ITERATOR_H
#define SYMTAB_ITERATOR_H

#include <stack>
#include <iterator>
#include "symtab.h"

using namespace std;

class SymTabIterator:

forward_iterator<SymTabScope<ContentType>::value_type,
    SymTabScope<ContentType>::difference_type>
{
protected:
    struct StackEntry
    {
        SymTabScope<ContentType>*              scope;
        SymTabScope<ContentType>::iterator  iter;
        StackEntry(SymTabScope<ContentType>* scp,
            SymTabScope<ContentType>::iterator it):
            scope(scp), iter(it) {}
        StackEntry(){scope = 0;}
    };
    stack<vector<StackEntry> >              backStack;
    SymTabScope<ContentType>*              currScope;
    SymTabScope<ContentType>::iterator  currIter;
    char                                    allDone;
public:
    SymTabIterator()
    {
        allDone = 0;
    }

    SymTabIterator(SymTabIterator& i1)
```

```
      {
         backStack = il.backStack;
         currScope = il.currScope;
         currIter = il.currIter;
         allDone = il.allDone;
      }

      SymTabIterator(SymTabScope<ContentType>* scp,
         SymTabScope<ContentType>::iterator it)
      {
         currScope = scp;
         currIter = it;
         allDone = currIter == currScope->end();
      }

      SymTabIterator operator=(SymTabIterator il)
      {
         if(this == &il) return *this;
            backStack = il.backStack;
         currScope = il.currScope;
         currIter = il.currIter;
         allDone = il.allDone;
            return *this;
      }

   pair<string, SymTabEntry<ContentType>* >
operator*()
      {
         return pair<string, SymTabEntry<ContentType>* >(
            (*currIter).first, (*currIter).second);
      }

   bool operator==(const SymTabIterator& il)  const
      {
            if(allDone && il.allDone) return(1);
            if((currScope == il.currScope) &&
               (currIter == il.currIter) )
               return(1);
         return(0);
      }

   SymTabIterator operator++(int)
      {
         SymbolTable<ContentType>::iterator tmp = *this;

         if((*currIter).second->IsScope()){
            backStack.push(StackEntry(
```

```
                currScope, currIter));
            currScope =
                (SymTabScope<ContentType>*)
                (*currIter).second;
            currIter = currScope->begin();
            return tmp;
        }

        currIter++;
        if(currIter == currScope->end()) {
            if(backStack.empty()) allDone = 1;
            else {
                currScope = backStack.top().scope;
                currIter = backStack.top().iter;
                currIter++;
            }
        }
        return tmp;
    }

    SymTabIterator& operator++()
    {
        if((*currIter).second->IsScope()) {
            backStack.push(
                StackEntry(currScope, currIter));
            currScope = (SymTabScope<ContentType>*)
                (*currIter).second;
            currIter = currScope->begin();
            return *this;
        }
        currIter++;
        if(currIter == currScope->end()) {
            if(backStack.empty()) allDone = 1;
            else {
                currScope = backStack.top().scope;
                currIter = backStack.top().iter;
                currIter++;
            }
        }
        return *this;
    }
};

#endif
```

Listing 11.9 — An Iterator for the Class SymbolTable [iterator.h]

Although much of the iterator code is unremarkable, the code for `opera-tor++()` warrants our attention. The symbol table itself is really a tree and must be traversed in some organized fashion. The iterator presented here traverses the symbol table in depth-first order, meaning that it traverses subscopes within a scope before it finishes traversing the scope containing the subscope. Whether this is the desired order or not depends on the application in which it is used.

There are several techniques for traversing trees: recursion, iteration, Deutsch-Schorr-Waite, and so on. The first point you have to realize about traversing a tree is that it is easier to go downward from the root to a leaf than it is to find your way back up to the root. The reason for this is that most trees maintain pointers from parent nodes to child nodes, but not pointers in the reverse direction. Thus, when you have finished traversing the subtree rooted at a node and wish to return to the node's parent, you must have some way of finding the parent of the node. The solution is to memorize your path down the tree by saving a pointer to every node you visit on the way down from the root.

If you think about this problem, you will realize that every time you go down a level in the tree a new node must be added to the path required to get back to the root. Each time you ascend one level in the tree, the pointer to the parent node is no longer needed and can be removed from the path. Thus, on descent, node pointers are appended to the path, whereas on ascent, they are removed from the same end of the path to which they were appended. These are the actions of a stack, which is the data structure required to save the path through a tree so that it can be traversed successfully.

A recursive function is one that calls itself. Each time a function calls another function, the state of the calling function is saved in a data structure called the run-time stack. The state information includes the values of the local variables, the machine registers, and the location of the next instruction to be executed. When the called function returns, the state values are popped off the run-time stack, local variables are restored, and a branch is taken to the saved location of the next instruction. The result is that the calling function continues to execute as if nothing had interrupted it.

Recursion can be used to traverse a tree by ensuring that one of the local variables saved on the run-time stack is a pointer to the tree node being visited. This series of pointers saved on the run-time stack forms the back-path necessary for the traversal to find its way back to the root of the tree. The popularity of recursion for tree traversal is due to the fact that the programmer does not have to worry about maintaining the stack—it is done automatically by the programming language.

The problem with recursion is that the entire traversal is done with a single recursive function call. This is very different from the way an iterator works. Each time operator++() is invoked on an iterator, it must advance one step in the traversal and return a reference to the new node being visited. There is no opportunity to take advantage of the run-time stack, so the iterator must maintain its own stack internally.

The Deutch-Schorr-Waite algorithm is a clever way of traversing a tree without using a stack. It manipulates the tree's own pointers so that they form a path back up the tree. The trick is that after you follow a downward-pointing link, you reverse it so that it points upward to the parent node. When you have finished visiting a node, you follow the upward link to the parent node and then reverse the link so that it points downward as it did originally.

An iterator could use the Deutch-Schorr-Waite algorithm if it had access to the links in the tree. We could use this algorithm to traverse the symbol table, but it would mean that only one traversal of the tree could be performed at once. If two iterators were active at once, they would each be changing different links, and mayhem would result. The only way to allow more than one iterator to be active simultaneously is to have each of them store their own state internally in a stack.

Examining the iterator, we see that it defines the structure StackEntry containing a scope pointer and the iterator for that scope. It also defines a stack based upon a vector of StackEntrys. operator++() uses a SymTabScope::iterator to traverse a scope and examines each SymTabEntry returned by the iterator. If the entry is a scope, it saves the current scope and iterator on the stack and sets its current scope and iterator pointers to be those of the subscope. It iterates through this new scope until it reaches the past-the-end iterator. Then it pops the previous scope and iterator off the stack and continues to iterate through the previous level of the symbol table. When it tries to pop the stack and finds it to be empty, the symbol table traversal is complete, and it returns its own past-the-end iterator.

The SymbolTable iterator has a member allDone, used to indicate if it is the past-the-end iterator. As long as this value is false, it is a valid iterator, but when it becomes true, it is a past-the-end iterator. The iterator constructor shown below will construct a past-the-end iterator when passed a scope and the past-the-end iterator for that scope:

```
SymTabIterator(SymTabScope<ContentType>*      scp,
   SymTabScope<ContentType>::iterator   it)
{
   currScope = scp;
```

Container Type	Expression	Explanation
Any Container	`value_type`	Type of the values stored in the container.
	`reference`	Type of a reference to container elements.
	`const_reference`	Type of a constant reference to container elements.
	`iterator`	Type of an iterator for the container.
	`const_iterator`	Type of a constant iterator for the container.
	`difference_type`	Type used to measure the distance between container elements.
	`size_type`	Usually used to state numbers of elements.
Reversible Containers	`reverse_iterator`	Type of a reverse iterator for the container.
	`const_reverse_iterator`	Type of a constant reverse iterator for the container.
Associative Containers	`key_type`	Type of the container key.
	`key_compare`	Type of a function to compare container keys.
	`value_compare`	Type of a function to compare container values.
	`key_comp()`	Returns the key comparison object.
	`value_comp()`	Returns the value comparison object.

Table 11.1—Required Container Type Definitions

```
    currIter = it;
    allDone = currIter == currScope->end();
}
```

In addition to providing the new iterator for the class, the `SymbolTable` must redefine its own methods `begin()` and `end()` to make proper use of the new iterator, as in Listing 11.10.

```
typedef SymTabIterator<ContentType> iterator;

iterator begin()
{
    return SymTabIterator<ContentType>(
```

```
        &subScope, subScope.begin());
}

iterator end()
{
    return SymTabIterator<ContentType>(
        &subScope, subScope.end());
}
```

Listing 11.10 — Revised SymbolTable Methods begin() and end()
[isymtab.h]

The method SymbolTable::end() passes the constructor the past-the-end constructor for the top-level scope of the symbol table, guaranteeing that a past-the-end iterator for the symbol table will be created. The final step is to have SymbolTable::operator==() compare the allDone members first and declare the two iterators equal if both allDone members are true.

All of the STL containers provide definitions for types that provide algorithms using the containers with important information about the type stored in the container. Iterators are also defined that can be used directly by code outside the class. Different container classes require that different types be defined, as summarized in Table 11.1.

These types are usually defined in terms of more basic types using a typedef, as was done in SymTabScope in Listing 11.8. The following short program in Listing 11.11 demonstrates how these types can be used.

```
#include <set>
#include <functional>
#include <iostream>

using namespace std;

main()
{
    set<int, less<int> >               s1;
    set<int, less<int> >::value_type value;

    s1.insert(1);
    s1.insert(2);

    value = *(s1.find(1));
    cout << "value = " << value << endl;

    set<int, less<int> >::reference valRef =
        *(s1.find(2));
    cout << "reference = " << valRef << endl;

    set<int,less<int> >::value_compare comp;
    if(comp(value, valRef)) cout << "less" << endl;
    else cout << "not less" << endl;

    return(0);
}
```

```
value = 1
reference = 2
less
```

Listing 11.11 — Using Class Types [cl_type.cpp]

If we want to create a new container type and have it behave in the same way as the STL containers, we must define all of the appropriate types listed in Table 11.1. We must also provide all of the methods required by the container category to which it belongs.

This has not been done in the case of the class SymbolTable, since it can be argued that this is not a general-purpose class but is specialized for a specific application. The key type is fixed to be a string and nothing else. To achieve generality, the class would have to be defined to be a map of maps and both the key type and the value type would need to be passed as template parameters.

The question that faces any software designer is, "Should this be defined as a generic class or written as a special-purpose class?" The answer depends on the probability of reuse of such a class, the additional effort required to make it generic, and any ease of use that will be sacrificed in the pursuit of generality. The only time I have used a map of maps is as a symbol table, so I can argue that for the applications that I usually write, the probability of reuse of a more generic class would be low. These are questions that every designer must ask, since the answers depend greatly on the type of applications being built.

12
The Story Continues

12.1 Introduction

In the mid-1980s, many of the workstation vendors had their own windowing systems. These were all proprietary and mutually incompatible. In the late 1980s, the X Window System [SG86] appeared. This was produced by MIT, placed in the public domain, and able to run on workstations from all the major vendors. It was also designed to be easily ported to platforms on which it did not run at that time.

In less than five years, the proprietary windowing systems had all but disappeared and all vendors were supporting the X Window System. It had become the defacto industry standard. What led to this popularity? The factors can be summarized as follows:

- an excellent design that could be extended,
- high dependability through years of use,
- cross-platform portability, and
- public domain so that any company could adopt it without high cost.

The Standard Template Library shares many of the qualities that made the X Window System so successful. It is based on a solid design, is highly portable, is in the public domain, and has been adopted as an ISO standard. As its usage increases, it will become highly robust. Although most compiler vendors offer their own C++ libraries, I believe these are destined for the same fate as the proprietary windowing systems.

What the STL offers the programmer is not as revolutionary as the way it is offered. The STL is based on a solid design in which all functions, containers, and iterators work the same way. This is a strong point that makes the library relatively easy to learn and to extend. Extensions from various vendors are already appearing. All of these work with the current STL components and are much easier to learn and use than libraries developed independently.

I believe that the STL is destined for success and that the time to adopt it for use in your applications is now. I think that you will be pleased that you made this decision.

12.2 The Future

Nothing ever stays the same, and this is particularly true if you work in the field of computing. Sometimes things change so quickly that it is all we can do to keep up. The STL is no different. Although the basics covered in this book will remain the same, the standards committee and the vendors are not resting on their laurels but are instead working on ways to improve and extend the STL.

The set of functions provided by the STL is far from exhaustive. Development continues, but additions to the library will be slow and carefully considered. When dealing with standardized software, it is easy to add new functionality to the standard but virtually impossible to remove something once it has been added to the standard. The developers and standardization bodies realize this and are proceeding slowly to avoid the inclusion of unnecessary or redundant components.

Nonetheless, experimental development of the STL is proceeding on a couple of fronts. Two of the main efforts are in the areas of persistence and safety. Persistence involves being able to save STL objects to secondary storage and then retrieve them in the same state in which they were written. Safety concerns having STL containers check references to them to determine if they are valid. Some of the work in these two areas is outlined in the following paragraphs.

Objects are said to have persistence if they can continue to exist past the termination of the program that created them. In most cases, this involves saving the object's contents to disk and reading it back at a later time. Although you can always iterate through a container, writing out the contents and later reading it back and inserting the objects into a new container, it is much easier if the objects can do this themselves. Several vendors provide STL implementations with persistence. Whether this will be included in the standard at some point remains to be seen.

The STL vector is a slightly enhanced array, and the programmer can make the same mistakes using it that can be made with any array. These mistakes usually involve accessing members that have not been allocated, and they result in either strange behavior or program termination. It is a relatively simple matter to modify the code so that it checks references for validity before the references are used. The container can then warn the programmer of the problem, leading to reduced debugging time.

It is possible to modify the code of every container to make these checks, but this would involve changing a lot of code. Since all references to containers ultimately involve iterators, it is easier to modify the iterators themselves so that they make the checks. Regardless of the technique used, there is a time penalty to be paid for these run-time checks, making them primarily suited for debugging.

There are two efforts under way in this regard. One is an iterator package distributed with the HP STL distribution in a header file called `safeit.h`. The other is a package by Cay Horstman called safe STL [HOR95].

12.3 Summary

In the 1950s, libraries of reusable software components were in common use. One of the more successful libraries of this period was SHARE, a public-domain library of functions contributed by individuals and organizations. This library was able to succeed due to the limited number of languages and data types in use at the time. Over the years, such organizations of programmers fell into disuse as major hardware vendors assumed the responsibility of providing all system software to accompany the hardware they sold. These vendors paid little attention to reusable components and, as languages and operating systems evolved, the old ones fell into disuse.

The C family of languages is available on virtually every platform and is one of the most portable families of programming languages. During the 1980s the family gained immense popularity, and this trend continued with the adoption of object-oriented techniques and C++. Once templates were added to C++, the programming community again had the means to produce reusable software components that could be used by a significant fraction of its members.

The introduction of the STL brings reusable components to the C++ community. Whereas the SHARE effort had been an uncoordinated collection of functions championed by individuals, the STL is an organized, well-designed framework on which more extensive libraries can be based. Furthermore, it is sanctioned by standards organizations and must be supported by all compiler vendors who wish to claim compliance with standards.

The current version of the STL provides a well-designed framework for a library of reusable components as well as a collection of useful data structures and algorithms. Over time, this collection will be augmented as vendors provide libraries to extend the capabilities of the STL. This will probably lead to the classification of algorithms and data structures and the adoption of a standard taxonomy.

The result could well revolutionize the practice of programming as we know it today. The programmer of the future would no more consider writing low-level algorithms by hand than the programmers of today would consider building a loop from `if` statements and `goto`s. The training of programmers will change from teaching them how to code low-level algorithms to teaching them the theory of various algorithms and the names of reusable implementations of those algorithms. This has already happened in the area of numerical methods, where extensive libraries have been available for some time, and will be extended to more general algorithms and data structures.

The STL brings to fruition one of the most sought-after goals of computer science in the last decade—software reuse. The programmer's job will get easier, and both productivity and maintainability will be enhanced. Software engineering comes a step closer to understanding how computer programs should be written and making programs robust and dependable.

Appendix A
STL Header Files

The following table lists the STL header files that you will need to include in programs using the STL. This is the list used by the C++ standard. Other implementations might use other header files:

Header File	Description
`<algorithm>`	Defines the non-numeric STL algorithms.
`<deque>`	Defines the `deque` container.
`<functional>`	Defines predefined function objects such as `unary_function`, `binary_function`, and `less`.
`<iterator>`	Defines iterator categories, functions, adaptors, and stream iterators.
`<list>`	Defines the `list` container.
`<map>`	Defines the `map` and `multimap` containers.
`<numeric>`	Defines the numeric functions and `valarray`.
`<queue>`	Defines the `queue` and `priority_queue` adaptors.
`<set>`	Defines the `set` and `multiset` containers.
`<stack>`	Defines the `stack` adaptor.
`<string>`	Defines the `string` class.
`<utility>`	Defines utilities such as the `pair`.
`<vector>`	Defines the `vector` class.

Appendix B
The STL Reference

This appendix is a reference to all of the types, functions, and containers in the Standard Template Library. It is designed to be used in conjunction with the main text as a handy reference for the working programmer. The descriptions in this reference are much briefer than those provided in the main text, which should be consulted when a more detailed discussion is required.

The reference is organized in a purely alphabetical fashion without regard for whether an object is a function or container. This will make it easier to find functions and containers since there are no sections within the reference.

Header files for implementations conforming to the C++ standard are enclosed in angle brackets (<>). Header files for the HP implementation are enclosed in square brackets ([]). Header files for other implementations are in curly brackets ({}). An empty set of brackets indicates that the STL component is not available in that implementation.

---

accumulate

TYPE: function   **HEADER:** <numeric> [algo.h]
TIME: linear   **SPACE:** constant

```
namespace std{
   template <class InputIterator, class T>
   T accumulate(InputIterator    first,
       InputIterator             last,
       T                         init);

   template <class InputIterator, class T, class
   BinaryOperation>
   T accumulate(InputIterator    first,
       InputIterator             last,
       T                         init,
       BinaryOperation           binary_op);
}
```

DESCRIPTION: The first form sums the values from `first` up to, but not including, `last`, adds the value of `init`, and returns the result. The second form allows the user to supply a binary operation that will be used in place of addition.

adjacent_difference

TYPE: function   **HEADER:** <numeric> [algo.h]
TIME: linear   **SPACE:** constant

```
namespace std{
template <class InputIterator, class OutputIterator>
OutputIterator adjacent_difference(
                InputIterator first,
                InputIterator last,
                OutputIterator result);

template <class InputIterator, class OutputIterator,
   class BinaryOperation>
OutputIterator adjacent_difference(
                InputIterator       first,
                InputIterator       last,
                OutputIterator      result,
                BinaryOperation     binary_op);
}
```

DESCRIPTION: Calculates the difference between each pair of elements in the sequence from `first` up to `last`. The result is of the same length as the input sequence. Since the number of differences is one less than the number of elements in the input sequence, a zero is inserted at the front of the result to make the sequences the same length. Thus, the difference between the first two elements in the input sequence is in the second position of the output sequence. The second form of the function allows the specification of an operation other than the default `operator-`.

adjacent_find

TYPE: function   **HEADER:** <algorithm> [algo.h]
TIME: linear   **SPACE:** constant

```
namespace std{
template <class InputIterator>
InputIterator adjacent_find(InputIterator    first,
```

```
                        InputIterator        last);

template <class InputIterator, class BinaryPredicate>
InputIterator adjacent_find(
                    InputIterator        first,
                    InputIterator        last,
                    BinaryPredicate      binary_pred);
}
```

DESCRIPTION: These functions find the first pair of duplicate elements in the range first to last. If a duplicate is found, then the functions return an iterator referring to the first element in the duplicate. If no duplicate is found, an iterator equal to last is returned. In the first form of the function, operator== is used to compare elements. The second form allows the user to specify an arbitrary binary predicate function to use to compare elements.

advance

TYPE: function   **HEADER:** <iterator> [algobase.h]
TIME: linear   **SPACE:** constant

```
namespace std{
template <class InputIterator, class Distance>
void advance(InputIterator&    i,
          Distance            n);
}
```

DESCRIPTION: Moves the iterator i by n positions by repeated application of operator++ or operator--. The iterator must be an input, forward, bidirectional, or random access iterator. The distance can be negative only if the iterator is bidirectional or random access. This function is usually used with input, forward, and bidirectional operators where it takes linear time. When used with random access iterators, operator+ or operator- are used, yielding a constant time operation.

auto_ptr

TYPE: class   **HEADER:** <memory> []

```
namespace std{
  template<class X>
```

```
        class auto_ptr;
}
```

DESCRIPTION: An `auto_ptr` encapsulates a pointer to a dynamically allocated object and destroys the object when the `auto_ptr` itself is destroyed. This can be used to avoid memory leaks by associating an `auto_ptr` allocated on the run-time stack with a dynamically allocated object. The dynamically allocated object will be destroyed by the `auto_ptr` when the scope in which the `auto_ptr` is declared is exited. The `auto_ptr` class defines operators that make it indistinguishable from the encapsulated pointer.

Public Members:

```
typedef X auto_ptr<X>::element_type;
```

`element_type` is a synonymn for the object type referenced by the `auto_ptr`.

Public Methods:

```
explicit auto_ptr<X>::auto_ptr(X* p =0) throw();
auto_ptr<X>::auto_ptr(const auto_ptr&) throw();
template<class Y>
auto_ptr<X>::auto_ptr(const auto_ptr<Y>&) throw();
```

These are the class constructors. The first associates the `auto_ptr` with the parameter. If no parameter is provided, a null pointer is assumed. The `auto_ptr` never takes ownership of a null pointer. The second and third forms are the copy constructors, which copy the value of the pointer referenced by the parameter and assume ownership if the pointer is non-null. The third form is able to convert `Y*` to `X*`.

```
auto_ptr& auto_ptr<X>::operator=(
    const auto_ptr&) throw();
template<class Y>
auto_ptr& auto_ptr<X>::operator=(
    const auto_ptr<Y>&) throw();
```

This operator assigns the parameter to `*this`. If the value of the pointer referenced by the parameter is non-null, `*this` will assume ownership of the pointer. The object referenced by the pointer will be destroyed when the `auto_ptr` that owns it is destroyed.

```
auto_ptr<X>::~auto_ptr();
```

The class destructor. This will destroy the object referenced by the encapsulated pointer if `*this` is the owner of the encapsulated pointer.

```
X& auto_ptr<X>::operator*() const throw();
```

Returns a reference to the object referenced by the encapsulated pointer.

```
X* auto_ptr<X>::operator->() const throw();
```

Returns the encapsulated pointer.

```
X* auto_ptr<X>::get() const throw();
```

Returns the encapsulated pointer.

```
X* auto_ptr<X>::release() const throw();
```

Relinquishes ownership of the encapsulated pointer.

back_insert_iterator

TYPE: adaptor   **HEADER:** <iterator> [iterator.h]

```
namespace std{
  template <class Container>
  class back_insert_iterator : public iterator<
  output_iterator_tag, void, void, void, void>;
}
```

DESCRIPTION: Unlike other iterators, when assigned a value the insert iterators insert a new value into a container rather than overwriting an existing value. The `back_insert_iterator` accomplishes this by invoking `push_back()` on the underlying container. Of course, this means that the underlying container must support the `push_back()` operation. Insert iterators are useful with the STL algorithms to copy values to a container without having to worry if sufficient space exists.

SEE ALSO: back_inserter, front_insert_iterator, insert_iterator

Public Members:

```
back_insert_iterator<Container>::container_type;
```

The same as the template parameter.

Public Methods:

```
back_insert_iterator<Container>&
back_insert_iterator<Container>::operator=(
  typename Container::const_reference value);
```

Inserts the value at the end of the container by invoking push_back().

```
back_insert_iterator<Container>&
back_insert_iterator<Container>::operator++();
```

Does nothing but is provided for compatibility with other iterators.

```
back_insert_iterator<Container>
back_insert_iterator<Container>::operator++(int);
```

Does nothing but is provided for compatibility with other iterators.

```
back_insert_iterator<Container>&
back_insert_iterator<Container>::operator*();
```

Dereference operator to return a reference to the back_insert_iterator itself.

```
explicit back_insert_iterator::back_insert_iterator(
  Container& x);
```

Constructor to create a back_insert_operator for a container.

back_inserter

TYPE: function   **HEADER:** <iterator> [iterator.h]

```
namespace std{
  template <class Container>
```

```
back_insert_iterator<Container>
back_inserter(Container& x);
}
```

DESCRIPTION: Creates and returns a back_insert_iterator for the container passed to it. This is a convenience function that is easier to use rather than creating the iterator yourself.

SEE ALSO: back_insert_iterator

---

basic_string

TYPE: class   **HEADER:** <string> []

```
template<class charT,
  class traits = char_traits<charT>,
  class Allocator = allocator<charT> >
  class basic_string;
```

DESCRIPTION: This class is a sequence container that stores objects in the same manner as a zero-terminated array stores characters. Numerous methods and operators are defined to provide capabilities similar to the string handling functions of the standard C library. This class has been generalized so that it can contain string-like types other than char. It defines two specializations: string, which is predefined to contain type char, and wstring which is predefined to contain type wchar_t. These can be used to store regular strings of characters and wide characters, respectively.

Public Methods:

```
basic_string<charT,traits,Allocator>&
basic_string<charT,traits,Allocator>::append(
const basic_string<charT,traits,Allocator>&  str);

basic_string<charT,traits,Allocator>&
basic_string<charT,traits,Allocator>::append(
const basic_string<charT,traits,Allocator>&  str,
size_type                                     pos,
size_type                                     n);

basic_string<charT,traits,Allocator>&
basic_string<charT,traits,Allocator>::append(
                  const charT*  s,
                  size_type     n);
```

```
basic_string<charT,traits,Allocator>&
basic_string<charT,traits,Allocator>::append(
                              const charT* s);

basic_string<charT,traits,Allocator>&
basic_string<charT,traits,Allocator>::append(
                    size_type      n,
                    charT          c);

basic_string<charT,traits,Allocator>&
basic_string<charT,traits,Allocator>::append(
                    InputIterator first,
                    InputIterator last);
```

Appends a string to the current string. The first form appends the entire parameter string. The second form appends n elements from str, starting at pos or until the end of the string is reached, whichever comes first. It can throw length_error or out_of_range exceptions depending on the parameter values. The third form appends n elements from s. The fourth form appends the entire array s. The fifth form appends n copies of c. The final form appends the elements from first up to last.

```
basic_string<charT,traits,Allocator>&
basic_string<charT,traits,Allocator>::assign(
  const basic_string<charT,traits,Allocator>&);

basic_string<charT,traits,Allocator>&
basic_string<charT,traits,Allocator>::assign(
const basic_string<charT,traits,Allocator>&  str,
size_type                                    pos,
size_type                                    n);

basic_string<charT,traits,Allocator>&
basic_string<charT,traits,Allocator>::assign(
                    const charT*  s,
                    size_type     n);

basic_string<charT,traits,Allocator>&
basic_string<charT,traits,Allocator>::assign(
                    const charT*  s);

basic_string<charT,traits,Allocator>&
basic_string<charT,traits,Allocator>::assign(
                    size_type     n,
                    charT         c);
```

```
basic_string<charT,traits,Allocator>&
basic_string<charT,traits,Allocator>::assign(
                    InputIterator first,
                    InputIterator last);
```

Assigns a string to the current string. The first form assigns the entire parameter string. The second form assigns n elements from str, starting at pos or until the end of the string is reached, whichever comes first. It can throw an out_of_range exception if pos is greater than the size of the parameter string. The third form assigns n elements from s. The fourth form assigns the entire array s. The fifth form assigns n copies of c. The final form assigns the elements from first up to last.

```
reference
   basic_string<charT,traits,Allocator>::at(
                            size_type pos);
const_reference
   basic_string<charT,traits,Allocator>::at(
                            size_type pos) const;
```

Returns a reference to the element at pos. It can throw an out_of_range exception.

```
explicit
basic_string<charT,traits,Allocator>::basic_string(
            const Allocator&   a = Allocator());

basic_string<charT,traits,Allocator>::basic_string(
const basic_string<charT,traits,Allocator>&   str,
size_type                          pos = 0,
size_type                          n = npos,
const Allocator&                   a = Allocator());

basic_string<charT,traits,Allocator>::basic_string(
            const charT*      s,
            size_type         n,
            const Allocator&  a = Allocator());

basic_string<charT,traits,Allocator>::basic_string(
            const charT*      s,
            const Allocator&  a = Allocator());

basic_string<charT,traits,Allocator>::basic_string(
            size_type         n,
```

```
                    charT             c,
                    const Allocator&  a = Allocator());

basic_string<charT,traits,Allocator>::basic_string(
         InputIterator     begin,
         InputIterator     end,
         const Allocator&  a = Allocator());
```

These are the class constructors. The first form constructs an empty string. The second form constructs a basic_string and initializes it to contain the elements from str, starting at pos and continuing for n elements or to the end of str, whichever is reached first. The third form constructs a basic_string, initializing it with the first n characters from s . The fourth form constructs a basic_string, initializing it with the contents of s. The fifth form initializes a basic_string to contain n copies of c. The final form constructs a basic_string and initializes it to contain the elements from begin up to end. None of the pointers to arrays can be NULL.

```
iterator
  basic_string<charT,traits,Allocator>::begin();
const_iterator
  basic_string<charT,traits,Allocator>::begin();
```

Returns an iterator referencing the start of the basic_string.

```
size_type
basic_string<charT,traits,Allocator>::capacity()
const;
```

Returns the size of the currently allocated storage for the string, which will be greater than or equal to size().

```
void basic_string<charT,traits,Allocator>::clear();
```

Removes all elements from the string, invalidating all pointers, references, and iterators.

```
const charT*
basic_string<charT,traits,Allocator>::c_str();
```

Returns a pointer to a zero-terminated array containing the string contents.

```
int basic_string<charT,traits,Allocator>::compare(
const basic_string<charT,traits,Allocator>& str)
```

```
const;

int basic_string<charT,traits,Allocator>::compare(
size_type                                      pos1,
size_type                                      n1,
const basic_string<charT,traits,Allocator>&   str)
const;

int basic_string<charT,traits,Allocator>::compare(
size_type                                      pos1,
size_type                                      n1,
const basic_string<charT,traits,Allocator>&   str,
size_type                                      pos2,
size_type                                      n2)
const;

int basic_string<charT,traits,Allocator>::compare(
          const charT* s) const;

int basic_string<charT,traits,Allocator>::compare(
          size_type    pos1,
          size_type    n1,
          const charT* s,
          size_type    n2 = npos)
          const;
```

Lexicographically compares the parameter to the string and returns a negative
value if the string is less than the parameter, zero if they are equal, and a
positive value if the string is greater than the parameter. The first form compares the string to the parameter string. The second form compares the string
with the parameter starting at pos1 for n1 elements, or until the end of the
string is reached. The third form compares the string starting at pos1 for
length n1, or end of string, to the n2 elements of str starting at pos2, or
until the end of str. The fourth form compares the string to the array s.
The fifth form compares the n1 elements of the string with the n2 elements
of the array s starting at pos1, or until the end of the string. If the default
value of n2 is used, it will compare all elements in the array.

```
size_type
basic_string<charT,traits,Allocator>::copy(
          charT*       s,
          size_type    n,
          size_type    pos = 0)
          const;
```

Copies n elements, or until the end of string, from the string starting at pos to the array s. This can throw an out_of_range exception if pos is greater than the length of the string.

```
const charT*
basic_string<charT,traits,Allocator>::data();
```

Returns a reference to the first element in the string. If the string is empty, a pointer that cannot be dereferenced is returned.

```
iterator basic_string<charT,traits,Allocator>::end();
const_iterator
    basic_string<charT,traits,Allocator>::end();
```

Returns a past-the-end iterator for the string.

```
bool
basic_string<charT,traits,Allocator>::empty() const;
```

Returns true if the string has no elements.

```
basic_string&
basic_string<charT,traits,Allocator>::erase(
                size_type      pos = 0,
                size_type      n = npos);

iterator
basic_string<charT,traits,Allocator>::erase(
                iterator position);

iterator
basic_string<charT,traits,Allocator>::erase(
                iterator       first,
                iterator       last);
```

Removes the indicated element(s) from the string. The first form removes the n elements, beginning at pos or until the end of the string is reached. It throws an out_of_range exception if pos is greater than the length of the string. The method returns *this. The second form removes the single element referenced by position and returns an iterator referencing the element after the one removed or a past-the-end iterator if the last element is removed. The third form removes the elements from first up to last and returns an iterator referencing the element after the last one removed or a past-the-end iterator if the last element was removed.

```
size_type
basic_string<charT,traits,Allocator>::find(
const basic_string<charT,traits,Allocator>&  str,
size_type                                    pos = 0)
const;

size_type
basic_string<charT,traits,Allocator>::find(
                const charT*    s,
                size_type       pos,
                size_type       n)
                const;

size_type
basic_string<charT,traits,Allocator>::find(
                const charT*    s,
                size_type       pos = 0)
                const;

size_type
basic_string<charT,traits,Allocator>::find(
                charT           c,
                size_type       pos = 0)
                const;
```

Finds the first location of a substring within the string. It either returns the location of the first element of the substring or returns `basic_string::npos`
if the substring is not found. The second form searches for the n elements
from s or until the end of string. The search begins at pos. The third form
searches for all the elements of s starting at pos. The fourth form searches
for the single element c starting at pos.

```
size_type basic_string<charT,traits,Allocator>::
find_first_of(
const basic_string<charT,traits,Allocator>&  str,
size_type                                    pos = 0)
const;

size_type basic_string<charT,traits,Allocator>::
find_first_of(
                const charT*    s,
                size_type       pos,
                size_type       n)
                const;
```

```
size_type basic_string<charT,traits,Allocator>::
find_first_of(
                    const charT*    s,
                    size_type       pos = 0)
                    const;
```

```
size_type basic_string<charT,traits,Allocator>::
find_first_of(
                    charT           c,
                    size_type       pos = 0)
                    const;
```

Returns the first position at which any of the elements in the parameter occur in the string. If none of the elements of the parameter occur in the string, basic_string::npos is returned. The first form searches the string for any of the elements in str from pos onward. The second form searches the string for the n elements in s, starting at pos in the string or until the end of s. The third form searches the string from pos for all elements of s. The fourth form searches the string, starting at pos, for the single element c.

```
size_type basic_string<charT,traits,Allocator>::
find_last_of(
const basic_string<charT,traits,Allocator>&   str,
size_type                             pos = npos)
const;
```

```
size_type basic_string<charT,traits,Allocator>::
find_last_of(
                    const charT*    s,
                    size_type       pos,
                    size_type       n)
                    const;
```

```
size_type basic_string<charT,traits,Allocator>::
find_last_of(
                    const charT*    s,
                    size_type       pos = npos)
                    const;
```

```
size_type basic_string<charT,traits,Allocator>::
find_last_of(
                    charT           c,
                    size_type       pos = npos)
                    const;
```

Finds the last element in the string that matches one of the elements in the parameter. It returns the position or `basic_string::npos` if there is no such element. The first form searches the string for any of the elements in `str` from `pos` onward. The second form searches the string for the n elements in `s`, starting at `pos` in the string or until the end of `s`. The third form searches the string from `pos` for all elements of `s`. The fourth form searches the string, starting at `pos`, for the single element c.

```
size_type basic_string<charT,traits,Allocator>::
find_first_not_of(
const basic_string<charT,traits,Allocator>&  str,
size_type                                    pos = 0)
const;


size_type basic_string<charT,traits,Allocator>::
find_first_not_of(
            const charT*   s,
            size_type      pos,
            size_type      n)
            const;


size_type basic_string<charT,traits,Allocator>::
find_first_not_of(
            const charT*   s,
            size_type      pos = 0)
            const;


size_type basic_string<charT,traits,Allocator>::
find_first_not_of(
            charT          c,
            size_type      pos = 0)
            const;
```

Finds the position of the first element in the string that does not occur in the parameter string. If such an element exists, its position is returned, otherwise `basic_string::npos` is returned. The first form searches the string for any of the elements not in `str` from `pos` onward. The second form searches the string for the n elements not in `s`, starting at `pos` in the string or until the end of `s`. The third form searches the string from `pos` for all elements not in `s`. The fourth form searches the string, starting at `pos`, for the element not equal to the single element c.

```
size_type basic_string<charT,traits,Allocator>::
find_last_not_of(
const basic_string<charT,traits,Allocator>&  str,
size_type                                    pos = npos)
const;

size_type basic_string<charT,traits,Allocator>::
find_last_not_of(
            const charT*  s,
            size_type     pos,
            size_type     n)
            const;

size_type basic_string<charT,traits,Allocator>::
find_last_not_of(
            const charT*  s,
            size_type     pos = npos)
            const;

size_type basic_string<charT,traits,Allocator>::
find_last_not_of(
            charT         c,
            size_type     pos = npos)
            const;
```

Finds the last element in the string that is not in the parameter string. It returns
the position of the element found or `basic_string::npos` if there is no
such element. The first form searches the string for any of the elements not
in str from pos onward. The second form searches the string for the n elements not in s, starting at pos in the string or until the end of s. The third
form searches the string from pos for all elements not in s. The fourth form
searches the string, starting at pos, for the element not equal to the single
element c.

```
allocator_type
basic_string<charT,traits,Allocator>::get_allocator()
   const;
```

Returns a copy of the allocator for the string.

```
basic_string<charT,traits,Allocator>&
basic_string<charT,traits,Allocator>::insert(
size_type                                    pos1,
const basic_string<charT,traits,Allocator>&  str);
```

```
basic_string<charT,traits,Allocator>&
basic_string<charT,traits,Allocator>::insert(
size_type                                       pos1,
const basic_string<charT,traits,Allocator>&     str,
size_type                                       pos2,
size_type                                       n);

basic_string<charT,traits,Allocator>&
basic_string<charT,traits,Allocator>::insert(
          size_type     pos,
          const charT*  s,
          size_type     n);

basic_string<charT,traits,Allocator>&
basic_string<charT,traits,Allocator>::insert(
          size_type     pos,
          const charT*  s);

basic_string<charT,traits,Allocator>&
basic_string<charT,traits,Allocator>::insert(
          size_type     pos,
          size_type     n,
          charT         c);

iterator
basic_string<charT,traits,Allocator>::insert(
          iterator  p,
          charT     c = charT());

void
basic_string<charT,traits,Allocator>::insert(
      iterator      p,
      size_type     n,
      charT         c);

void
basic_string<charT,traits,Allocator>::insert(
      iterator      p,
      InputIterator first,
      InputIterator last);
```

Inserts the parameter string into the string immediately before the indicated position. It returns *this, the string itself, when a nonvoid return type is indicated. Where the number of elements from the parameter string is indicated, it will insert that number of elements or until the end of the parameter string, whichever comes first. The first form inserts the entire contents of str. The second form inserts the n elements of str beginning at pos2. The third form inserts the first n elements of s. The fourth form inserts the entire array s. The fifth form inserts n copies of the element c. The sixth form inserts the single element c. The seventh form inserts n copies of the element c. The eighth form inserts the elements from first up to last.

```
size_type
basic_string<charT,traits,Allocator>::length() const;
```

Returns the number of elements stored in the string.

```
size_type
basic_string<charT,traits,Allocator>::max_size()
const;
```

The maximum number of elements that can be stored in the string.

```
basic_string<charT,traits,Allocator>&
basic_string<charT,traits,Allocator>::replace(
size_type                                     pos1,
size_type                                     n1,
const basic_string<charT,traits,Allocator>&   str);

basic_string<charT,traits,Allocator>&
basic_string<charT,traits,Allocator>::replace(
size_type                                     pos1,
size_type                                     n1,
const basic_string<charT,traits,Allocator>&   str,
size_type                                     pos2,
size_type                                     n2);

basic_string<charT,traits,Allocator>&
basic_string<charT,traits,Allocator>::replace(
              size_type       pos,
              size_type       n1,
              const charT*    s,
              size_type       n2);

basic_string<charT,traits,Allocator>&
basic_string<charT,traits,Allocator>::replace(
```

```
                size_type      pos,
                size_type      n1,
                const charT*   s);

basic_string<charT,traits,Allocator>&
basic_string<charT,traits,Allocator>::replace(
                size_type      pos,
                size_type      n1,
                size_type      n2,
                charT          c);

basic_string<charT,traits,Allocator>&
basic_string<charT,traits,Allocator>::replace(
iterator                                          i1,
iterator                                          i2,
const basic_string<charT,traits,Allocator>&  str);

basic_string<charT,traits,Allocator>&
basic_string<charT,traits,Allocator>::replace(
                iterator       i1,
                iterator       i2,
                const charT*   s,
                size_type      n);

basic_string<charT,traits,Allocator>&
basic_string<charT,traits,Allocator>::replace(
                iterator       i1,
                iterator       i2,
                const charT*   s);

basic_string<charT,traits,Allocator>&
basic_string<charT,traits,Allocator>::replace(
                iterator       i1,
                iterator       i2,
                size_type      n,
                charT          c);

basic_string<charT,traits,Allocator>&
basic_string<charT,traits,Allocator>::replace(
                iterator       i1,
                iterator       i2,
                InputIterator  j1,
                InputIterator  j2);
```

Replaces the indicated range of elements in the string with the replacement elements specified in the parameters. Methods that use a parameter indicating the number of elements will consume this number unless the end of the string is reached. In such a case, the maximum number of elements possible will be used. Use of these methods invalidates pointers, references, and iterators.

The first form replaces the n1 elements in the string from pos1 onward with the elements of str. The second form replaces the n1 elements in the string from pos1 onward with the n2 elements of str from pos2 onward. The third form replaces the n1 elements from pos onward with the n2 elements of the array s. The fourth form replaces the n1 elements of the string from pos onward with all the elements in s. The fifth form replaces the n1 elements of the string from pos onward with the element c. The sixth form replaces the n1 elements of the string from pos onward with n2 copies of the element c. The seventh form replaces the elements from i1 up to i2 by the contents of str. The eighth form replaces the elements from i1 up to i2 with n elements of s. The ninth form replaces the elements from i1 up to i2 by the contents of s. The tenth form replaces the elements from i1 up to i2 by n copies of the element c. The eleventh form replaces the elements from i1 up to i2 by the elements from j1 up to j2.

```
void basic_string<charT,traits,Allocator>::reserve(
          size_type res_arg=0);
```

This is used prior to a change in the size of the string to ensure that adequate memory is allocated. After it is executed, capacity() >= res_arg. All references, pointers, and iterators are invalidated.

```
void basic_string<charT,traits,Allocator>::resize(
          size_type n, charT c);
```

Alters the size of the string. If n is less than or equal to the current size of the string, the string is truncated to the first n characters. If n is greater than the size of the string, a longer string is created whose first size() elements are a copy of the current string contents and whose remaining elements are initialized to c. n must be less than or equal to max_size().

```
size_type
basic_string<charT,traits,Allocator>::rfind(
const basic_string<charT,traits,Allocator>&  str,
size_type                                 pos = npos)
const;
```

```
size_type
basic_string<charT,traits,Allocator>::rfind(
            const charT*   s,
            size_type      pos,
            size_type      n)
            const;

size_type
basic_string<charT,traits,Allocator>::rfind(
            const charT*   s,
            size_type      pos = npos)
            const;

size_type
basic_string<charT,traits,Allocator>::rfind(
            charT          c,
            size_type      pos = npos)
            const;
```

Searches in the reverse direction for the first occurrence of the subsequence specified by the parameter. It begins seraching at pos, which is an offset from the end of the string. It returns the position where the matching subsequence begins in the string or basic_string::npos if there is no occurrence. The first form searches for the contents of str. The second form searches for the first n elements of s or until the end of s if n is greater than the length of s. The third form searches for the entire array s. The fourth form searches for the single element c.

```
size_type
basic_string<charT,traits,Allocator>::size() const;
```

Returns the number of elements stored in the string.

```
basic_string
basic_string<charT,traits,Allocator>::substr(
            size_type      pos = 0,
            size_type      n = npos)
            const;
```

Returns a subsequence of the string whose first element begins at pos and has n elements or until the end of the string is reached. It can throw an out_of_- range exception if pos is greater than the length of the string.

```
void basic_string<charT,traits,Allocator>::swap(
    basic_string<charT,traits,Allocator>& s);
```

Swaps the contents of the string with the string s so that each has the content of
the other.

Nonmember Functions:

```
template<class charT, class traits,
   class Allocator>
basic_string<charT,traits,Allocator>
operator+(
const basic_string<charT,traits,Allocator>&  lhs,
const basic_string<charT,traits,Allocator>&  rhs);

template<class charT, class traits,
   class Allocator>
basic_string<charT,traits,Allocator>
operator+(
const charT*                                 lhs,
const basic_string<charT,traits,Allocator>&  rhs);

template<class charT, class traits,
   class Allocator>
basic_string<charT,traits,Allocator>
operator+(
charT                                        lhs,
const basic_string<charT,traits,Allocator>&  rhs);

template<class charT, class traits,
   class Allocator>
basic_string<charT,traits,Allocator>
operator+(
const basic_string<charT,traits,Allocator>&  lhs,
const charT*                                 rhs);

template<class charT, class traits,
   class Allocator>
basic_string<charT,traits,Allocator>
operator+(
const basic_string<charT,traits,Allocator>&  lhs,
charT                                        rhs);
```

Returns the result of appending rhs to lhs.

```
template<class charT, class traits,
   class Allocator>
bool operator==(
const basic_string<charT,traits,Allocator>&  lhs,
```

```
                    const basic_string<charT,traits,Allocator>&  rhs);

template<class charT, class traits,
   class Allocator>
bool operator==(
const charT*                                             lhs,
const basic_string<charT,traits,Allocator>&  rhs);

template<class charT, class traits,
   class Allocator>
bool operator==(
const basic_string<charT,traits,Allocator>&  lhs,
const charT*                                             rhs);
```

Returns true if lhs is equal to rhs.

```
template<class charT, class traits,
   class Allocator>
bool operator!=(
const basic_string<charT,traits,Allocator>&  lhs,
const basic_string<charT,traits,Allocator>&  rhs);

template<class charT, class traits,
   class Allocator>
bool operator!=(
const charT*                                             lhs,
const basic_string<charT,traits,Allocator>&  rhs);

template<class charT, class traits,
   class Allocator>
bool operator!=(
const basic_string<charT,traits,Allocator>&  lhs,
const charT*                                             rhs);
```

Returns true if lhs is not equal to rhs.

```
template<class charT, class traits,
   class Allocator>
bool operator<(
const basic_string<charT,traits,Allocator>&  lhs,
const basic_string<charT,traits,Allocator>&  rhs);

template<class charT, class traits,
   class Allocator>
bool operator<(
const charT*                                             lhs,
```

```
                              const basic_string<charT,traits,Allocator>&  rhs);

template<class charT, class traits,
   class Allocator>
bool operator<(
const basic_string<charT,traits,Allocator>&  lhs,
const charT*                                 rhs);
```

Returns true if lhs is lexicographically less than rhs.

```
template<class charT, class traits,
   class Allocator>
bool operator>(
const basic_string<charT,traits,Allocator>&  lhs,
const basic_string<charT,traits,Allocator>&  rhs);

template<class charT, class traits,
   class Allocator>
bool operator>(
const charT*                                 lhs,
const basic_string<charT,traits,Allocator>&  rhs);

template<class charT, class traits,
   class Allocator>
bool operator>(
const basic_string<charT,traits,Allocator>&  lhs,
const charT*                                 rhs);
```

Returns true if lhs is lexicographically greater than rhs.

```
template<class charT, class traits,
   class Allocator>
bool operator<=(
const basic_string<charT,traits,Allocator>&  lhs,
const basic_string<charT,traits,Allocator>&  rhs);

template<class charT, class traits,
   class Allocator>
bool operator<=(
const charT*                                 lhs,
const basic_string<charT,traits,Allocator>&  rhs);

template<class charT, class traits,
   class Allocator>
bool operator<=(
```

```
const basic_string<charT,traits,Allocator>&   lhs,
const charT*                                   rhs);
```

Returns `true` if `lhs` is lexicographically less than or equal to `rhs`.

```
template<class charT, class traits,
   class Allocator>
bool operator>=(
const basic_string<charT,traits,Allocator>&   lhs,
const basic_string<charT,traits,Allocator>&   rhs);

template<class charT, class traits,
   class Allocator>
bool operator>=(
const charT*                                   lhs,
const basic_string<charT,traits,Allocator>&   rhs);

template<class charT, class traits,
   class Allocator>
bool operator>=(
const basic_string<charT,traits,Allocator>&   lhs,
const charT*                                   rhs);
```

Returns `true` if `lhs` is lexicographically greater than or equal to `rhs`.

```
template<class charT, class traits,
   class Allocator>
void swap(
basic_string<charT,traits,Allocator>&   lhs,
basic_string<charT,traits,Allocator>&   rhs);
```

Swaps the contents of `lhs` with `rhs`.

```
template<class charT, class traits,
   class Allocator>
basic_istream<charT,traits>& operator>>(
basic_istream<charT,traits>&            is,
basic_string<charT,traits,Allocator>&   str);
```

Extracts a string from `is` into `str` until either `is.width()` elements are extracted, `str.max_size()` elements are extracted, EOF is encountered, or a space is found in the input stream. `isspace()` is used to determine if the element is a space.

```
template<class charT, class traits,
   class Allocator>
basic_ostream<charT, traits>& operator<<(
basic_ostream<charT, traits>&                os,
const basic_string<charT,traits,Allocator>&  str);
```

Inserts the string str into the stream os.

```
template<class charT, class traits,
   class Allocator>
basic_istream<charT,traits>& getline(
   basic_istream<charT,traits>&              is,
   basic_string<charT,traits,Allocator>&  str,
   charT                                  delim);

template<class charT, class traits,
   class Allocator>
basic_istream<charT,traits>& getline(
   basic_istream<charT,traits>&              is,
   basic_string<charT,traits,Allocator>&  str);
```

The first form extracts elements from is into str, replacing the contents of str, until EOF is encountered, is.max_size() elements are extracted, or delim is encountered. The second form does the same thing but uses '\n' as a delimiter.

binary_function

TYPE: struct   **HEADER:** <functional> [function.h]

```
namespace std{
template <class Arg1, class Arg2, class Result>
   struct binary_function;
}
```

DESCRIPTION: This is a base struct from which all the function objects that are binary_functions are derived. It models a function that requires two parameters. Any function conforming to the definition of a binary_function must define first_argument_type, second_argument_type, and result_type.

SEE ALSO: unary_function

Public Members:

```
binary_function<class Arg1, class Arg2,
   class Result>::
   first_argument_type;
```

The type of the first argument to the function.

```
binary_function<class Arg1, class Arg2,
   class Result>::
   second_argument_type;
```

The type of the second argument to the function.

```
binary_function<class Arg1, class Arg2,
   class Result>::
   result_type;
```

The type of the result of the function.

binary_negate

TYPE: adaptor   **HEADER:** <functional> [function.h]

```
namespace std{
   template <class Predicate>
   class binary_negate
   : public binary_function<
        typename Predicate::first_argument_type,
        typename Predicate::second_argument_type,
        bool>;
}
```

DESCRIPTION: This is a function adaptor that logically negates the result of a binary predicate. The predicate must satisfy the requirements of a binary_function. The adaptor not2 is more convenient to use and performs the same operation.

SEE ALSO: binary_function, not2, unary_negate

Public Methods:

```
explicit binary_negate<Predicate>::binary_negate(
                  const Predicate& pred);
```

This is the constructor to which is passed the function object to be negated.

```
bool binary_negate<Predicate>::operator()(
            const first_argument_type&  x,
            const second_argument_type& y) const;
```

This is the `operator()` which is the way all function objects are invoked. This returns the negation of the result returned by `pred(x, y)`.

binary_search

TYPE: function   **HEADER:** <algorithm> [algo.h]
TIME: logarithmic   **SPACE:** constant

```
namespace std{
template <class ForwardIterator, class T>
bool binary_search(ForwardIterator  first,
                   ForwardIterator  last,
                   const T&         value);

template <class ForwardIterator, class T,
    class Compare>
bool binary_search(ForwardIterator  first,
                   ForwardIterator  last,
                   const T&         value,
                   Compare          comp);
}
```

DESCRIPTION: This performs a binary search of the range from `first` to `last` for `value`. It returns a Boolean `true` if `value` is found, otherwise `false`.

bind1st

TYPE: adaptor   **HEADER:** <functional> [function.h]

```
namespace std{
template <class Operation, class T>
binder1st<Operation> bind1st(
      const Operation&  op,
      const T&          x);
}
```

DESCRIPTION: This creates a new function object that is identical to `op`, but that has x bound as the first parameter of the function object `op`.

SEE ALSO: binder1st, bind2nd

bind2nd

TYPE: adaptor   **HEADER:** <functional> [function.h]

```
namespace std{
template <class Operation, class T>
binder2nd<Operation> bind2nd(
      const Operation&    op,
      const T&            x);
}
```

DESCRIPTION: This creates and returns a function object that accepts two parameters. When invoked, this function object will apply op to the first parameter, using x as the second parameter, and return the result.

SEE ALSO: binder2nd, bind1st

binder1st

TYPE: adaptor   **HEADER:** <functional> [function.h]

```
namespace std{
  template <class Operation>
  class binder1st
  : public unary_function<
       typename Operation::second_argument_type,
       typename Operation::result_type>;
}
```

DESCRIPTION: This is a function object adaptor that is returned as the result of the function bind1st(). It binds a constant to the first parameter of a function object. binder1st can itself be adapted, since it is a unary_function.

SEE ALSO: bind1st, binder2nd

Public Methods:

```
binder1st<Operation>::binder1st(
   const Operation&                     x,
   const Operation::first_argument_type& y);
```

The class constructor that requires x to be a `binary_function` and y to be a valid value for the first argument of x. It binds y as the value of the first argument of x.

```
typename Operation::result_type
binder1st<Operation>::operator()(
    const argument_type& v) const;
```

Since `binder1st` is itself a function object, it defines `operator()`. This invokes the operation as `x(y, v)`, where v is the argument to `operator()` and y is the value bound to the first parameter.

binder2nd

TYPE: adaptor   **HEADER:** <functional> [function.h]

```
namespace std{
    template <class Operation>
    class binder2nd
    : public unary_function<
        typename Operation::first_argument_type,
        typename Operation::result_type>;
}
```

DESCRIPTION: This is a function object adaptor that is returned as the result of the function `bind2nd()`. It binds a constant to the second parameter of a function object. `binder2nd` can itself be adapted, since it is a `unary_function`.

SEE ALSO: bind2nd, binder1st

Public Members:

```
binder2nd<Operation>::value;
```

Defined as `Operation::second_argument_type`.

Public Methods:

```
binder2nd<Operation>::binder2nd(
    const Operation&                          x,
    const Operation::second_argument_type&    y);
```

The class constructor that requires x to be a `binary_function` and y to be a valid value for the second argument of x. It binds y as the value of the second argument of x.

```
typename Operation::result_type
binder2nd<Operation>::operator()(
    const Operation::first_argument_type& v) const;
```

Since binder2nd is itself a function object, it defines `operator()`. This invokes the operation as `x(v, y)`, where v is the argument to `operator()` and y is the value bound to the second parameter.

bitset

TYPE: class   **HEADER:** <bitset> [bvector.h]

```
namespace std {
    template<size_t N>
    class bitset;
}
```

DESCRIPTION: The bitset is a substitute for `vector<bool>` that is provided for compilers that do not fully support the type `bool`. It is very similar to a `vector`, with the addition of a few operators that are specific to Boolean operations.

SEE ALSO: vector

Public Members:

```
bitset<N>::reference;
```

A reference to a member of the bitset.

Public Methods:

```
bool bitset<N>::any() const;
```

Returns `true` if any bit in `*this` is 1.

```
size_t bitset<N>::count() const;
```

Returns a count of the number of bits set to 1.

```
bitset<N>& bitset<N>::flip();
bitset<N>& bitset<N>::flip(size_t pos);
```

The first form negates all of the bits in *this. The second form negates the bit in position pos. out_of_range will be thrown if pos is invalid.

```
bool bitset<N>::none() const;
```

Returns true if no bit in *this is 1.

```
bitset<N> bitset<N>::operator<<(size_t pos) const;
```

Returns (*this) <<= pos.

```
bitset<N> bitset<N>::operator>>(size_t pos) const;
```

Returns (*this) >>= pos.

```
bitset<N>& bitset<N>::operator&=(
        const bitset<N>& rhs);
```

AND's rhs into *this.

```
bitset<N>& bitset<N>::operator|=(
        const bitset<N>& rhs);
```

OR's rhs into *this.

```
bitset<N>& bitset<N>::operator^=(
        const bitset<N>& rhs);
```

Exclusive OR's rhs into *this.

```
bitset<N>& bitset<N>::operator<<=(size_t pos);
```

Replaces each bit with the bit pos positions before it. Bits whose position is less than pos are replaced by zero.

```
bitset<N>& bitset<N>::operator>>=(size_t pos);
```

Replaces each bit with the bit pos positions after it. Bits whose position is greater than or equal to N - pos are replaced by 0.

```
bitset<N> bitset<N>::operator~() const;
```

Returns a bitset equal to *this with all the bits negated.

```
bool bitset<N>::operator==(const bitset<N>& rhs)
    const;
```

Returns true if every bit in *this equals the corresponding bit in rhs.

```
bool bitset<N>::operator!=(const bitset<N>& rhs)
    const;
```

Returns !(*this == rhs).

```
bitset<N>& bitset<N>::reset();
bitset<N>& bitset<N>::reset(size_t pos);
```

The first form sets all the bits to 0. The second form sets the bit at position pos to 0. out_of_range will be thrown if pos is invalid.

```
bitset<N>& bitset<N>::set();
bitset<N>& bitset<N>::set(size_t pos, int val = 1);
```

The first form sets all bits to 1. The second form sets the bit at position pos to 0 or 1, depending on whether val is zero or nonzero. out_of_range will be thrown if pos is invalid.

```
size_t bitset<N>::size() const;
```

Returns the number of bits in *this.

```
bool bitset<N>::test(size_t pos) const;
```

Returns true if the bit at position pos is 1. out_of_range will be thrown if pos is invalid.

```
template <class charT, class traits, class Allocator>
basic_string<charT, traits, Allocator>
bitset<N>::to_string() const;
```

Converts the bitset to a character string with 1 bits represented as the character "1" and 0 bits represented as "0". The order of the characters is the reverse of the order of the bits.

```
unsigned long bitset<N>::to_ulong() const;
```

Converts the bits to a long value. Throws overflow_error if the bits cannot be represented as a long.

Nonmember Functions:

```
bitset<N> operator&(const bitset<N>&    lhs,
                    const bitset<N>&    rhs);
```

Returns the AND of the two bitsets.

```
bitset<N> operator|(const bitset<N>&    lhs,
                    const bitset<N>&    rhs);
```

Returns the OR of the two bitsets.

```
bitset<N> operator^(const bitset<N>&    lhs,
                    const bitset<N>&    rhs);
```

Returns the exclusive OR of the two bitsets.

```
template <class charT, class traits, size_t N>
basic_istream<charT, traits>&
operator>>(basic_istream<charT, traits>&    is,
                    bitset<N>&               x);
```

Reads up to N single byte characters from the stream terminating when N characters have been read, end-of-file is found, or a character that is neither 0 nor 1 is found. The result is converted to a bitset and returned in x.

```
template <class charT, class traits, size_t N>
basic_ostream<charT, traits>&
operator<<(basic_ostream<charT, traits>&    os,
                    const bitset<N>&          x);
```

Inserts the string representation of the bitset, as returned by x.to_string(), into the stream os.

char_traits

TYPE: struct   **HEADER:** <string> []

```
namespace std{
  template<class T>
  struct char_traits;
}
```

DESCRIPTION: A structure defining types and methods that allow string operations to be performed on a string-like type. Specializations are provided for actual types commonly used to represent characters. It is used as a template parameter of other classes, such as `basic_string`, so that they can handle different character representations.

Public Members:

```
char_traits<T>::char_type;
```

The type T that is the type of the character.

```
char_traits<T>::int_type;
```

A type that can represent all the valid characters in T as well as an end-of-file character.

```
char_traits<T>::off_type;
```

A type that can represent the difference between two `char_traits<T>::pos_type` values.

```
char_traits<T>::pos_type;
```

A type that can represent the position of a character in a file.

```
char_traits<T>::state_type;
```

A type that can represent a state in a multibyte character encoding.

Public Methods:

```
void char_traits<T>::assign(char_type&      x,
                            const char_type&  y);
```

Assigns x = y.

```
char_type* char_traits<T>::assign(char_type* s,
                                  size_t     n,
                                  char_type  c);
```

Assigns the n characters in s the value c. It returns s.

```
int char_traits<T>::compare(const char_type* s1,
                            const char_type* s2,
                            size_t           n);
```

Compares two arrays s1 and s2 of length n and returns a negative value if s1 is lexicographically less than s1, zero if s1 is equal to s2, and a positive value if s1 is greater than s2.

```
char_type*
char_traits<T>::copy(char_type*       s1,
                     const char_type* s2,
                     size_t           n);
```

Copies the first n characters from s2 to s1. s1 and s2 cannot overlap. It returns s1 + n.

```
int_type char_traits<T>::eof();
```

Returns the end-of-file value.

```
bool char_traits<T>::eq(const char_type& c,
                        const char_type& d);
```

Returns true if c is equal to d.

```
bool
char_traits<T>::eq_int_type(const int_type& c,
                            const int_type& d);
```

Returns true if c equals d.

```
char_type*
char_traits<T>::find(const char_type* s,
                     size_t           n,
                     const char_type& c);
```

Returns a pointer to the first occurrence of c in s, or 0 if not found.

```
state_type char_traits<T>::get_state(pos_type p);
```

Returns the state of the character in position p.

```
bool char_traits<T>::lt(const char_type&    c,
                        const char_type&    d);
```

Returns true if c is less than d.

```
char_type*
char_traits<T>::move(char_type*        s1,
                     const char_type*  s2,
                     size_t            n);
```

Copies the first n values from s2 to s1. s1 and s2 can overlap. It returns s1
   + n.

```
int_type char_traits<T>::not_eof(const int_type& c);
```

Returns c if c is not the end-of-file (EOF) value; otherwise, returns a value that
   is not the EOF value.

```
char_type
char_traits<T>::to_char_type(const int_type& i);
```

Returns the char_type value representing i.

```
int_type
char_traits<T>::to_int_type(const char_type& c);
```

Returns the int_type value representing c.

compose1

TYPE: adaptor   **HEADER:** <> [function.h]

```
template <class Operation1, class Operation2>
unary_compose<Operation1, Operation2>
compose1(const Operation1&    op1,
   const Operation2&         op2);
```

DESCRIPTION: Returns a new function object that is the combination of the two function objects passed as parameters. The effect is to first apply `op2` and then apply `op1` to the result of the first function object. This is only in the HP implementation and has been removed from the C++ standard.

SEE ALSO: compose2

---

compose2

TYPE: adaptor   **HEADER:** <> [function.h]

```
template <class Operation1, class Operation2,
    class Operation3>
binary_compose<Operation1, Operation2, Operation3>
compose2(const Operation1& op1,
        const Operation2& op2,
        const Operation3& op3);
```

DESCRIPTION: This combines the three separate function objects into a single function object. The resultant function applies the parameter functions in the order `op1(op2(x), op2(x))`. This is only in the HP implementation and has been removed from the C++ standard.

SEE ALSO: compose1

---

const_iterator

TYPE: typedef   **REQUIRED BY:** all containers

DESCRIPTION: A typedef provided by all containers defining a constant iterator for the container.

SEE ALSO: iterator

---

const_reference

TYPE: typedef   **REQUIRED BY:** all containers

DESCRIPTION: A typedef provided by all containers that is a constant reference to the object type stored in the container.

SEE ALSO: reference

copy

TYPE: function   **HEADER:** <algorithm> [algobase.h]
TIME: linear   **SPACE:** constant

```
namespace std{
template <class InputIterator, class OutputIterator>
OutputIterator copy(InputIterator    first,
                    InputIterator    last,
                    OutputIterator   result);
}
```

DESCRIPTION: This copies all elements from first up to but not including last to the location referred to by result. It returns an iterator that refers to the location one past the end of the destination. The source and destination ranges may overlap only if result <= first.

copy_backward

TYPE: function   **HEADER:** <algorithm> [algobase.h]
TIME: linear   **SPACE:** constant

```
namespace std{
template <class BidirectionalIterator1,
  class BidirectionalIterator2>
BidirectionalIterator2
copy_backward(BidirectionalIterator1    first,
              BidirectionalIterator1    last,
              BidirectionalIterator2    result);
}
```

DESCRIPTION: This copies the sequence from first up to but not including last to a location whose upper end is indicated by result. It returns an iterator that references the last element copied, which will be the start of the sequence in the destination. The source and destination ranges may overlap only if result >= last.

count

TYPE: function   **HEADER:** <algorithm> [algo.h]
TIME: linear   **SPACE:** constant

```
namespace std{
  template <class InputIterator, class T>
  typename
  iterator_traits<InputIterator>::difference_type
  count(InputIterator    first,
       InputIterator    last,
       const T&         value);
}
```

DESCRIPTION: Traverses the range from first up to last and produces a count of all elements equal to value. No order of the elements is assumed, and the entire range is searched.

count_if

TYPE: function	**HEADER:** <algorithm> [algo.h]
TIME: linear	**SPACE:** constant

```
namespace std{
  template <class InputIterator, class Predicate>
  typename
  iterator_traits<InputIterator>::difference_type
  count_if(InputIterator  first,
       InputIterator    last,
       Predicate        pred);
}
```

DESCRIPTION: Counts all the elements in the range first up to last that satisfy the predicate pred. No order of the elements is assumed, and the entire range is searched.

deque

TYPE: class   **HEADER:** <deque> [deque.h]

```
namespace std {
  template <class T, class Allocator = allocator<T> >
  class deque;
}
```

DESCRIPTION: A deque is a container that can store a sequence of objects. It provides constant time insertion and deletion at the beginning and end of the sequence. Linear time insertion and deletion are provided for elements in the interior of the sequence. Deques support random access iterators so that you can access the contents in a nonsequential fashion. Deques are optimized for insertion and deletion at either end of the sequence and should be used in applications requiring this behavior.

SEE ALSO: list, vector

Public Members:

```
deque<T, Allocator>::allocator_type;
```

The type of the allocator.

```
deque<T, Allocator>::const_iterator;
```

A constant iterator for the container.

```
deque<T, Allocator>::const_pointer;
```

The type of a constant pointer to the content.

```
deque<T, Allocator>::const_reference;
```

The type of a constant reference to the content.

```
deque<T, Allocator>::const_reverse_iterator;
```

A constant reverse iterator for the container.

```
deque<T, Allocator>::difference_type;
```

Able to represent the difference between any two iterators.

```
deque<T, Allocator>::iterator;
```

An iterator for the container.

```
deque<T, Allocator>::pointer;
```

The type of a pointer to the content.

```
deque<T, Allocator>::reference;
```

The type of a reference to the content.

```
deque<T, Allocator>::reverse_iterator;
```

A reverse iterator for the container.

```
deque<T, Allocator>::size_type;
```

Able to represent any non-negative value of difference_type.

```
deque<T, Allocator>::value_type;
```

The type stored in the container.

Public Methods:

```
void deque<T, Allocator>::assign(
          size_type    n,
          const T&     value);

template<class InputIterator>
void deque<T, Allocator>::assign(
          InputIterator first,
          InputIterator last);
```

These methods erase the content of the deque and replace it with new values
    specified by the parameters. The first form fills the deque with n copies of
    value. The second form inserts the values from first up to last.

```
reference deque<T, Allocator>::at(size_type n);
const_reference deque<T, Allocator>::at( size_type n)
    const;
```

Returns a reference to the nth element of the deque. n must be less than
    size().

```
reference deque<T, Allocator>::back();
const_reference deque<T, Allocator>::back() const;
```

Returns the last element in the deque.

```
iterator deque<T, Allocator>::begin();
const_iterator deque<T, Allocator>::begin() const;
```

Returns an iterator that references the first element in the deque.

```
void deque<T, Allocator>::clear();
```

Erases all elements in the deque.

```
explicit deque<T, Allocator>::deque(
          const Allocator& = allocator());
deque<T, Allocator>::deque(
          size_type           n,
          const T&            value = T(),
          const Allocator& = allocator());
template<class InputIterator>
deque<T, Allocator>::deque(
          InputIterator       first,
          InputIterator       last,
          const Allocator& = allocator());
deque<T, Allocator>::deque(
          const deque<T, Allocator>& x);
```

The first form constructs an empty deque. The second form constructs a deque
   containing n copies of value. The third form constructs a deque containing
   the elements from first up to last. The fourth form is the copy
   constructor.

```
deque<T, Allocator>::~deque();
```

Destroys the deque and its contents.

```
bool deque<T, Allocator>::empty() const;
```

Returns a Boolean value indicating if the deque is empty.

```
iterator deque<T, Allocator>::end();
const_iterator deque<T, Allocator>::end() const;
```

Returns an iterator that is one past the last element in the deque.

```
iterator deque<T, Allocator>::erase(
                iterator position);
iterator deque<T, Allocator>::erase(
```

```
              iterator      first,
              iterator      last);
```

Deletes the element at the indicated position from the deque. The second form
deletes all elements in the range from first up to last. An iterator referencing the element after the last element erased is returned. Only iterators,
pointers, and references to the erased elements are invalidated.

```
reference deque<T, Allocator>::front();
const_reference deque<T, Allocator>::front() const;
```

Returns the first element in the deque.

```
allocator_type deque<T, Allocator>::get_allocator()
    const;
```

Returns the allocator for the container.

```
iterator deque<T, Allocator>::insert(
                iterator  position,
                const T&  x);
template<class InputIterator>
void deque<T, Allocator>::insert(
                iterator              position,
                InputIterator         first,
                Inputterator          last);
void deque<T, Allocator>::insert(
                iterator          position,
                size_type         n,
                const T&          x);
```

Inserts the element x just before position. The first form returns an iterator
that references the element just inserted. The second form inserts the elements from first up to last just before position. The third form inserts n copies of the element x just before position.

```
size_type deque<T, Allocator>::max_size() const;
```

Returns the maximum number of elements that can be stored in the deque.

```
reference deque<T, Allocator>::operator[](
    size_type n);
const_reference deque<T, Allocator>::operator[](
    size_type n) const;
```

Returns a reference to the nth element of the deque. n must be less than
  `size()`.

```
deque<T, Allocator>& deque<T, Allocator>::operator=(
           const deque<T, Allocator>& x);
```

Assigns `*this` the contents of the deque x.

```
void deque<T, Allocator>::pop_back();
```

Deletes the last element in the deque.

```
void deque<T, Allocator>::pop_front();
```

Deletes the first element in the deque.

```
void deque<T, Allocator>::push_back(const T& x);
```

Appends the element x to the end of the deque.

```
void deque<T, Allocator>::push_front(const T& x);
```

Inserts the element x at the beginning of the deque.

```
reverse_iterator deque<T, Allocator>::rbegin();
const_reverse_iterator deque<T, Allocator>::rbegin()
  const;
```

Returns an iterator that is one past the end of the deque and can be used as the
  starting value for a reverse iterator.

```
reverse_iterator deque<T, Allocator>::rend();
const_reverse_iterator deque<T, Allocator>::rend()
  const;
```

Returns an iterator that can be used to find the end for a reverse iteration.

```
void deque<T, Allocator>::resize(
                          size_type size,
                          T         value = T());
```

Changes the size of the deque so that it contains `size` members. If the deque has less than `size` elements, new elements are appended to make it the desired length, with the new elements assigned `value`. If the deque has more than `size` elements, elements are removed from the end to make it the desired length. If the deque is the desired length, nothing is done.

```
size_type deque<T, Allocator>::size() const;
```

Returns the number of elements currently stored in the deque.

```
void deque<T, Allocator>::swap(
                        deque<T, Allocator>& x);
```

Swaps the contents of the object deque with the deque x so that each has the contents of the other.

Nonmember Functions:

```
template <class T, Allocator>
bool operator==(const deque<T, Allocator>& x,
                const deque<T, Allocator>& y);
```

Returns a Boolean indicating if the two deques are equal.

```
template <class T, Allocator>
bool operator!=(const deque<T, Allocator>& x,
                const deque<T, Allocator>& y);
```

Returns a Boolean indicating if the two deques are not equal.

```
template <class T, Allocator>
bool operator<(const deque<T, Allocator>& x,
               const deque<T, Allocator>& y);
```

Performs a lexicographical comparison to determine if the first deque is less than the second.

```
template <class T, Allocator>
bool operator>(const deque<T, Allocator>& x,
               const deque<T, Allocator>& y);
```

Performs a lexicographical comparison to determine if the first deque is greater than the second.

```
template <class T, Allocator>
bool operator>=(const deque<T, Allocator>&   x,
                const deque<T, Allocator>&   y);
```

Performs a lexicographical comparison to determine if the first deque is greater than or equal to the second.

```
template <class T, Allocator>
bool operator<=(const deque<T, Allocator>&   x,
                const deque<T, Allocator>&   y);
```

Performs a lexicographical comparison to determine if the first deque is less than or equal to the second.

```
template<class T, class Allocator>
void swap(deque<T, Allocator>& a,
          deque<T, Allocator>&    b);
```

Swaps the contents of the deque a with the deque b.

difference_type

TYPE: typedef   **REQUIRED BY:** all containers

DESCRIPTION: A typedef provided by all containers defining the type for the difference of two iterators.

distance

TYPE: function   **HEADER:** <iterator> [algobase.h]
TIME: linear   **SPACE:** constant

```
namespace std{
  template <class InputIterator>
  typename
  iterator_traits<InputIterator>::difference_type
  distance(InputIterator        first,
           InputIterator        last);
}
```

DESCRIPTION: Determines the distance between the iterators `first` and `last` and returns this. The distance is the number of times the iterator `first` must be incremented to become equal to `last`. The function uses `operator+` and `operator-` for random access iterators yielding a constant time implementation. Input, forward, and bidirectional iterators use `operator++` and `operator--`, yielding a linear time implementation. The signature of this function has been changed from the HP implementation.

distance_type

TYPE: function   **HEADER:** <> [iterator.h]
TIME: constant   **SPACE:** constant

```
template <class T, class Distance>
inline Distance* distance_type(
  const input_iterator<T, Distance>&);

template <class T, class Distance>
inline Distance* distance_type(
  const forward_iterator<T, Distance>&);

template <class T, class Distance>
inline Distance* distance_type(
  const bidirectional_iterator<T, Distance>&);

template <class T, class Distance>
inline Distance* distance_type(
  const random_access_iterator<T, Distance>&);

template <class T>
inline ptrdiff_t* distance_type(const T*);
```

DESCRIPTION: When an iterator is passed to this function, it returns a pointer to the type that the iterator uses to represent the difference between pointers. The value of this pointer is always zero and is not intended to be used—only the type is important. This function is used to specialize algorithms to take advantage of the capabilities of specific iterator categories. This function might not exist in all implementations, and it has been removed from the C++ standard. The same functionality can be obtained using the expression `iterator_traits<iter>::difference_type`.

SEE ALSO: iterator_category, value_type

divides

TYPE: function object   **HEADER:** <functional> [function.h]
TIME: constant   **SPACE:** constant

```
namespace std{
  template <class T>
  struct divides: binary_function<T, T, T> {
    T operator()(const T& x, const T& y) const;
  };
}
```

DESCRIPTION: A function object that can be passed to another function as a substitute for operator/. It applies operator/ to its two parameters and returns the result.

SEE ALSO: minus, multiplies, plus, modulus

equal

TYPE: function   **HEADER:** <algorithm> [algobase.h]
TIME: linear   **SPACE:** constant

```
namespace std{
template <class InputIterator1,
      class InputIterator2>
  bool equal(InputIterator1    first1,
         InputIterator1    last1,
       InputIterator2    first2);

template <class InputIterator1, class InputIterator2,
      class BinaryPredicate>
bool equal(InputIterator1 first1,
      InputIterator1    last1,
      InputIterator2    first2,
      BinaryPredicate    binary_pred);
}
```

DESCRIPTION: Compares two ranges and returns a Boolean indicating if they are equal on an element-by-element basis. The first range begins with first1 and continues up to last1. The second range begins at first2 and has the same length as the first range. The first form performs the comparison using operator==, and the second allows the specification of an alternate comparison operator.

equal_range

TYPE: function   **HEADER:** <algorithm> [algo.h]
TIME: logarithmic   **SPACE:** constant

```
namespace std{
  template <class ForwardIterator, class T>
  pair<ForwardIterator,ForwardIterator>
  equal_range(ForwardIterator  first,
              ForwardIterator  last,
              const T&         value);

  template <class ForwardIterator, class T, class
  Compare>
  pair<ForwardIterator,ForwardIterator>
  equal_range(ForwardIterator  first,
      ForwardIterator          last,
      const T&                 value,
      Compare                  comp);
}
```

DESCRIPTION: Searches the range from `first` up to `last` looking for a range of elements, all of which are equal to `value`. It returns a pair of iterators that indicate the start and end of the range meeting the requirements. If no such range exists, the pair contains two iterators equal to `first`. The sequence being searched is assumed to be sorted into ascending order. The second form allows you to specify a comparison operator other than the default, `operator<`.

fill

TYPE: function   **HEADER:** <algorithm> [algobase.h]
TIME: linear   **SPACE:** constant

```
namespace std{
  template <class ForwardIterator, class T>
  void fill(ForwardIterator  first,
            ForwardIterator  last,
            const T&         value);
}
```

DESCRIPTION: Assigns `value` to all elements in the range from `first` up to `last`.

fill_n

TYPE: function   **HEADER:** <algorithm> [algobase.h]
TIME: linear   **SPACE:** constant

```
namespace std{
  template <class OutputIterator, class Size,
  class T>
  void fill_n(OutputIterator  first,
      Size                n,
      const T&            value);
}
```

DESCRIPTION: Assigns value to the next n elements beginning with first.

find

TYPE: function   **HEADER:** <algorithm> [algo.h]
TIME: linear   **SPACE:** constant

```
namespace std{
  template <class InputIterator, class T>
  InputIterator find(InputIterator first,
                     InputIterator  last,
                     const T&       value);
}
```

DESCRIPTION: Searches the range from first up to last for value. If found, it returns an iterator referring to the first occurrence of value. If not found, it returns an iterator equal to last. No assumptions about the order of the sequence are made.

find_end

TYPE: function   **HEADER:** <algorithm> []
TIME: (last1 - first1) * (last2 - first2)   **SPACE:** constant

```
namespace std{
    template <class ForwardIterator1,
        class ForwardIterator2>
    ForwardIterator1 find_end(
                ForwardIterator1  first1,
                ForwardIterator1  last1,
                ForwardIterator2  first2,
```

```
                              ForwardIterator2   last2);

      template <class ForwardIterator1,
          class ForwardIterator2,
          class BinaryPredicate>
      ForwardIterator1 find_end(
              ForwardIterator1   first1,
              ForwardIterator1   last1,
              ForwardIterator2   first2,
              ForwardIterator2   last2,
              BinaryPredicate    comp);
  }
```

DESCRIPTION: This searches the sequence from first1 up to last1 to find the last occurrence of the subsequence from first2 up to last2. It either returns an iterator referencing the start of the subsequence in the sequence from first1 up to last1, or last1 if the subsequence is not found. This is similar to the search() function, which finds the first occurrence of a subsequence in a sequence. The predicate version uses the function object pred instead of the default operator==.

SEE ALSO: search

find_first_of

TYPE: function   **HEADER:** <algorithm> []
TIME: n * m   **SPACE:** constant

```
namespace std{
  template<class ForwardIterator1, class
      ForwardIterator2>
  ForwardIterator1 find_first_of(
          ForwardIterator1   first1,
          ForwardIterator1   last1,
          ForwardIterator2   first2,
          ForwardIterator2   last2);

  template<class ForwardIterator1, class
      ForwardIterator2, class BinaryPredicate>
  ForwardIterator1 find_first_of(
          ForwardIterator1   first1,
          ForwardIterator1   last1,
          ForwardIterator2   first2,
          ForwardIterator2   last2,
```

```
                  BinaryPredicate      pred);
}
```

DESCRIPTION: find_first_of() locates the first occurrence of any member of the subsequence from first2 up to last2, of length m, within the sequence from first1 up to last1, of length n. It returns an iterator referencing the location of the first occurrence of an element of the subsequence within the sequence, or last1 if there is no such element. The second form of the function allows the specification of a comparison function other than the default, operator==.

SEE ALSO: find

find_if

TYPE: function   **HEADER:** <algorithm> [algo.h]
TIME: linear   **SPACE:** constant

```
namespace std{
  template <class InputIterator, class Predicate>
  InputIterator find_if(InputIterator     first,
                        InputIterator last,
                        Predicate       pred);
}
```

DESCRIPTION: Searches the range from first up to last for an element that satisfies the predicate. If found, it returns an iterator referring to the first element satisfying the predicate. If not found, it returns an iterator equal to last. No assumptions about the order of the sequence are made.

for_each

TYPE: function   **HEADER:** <algorithm> [algo.h]
TIME: linear   **SPACE:** constant

```
namespace std{
  template <class InputIterator, class Function>
  Function for_each(InputIterator     first,
                    InputIterator     last,
                    Function          f);
}
```

DESCRIPTION: This traverses the sequence from `first` up to `last`, applying the function `f` to each member of the sequence. It returns the function `f` that was passed to it.

forward_iterator

TYPE: structure   **HEADER:** <> [iterator.h]

```
template <class T, class Distance>
struct forward_iterator;
```

DESCRIPTION: Forward iterators can both assign and retrieve values but are restricted in that they can move only in the forward direction. This structure has been removed from the C++ standard.

Operators:

```
T forward_iterator<T, Distance>::operator=(
   const forward_iterator& x);
```

Assigns the value of one iterator to another.

```
bool forward_iterator<T, Distance>::operator==(
   const forward_iterator& x);
```

Returns `true` if the two iterators are equal.

```
bool forward_iterator<T, Distance>::operator!=(
   const forward_iterator& x);
```

Returns `true` if the two iterators are unequal.

```
forward_iterator& forward_iterator<T,
Distance>::operator++();
```

Increments the iterator and returns a reference to the new value.

```
forward_iterator<T, Distance>::operator++(int);
```

Returns the current value of the iterator and then increments the iterator.

```
T forward_iterator<T, Distance>::operator*();
```

Dereferences the iterator and allows a value to be assigned to it.

front_insert_iterator

TYPE: adaptor   **HEADER:** <iterator> [iterator.h]

```
namespace std{
   template <class Container>
   class front_insert_iterator : public iterator<
   output_iterator_tag, void, void, void, void>;
}
```

DESCRIPTION: The insert iterators differ from other iterators in that they insert a new object into the container when assigned a value, rather than overwriting an existing object. This adaptor uses the push_front() method of the underlying class to insert values at the front of a container. It is, therefore, restricted to use with classes that provide the push_front() method. The insert iterators are particularly useful as output iterators when used in conjunction with the STL algorithms so that results can be written to a container that does not have sufficient space currently allocated.

SEE ALSO: back_insert_iterator, insert_iterator, front_inserter

Public Members:

```
front_insert_iterator<Container>::container_type;
```

The type of the adapted container.

Public Methods:

```
explicit front_insert_iterator<Container>::
front_insert_iterator(Container& x);
```

Constructor to create a front insert iterator for the given container.

```
front_insert_iterator<Container>&
front_insert_iterator<Container>::operator=(
   typename Container::const_reference value);
```

Assignment operator that uses `push_front()` to insert a new value into the container.

```
front_insert_iterator<Container>&
front_insert_iterator<Container>::operator++();
```

Does nothing but is provided to be compatible with other iterators.

```
front_insert_iterator<Container>
front_insert_iterator<Container>::operator++(int);
```

Does nothing but is provided to be compatible with other iterators.

```
front_insert_iterator<Container>&
front_insert_iterator<Container>::operator*();
```

Dereference operator to return a reference to the iterator itself.

front_inserter

TYPE: function   **HEADER:** <iterator> [iterator.h]

```
namespace std{
   template <class Container>
   front_insert_iterator<Container>
   front_inserter(Container& x);
}
```

DESCRIPTION: Convenience function that creates and returns a front-_insert_iterator for the given container.

SEE ALSO: front_insert_iterator

generate

TYPE: function   **HEADER:** <algorithm> [algo.h]
TIME: linear   **SPACE:** constant

```
namespace std{
   template <class ForwardIterator, class Generator>
   void generate(ForwardIterator    first,
                 ForwardIterator    last,
                 Generator          gen);
}
```

DESCRIPTION: Fills the object referenced by the iterators with the successive values returned by `gen`. The range to be filled goes from `first` to up to `last`.

generate_n

TYPE: function   **HEADER:** <algorithm> [algo.h]
TIME: linear   **SPACE:** constant

```
namespace std{
  template <class OutputIterator, class Size,
      class Generator>
  void generate_n(OutputIterator      first,
                  Size                 n,
                  Generator            gen);
}
```

DESCRIPTION: Fills n locations of the container referenced by the output iterator with the values obtained by n successive calls to `gen`.

greater

TYPE: function object   **HEADER:** <functional> [function.h]
TIME: constant   **SPACE:** constant

```
namespace std{
  template <class T>
  struct greater: binary_function<T, T, bool> {
    bool operator()(const T& x, const T& y) const;
  };
}
```

DESCRIPTION: A function object that can be used as a substitute for `operator>` and passed as a parameter to functions expecting a function object. It compares its two parameters using `operator>` and returns the result.

SEE ALSO: equal_to, not_equal_to, less, less_equal, greater_equal

greater_equal

TYPE: function object   **HEADER:** <functional> [function.h]
TIME: constant   **SPACE:** constant

```
namespace std{
  template <class T>
  struct greater_equal: binary_function<T, T, bool> {
    bool operator()(const T& x, const T& y) const;
  };
}
```

DESCRIPTION: A function object that can be used as a substitute for opera-
tor>= and passed as a parameter to functions expecting a function object.
It compares its two parameters using operator>= and returns the result.

SEE ALSO: equal_to, not_equal_to, less, less_equal, greater

gslice

TYPE: class   **HEADER:** <numeric> []

```
namespace std {
  class gslice;
}
```

DESCRIPTION: A gslice represents a generalized slice through a multi-
dimensional array. It generates a series of indices that can be used to map a
multi-dimensional array onto a one-dimensional array. It specifies the slice
in terms of a starting index, a series of lengths, and a series of strides. The
final indices are generated by incrementing the starting index by each of the
stride values to generate the corresponding lengths of indices. It iterates
through all members of the length and slice arrays, which must both have the
same length.

Public Methods:

```
size_t gslice::start() const;
```

Returns the starting index for the gslice.

```
valarray<size_t> gslice::size() const;
```

Returns the array of lengths used by the gslice.

```
valarray<size_t> gslice::stride() const;
```

Returns the array of strides used by the gslice.

```
gslice::gslice();
gslice::gslice(size_t                     start,
           const valarray<size_t>& lengths,
           const valarray<size_t>& strides);
gslice::gslice(const gslice&);
```

These are the gslice constructors. The first creates an empty gslice. The second is the most commonly used constructor. The final one is the copy constructor.

---

gslice_array

TYPE: class   **HEADER:** <numeric> []

```
namespace std {
  template <class T>
     class gslice_array;
}
```

DESCRIPTION: The gslice_array is a helper class used for subscripting by the valarray. It contains a reference to the container being subscripted along with a list of the subscripts. It has no public constructors and can be instantiated only by subscripting a valarray with a gslice.

SEE ALSO: gslice, slice_array, mask_array, indirect_array

Public Methods:

```
void gslice_array<T>::operator=(
   const valarray<T>& a) const;
slice_array& gslice_array<T>::operator=(
   const slice_array& a);
```

The first form assigns the subscripted members of the valarray referenced by *this the values in a. The second form is private and allows one slice_array to be assigned to another.

```
void gslice_array<T>::operator*=(
   const valarray<T>& a) const;
```

Multiplies the subscripted members of the valarray referenced by *this by the values in a.

```
void gslice_array<T>::operator/=(
  const valarray<T>& a) const;
```

Divides the subscripted members of the valarray referenced by *this by the values in a.

```
void gslice_array<T>::operator%=(
  const valarray<T>& a) const;
```

Replaces the subscripted members of the valarray referenced by *this by the remainder upon division of these values by the values in a.

```
void gslice_array<T>::operator+=(
  const valarray<T>& a) const;
```

Adds the values in a onto the subscripted members of the valarray referenced by *this.

```
void gslice_array<T>::operator-=(
  const valarray<T>& a) const;
```

Subtracts the values in a from the subscripted members of the valarray referenced by *this.

```
void gslice_array<T>::operator^=(
  const valarray<T>& a) const;
```

Replaces each of the subscripted members of the valarray referenced by *this with itself exclusive OR'ed with the corresponding value from a.

```
void gslice_array<T>::operator&=(
  const valarray<T>& a) const;
```

Replaces each of the subscripted members of the valarray referenced by *this with itself, bitwise AND'ed with the corresponding value from a.

```
void gslice_array<T>::operator|=(
  const valarray<T>& a) const;
```

Replaces each of the subscripted members of the valarray referenced by *this with itself, inclusive OR'ed with the corresponding value from a.

```
void gslice_array<T>::operator<<=(
    const valarray<T>& a) const;
```

Replaces each of the subscripted members of the valarray referenced by *this with itself, shifted left by the corresponding value from a.

```
void gslice_array<T>::operator>>=(
    const valarray<T>& a) const;
```

Replaces each of the subscripted members of the valarray referenced by *this with itself, shifted right by the corresponding value from a.

```
void gslice_array<T>::fill(const T& v);
```

Assigns the value v to the subscripted elements of the valarray referenced by *this.

```
gslice_array<T>::gslice_array();
gslice_array<T>::gslice_array(const gslice_array& a);
```

These are the private constructors. The first is the default constructor and the second is the copy constructor. These might not be defined by all implementations.

```
gslice_array<T>::~gslice_array();
```

The class destructor.

includes

TYPE: function   **HEADER:** <algorithm> [algo.h]
TIME: linear   **SPACE:** constant

```
namespace std{
  template <class InputIterator1,
      class InputIterator2>
  bool includes(InputIterator1 first1,
          InputIterator1    last1,
          InputIterator2    first2,
          InputIterator2    last2);

  template <class InputIterator1,
      class InputIterator2, class Compare>
```

```
bool includes(InputIterator1 first1,
        InputIterator1      last1,
        InputIterator2      first2,
        InputIterator2      last2,
        Compare             comp);
}
```

DESCRIPTION: Returns `true` if the set or multiset represented by the sequence `first1` up to `last1` is a subset of the set or multiset represented by the sequence from `first2` up to `last2`. Each of the sequences must be in ascending order and may contain duplicate values. The first sequence is a subset of the second if the number of occurrences of each element in the first set is less than or equal to the number of occurrences in the second set. The second form of the function allows the specification of a comparison operator other than the default, `operator<`.

SEE ALSO: set_intersection, set_difference, set_symmetric_difference, set_union

indirect_array

TYPE: class   **HEADER:** <numeric> []

```
namespace std {
  template <class T>
      class indirect_array;
}
```

DESCRIPTION: The `indirect_array` is a helper class used for subscripting by the `valarray`. It contains a reference to the container being subscripted along with a list of the subscripts. It has no public constructors and can only be instantiated by subscripting a `valarray` with a `valarray` <size_t>.

SEE ALSO: slice_array, mask_array, gslice_array, valarray

Public Methods:

```
void indirect_array<T>::operator=(
                    const valarray<T>& a) const;
indirect_array<T>& indirect_array<T>::operator=(
                    const indirect_array<T>& a);
```

The first form assigns the subscripted members of the `valarray` referenced by
`*this` the values in a. The second form is private and allows one `indi-
rect_array` to be assigned to another.

```
void indirect_array<T>::operator*=(
                const valarray<T>& a) const;
```

Multiplies the subscripted members of the `valarray` referenced by `*this` by
the values in a.

```
void indirect_array<T>::operator/=(
                const valarray<T>& a) const;
```

Divides the subscripted members of the `valarray` referenced by `*this` by
the values in a.

```
void indirect_array<T>::operator%=(
                const valarray<T>& a) const;
```

Replaces the subscripted members of the `valarray` referenced by `*this` by
the remainder upon division of these values by the values in a.

```
void indirect_array<T>::operator+=(
                const valarray<T>& a) const;
```

Adds the values in a onto the subscripted members of the `valarray` referenced by `*this`.

```
void indirect_array<T>::operator-=(
                const valarray<T>& a) const;
```

Subtracts the values in a from the subscripted members of the `valarray` referenced by `*this`.

```
void indirect_array<T>::operator^=(
                const valarray<T>& a) const;
```

Replaces each of the subscripted members of the `valarray` referenced by
`*this` with itself, exclusive OR'ed with the corresponding value from a.

```
void indirect_array<T>::operator&=(
                const valarray<T>& a) const;
```

Replaces each of the subscripted members of the `valarray` referenced by `*this` with itself, bitwise AND'ed with the corresponding value from a.

```
void indirect_array<T>::operator|=(
              const valarray<T>& a) const;
```

Replaces each of the subscripted members of the `valarray` referenced by `*this` with itself, inclusive OR'ed with the corresponding value from a.

```
void indirect_array<T>::operator<<=(
              const valarray<T>& a) const;
```

Replaces each of the subscripted members of the `valarray` referenced by `*this` with itself, shifted left by the corresponding value from a.

```
void indirect_array<T>::operator>>=(
              const valarray<T>& a) const;
```

Replaces each of the subscripted members of the `valarray` referenced by `*this` with itself, shifted right by the corresponding value from a.

```
void indirect_array<T>::fill(const T& v);
```

Assigns the value v to the subscripted elements of the `valarray` referenced by `*this`.

```
indirect_array<T>::indirect_array();
indirect_array<T>::indirect_array(
              const indirect_array<T>& a);
```

These are the private constructors. The first is the default constructor, and the second is the copy constructor. These might not be defined by all implementations.

```
indirect_array<T>::~indirect_array();
```

The class destructor.

inner_product

TYPE: function   **HEADER:** <numeric> [algo.h]
TIME: linear   **SPACE:** constant

```
namespace std{
  template <class InputIterator1,
      class InputIterator2, class T>
  T inner_product(InputIterator1   first1,
                  InputIterator1   last1,
                  InputIterator2   first2,
                  T                init);

  template <class InputIterator1,
      class InputIterator2,
      class T, class BinaryOperation1,
      class BinaryOperation2>
  T inner_product(InputIterator1   first1,
                  InputIterator1   last1,
                  InputIterator2   first2,
                  T                init,
                  BinaryOperation1 binary_op1,
                  BinaryOperation2 binary_op2);
}
```

DESCRIPTION: Computes the inner product of two ranges. The first range goes from `first1` up to `last1`, and the second range starts with `first2` and is of the same length as the first range. The first form computes the inner product by multiplying the ranges on an element-by-element basis, summing the results, and adding the value `init`. The second form allows the substitution of other operations where `op1` replaces `operator+` and `op2` replaces `operator*`.

inplace_merge

TYPE: function   **HEADER:** <algorithm> [algo.h]
TIME: linear   **SPACE:** constant

```
namespace std{
  template <class BidirectionalIterator>
  void inplace_merge(
          BidirectionalIterator   first,
          BidirectionalIterator   middle,
          BidirectionalIterator   last);

  template <class BidirectionalIterator,
      class Compare>
  void inplace_merge(
          BidirectionalIterator   first,
          BidirectionalIterator   middle,
          BidirectionalIterator   last,
```

```
            Compare                    comp);
}
```

DESCRIPTION: Merges the sequence from `first` up to `middle` with the sequence from `middle` up to `last`. The result is placed at `first`. It is assumed that the input sequences are sorted. The second form allows the specification of a comparison operator other than the default, `operator<`.

input_iterator

TYPE: structure   **HEADER:** <> [iterator.h]

```
template <class T, class Distance>
struct input_iterator;
```

DESCRIPTION: Input iterators are used only to obtain values from an input source. One of their main uses is to implement stream iterators for the reading of values from streams. They move only in the forward direction and can only be dereferenced to obtain the value associated with the iterator, never to set it. This structure has been removed from the C++ standard.

Operators:

```
bool input_iterator<T, Distance>::operator==(
   const input_iterator& x);
```

Returns `true` if the two iterators are equal.

```
bool input_iterator<T, Distance>::operator!=(
   const input_iterator& x);
```

Returns `true` if the two iterators are not equal.

```
input_iterator& input_iterator<T,
Distance>::operator++();
```

Increments the iterator and returns a reference to the new value.

```
input_iterator<T, Distance>::operator++(int);
```

Returns the current value of the iterator and then increments the iterator.

```
T input_iterator<T, Distance>::operator*();
```

Dereferences the iterator and returns the value associated with it.

inserter

TYPE: function   **HEADER:** <iterator> [iterator.h]

```
namespace std{
  template <class Container, class Iterator>
  insert_iterator<Container> inserter(
      Container& x, Iterator i);
}
```

DESCRIPTION: Convenience function to create an `insert_iterator` and position it at the location of i.

SEE ALSO: insert_iterator

insert_iterator

TYPE: adaptor   **HEADER:** <iterator> [iterator.h]

```
namespace std{
  template <class Container>
  class insert_iterator : public iterator<
  output_iterator_tag, void, void, void, void>;
}
```

DESCRIPTION: The insert iterators differ from other iterators in that when a value is assigned to them, they insert a new value into the container rather than overwriting an existing value. An insert iterator is positioned within a container, and all values assigned to it are inserted in front of this position. This is particularly useful as an output iterator for one of the STL algorithms to write output to a container that does not have a sufficient number of values already allocated.

SEE ALSO: inserter, front_insert_iterator, back_insert_iterator

Public Members:

```
insert_iterator<Container>::container_type;
```

The type of the adapted container.

Public Methods:

```
insert_iterator<Container>::insert_iterator(
        Container&             x,
        typename Container::iterator i);
```

Constructor that initializes an insert iterator at the given position in the container.

```
insert_iterator<Container>&
insert_iterator<Container>::operator=(
  typename Container::const_reference value);
```

Assignment operator that uses `insert()` on the underlying container to insert an object into the container. The iterator is then advanced so that the next value inserted will be after the one just inserted.

```
insert_iterator<Container>&
insert_iterator<Container>::operator++();
```

Does nothing but is provided to be compatible with the other iterators.

```
insert_iterator<Container>&
insert_iterator<Container>::operator++(int);
```

Does nothing but is provided to be compatible with the other iterators.

```
insert_iterator<Container>&
insert_iterator<Container>::operator*();
```

Dereference operator to return a reference to the iterator itself.

IotaGen

TYPE: class   **HEADER:** <> [iota.h]
TIME: constant   **SPACE:** constant

```
template <class T>
class IotaGen {
    public:
        IotaGen(const T& init);
        T operator()();
};
```

DESCRIPTION: IotaGen is a generator that is given an initial value and returns successive values, starting with the initial value, each time `opera-tor()` is invoked. The successive values are obtained by applying `operator++` to type T. (NOTE: This is distributed by Rensselaer Polytechnic Institute as a convenience function to be used with their examples and is not part of the STL. The SGI implementation provides similar functionality with the function `iota()`)

iterator

TYPE: typedef   **REQUIRED BY:** all containers

DESCRIPTION: A typedef provided by all containers that defines the type of an iterator for the container.

SEE ALSO: const_iterator

iterator

TYPE: struct   **HEADER:** <iterator> []

```
namespace std {
  template<class Category, class T,
  class Distance = ptrdiff_t,
  class Pointer = T*, class Reference = T&>
  struct iterator;
}
```

DESCRIPTION: This is a base class from which most iterators are derived.

Public Members:

```
iterator<Category, T>::difference_type;
```

A type that can represent the difference between two iterators.

```
iterator<Category, T>::iterator_category;
```

One of the iterator tags representing the category of the iterator.

```
iterator<Category, T>::pointer;
```

The type of a pointer to the type referenced by the iterator.

```
iterator<Category, T>::reference;
```

A reference to the type referenced by the iterator.

```
iterator<Category, T>::iterator_category;
```

One of the iterator tags representing the category of the iterator.

```
iterator<Category, T>::value_type;
```

The type referenced by the iterator.

iterator_category

TYPE: function   **HEADER:** <> [iterator.h]
TIME: constant   **SPACE:** constant

```
template <class T, class Distance>
inline input_iterator_tag iterator_category(
    const input_iterator<T, Distance>&);

inline output_iterator_tag iterator_category(const
output_iterator&);

template <class T, class Distance>
inline forward_iterator_tag iterator_category(
    const forward_iterator<T, Distance>&);

template <class T, class Distance>
inline bidirectional_iterator_tag iterator_category(
    const bidirectional_iterator<T, Distance>&);

template <class T, class Distance>
inline random_access_iterator_tag iterator_category(
    const random_access_iterator<T, Distance>&);

template <class T>
inline random_access_iterator_tag
iterator_category(const T*);
```

DESCRIPTION: Each of the iterator categories has an iterator tag associated with it that can be used to identify the category to which an iterator belongs. An instance of an iterator is passed to this function that returns the iterator tag for the iterator. The main use of this function is to allow algorithms to be specialized to take advantage of the capabilities of specific iterator categories. This function has been removed from the C++ standard, and the same functionality can be obtained using the expression `iterator_traits <iter>::iterator_category`.

SEE ALSO: iterator_tag, value_type, distance_type

iterator_tag

TYPE: structure   **HEADER:** <iterator> [iterator.h]

```
namespace std{
   struct input_iterator_tag {};
   struct output_iterator_tag {};
   struct forward_iterator_tag {}:
       public input_iterator_tag;
   struct bidirectional_iterator_tag {}:
       public forward_iterator_tag;
   struct random_access_iterator_tag {}:
       public bidirectional_iterator_tag;
}
```

DESCRIPTION: the iterator tags are a series of empty structures used to identify the category to which an iterator belongs. The expression `iterator_traits<iter>::iterator_category` returns an iterator tag, indicating the category to which `iter` belongs. No values are contained within the iterator tags since their type alone is sufficient to identify the iterator category.

Note that `iterator_traits` is available only in implementations supporting the C++ standard. Older implementations might use the function `iterator_category()` or an implementation-specific function to determine the category of an iterator.

SEE ALSO: iterator_category

iterator_traits

TYPE: struct   **HEADER:** <iterator> []

```
namespace std{
  template<class T>
  struct iterator_traits;
}
```

DESCRIPTION: This is a structure that is able to return information about the type referenced by an iterator. It has specializations to deal with different template parameters.

Public Members:

```
iterator_traits::difference_type;
```

A type which can be used to represent the difference between two iterators.

```
iterator_traits::iterator_category;
```

One of the iterator tags that determines the category of the iterator.

```
iterator_traits::pointer;
```

The type of a pointer to the type referenced by the iterator.

```
iterator_traits::reference;
```

The type of a reference to the type referenced by the iterator.

```
iterator_traits::value_type;
```

The type referenced by the iterator.

iter_swap

TYPE: class   **HEADER:** <algorithm> [algobase.h]
TIME: constant   **SPACE:** constant

```
namespace std{
  template <class ForwardIterator1,
      class ForwardIterator2>
```

```
void iter_swap(ForwardIterator1   a,
            ForwardIterator2        b);
}
```

DESCRIPTION: Swaps the contents of the two iterators a and b.

SEE ALSO: swap, swap_ranges

key_compare

TYPE: typedef   **REQUIRED BY:** associative containers

DESCRIPTION: This is a typedef provided by all associative containers that returns the function object used by the container to compare keys.

SEE ALSO: key_type, value_compare

key_type

TYPE: typedef   **REQUIRED BY:** associative containers

DESCRIPTION: A type defined by all associative containers that is the type of the key used by the container.

SEE ALSO: key_compare, value_type

less

TYPE: function object   **HEADER:** <functional> [function.h]
TIME: constant   **SPACE:** constant

```
namespace std{
  template <class T>
  struct less : binary_function<T, T, bool> {
    bool operator()(const T& x, const T& y) const;
  };
}
```

DESCRIPTION: A function object that can be used as a substitute for operator< and passed as a parameter to functions expecting a function object. It compares its two parameters using operator< and returns the result.

SEE ALSO: equal_to, not_equal_to, greater, less_equal, greater_equal

less_equal

TYPE: function object   **HEADER:** <functional> [function.h]
TIME: constant   **SPACE:** constant

```
namespace std{
  template <class T>
  struct less_equal : binary_function<T, T, bool> {
    bool operator()(const T& x, const T& y) const;
  };
}
```

DESCRIPTION: A function object that can be used as a substitute for opera-tor<= and passed as a parameter to functions expecting a function object. It compares its two parameters using operator<= and returns the result.

SEE ALSO: equal_to, not_equal_to, greater, less, greater_equal

lexicographical_compare

TYPE: function   **HEADER:** <algorithm> [algobase.h]
TIME: linear   **SPACE:** constant

```
namespace std{
  template <class InputIterator1,
      class InputIterator2>
  bool lexicographical_compare(
                    InputIterator1    first1,
                    InputIterator1    last1,
                    InputIterator2    first2,
                    InputIterator2    last2);

  template <class InputIterator1,
      class InputIterator2, class Compare>
  bool lexicographical_compare(
                    InputIterator1    first1,
                    InputIterator1    last1,
                    InputIterator2    first2,
                    InputIterator2    last2,
                    Compare           comp);
}
```

DESCRIPTION: Performs a lexicographical comparison (similar to alphabetical order) on the sequence from `first1` up to `last1` and from `first2` up to `last2`. It returns `true` if the first sequence is less than the second. The second form allows the specification of a comparison operator other than `operator<`.

list

TYPE: class   **HEADER:** <list> [list.h]

```
namespace std {
   template <class T, class Allocator = allocator<T> >
   class list;
}
```

DESCRIPTION: A doubly linked list of elements of arbitrary type *T*. The list is a sequence container that provides constant time insertion and deletion at any point in the list. Only linear access to the elements is supported via bidirectional iterators. Lists should be used when large numbers of insertions and deletions will be made at any point in the sequence.

SEE ALSO: deque, vector

Public Members:

`list<T, Allocator>::allocator_type;`

The type of the allocator.

`list<T, Allocator>::const_iterator;`

A constant iterator for the container.

`list<T, Allocator>::const_pointer;`

The type of a constant pointer to the content.

`list<T, Allocator>::const_reference;`

The type of a constant reference to the content.

`list<T, Allocator>::const_reverse_iterator;`

A constant reverse iterator for the container.

```
list<T, Allocator>::difference_type;
```

Able to represent the difference between any two iterators.

```
list<T, Allocator>::iterator;
```

An iterator for the container.

```
list<T, Allocator>::pointer;
```

The type of a pointer to the content.

```
list<T, Allocator>::reference;
```

The type of a reference to the content.

```
list<T, Allocator>::reverse_iterator;
```

A reverse iterator for the container.

```
list<T, Allocator>::size_type;
```

Able to represent any non-negative value of difference_type.

```
list<T, Allocator>::value_type;
```

The type stored in the container.

Public Methods:

```
void list<T, Allocator>::assign(
            size_type    n,
            const T&     value);

template<class InputIterator>
void list<T, Allocator>::assign(
            InputIterator first,
            InputIterator last);
```

These methods erase the content of the list and replace it with new values specified by the parameters. The first form fills the list with n copies of value. The second form inserts the values from first up to last.

```
reference list<T, Allocator>::back();
const_reference list<T>::back() const;
```

Returns the last element in the list.

```
iterator list<T, Allocator>::begin();
const_iterator list<T, Allocator>::begin() const;
```

Returns an iterator that references the first element in the list.

```
void list<T, Allocator>::clear();
```

Erases all elements in the list.

```
bool list<T, Allocator>::empty() const;
```

Returns a Boolean value indicating if the list is empty.

```
iterator list<T, Allocator>::end();
const_iterator list<T, Allocator>::end() const;
```

Returns an iterator that is one past the last element in the list.

```
iterator list<T, Allocator>::erase(iterator position);
iterator list<T, Allocator>::erase(iterator  first,
                                   iterator  last);
```

Deletes the element at the indicated position from the list. The second form deletes all elements in the range from first up to last. An iterator referencing the element after the last element erased is returned. Only iterators, pointers, and references to the erased elements are invalidated.

```
reference list<T, Allocator>::front();
const_reference list<T, Allocator>::front() const;
```

Returns the first element in the list.

```
allocator_type list<T, Allocator>::get_allocator()
const;
```

Returns the allocator for the container.

```
iterator list<T, Allocator>::insert(iterator position,
                                     const T&  x);
template<class InputIterator>
void list<T, Allocator>::insert(
                    iterator         position,
                    InputIterator    first,
                    InputIterator    last);
void list<T, Allocator>::insert(
                    iterator     position,
                    size_type    n,
                    const T&     x);
```

Inserts the element x just before position. The first form returns an iterator
that references the element just inserted. The second form inserts the elements from first up to last just before position. The third form inserts n copies of the element x just before position.

```
explicit list<T, Allocator>::list(
                const Allocator& = Allocator());

list<T, Allocator>::list(
            size_type    n,
            const T&     value = T(),
            const        Allocator& = Allocator());

template<class InputIterator>
list<T, Allocator>::list(
    const InputIterator    first,
    const InputIterator    last);
    const                  Allocator& = Allocator());

list<T, Allocator>::list(
    const list<T, Allocator>& x);
```

The first form constructs an empty list. The second form constructs a list containing n copies of value. The third form constructs a list containing the
elements from first up to last. The fourth form is the copy constructor.

```
list<T, Allocator>::~list();
```

Destroys the list and its contents.

```
size_type list<T, Allocator>::max_size() const;
```

Returns the maximum number of elements that can be stored in the list.

```
void list<T, Allocator>::merge(list<T, Allocator>& x);
template<class Compare>
void list<T, Allocator>::merge(
                    list<T, Allocator>&    x,
                    Compare                comp);
```

Merges the sorted list x into the current list, which is assumed to be sorted. After the merge, the list x has no elements, and its length is reduced to zero. The merge operation does not remove duplicates. The second form uses comp to compare elements rather than operator<.

```
list<T, Allocator>& list<T, Allocator>::operator=(
            const list<T, Allocator>& x);
```

Assigns *this the contents of the list x.

```
void list<T, Allocator>::pop_back();
```

Deletes the last element in the list.

```
void list<T, Allocator>::pop_front();
```

Deletes the first element in the list.

```
void list<T, Allocator>::push_back(const T& x);
```

Appends the element x to the end of the list.

```
void list<T, Allocator>::push_front(const T& x);
```

Inserts the element x at the beginning of the list.

```
reverse_iterator list<T, Allocator>::rbegin();
const_reverse_iterator list<T, Allocator>::rbegin()
const;
```

Returns an iterator that is one past the end of the list and can be used as the starting value for a reverse iterator.

```
void list<T, Allocator>::remove(const T& value);
```

Removes all elements equal to value from the list.

```
template<class Predicate>
void list<T, Allocator>::remove_if(Predicate p);
```

Removes all elements for which the predicate is true.

```
reverse_iterator list<T, Allocator>::rend();
const_reverse_iterator list<T, Allocator>::rend()
const;
```

Returns an iterator that can be used to find the end for a reverse iteration.

```
void list<T, Allocator>::resize(
                        size_type size,
                        T          value = T());
```

Changes the size of the list so that it contains size members. If the list has less than size elements, new elements are appended to make it the desired length, with the new elements assigned value. If the list has more than size elements, elements are removed from the end to make it the desired length. If the list is the desired length, nothing is done.

```
void list<T, Allocator>::reverse();
```

Reverses the order of the elements in the list.

```
size_type list<T, Allocator>::size() const;
```

Returns the number of elements currently stored in the list.

```
void list<T, Allocator>::sort();
template<class Compare>
void list<T, Allocator>::sort(Compare comp);
```

Sorts the elements of the list into ascending order. This is an order *n log n* sort. The second form uses comp to compare elements rather than operator<.

```
void list<T, Allocator>::splice(iterator       position,
                    list<T, Allocator>&       x);
void list<T, Allocator>::splice(
              iterator                  position,
              list<T, Allocator>&       x,
              iterator                  i);
void list<T, Allocator>::splice(
              iterator                  position,
```

```
list<T, Allocator>&      x,
iterator                 first,
iterator                 last);
```

Inserts the entire list x into the list so that it is placed immediately before position and removes the inserted elements from x. The second form inserts
the element from the list x referenced by i just before position. It also
removes the element referenced by i from the list x. The third form places
the elements from first up to last from the list x just before position
and removes them from the list x.

```
void list<T, Allocator>::swap(list<T, Allocator>& x);
```

Swaps the contents of the object list with the list x so that each has the contents
of the other.

```
void list<T, Allocator>::unique();
template<class BinaryPredicate>
void list<T, Allocator>::unique(BinaryPredicate p);
```

Removes adjacent duplicates from a sorted list so that only a single copy of each
element remains. The second form uses p to determine equivalence.

Nonmember Functions:

```
template <class T, Allocator>
bool operator==(const list<T, Allocator>& x,
                const list<T, Allocator>& y);
```

Returns a Boolean indicating if the two lists are equal.

```
template <class T, Allocator>
bool operator!=(const list<T, Allocator>& x,
                const list<T, Allocator>& y);
```

Returns a Boolean indicating if the two lists are not equal.

```
template <class T, Allocator>
bool operator<(const list<T, Allocator>& x,
               const list<T, Allocator>& y);
```

Performs a lexicographical comparison to determine if the first list is less than
the second.

```
template <class T, Allocator>
bool operator>(const list<T, Allocator>& x,
               const list<T, Allocator>& y);
```

Performs a lexicographical comparison to determine if the first list is greater than the second.

```
template <class T, Allocator>
bool operator>=(const list<T, Allocator>&   x,
                const list<T, Allocator>&   y);
```

Performs a lexicographical comparison to determine if the first list is greater than or equal to the second.

```
template <class T, Allocator>
bool operator<=(const list<T, Allocator>&   x,
                const list<T, Allocator>&   y);
```

Performs a lexicographical comparison to determine if the first list is less than or equal to the second.

```
template<class T, class Allocator>
void swap(list<T, Allocator>&   a,
          list<T, Allocator>&   b);
```

Swaps the contents of list a with list b.

logical_and

TYPE: function object   **HEADER:** <functional> [function.h]
TIME: constant   **SPACE:** constant

```
namespace std{
  template <class T>
  struct logical_and : binary_function<T, T, bool> {
    bool operator()(const T& x, const T& y) const;
  };
}
```

DESCRIPTION: A function object that can be passed to any function expecting a function object as a substitute for operator&&. It performs operator&& on its two parameters and returns the result.

SEE ALSO: logical_or, logical_not

logical_not

TYPE: function object   **HEADER:** <functional> [function.h]
TIME: constant   **SPACE:** constant

```
namespace std{
  template <class T>
  struct logical_not : binary_function<T, T, bool> {
   bool operator()(const T& x) const;
  };
}
```

DESCRIPTION: A function object that can be passed to any function expecting a function object as a substitute for operator!. It performs operator! on its parameter and returns the result.

SEE ALSO: logical_and, logical_or

logical_or

TYPE: function object   **HEADER:** <functional> [function.h]
TIME: constant   **SPACE:** constant

```
namespace std{
  template <class T>
  struct logical_or : binary_function<T, T, bool> {
   bool operator()(const T& x, const T& y) const;
  };
}
```

DESCRIPTION: A function object that can be passed to any function expecting a function object as a substitute for operator||. It performs operator|| on its two parameters and returns the result.

SEE ALSO: logical_and, logical_not

lower_bound

TYPE: function   **HEADER:** <algorithm> [algo.h]
TIME: logarithmic **SPACE:** constant

```
namespace std{
  template <class ForwardIterator, class T>
  ForwardIterator lower_bound(
```

```
                        ForwardIterator      first,
                        ForwardIterator      last,
                        const T&             value);

template <class ForwardIterator, class T,
     class Compare>
ForwardIterator lower_bound(
                        ForwardIterator      first,
                        ForwardIterator      last,
                        const T&             value,
                        Compare              comp);
}
```

DESCRIPTION: Returns an iterator that references the first element in the range from first up to but not including last that is >= value. If no such element exists, it returns last. The elements in the range first to last are assumed to be sorted in ascending order. The second form allows the specification of a comparison function other than the default, operator<.

make_heap

TYPE: function   **TYPE:** <algorithm> [heap.h]
TIME: linear   **SPACE:** constant

```
namespace std{
  template <class RandomAccessIterator>
  void make_heap(RandomAccessIterator    first,
                 RandomAccessIterator    last);

  template <class RandomAccessIterator,
       class Compare>
  void make_heap(RandomAccessIterator    first,
                 RandomAccessIterator    last,
                 Compare                 comp);
}
```

DESCRIPTION: Rearranges the elements in the sequence from first up to last so that they form a heap. A heap is a data structure that looks like a binary tree and is sorted so that the parent of every node is greater than the node itself. This function must be used to create a heap from a sequence before any of the other heap functions can be used.

SEE ALSO: push_heap, pop_heap, sort_heap

map

TYPE: class   **HEADER:** <map> [map.h]

```
namespace std {
  template <class Key, class T,
  class Compare = less<Key>,
  class Allocator = allocator<pair<const Key, T> > >
  class map;
}
```

DESCRIPTION: The map stores and retrieves objects based on a key provided when the object is inserted. The key can be of any type, and it does not have to be contained within the object. The keys for the map must be unique, but the multimap supports duplicate keys. The map allows you to insert objects and provides fast retrieval using a comparison function to determine the equality of objects. The objects are actually stored in a tree so that insertion and retrieval take logarithmic time. The map is useful for applications that implement the concept of associative arrays. Internally, the objects in the map are always ordered so that an iterator will retrieve the objects in sorted order.

SEE ALSO: multiset, set, multimap

Public Members:

```
map<Key, T, Compare, Allocator>::allocator_type;
```

The type of the allocator.

```
map<Key, T, Compare, Allocator>::const_iterator;
```

A constant iterator for the container.

```
map<Key, T, Compare, Allocator>::const_pointer;
```

The type of a constant pointer to the content.

```
map<Key, T, Compare, Allocator>::const_reference;
```

The type of a constant reference to the content.

```
map<Key, T, Compare,
  Allocator>::const_reverse_iterator;
```

A constant reverse iterator for the container.

```
map<Key, T, Compare, Allocator>::difference_type;
```

Able to represent the difference between any two iterators.

```
map<Key, T, Compare, Allocator>::iterator;
```

An iterator for the container.

```
map<Key, T, Compare, Allocator>::key_compare;
```

The type of the key comparison function.

```
map<Key, T, Compare, Allocator>::key_type;
```

The type of the key.

```
map<Key, T, Compare, Allocator>::mapped_type;
```

The type of the values stored in the container.

```
map<Key, T, Compare, Allocator>::pointer;
```

The type of a pointer to the content.

```
map<Key, T, Compare, Allocator>::reference;
```

The type of a reference to the content.

```
map<Key, T, Compare, Allocator>::reverse_iterator;
```

A reverse iterator for the container.

```
map<Key, T, Compare, Allocator>::size_type;
```

Represents any non-negative value of `difference_type`.

```
multimap<Key, T, Compare, Allocator>::value_compare;
```

The value comparison object.

```
map<Key, T, Compare, Allocator>::value_type;
```

A pair<const Key, T>.

Public Methods:

```
iterator map<Key, T, Compare, Allocator>::begin();
const_iterator map<Key, T, Compare, Allocator>::
  begin() const;
```

Returns an iterator referencing the first value in the map.

```
void map<Key, T, Compare, Allocator>::clear();
```

Deletes all elements from the map.

```
size_type map<Key, T, Compare, Allocator>::count(
  const key_type& x) const;
```

Returns a count of the number of objects equal to x. For a map this will be zero or one.

```
bool map<Key, T, Compare, Allocator>::empty() const;
```

Returns a Boolean indicating if the map is empty.

```
iterator map<Key, T, Compare, Allocator>::end();
const_iterator map<Key, T, Compare, Allocator>::
  end() const;
```

Returns a past-the-end iterator for the map.

```
void map<Key, T, Compare, Allocator>::
  erase(iterator position);
size_type map<Key, T, Compare, Allocator>::erase(
  const key_type& x);
void map<Key, T, Compare, Allocator>::erase(
                              iterator first,
                              iterator last);
```

The first form deletes the object referenced by the iterator `position`. The second form deletes all occurrences of the object x and returns the number of objects deleted. The third form deletes all the objects in the range from `first` up to `last`.

```
pair<iterator, iterator>
map<Key, T, Compare, Allocator>::
  equal_range(const key_type& x);

pair<const_iterator, const_iterator>
map<Key, T, Compare, Allocator>::
equal_range(const key_type& x) const;
```

Returns a pair of iterators delimiting a range of values equal to x.

```
iterator map<Key, T, Compare, Allocator>::find(
  const key_type& x);
const_iterator map<Key, T, Compare, Allocator>::find(
  const key_type& x) const;
```

Finds the first object equal to x and returns an iterator referencing it. If not found, it returns a past-the-end iterator.

```
allocator_type map<Key, T, Compare, Allocator>::
  get_allocator();
```

Returns the allocator object.

```
pair<iterator, bool> map<Key, T, Compare, Allocator>::
  insert(const value_type& x);
iterator map<Key, T, Compare, Allocator>::
  insert(iterator posn, const value_type& x);
template<class InputIterator>
void map<Key, T, Compare, Allocator>::insert(
      InputIterator first,
      InputIterator last);
```

Inserts a new value into the map. The first form returns a `pair` whose second member is a `bool` indicating if the insertion was successful. An insertion can fail if the object being inserted is already in the map. The first member is an iterator referencing the newly inserted object or the existing object if the object being inserted is a duplicate. The second form inserts x into the container if it is not already present. It returns an iterator referencing the element equal to x in the map. `posn` is a hint as to where the search for the insertion position should begin. The third form inserts the elements from `first` up to `last`, providing each element is not already in the map.

```
key_compare map<Key, T, Compare, Allocator>::
  key_comp() const;
```

Returns the comparison function for the map.

```
iterator map<Key, T, Compare, Allocator>::
  lower_bound(const key_type& x);
const_iterator map<Key, T, Compare, Allocator>::
  lower_bound(const key_type& x) const;
```

Returns an iterator referencing the lower bound on a range of values equal to x.

```
map<Key, T, Compare, Allocator>::map(
  const Compare& comp = Compare(),
  const Allocator& = allocator());
template<class InputIterator>
map<Key, T, Compare, Allocator>::map(
          InputIterator     first,
          InputIterator     last,
          const Compare&    comp = Compare(),
          const Allocator&  = allocator());
map<Key, T, Compare>::map(
  const map<Key, T, Compare, Allocator>& x);
```

These are the map constructors. The first two allow the specification of an alternate comparison function. The first form constructs an empty map and the second constructs a map and inserts the values from the range of the interators `first` up to `last`. The third form is the copy constructor.

```
map<Key, T, Compare, Allocator>::~Map();
```

The class destructor.

```
size_type map<Key, T, Compare, Allocator>::max_size()
    const;
```

Returns the maximum size of the container.

```
map<Key, T, Compare, Allocator>&
map<Key, T, Compare, Allocator>::operator=(
    const map<Key, T, Compare, Allocator>& x);
```

Assignment operator to assign the value of one map to another.

```
T& map<Key, T, Compare, Allocator>::operator[](
    const key_type& k);
```

Returns a reference to the object in the container that matches the given key.

```
reverse_iterator map<Key, T, Compare, Allocator>::
    rbegin();
const_reverse_iterator
map<Key, T, Compare, Allocator>::rbegin() const;
```

Returns a reverse iterator referencing the last object in the map.

```
reverse_iterator map<Key, T, Compare, Allocator>::
    rend();
const_reverse_iterator
map<Key, T, Compare, Allocator>::rend() const;
```

Returns a past-the-end iterator for a reverse iteration.

```
size_type map<Key, T, Compare, Allocator>::size()
    const;
```

Returns the current number of objects in the container.

```
void map<Key, T, Compare, Allocator>::swap(
    map<Key, T, Compare, Allocator>& x);
```

Swaps the contents of two sets.

```
iterator map<Key, T, Compare, Allocator>::upper_bound(
    const key_type& x);
const_iterator map<Key, T, Compare, Allocator>::
upper_bound(const key_type& x) const;
```

Returns the upper bound on a range of values equal to x.

```
value_compare map<Key, T, Compare, Allocator>::
  value_comp() const;
```

Returns the value comparison object.

Nonmember Functions:

```
template <class Key, class Compare, class Allocator>
bool operator==(
  const map<Key, T, Compare, Allocator>&    x,
  const map<Key, T, Compare, Allocator>&    y);
```

Compares two sets for equality.

```
template <class Key, class Compare, class Allocator>
bool operator<(
  const map<Key, T, Compare, Allocator>&    x,
  const map<Key, T, Compare, Allocator>&    y);
```

Returns true if the set x is less than the set y.

```
template <class Key, class Compare, class Allocator>
bool operator!=(
  const map<Key, T, Compare, Allocator>&    x,
  const map<Key, T, Compare, Allocator>&    y);
```

Returns true if the two sets are not equal.

```
template <class Key, class Compare, class Allocator>
bool operator<=(
  const map<Key, T, Compare, Allocator>&    x,
  const map<Key, T, Compare, Allocator>&    y);
```

Returns true if x is less than or equal to y.

```
template <class Key, class Compare, class Allocator>
bool operator>=(
  const map<Key, T, Compare, Allocator>&    x,
  const map<Key, T, Compare, Allocator>&    y);
```

Returns true if x is greater than or equal to y.

```
template <class Key, class Compare, class Allocator>
void swap(
    const map<Key, T, Compare, Allocator>&    x,
    const map<Key, T, Compare, Allocator>&    y);
```

Swaps the contents of two sets.

mask_array

TYPE: class   **HEADER:** <numeric> []

```
namespace std {
    template <class T>
        class mask_array;
}
```

DESCRIPTION: The mask_array is a helper class used for subscripting by the valarray. It contains a reference to the container being subscripted along with a list of the subscripts. It has no public constructors and can be instantiated only by subscripting a valarray with a Boolean array.

SEE ALSO: slice_array, gslice_array, indirect_array

Public Methods:

```
void mask_array<T>::operator=(
    const valarray<T>& a) const;
mask_array& mask_array<T>::operator=(
    const mask_array& a);
```

The first form assigns the subscripted members of the valarray referenced by *this the values in a. The second form is private and allows one mask_array to be assigned to another.

```
void mask_array<T>::operator*=(
    const valarray<T>& a) const;
```

Multiplies the subscripted members of the valarray referenced by *this by the values in a.

```
void mask_array<T>::operator/=(
    const valarray<T>& a) const;
```

Divides the subscripted members of the `valarray` referenced by `*this` by the values in a.

```
void mask_array<T>::operator%=(
    const valarray<T>& a) const;
```

Replaces the subscripted members of the `valarray` referenced by `*this` by the remainder upon division of these values by the values in a.

```
void mask_array<T>::operator+=(
    const valarray<T>& a) const;
```

Adds the values in a onto the subscripted members of the `valarray` referenced by `*this`.

```
void mask_array<T>::operator-=(
    const valarray<T>& a) const;
```

Subtracts the values in a from the subscripted members of the `valarray` referenced by `*this`.

```
void mask_array<T>::operator^=(
    const valarray<T>& a) const;
```

Replaces each of the subscripted members of the `valarray` referenced by `*this` with itself, exclusive OR'ed with the corresponding value from a.

```
void mask_array<T>::operator&=(
    const valarray<T>& a) const;
```

Replaces each of the subscripted members of the `valarray` referenced by `*this` with itself, bitwise AND'ed with the corresponding value from a.

```
void mask_array<T>::operator|=(
    const valarray<T>& a) const;
```

Replaces each of the subscripted members of the `valarray` referenced by `*this` with itself, inclusive OR'ed with the corresponding value from a.

```
void mask_array<T>::operator<<=(
    const valarray<T>& a) const;
```

Replaces each of the subscripted members of the `valarray` referenced by `*this` with itself, shifted left by the corresponding value from a.

```
void mask_array<T>::operator>>=(
  const valarray<T>& a) const;
```

Replaces each of the subscripted members of the `valarray` referenced by `*this` with itself, shifted right by the corresponding value from a.

```
void mask_array<T>::fill(const T& v);
```

Assigns the value v to the subscripted elements of the `valarray` referenced by `*this`.

```
mask_array<T>::mask_array();
mask_array<T>::mask_array(
  const mask_array<T>& a);
```

These are the private constructors. The first is the default constructor, and the second is the copy constructor. These might not be defined by all implementations.

```
mask_array<T>::~mask_array();
```

The class destructor.

max

TYPE: function   **HEADER:** <algorithm> [algobase.h]
TIME: constant   **SPACE:** constant

```
namespace std{
  template <class T>
  const T& max(const T&   a,
              const T&   b);

  template <class T, class Compare>
  const T& max(const T&   a,
               const T&   b,
               Compare    comp);
}
```

DESCRIPTION: Returns the maximum of the values a and b. The second form allows the specification of a comparison other than the default, `operator<`.

max_element

TYPE: function   **HEADER:** <algorithm> [algo.h]
TIME: linear   **SPACE:** constant

```
namespace std{
  template <class ForwardIterator>
  InputIterator max_element(ForwardIterator  first,
                            ForwardIterator  last);

  template <class ForwardIterator, class Compare>
  InputIterator max_element(ForwardIterator  first,
                            ForwardIterator  last,
                            Compare          comp);
}
```

DESCRIPTION: Traverses the sequence from `first` up to `last` and returns an iterator that refers to the largest element found. The second form allows the specification of a comparison other than the default, `operator<`.

mem_fun

TYPE: function   **HEADER:** <functional> [function.h]

```
namespace std{
  template<class S, class T>
  mem_fun_t<S,T>
  mem_fun(S (T::*mth)());
}
```

DESCRIPTION: This is a convenience function for adapting a parameterless method to a function object. It returns a function object of type `mem_fun_t` whose `operator()` will invoke the adapted method.

SEE ALSO: mem_fun1, mem_fun_t

mem_fun1

TYPE: function   **HEADER:** <functional> [function.h]

```
namespace std{
  template<class S, class T, class A>
  mem_fun1_t<S,T,A>
  mem_fun1(S (T::*f)(A));
}
```

DESCRIPTION: This is a convenience function for adapting a method requiring a single parameter to a function object. It returns a function object of type mem_fun1_t whose operator() will invoke the adapted method.

SEE ALSO: mem_fun_ref, mem_fun1_ref_t

mem_fun_ref

TYPE: function   **HEADER:** <functional> [function.h]

```
namespace std{
  template<class S, class T>
  mem_fun_ref_t<S,T>
  mem_fun_ref(S (T::*mth)());
}
```

DESCRIPTION: This convenience function returns a function object that adapts a parameterless class method so that it can be called as a regular function. It is useful for transforming a method into a function object.

SEE ALSO: mem_fun_ref_t, mem_fun1_ref

mem_fun1_ref

TYPE: function   **HEADER:** <functional> [function.h]

```
namespace std{
  template<class S, class T, class A>
  mem_fun1_ref_t<S,T,A>
  mem_fun1_ref(S (T::*mth)(A));
}
```

DESCRIPTION: This convenience function returns a function object that adapts a class method with one parameter so that it can be called as a regular function. It is useful for transforming a method into a function object.

SEE ALSO: mem_fun1_ref_t, mem_fun_ref

mem_fun_ref_t

TYPE: adaptor   **HEADER:** <functional> [function.h]

```
namespace std{
  template <class S, class T>
  class mem_fun_ref_t
  : public unary_function<T, S>;
}
```

DESCRIPTION: This function object adapts a parameterless method, transforming it into a function object that can be used by the STL algorithms. It differs from mem_fun_t in that it can be used with containers of objects rather than containers of pointers to objects.

SEE ALSO: mem_fun_ref, mem_fun1_ref_t

Public Members:

```
explicit mem_fun_ref_t(S (T::*mth)());
```

This constructs an instance to adapt mth().

```
S operator()(T& r);
```

This invokes the adapted function as (r.*mth)(), where r is a reference to the object on which to invoke the method. This should be used with containers of objects rather than containers of object pointers.

mem_fun1_ref_t

TYPE: adaptor   **HEADER:** <functional> [function.h]

```
namespace std{
  template <class S, class T, class A>
  class mem_fun1_ref_t
  : public binary_function<T, A, S>;
}
```

DESCRIPTION: This function object adapts a method with one parameter, transforming it into a function object that can be used by the STL algorithms. It differs from mem_fun1_t in that it can be used with containers of objects rather than containers of pointers to objects.

SEE ALSO: mem_fun1_ref, mem_fun_ref_t

Public Members:

```
explicit mem_fun1_ref_t(S (T::*mth)(A));
```

This constructs an instance to adapt mth().

```
S operator()(T& r, A x);
```

This invokes the adapted function as (r.*mth)(x), where r is a reference to the object on which to invoke the method. This should be used with containers of objects rather than containers of object pointers.

mem_fun_t

TYPE: adaptor   **HEADER:** <functional> [function.h]

```
namespace std{
  template <class S, class T>
  class mem_fun_t
  : public unary_function<T*, S>;
}
```

DESCRIPTION: mem_fun_t is a function adaptor that allows a pointer to a class method to be called as if it were a function. mem_fun_t is a function object in its own right. mem_fun_t is usually created using the convenience function mem_fun().

SEE ALSO: mem_fun, mem_fun1_t, mem_fun_ref_t

Public Methods:

```
explicit mem_fun_t(S (T::*mth)());
```

This constructs an instance to adapt T::mth() so that it can be called as a regular function. mth must be a unary method that returns a result.

```
S operator()(T* p);
```

This invokes the adapted method as (p->*mth)() so that p is a pointer to the object on which the method should be invoked. Since a pointer to an object is required, this is suitable only for containers of object pointers.

mem_fun1_t

TYPE: adaptor   **HEADER:** <functional> [function.h]

```
namespace std{
  template <class S, class T, class A>
  class mem_fun1_t
  : public binary_function<T*, A, S>;
}
```

DESCRIPTION: mem_fun1_t is a function adaptor that allows a pointer to a class method with one parameter to be called as if it were a function. mem_fun1_t is a function object in its own right. mem_fun1_t is usually created using the convenience function mem_fun1().

SEE ALSO: mem_fun1, mem_fun_t, mem_fun1_ref_t

Public Methods:

```
explicit mem_fun1_t(S (T::*mth)(A));
```

This constructs an instance to adapt T::mth() so that it can be called as a regular function. mth must be a unary method that returns a result.

```
S operator()(T* p, A x);
```

This invokes the adapted method as (p->*mth)(x) so that p is a pointer to the object on which the method should be invoked. Since a pointer to an object is required, this is suitable only for containers of object pointers.

merge

TYPE: function   **HEADER:** <algorithm> [algo.h]
TIME: linear   **SPACE:** constant

```
namespace std{
  template <class InputIterator1,
      class InputIterator2, class OutputIterator>
  OutputIterator merge(InputIterator1    first1,
                       InputIterator1    last1,
                       InputIterator2    first2,
                       InputIterator2    last2,
                       OutputIterator    result);
```

```
template <class InputIterator1,
    class InputIterator2, class OutputIterator,
    class Compare>
OutputIterator merge(InputIterator1      first1,
                     InputIterator1      last1,
                     InputIterator2      first2,
                     InputIterator2      last2,
                     OutputIterator      result,
                     Compare             comp);
}
```

DESCRIPTION: Merges the sequence starting with first1 up to last1 with the sequence starting with first2 up to last2. The merged sequence is placed starting at the position referred to by result. The resultant sequence is sorted and assumes that both of the input sequences are sorted. The second form allows the specification of a comparison operator other than the default, operator<.

min

TYPE: function   **HEADER:** <algorithm> [algobase.h]
TIME: constant   **SPACE:** constant

```
namespace std{
  template <class T>
  const T& min(const T&   a,
               const T&   b);

  template <class T, class Compare>
  const T& min(const T&   a,
               const T&   b,
               Compare    comp);
}
```

DESCRIPTION: Returns the minimum of the values a and b. The second form allows the specification of a comparison other than the default operator<.

min_element

TYPE: function   **HEADER:** <algorithm> [algo.h]
TIME: linear   **SPACE:** constant

```
namespace std{
  template <class ForwardIterator>
  InputIterator min_element(ForwardIterator  first,
```

```
                              ForwardIterator    last);

   template <class ForwardIterator, class Compare>
   InputIterator min_element(ForwardIterator  first,
                             ForwardIterator  last,
                             Compare          comp);
}
```

DESCRIPTION: Traverses the sequence from first up to last and returns an iterator that refers to the smallest element found. The second form allows the specification of a comparison other than the default operator<.

minus

TYPE: function object   **HEADER:** <functional> [function.h]
TIME: constant   **SPACE:** constant

```
namespace std{
   template <class T>
   struct minus: binary_function<T, T, T> {
     T operator()(const T& x, const T& y) const;
   };
}
```

DESCRIPTION: A function object that can be passed to another function as a substitute for operator-. It applies operator- to its two parameters and returns the result.

SEE ALSO: plus, multiplies, divides, modulus

mismatch

TYPE: function   **HEADER:** <algorithm> [algobase.h]
TIME: linear   **SPACE:** constant

```
namespace std{
   template <class InputIterator1,
       class InputIterator2>
   pair<InputIterator1, InputIterator2>
   mismatch(InputIterator1 first1,
       InputIterator1    last1,
       InputIterator2    first2);

   template <class InputIterator1,
       class InputIterator2, class BinaryPredicate>
```

```
        pair<InputIterator1, InputIterator2>
        mismatch(InputIterator1 first1,
            InputIterator1    last1,
            InputIterator2    first2,
            BinaryPredicate   binary_pred);
}
```

DESCRIPTION: Compares each element in the sequence from `first1` up to `last1` with the elements in the sequence of the same length beginning with `first2`. It returns a pair of iterators that refers to the first mismatching elements in each sequence. The first member of the pair refers to the element in the first sequence, and the second member refers to the element in the second sequence. If there are no mismatches, an iterator pair is returned whose first member is `last1` and whose second member is a past-the-end iterator for the sequence starting at `first2`. No assumption about the order of the sequences is made. The second form allows the specification of a comparison operator other than the default, `operator==`.

modulus

TYPE: function object   **HEADER:** <functional> [function.h]
TIME: constant   **SPACE:** constant

```
namespace std{
  template <class T>
  struct modulus: binary_function<T, T, T> {
    T operator()(const T& x, const T& y) const;
  };
}
```

DESCRIPTION: A function object that can be passed to another function as a substitute for `operator%`. It applies `operator%` to its two parameters and returns the result.

SEE ALSO: minus, multiplies, divides, plus

multimap

TYPE: class   **HEADER:** <map> [multimap.h]

```
namespace std {
  template <class Key, class T,
  class Compare = less<Key>,
```

```
   class Allocator = allocator<pair<const Key, T> > >
   class multimap;
}
```

DESCRIPTION: The multimap stores and retrieves objects based on a key provided when the object is inserted. The key can be of any type, and it does not have to be contained within the object. The multimap supports duplicate keys. The multimap allows you to insert objects and provides fast retrieval using a comparison function to determine the equality of objects. The objects are actually stored in a tree so that insertion and retrieval take logarithmic time. The multimap is useful for applications that want to implement the concept of associative arrays. Internally, the objects in the multimap are always ordered so that an iterator will retrieve the objects in sorted order.

SEE ALSO: multiset, set, map

Public Members:

```
multimap<Key, T, Compare, Allocator>::allocator_type;
```

The type of the allocator.

```
multimap<Key, T, Compare, Allocator>::const_iterator;
```

A constant iterator for the container.

```
multimap<Key, T, Compare, Allocator>::const_pointer;
```

The type of a constant pointer to the content.

```
multimap<Key, T, Compare, Allocator>::const_reference;
```

The type of a constant reference to the content.

```
multimap<Key, T, Compare,
   Allocator>::const_reverse_iterator;
```

A constant reverse iterator for the container.

```
multimap<Key, T, Compare, Allocator>::difference_type;
```

Able to represent the difference between any two iterators.

```
multimap<Key, T, Compare, Allocator>::iterator;
```

An iterator for the container.

```
multimap<Key, T, Compare, Allocator>::key_compare;
```

The type of the key comparison function.

```
multimap<Key, T, Compare, Allocator>::key_type;
```

The type of the key.

```
multimap<Key, T, Compare, Allocator>::mapped_type;
```

The type of the values stored in the container.

```
multimap<Key, T, Compare, Allocator>::pointer;
```

The type of a pointer to the content.

```
multimap<Key, T, Compare, Allocator>::reference;
```

The type of a reference to the content.

```
multimap<Key, T, Compare, Allocator>::
   reverse_iterator;
```

A reverse iterator for the container.

```
multimap<Key, T, Compare, Allocator>::size_type;
```

Able to represent any non-negative value of `difference_type`.

```
multimap<Key, T, Compare, Allocator>::value_compare;
```

The value comparison object.

```
multimap<Key, T, Compare, Allocator>::value_type;
```

A `pair<const Key, T>`.

Public Methods:

```
iterator multimap<Key, T, Compare, Allocator>::
   begin();
```

```
const_iterator multimap<Key, T, Compare, Allocator>::
  begin() const;
```

Returns an iterator referencing the first value in the multimap.

```
void multimap<Key, T, Compare, Allocator>::clear();
```

Deletes all elements from the multimap.

```
size_type multimap<Key, T, Compare, Allocator>::count(
  const key_type& x) const;
```

Returns a count of the number of objects equal to x.

```
bool multimap<Key, T, Compare, Allocator>::empty()
  const;
```

Returns a Boolean indicating if the multimap is empty.

```
iterator multimap<Key, T, Compare, Allocator>::end();
const_iterator multimap<Key, T, Compare, Allocator>::
  end() const;
```

Returns a past-the-end iterator for the multimap.

```
void multimap<Key, T, Compare, Allocator>::erase(
  iterator position);
size_type multimap<Key, T, Compare, Allocator>::erase(
  const key_type& x);
void multimap<Key, T, Compare, Allocator>::erase(
                    iterator first,
                    iterator last);
```

The first form deletes the object referenced by the iterator position. The second form deletes all occurrences of the object x and returns the number of objects deleted. The third form deletes all the objects in the range from first up to last.

```
pair<iterator, iterator>
multimap<Key, T, Compare, Allocator>::equal_range(
  const key_type& x);

pair<const_iterator, const_iterator>
```

```
multimap<Key, T, Compare, Allocator>::
equal_range(const key_type& x) const;
```

Returns a pair of iterators delimiting a range of values equal to x.

```
iterator multimap<Key, T, Compare, Allocator>::
  find(const key_type& x);
const_iterator multimap<Key, T, Compare, Allocator>::
  find(const key_type& x) const;
```

Finds the first object equal to x and returns an iterator referencing it. If not found, it returns a past-the-end iterator.

```
allocator_type multimap<Key, T, Compare, Allocator>::
  get_allocator();
```

Returns the allocator object.

```
iterator multimap<Key, T, Compare, Allocator>::
  insert(const value_type& x);
template<class InputIterator>
void multimap<Key, T, Compare, Allocator>::insert(
                   InputIterator first,
                   InputIterator last);
iterator multimap<Key, T, Compare, Allocator>::insert(
                   iterator           position,
                   const value_type&  x);
```

The first form inserts a new value into the multimap. It returns an iterator referencing the newly inserted element. The second form inserts the series of values from first up to last. The third form inserts the value x into the multimap. The iterator position is used as a hint about where to start searching for the insertion position. It returns an iterator referencing the newly inserted element.

```
key_compare multimap<Key, T, Compare, Allocator>::
  key_comp()const;
```

Returns the key comparison function for the multimap.

```
iterator multimap<Key, T, Compare, Allocator>::
  lower_bound(const key_type& x);
const_iterator multimap<Key, T, Compare, Allocator>::
  lower_bound(const key_type& x) const;
```

Returns an iterator referencing the lower bound on a range of values equal to x.

```
size_type multimap<Key, T, Compare, Allocator>::
   max_size() const;
```

Returns the maximum size of the container.

```
multimap<Key, T, Compare, Allocator>::multimap(
   const Compare& comp = Compare(),
   const Allocator& = allocator());
template<class InputIterator>
multimap<Key, T, Compare, Allocator>::multimap(
             InputIterator      first,
             InputIterator      last,
             const Compare&     comp = Compare(),
             const Allocator& = allocator());
multimap<Key, T, Compare, Allocator>::multimap(
   const multimap<Key, T, Compare, Allocator>& x);
```

These are the multimap constructors. Two of these allow the specification of an alternate comparison function other than the one specified in the template parameters. The first form constructs an empty multimap, and the second constructs a multimap and inserts the values from the range of the iterators first up to last. The third form is the copy constructor.

```
multimap<Key, T, Compare, Allocator>::~multimap();
```

The class destructor.

```
multimap<Key, T, Compare, Allocator>&
multimap<Key, T, Compare, Allocator>::operator=(
   const multimap<Key, T, Compare, Allocator>& x);
```

Assignment operator to assign the value of one multimap to another.

```
Allocator<T>::reference multimap<Key, T, Compare,
   Allocator>::
operator[](const key_type& k);
```

Returns a reference to the object in the container that matches the given key.

```
reverse_iterator multimap<Key, T, Compare, Allocator>
   ::rbegin();
```

```
const_reverse_iterator
multimap<Key, T, Compare, Allocator>::rbegin() const;
```

Returns a reverse iterator referencing the last object in the multimap.

```
reverse_iterator multimap<Key, T, Compare, Allocator>
  ::rend();

const_reverse_iterator
multimap<Key, T, Compare, Allocator>::rend() const;
```

Returns a past-the-end iterator for a reverse iteration.

```
size_type multimap<Key, T, Compare, Allocator>::
  size() const;
```

Returns the current number of objects in the container.

```
void multimap<Key, T, Compare, Allocator>::swap(
  multimap<Key, T, Compare, Allocator>& x);
```

Swaps the contents of two sets.

```
iterator multimap<Key, T, Compare, Allocator>::
  upper_bound(const key_type& x);
const_iterator multimap<Key, T, Compare, Allocator>::
  upper_bound(const key_type& x) const;
```

Returns the upper bound on a range of values equal to x.

```
value_compare multimap<Key, T, Compare, Allocator>::
  value_comp() const;
```

Returns the value comparison object.

Nonmember Functions:

```
template <class Key, class Compare, class Allocator>
bool operator==(
  const multimap<Key, T, Compare, Allocator>& x,
  const multimap<Key, T, Compare, Allocator>& y);
```

Compares two sets for equality.

```
template <class Key, class Compare, class Allocator>
bool operator<(
   const multimap<Key, T, Compare, Allocator>& x,
   const multimap<Key, T, Compare, Allocator>& y);
```

Returns true if the set x is less than the set y.

```
template <class Key, class Compare, class Allocator>
bool operator!=(
   const multimap<Key, T, Compare, Allocator>& x,
   const multimap<Key, T, Compare, Allocator>& y);
```

Returns true if the two sets are not equal.

```
template <class Key, class Compare, class Allocator>
bool operator<=(
   const multimap<Key, T, Compare, Allocator>& x,
   const multimap<Key, T, Compare, Allocator>& y);
```

Returns true if x is less than or equal to y.

```
template <class Key, class Compare, class Allocator>
bool operator>=(
   const multimap<Key, T, Compare, Allocator>& x,
   const multimap<Key, T, Compare, Allocator>& y);
```

Returns true if x is greater than or equal to y.

```
template <class Key, class Compare, class Allocator>
void swap(
   const multimap<Key, T, Compare, Allocator>& x,
   const multimap<Key, T, Compare, Allocator>& y);
```

Swaps the contents of two sets.

multiplies

TYPE: function object   **HEADER:** <functional> [ ]
TIME: constant   **SPACE:** constant

```
namespace std{
   template <class T>
   struct multiplies: binary_function<T, T, T> {
    T operator()(const T& x, const T& y);
```

```
      };
}
```

DESCRIPTION: A function object that can be passed to another function as a substitute for `operator*`. It applies `operator*` to its two parameters and returns the result. This function object replaces `times` in the HP implementation.

SEE ALSO: minus, plus, divides, modulus, times

multiset

TYPE: class   **HEADER:** <set> [multiset.h]

```
namespace std {
  template <class Key, class Compare = less<Key>,
  class Allocator = allocator<Key> >
  class multiset;
}
```

DESCRIPTION: This is an associative container and should not be confused with the mathematical concept of a set. The multiset is very similar to the set container except that it allows duplicate objects to be stored, whereas a set does not. The multiset allows you to insert objects and provides fast retrieval using a comparison function to determine the order of objects. The objects are actually stored in a tree so that insertion and retrieval take logarithmic time. The multiset is useful for applications that require fast storage and retrieval of objects in random order. Internally, the objects in the multiset are always ordered so that an iterator will retrieve the objects in sorted order.

SEE ALSO: set, map, multimap

Public Members:

```
multiset<Key, Compare, Allocator>::allocator_type;
```

The type of the allocator.

```
multiset<Key, Compare, Allocator>::const_iterator;
```

A constant iterator for the container.

```
multiset<Key, Compare, Allocator>::const_pointer;
```

The type of a constant pointer to the content.

```
multiset<Key, Compare, Allocator>::const_reference;
```

The type of a constant reference to the content.

```
multiset<Key, Compare, Allocator>::
  const_reverse_iterator;
```

A constant reverse iterator for the container.

```
multiset<Key, Compare, Allocator>::difference_type;
```

Able to represent the difference between any two iterators.

```
multiset<Key, Compare, Allocator>::iterator;
```

An iterator for the container.

```
multiset<Key, Compare, Allocator>::key_compare;
```

The type of the key comparison function.

```
multiset<Key, Compare, Allocator>::key_type;
```

The type of the key.

```
multiset<Key, Compare, Allocator>::pointer;
```

The type of a pointer to the content.

```
multiset<Key, Compare, Allocator>::reference;
```

The type of a reference to the content.

```
multiset<Key, Compare, Allocator>::reverse_iterator;
```

A reverse iterator for the container.

```
multiset<Key, Compare, Allocator>::size_type;
```

Able to represent any non-negative value of difference_type.

```
multiset<Key, Compare, Allocator>::value_compare;
```

The value comparison object.

```
multiset<Key, Compare, Allocator>::value_type;
```

The same type as the key.

Public Methods:

```
iterator multiset<Key, Compare, Allocator>::begin();
const_iterator multiset<Key, Compare, Allocator>::
    begin() const;
```

Returns an iterator referencing the first value in the multiset.

```
void multiset<Key, Compare, Allocator>::clear();
```

Removes all elements from the container.

```
size_type multiset<Key, Compare, Allocator>::
    count(const key_type& x) const;
```

Returns a count of the number of objects equal to x.

```
bool multiset<Key, Compare, Allocator>::empty() const;
```

Returns a Boolean indicating if the multiset is empty.

```
iterator multiset<Key, Compare, Allocator>::end();
const_iterator multiset<Key, Compare, Allocator>::
    end() const;
```

Returns a past-the-end iterator for the multiset.

```
void multiset<Key, Compare, Allocator>::erase(
    iterator position);
```

```
size_type multiset<Key, Compare, Allocator>::erase(
    const key_type& x);
```

```
void multiset<Key, Compare, Allocator>::erase(
        iterator first,
        iterator last);
```

The first form deletes the object referenced by the iterator `position`. The second deletes all occurrences of the object x and returns the number of objects deleted. Finally, the third form deletes all the objects in the range from `first` up to `last`.

```
pair<iterator, iterator>
multiset<Key, Compare, Allocator>::equal_range(
    const key_type& x) const;
```

Returns a pair of iterators delimiting a range of values equal to x.

```
iterator multiset<Key, Compare, Allocator>::find(
    const key_type& x) const;
```

Finds the first object equal to x and returns an iterator referencing it. If not found, it returns a past-the-end iterator.

```
allocator_type multiset<Key, Compare, Allocator>::
    get_allocator() const;
```

Returns the class allocator.

```
iterator multiset<Key, Compare, Allocator>::insert(
                    const value_type& x);
iterator multiset<Key, Compare, Allocator>::insert(
                    iterator        posn,
                    const value_type&  x);
template<class InputIterator>
void multiset<Key, Compare, Allocator>::insert(
                    InputIterator first,
                    InputIterator last);
```

The first form inserts a new value into the multiset and returns an iterator that references the newly inserted object. The second form inserts a new value, using `posn` as a hint about where to start searching for the insertion position. The third form inserts the series of values from `first` up to `last`.

```
key_compare multiset<Key, Compare, Allocator>::
    key_comp() const;
```

Returns the comparison function for the multiset.

```
iterator multiset<Key, Compare, Allocator>::
    lower_bound(const key_type& x) const;
```

Returns an iterator referencing the lower bound on a range of values equal to x.

```
size_type multiset<Key, Compare, Allocator>::
  max_size() const;
```

Returns the maximum size of the container.

```
multiset<Key, Compare, Allocator>&
multiset<Key, Compare, Allocator>::operator=(
  const multiset<Key, Compare, Allocator>& x);
```

Assignment operator to assign the value of one multiset to another.

```
explicit multiset<Key, Compare, Allocator>::multiset(
  const Compare& comp = Compare(),
  const Allocator& = Allocator());
template<class InputIterator>
multiset<Key, Compare, Allocator>::multiset(
              InputIterator    first,
              InputIterator    last,
              const Compare&   comp = Compare()),
              const Allocator& = Allocator());
multiset<Key, Compare, Allocator>::multiset(
  const multiset<Key, Compare, Allocator>& x);
```

These are the multiset constructors. Two of these allow the specification of an alternate comparison function other than the one specified in the template parameters. The first form constructs an empty multiset, and the second constructs a multiset and inserts the values from the range of the iterators first up to last. The third form is the copy constructor.

```
multiset<Key, Compare, Allocator>::~multiset();
```

The class destructor.

```
reverse_iterator multiset<Key, Compare, Allocator>::
  rbegin();
const_reverse_iterator
multiset<Key, Compare, Allocator>:: rbegin() const;
```

Returns a reverse iterator referencing the last object in the multiset.

```
reverse_iterator multiset<Key, Compare, Allocator>::
  rend();
```

```
const_reverse_iterator
multiset<Key, Compare, Allocator>::rend() const;
```

Returns a past-the-end iterator for a reverse iteration.

```
size_type multiset<Key, Compare, Allocator>::
    size() const;
```

Returns the current number of objects in the container.

```
void multiset<Key, Compare, Allocator>::swap(
    multiset<Key, Compare, Allocator>& x);
```

Swaps the contents of two sets.

```
iterator multiset<Key, Compare, Allocator>::
    upper_bound(const key_type& x) const;
```

Returns the upper bound on a range of values equal to x.

```
value_compare multiset<Key, Compare, Allocator>::
    value_comp();
```

Returns the value comparison object.

Nonmember Functions:

```
template <class Key, class Compare, Allocator>
bool operator==(
    const multiset<Key, Compare, Allocator>&   x,
    const multiset<Key, Compare, Allocator>&   y);
```

Returns true if the two sets are equal on an element-by-element basis.

```
template <class Key, class Compare, Allocator>
bool operator<(
    const multiset<Key, Compare, Allocator>&   x,
    const multiset<Key, Compare, Allocator>&   y);
```

Returns true if the multiset x is lexicographically less than the multiset y.

```
template <class Key, class Compare, Allocator>
bool operator!=(
```

```
      const multiset<Key, Compare, Allocator>&   x,
      const multiset<Key, Compare, Allocator>&   y);
```

Returns true if the two sets are not equal on an element-by-element basis.

```
template <class Key, class Compare, Allocator>
bool operator>(
   const multiset<Key, Compare, Allocator>&   x,
   const multiset<Key, Compare, Allocator>&   y);
```

Returns true if the multiset x is lexicographically greater than the multiset y.

```
template <class Key, class Compare, Allocator>
bool operator<=(
   const multiset<Key, Compare, Allocator>&   x,
   const multiset<Key, Compare, Allocator>&   y);
```

Returns true if the multiset x is lexicographically less than or equal to the multiset y.

```
template <class Key, class Compare, Allocator>
bool operator>=(
   const multiset<Key, Compare, Allocator>&   x,
   const multiset<Key, Compare, Allocator>&   y);
```

Returns true if the multiset x is lexicographically greater than or equal to the multiset y.

```
template <class Key, class Compare, Allocator>
bool swap(
   const multiset<Key, Compare, Allocator>&   x,
   const multiset<Key, Compare, Allocator>&   y);
```

Swaps the contents of the two multisets.

negate

TYPE: function object   **HEADER:** <functional> [function.h]
TIME: constant   **SPACE:** constant

```
namespace std{
  template <class T>
  struct negate: unary_function<T, T> {
      T operator()(const T& x) const;
```

```
    };
}
```

DESCRIPTION: A function object that can be passed to another function as a substitute for the unary `operator-`. It applies `operator-` to its parameter and returns the result.

SEE ALSO: minus, multiplies, plus, modulus, divides

next_permutation

TYPE: function   **HEADER:** <algorithm> [algo.h]
TIME: linear   **SPACE:** constant

```
namespace std{
    template <class BidirectionalIterator>
    bool next_permutation(
            BidirectionalIterator    first,
            BidirectionalIterator    last);

    template <class BidirectionalIterator,
        class Compare>
    bool next_permutation(
            BidirectionalIterator    first,
            BidirectionalIterator    last,
            Compare                  comp);
}
```

DESCRIPTION: A permutation of a sequence is a member of the set of all arrangements of elements in the sequence such that no two of the sequences are equal on an element-by-element basis. The set of all permutations of a sequence is viewed as an ordered set, where each successive member is lexicographically greater than the previous member. Given the sequence from `first` up to `last`, the function `next_permutation()` will attempt to generate the next permutation that is lexicographically greater than the original. If such a permutation exists, the function returns `true`. If there is no such permutation, then `false` is returned, and the original sequence is reversed. The second form allows the specification of a comparison function to be used for the lexicographical comparison other than the default, `operator<`.

SEE ALSO: prev_permutation

not1

TYPE: function   HEADER: <functional> [function.h]

```
namespace std{
  template <class Predicate>
  unary_negate<Predicate>
  not1(const Predicate& pred);
}
```

DESCRIPTION: This takes a unary function as a parameter and logically negates the result of the function. It returns an instance of unary_negate, which is a function object that actually adapts pred.

SEE ALSO: not2, unary_negate

not2

TYPE: function   HEADER: <functional> [function.h]

```
namespace std{
  template <class Predicate>
  binary_negate<Predicate>
  not2(const Predicate& pred);
}
```

DESCRIPTION: Takes a binary function as a parameter and logically negates the result of the function. It returns an instance of binary_negate, which is a function object that actually adapts pred.

SEE ALSO: not1, binary_negate

not_equal_to

TYPE: function object   HEADER: <functional> [function.h]
TIME: constant   SPACE: constant

```
namespace std{
  template <class T>
  struct not_equal_to : binary_function<T, T, bool> {
      bool operator()(const T& x, const T& y) const;
  };
}
```

DESCRIPTION: A function object that can be used as a substitute for `opera-tor!=` and passed as a parameter to functions expecting a function object. It compares its two parameters using `operator!=` and returns the result.

SEE ALSO: equal_to, greater, less, less_equal, greater_equal

nth_element

TYPE: function   **HEADER:** <algorithm> [algo.h]
TIME: linear   **SPACE:** constant

```
namespace std{
   template <class RandomAccessIterator>
   void nth_element(
            RandomAccessIterator    first,
            RandomAccessIterator    nth,
            RandomAccessIterator    last);
   template <class RandomAccessIterator,
        class Compare>
   void nth_element(
            RandomAccessIterator    first,
            RandomAccessIterator    nth,
            RandomAccessIterator    last,
            Compare                 comp);
}
```

DESCRIPTION: Places the `nth` element in the range from `first` up to `last` in the position it would lie if the range had been sorted. It also ensures that all of the elements prior to the final location of the `nth` element are less than or equal to all of the elements that are after the final position of the `nth` element. It is assumed that `nth` is an iterator that lies within the range from `first` up to `last`. The second form allows an alternate comparison object other than the default, `operator<`.

operator>

TYPE: operator   **HEADER:** <utility> [function.h]
TIME: constant   **SPACE:** constant

```
namespace std{
   namespace rel_ops {
        template <class T>
```

```
                     bool operator>(const T& x, const T& y);
        }
    }
```

DESCRIPTION: Returns true if x is greater than y.

---

operator>=

    TYPE: operator   **HEADER:** <utility> [function.h]
    TIME: constant   **SPACE:** constant

```
namespace std{
  namespace rel_ops {
      template <class T>
      bool operator>=(const T& x, const T& y);
  }
}
```

DESCRIPTION: Returns true if x is greater than or equal to y.

---

operator<=

    TYPE: operator   **HEADER:** <utility> [function.h]
    TIME: constant   **SPACE:** constant

```
namespace std{
  namespace rel_ops {
      template <class T>
      bool operator<=(const T& x, const T& y);
  }
}
```

DESCRIPTION: returns true if x is less than or equal to y.

---

operator!=

    TYPE: operator   **HEADER:** <utility> [function.h]
    TIME: constant   **SPACE:** constant

```
namespace std{
  namespace rel_ops {
      template <class T>
      bool operator!=(const T& x, const T& y);
  }
}
```

DESCRIPTION: Returns `true` if x is not equal to y.

---

output_iterator

TYPE: structure   **HEADER:** <> [iterator.h]

```
struct output_iterator;
```

DESCRIPTION: Output iterators can only output values to a destination and are used primarily to implement output stream iterators. The operations are restricted so that values can be assigned to output iterators but not retrieved from them. This has been removed from the C++ standard as a class.

Operators:

```
bool output_iterator<T, Distance>::operator==(
  const output_iterator& x);
```

Returns `true` if the two iterators are equal.

```
output_iterator& output_iterator<T,
Distance>::operator++();
```

Rncrements the iterator and returns a reference to the new value of the iterator.

```
output_iterator<T, Distance>::operator++(int);
```

Returns the current value of the iterator and then increments the iterator.

```
T output_iterator<T, Distance>::operator*();
```

Dereferences the iterator and allows a value to be assigned to it.

---

pair

TYPE: struct   **HEADER:** <utility> [pair.h]

```
namespace std {
  template <class T1, class T2>
  struct pair;
}
```

DESCRIPTION: While this can be used to represent a pair of any two objects, it is commonly used to represent a pair of iterators that indicate the beginning and ending of a sequence. The header file also defines templates for op-erator== and operator< for use with pairs.

Public Members:

```
pair<T1, T2>::first_type;
```

The type of the first member.

```
pair<T1, T2>::second_type;
```

The type of the second member.

Public Methods:

```
pair<T1, T2>::pair();
pair<T1, T2>::pair(const T1& x, const T2& y);
template<class U, class V>
  pair<T1, T2>::pair(const pair<U, V> &p);
```

The first form is the default constructor that uses T1() and T2() to construct first and second, respectively. The second form is the most commonly used constructor and assigns the values x and y to first and second, re-spectively. The third form accepts a pair with different template parameters and uses implicit conversions to obtain the correct types.

Nonmember Functions:

```
template <class T1, class T2>
pair<T1, T2> make_pair(const T1&    x,
                       const T2&    y);
```

A convenience function to make a pair from two values. It returns pair<T1, T2>(x, y).

```
template<class T1, class T2>
bool operator==(const pair<T1, T2>&    x,
                const pair<T1, T2>&    y);
```

Returns a Boolean indicating if the pairs x and y are equal.

```
template<class T1, class T2>
bool operator<(const pair<T1, T2>& x,
               const pair<T1, T2>&     y);
```

Returns a Boolean indicating if the pair x is less than the pair y. This returns the result of the expression

```
x.first   < y.first || (!(y.first < x.first) &&
x.second < y.second)
```

partial_sort

TYPE: function   **HEADER:** <algorithm> [algo.h]
TIME: n log m   **SPACE:** constant

```
namespace std{
   template <class RandomAccessIterator>
   void partial_sort(RandomAccessIterator    first,
                     RandomAccessIterator    middle,
                     RandomAccessIterator    last);

   template <class RandomAccessIterator,
       class Compare>
   void partial_sort(RandomAccessIterator    first,
                     RandomAccessIterator    middle,
                     RandomAccessIterator    last,
                     Compare                 comp);
}
```

DESCRIPTION: Sorts the first *m* elements of the sequence from first up to last of length *n*. The sequence from first up to middle of length *m* is replaced by the first *m* elements of the sequence [first, last) in sorted order. The remaining elements from middle up to last are left in an undefined order. The second form of the function allows the specification of a comparison function object other than the default, operator<.

SEE ALSO: sort, stable_sort, partial_sort_copy

partial_sort_copy

TYPE: function   **HEADER:** <algorithm> [algo.h]
TIME: n log m   **SPACE:** constant

```
namespace std{
  template <class InputIterator,
       class      RandomAccessIterator>
  RandomAccessIterator partial_sort_copy(
            InputIterator              first,
            InputIterator              last,
            RandomAccessIterator       result_first,
            RandomAccessIterator       result_last);

  template <class InputIterator,
       class RandomAccessIterator, class Compare>
  RandomAccessIterator partial_sort_copy(
            InputIterator              first,
            InputIterator              last,
            RandomAccessIterator       result_first,
            RandomAccessIterator       result_last,
            Compare                    comp);
}
```

DESCRIPTION: Sorts the first m elements of the sequence from first up to last and places them at the location referred to by result_first. m is the length of the shorter of the two sequences from first up to last and from result_first up to result_last, and n is the length of the longer sequence. If the entire result sequence is not overwritten, then the remainder of the result sequence past the first n elements is in an undefined order. The second form of the function allows the specification of a comparison function object other than the default, operator<.

SEE ALSO: sort, stable_sort, partial_sort

partial_sum

TYPE: function   **HEADER:** <numeric> [algo.h]
TIME: linear   **SPACE:** constant

```
namespace std{
  template <class InputIterator,
       class OutputIterator>
  OutputIterator partial_sum(InputIterator    first,
                             InputIterator last,
                             OutputIteratorresult);
```

```
template <class InputIterator,
    class OutputIterator, class BinaryOperation>
OutputIterator partial_sum(
                InputIterator       first,
                InputIterator       last,
                OutputIterator      result,
                BinaryOperation     binary_op);
}
```

DESCRIPTION: Produces a sequence where each element in the sequence is the cumulative sum of the preceding corresponding elements in the sequence from first up to last. The resulting partial sum sequence is placed beginning at the location referenced by result. The function returns an iterator that refers to one past the final value in the result sequence. If first == result, then the original sequence will be replaced by its partial sum. This is usually the only case where the two sequences can overlap and produce meaningful results. The second form allows the specification of an operation to be used to compute the sum other than the default, operator+.

partition

TYPE: function   **HEADER:** <algorithm> [algo.h]
TIME: linear   **SPACE:** constant

```
namespace std{
  template <class BidirectionalIterator,
      class Predicate>
  BidirectionalIterator partition(
                  BidirectionalIterator   first,
                  BidirectionalIterator   last,
                  Predicate               pred);
}
```

DESCRIPTION: Rearranges the elements in the sequence from first up to last so that all elements that satisfy the predicate are placed before all elements that do not satisfy the predicate. The function returns an iterator i such that all elements in the range from first up to i satisfy the predicate and all elements from i up to last do not satisfy the predicate. The order of the elements in the subranges from first up to i and from i up to last is undefined.

plus

TYPE: function object   **HEADER:** <functional> [function.h]
TIME: constant   **SPACE:** constant

```
namespace std{
  template <class T>
  struct plus : binary_function<T, T, T> {
      T operator()(const T& x, const T& y) const;
  };
}
```

DESCRIPTION: A function object that can be passed to another function as a substitute for operator+. It applies operator+ to its two parameters and returns the result.

SEE ALSO: minus, multiplies, divides, modulus

pointer

TYPE: typedef   **REQUIRED BY:** all containers

DESCRIPTION: A typedef defined by all containers that returns the type of a pointer to an object in the container.

SEE ALSO: reference

pointer_to_binary_function

TYPE: adaptor   **HEADER:** <functional> [function.h]

```
namespace std{
  template <class Arg1, class Arg2, class Result>
  class pointer_to_binary_function :
  public binary_function<Arg1,Arg2,Result>;
}
```

DESCRIPTION: This is an adaptor that adapts a pointer to a binary function to a function object. It is used to convert an ordinary function into a function object as used by many of the STL algorithms. This is usually constructed using the convenience function ptr_fun().

SEE ALSO: ptr_fun, pointer_to_unary_function

Public Methods:

```
explicit pointer_to_binary_function(
            Result (*fun)(Arg1, Arg2));
```

This is the constructor that requires a pointer to a binary function.

```
Result operator()(Arg1 x, Arg2 y) const;
```

`operator()` is invoked to call the function being adapted. The adapted function is passed the arguments x and y.

---

pointer_to_unary_function

TYPE: adaptor   **HEADER:** <functional> [function.h]

```
namespace std{
  template <class Arg, class Result>
  class pointer_to_unary_function :
  public unary_function<Arg, Result>;
}
```

DESCRIPTION: This is an adaptor that adapts a pointer to a unary function to a function object. It is used to convert an ordinary function into a function object as used by many of the STL algorithms. This is usually constructed using the convenience function `ptr_fun()`.

SEE ALSO: ptr_fun, pointer_to_binary_function

Public Methods:

```
explicit pointer_to_unary_function(
                  Result (*fun)(Arg));
```

This is the constructor that requires a pointer to a unary function.

```
Result operator()(Arg x) const;
```

`operator()` is invoked to call the function being adapted. The adapted function is passed the argument x.

pop_heap

TYPE: function   **HEADER:** <algorithm> [heap.h]
TIME: logarithmic   **SPACE:** constant

```
namespace std{
  template <class RandomAccessIterator>
  void pop_heap(RandomAccessIterator    first,
                RandomAccessIterator    last);

  template <class RandomAccessIterator,
      class Compare>
  void pop_heap(RandomAccessIterator    first,
                RandomAccessIterator    last,
                Compare                 comp);
}
```

DESCRIPTION: Removes the root element from a heap stored as a sequence that was created with the function make_heap. The root element is swapped with the element at the end of the heap, and the sequence from first to last-1 is reformed into a heap. The resulting heap is one element shorter than the original, and the programmer is responsible for taking this difference into account.

SEE ALSO: make_heap, push_heap, sort_heap

prev_permutation

TYPE: function   **HEADER:** <algorithm> [algo.h]
TIME: linear   **SPACE:** constant

```
namespace std{
  template <class BidirectionalIterator>
  bool prev_permutation(
                BidirectionalIterator    first,
                BidirectionalIterator    last);

  template <class BidirectionalIterator,
      class Compare>
  bool prev_permutation(
                BidirectionalIterator    first,
                BidirectionalIterator    last,
                Compare                  comp);
}
```

DESCRIPTION: A permutation of a sequence is a member of the set of all arrangements of elements in the sequence such that no two of the sequences are
equal on an element-by-element basis. The set of all permutations of a sequence is viewed as an ordered set where each successive member is lexicographically greater than the previous member. Given the sequence from
`first` up to `last`, the function `prev_permutation` will attempt to
generate the previous permutation that is lexicographically less than the
original. If such a permutation exists, the function returns `true`. If there is
no such permutation, then `false` is returned, and the original sequence is
reversed. The second form allows the specification of a comparison function
to be used for the lexicographical comparison other than the default,
`operator<`.

SEE ALSO: next_permutation

ptr_fun

TYPE: adaptor   **HEADER:** <functional> [function.h]

```
namespace std{
  template <class Arg, class Result>
  pointer_to_unary_function<Arg, Result>
  ptr_fun(Result (*x)(Arg));

  template <class Arg1, class Arg2, class Result>
  pointer_to_binary_function<Arg1, Arg2, Result>
  ptr_fun(Result (*x)(Arg1, Arg2));
}
```

DESCRIPTION: An adaptor that accepts a pointer to a unary or binary function
and returns the equivalent function object. This is used to convert an ordinary function to a function object. It is more commonly used than the more
direct `pointer_to_unary_function` and `pointer_to_binary-
_function`.

SEE ALSO: pointer_to_unary_function, pointer_to_binary_function

push_heap

TYPE: function   **HEADER:** <algorithm> [heap.h]
TIME: logarithmic   **SPACE:** constant

```
namespace std{
  template <class RandomAccessIterator>
  void push_heap(RandomAccessIterator  first,
                 RandomAccessIterator  last);

  template <class RandomAccessIterator,
      class Compare>
  void push_heap(RandomAccessIterator  first,
                 RandomAccessIterator  last,
                 Compare               comp);
}
```

DESCRIPTION: Assumes that the sequence from first up to last is a heap created by the function make_heap(). It inserts the element in the position referenced by last into the heap so that the heap is one element longer. The resulting sequence is a valid heap. The second form allows you to specify a comparison function to create a heap where the smallest value is at the top or if nonscalar elements are stored in the heap.

SEE ALSO: make_heap, pop_heap, sort_heap

priority_queue

TYPE: adaptor   **HEADER:** <queue> [stack.h]

```
namespace std {
  template <class T, class Container = vector<T>,
  class Compare =
  less<typename Container::value_type> >
  class priority_queue;
}
```

DESCRIPTION: A priority queue is a special type of queue that allows values to be inserted onto the end of the queue in any order, but sorts them so that they emerge in sorted order. The effect is that the value at the front of the queue is always the greatest (or least) of all the values currently on the queue. This is useful for applications where you want the next value to be removed from the queue to be the highest value on the queue. You must pass a comparison function to the template that will be used to determine the order of values in the priority queue. You can change the comparison function to alter the order of values in the queue or to perform special comparisons on particular attributes of classes and structures. The priority queue must be based on one of the sequence containers and uses the heap algorithms to transform the sequence into a heap. For most applications, the vector is suitable as the underlying container.

SEE ALSO: queue, vector, make_heap

Public Members:

```
priority_queue<T, Container, Compare>::container_type;
```

The type of the container from which the priority queue was constructed.

```
priority_queue<T, Container, Compare>::size_type;
```

A type suitable for representing the difference between any two iterators.

```
priority_queue<T, Container, Compare>::value_type;
```

The type stored in the priority queue.

Public Methods:

```
bool priority_queue<T, Container, Compare>::empty()
   const;
```

Returns a Boolean indicating if the queue is empty.

```
void priority_queue<T, Container, Compare>::pop();
```

Removes the object at the front of the priority queue but does not return the value.

```
priority_queue<T, Container, Compare>::priority_queue(
   const Compare& x = Compare(),
   const Container& = Container());
template<class InputIterator>
priority_queue<T, Container, Compare>::priority_queue(
           InputIterator      first,
           InputIterator      last,
           const Compare&     x = Compare(),
           const Container&   = Container());
```

Constructors that allow you to change the comparison function for specific instances of the class. The first form creates an empty priority queue, and the second fills the new priority queue with objects stored in another container from the iterator first up to last.

```
void priority_queue<T, Container, Compare>::push(
   const value_type& x);
```

Adds a new object to the end of the priority queue.

```
size_type priority_queue<T, Container, Compare>::
   size() const;
```

Returns the number of objects currently stored in the priority queue.

```
const value_type&
priority_queue<T, Container, Compare>::top() const;
```

Returns the value at the top of the priority queue without removing it from the queue.

queue

TYPE: adaptor   **HEADER:** <queue> [stack.h]

```
namespace std {
   template <class T, class Container = deque<T> >
   class queue;
}
```

DESCRIPTION: Queues are based on sequence containers and are distinguished by having all additions to one end and all deletions from the other end. This means that the objects placed on the queue emerge in the same order in which they were inserted. This makes the queue suitable for applications where a sequence must be stored temporarily and have its order preserved. The queue makes frequent usage of the methods push_back() and pop_front() of the underlying container. This means that the container on which the queue is based must support these operations and do so efficiently. Thus, the queue should be based on the deque or list. For many applications, the deque will use memory more efficiently than the list.

SEE ALSO: deque, list, priority_queue, stack

Public Members:

```
priority_queue<T, Container, Compare>::container_type;
```

The type of the container from which the priority queue was constructed.

```
priority_queue<T, Container, Compare>::size_type;
```

A type suitable for representing the difference between any two iterators.

```
priority_queue<T, Container, Compare>::value_type;
```

The type stored in the priority queue.

Public Methods:

```
value_type& queue<T, Container>::back();
const value_type& queue<T, Container>::back() const;
```

These methods return a reference to the object at the back end of the queue.

```
bool queue<T, Container>::empty() const;
```

Returns a Boolean indicating if the queue is empty.

```
value_type& queue<T, Container>::front();
const value_type& queue<T, Container>::front() const;
```

These methods return a reference to the object at the front of the queue.

```
void queue<T, Container>::pop();
```

This removes the object at the head of the queue, but does not return its value.

```
void queue<T, Container>::push(const value_type& x);
```

This adds a new object onto the end of the queue.

```
explicit queue<T, Container>::queue(
   const Container& = Container());
```

The queue constructor.

```
size_type queue<T, Container>::size();
```

Returns the number of entries in the queue.

Nonmember Functions:

```
template <class T, class Container>
bool operator==(const queue<T, Container>&   x,
                const queue<T, Container>&   y);
```

Compares two queues for equality by invoking operator==() on the underlying container.

```
template <class T, class Container>
bool operator<(const queue<T, Container>&   x,
               const queue<T, Container>&   y);
```

Returns true if the queue x is less than the queue y as determined by invoking operator<() on the underlying container.

```
template <class T, class Container>
bool operator!=(const queue<T, Container>&   x,
                const queue<T, Container>&   y);
```

Compares two queues for inequality by invoking operator!=() on the underlying container.

```
template <class T, class Container>
bool operator>(const queue<T, Container>&   x,
               const queue<T, Container>&   y);
```

Returns true if queue x is greater than queue y.

```
template <class T, class Container>
bool operator>=(const queue<T, Container>&   x,
                const queue<T, Container>&   y);
```

Returns true if queue x is greater than or equal to queue y.

```
template <class T, class Container>
bool operator<=(const queue<T, Container>&   x,
                const queue<T, Container>&   y);
```

Returns true if queue x is less than or equal to queue y.

random_access_iterator

TYPE: structure   **HEADER:** <> [iterator.h]

```
template <class T, class Distance>
struct random_access_iterator;
```

DESCRIPTION: Random access iterators can both assign and retrieve values as well as be able to move in both the forward and reverse directions. In addition, they can be moved an arbitrary distance in either direction and can be added together, subtracted from one another, and compared for equality and inequality. This has been removed from the C++ standard as a class, but containers can return iterators meeting the requirements of a random access iterator.

Operators:

```
T random_access_iterator<T, Distance>::operator=(
    const random_access_iterator& x);
```

Assigns the value of one iterator to another.

```
bool random_access_iterator<T, Distance>::operator==(
    const random_access_iterator& x);
```

Returns true if the two iterators are equal.

```
bool random_access_iterator<T, Distance>::operator!=(
    const random_access_iterator& x);
```

Returns true if the two iterators are unequal.

```
bool random_access_iterator<T, Distance>::operator<(
    const random_access_iterator& x);
```

Returns true if the first iterator is less than the second.

```
bool random_access_iterator<T, Distance>::operator>(
    const random_access_iterator& x);
```

Returns true if the first iterator is greater than the second.

```
bool random_access_iterator<T, Distance>::operator<=(
    const random_access_iterator& x);
```

Returns `true` if the first iterator is less than or equal to the second.

```
bool random_access_iterator<T, Distance>::operator>=(
    const random_access_iterator& x);
```

Returns `true` if the first iterator is greater than or equal to the second.

```
random_access_iterator&
random_access_iterator<T, Distance>::operator+(
    random_access_iterator&);
```

Adds two iterators together and returns an iterator representing their sum.

```
random_access_iterator&
random_access_iterator<T, Distance>::operator++();
```

Increments the iterator and returns a reference to the new value.

```
random_access_iterator&
random_access_iterator<T, Distance>::operator++(int);
```

Returns the current value of the iterator and then increments the iterator.

```
random_access_iterator&
random_access_iterator<T, Distance>::operator+=(int);
```

Adds an arbitrary integer to the iterator to move it that number of positions in the forward direction. Negative values move the iterator backwards.

```
random_access_iterator&
random_access_iterator<T, Distance>::operator-(
    random_access_iterator&);
```

Subtracts two iterators from each other and returns an iterator representing their difference.

```
random_access_iterator&
random_access_iterator<T, Distance>::operator-=(int);
```

Subtracts an arbitrary integer from the iterator to move it that number of positions in the reverse direction.

```
random_access_iterator&
random_access_iterator<T, Distance>::operator--();
```

Decrements the iterator and returns a reference to the new value.

```
random_access_iterator<T, Distance>::operator--(int);
```

Returns the current value of the iterator and then decrements the iterator.

```
T& random_access_iterator<T, Distance>::operator*();
```

Dereferences the iterator and allows a value to be assigned to it or retrieved from it.

```
T& random_access_iterator<T,
Distance>::operator[](int);
```

Returns a reference to the object in the position of the container indicated by the offset from the iterator.

random_shuffle

TYPE: function   **HEADER:** <algorithm> [algo.h]
TIME: linear   **SPACE:** constant

```
namespace std{
   template <class RandomAccessIterator>
   void random_shuffle(
        RandomAccessIterator    first,
        RandomAccessIterator    last);

   template <class RandomAccessIterator, class
        RandomNumberGenerator>
   void random_shuffle(
                RandomAccessIterator    first,
                RandomAccessIterator    last,
                RandomNumberGenerator&  rand);
}
```

DESCRIPTION: Randomly rearranges the elements in the range from `first` up to `last`. The second form allows the user to provide an alternate random number function object. The random function object must provide `operator()(n)`, which returns a value of type `Distance` in the range from 0 up to n.

raw_storage_iterator

TYPE: adaptor   **HEADER:** <memory> [iterator.h]

```
namespace std {
  template <class OutputIterator, class T>
  class raw_storage_iterator
  : public iterator<output_iterator_tag,
  void, void, void, void>;
}
```

DESCRIPTION: Raw storage iterators allow a program to write objects into uninitialized memory. This is done by calling construct() for the type being written before the data are actually assigned. The result is that operator new is invoked with the placement syntax to initialize the memory before assignment. Since the raw storage iterator is derived from an output iterator, it cannot be used to retrieve values, only to write them.

Public Members:

```
raw_storage_iterator<OutputIterator, T>&
raw_storage_iterator<OutputIterator, T>::
operator=(const T& element);
```

Assignment operator that initializes memory by calling construct() before assigning the value to it.   Returns an iterator referencing the location that was assigned the value.

```
raw_storage_iterator<OutputIterator, T>&
raw_storage_iterator<OutputIterator, T>::operator++();
```

Increments the iterator to move it forward one position and returns its new value.

```
raw_storage_iterator<OutputIterator, T>
raw_storage_iterator<OutputIterator, T>
::operator++(int);
```

Returns the current value of the iterator and then increments its value to move it in the forward direction.

```
raw_storage_iterator<OutputIterator, T>&
raw_storage_iterator<OutputIterator, T>::operator*();
```

Dereference operator that returns a reference to the raw storage iterator to which it is applied.

```
explicit raw_storage_iterator<OutputIterator, T>
::raw_storage_iterator(OutputIterator x);
```

Constructor to create a raw storage iterator from an output iterator.

reference

TYPE: typedef   **REQUIRED BY:** all containers

DESCRIPTION: A typedef defined by all containers that returns the type of a reference to the value stored in the container.

SEE ALSO: const_reference

remove

TYPE: function   **HEADER:** <algorithm> [algo.h]
TIME: linear   **SPACE:** constant

```
namespace std{
   template <class ForwardIterator, class T>
   ForwardIterator remove(ForwardIterator    first,
                          ForwardIterator    last,
                          const T&           value);
}
```

DESCRIPTION: Removes all elements in the range from `first` up to `last` that are equal to `value`. The function returns an iterator that is one past the end of the new, possibly shorter sequence. No assumption is made about the order of elements in the original sequence.

SEE ALSO: remove_if, remove_copy, remove_copy_if

remove_copy

TYPE: function   **HEADER:** <algorithm> [algo.h]
TIME: linear   **SPACE:** constant

```
namespace std{
   template <class InputIterator,
```

```
            class OutputIterator, class T>
    OutputIterator remove_copy(
                    InputIterator      first,
                    InputIterator      last,
                    OutputIterator     result,
                    const T&           value);
}
```

DESCRIPTION: Copies all elements from `first` up to `last` that are not equal to `value` to the location referenced by `result`. The function returns an iterator that is one past the end of the result sequence. The original sequence is left unchanged. No assumption is made about the order of elements in the original sequence.

SEE ALSO: remove, remove_if, remove_copy_if

remove_copy_if

TYPE: function   **HEADER:** <algorithm> [algo.h]
TIME: linear   **SPACE:** constant

```
namespace std{
  template <class InputIterator,
      class OutputIterator, class Predicate>
  OutputIterator remove_copy_if(
                  InputIterator      first,
                  InputIterator      last,
                  OutputIterator     result,
                  Predicate          pred);
}
```

DESCRIPTION: Copies all elements in the range from `first` up to `last`, except those that satisfy the predicate `pred`, to the sequence beginning at `result`. The function returns an iterator that references the location one past the end of the new, possibly shorter result sequence. The original sequence is left unchanged, and no assumption is made about the order of the original sequence.

SEE ALSO: remove, remove_if, remove_copy

remove_if

TYPE: function   **HEADER:** <algorithm> [algo.h]
TIME: linear   **SPACE:** constant

```
namespace std{
   template <class ForwardIterator, class Predicate>
   ForwardIterator remove_if(ForwardIterator first,
                   ForwardIterator          last,
                   Predicate                pred);
}
```

DESCRIPTION: Removes all elements in the range from `first` up to `last` that satisfy the predicate `pred`. The function returns an iterator that references the location one past the end of the new, possibly shorter result sequence. No assumption is made about the order of the original sequence.

SEE ALSO: remove, remove_copy_if, remove_copy

replace

TYPE: function   **HEADER:** <algorithm> [algo.h]
TIME: linear   **SPACE:** constant

```
namespace std{
   template <class ForwardIterator, class T>
   void replace(ForwardIterator first,
           ForwardIterator     last,
           const T&            old_value,
           const T&            new_value);
}
```

DESCRIPTION: Replaces all occurrences of `old_value` by `new_value` in the sequence from `first` up to `last`.

SEE ALSO: replace_copy, replace_if, replace_copy_if

replace_copy

TYPE: function   **HEADER:** <algorithm> [algo.h]
TIME: linear   **SPACE:** constant

```
namespace std{
   template <class InputIterator,
        class OutputIterator, class T>
   OutputIterator replace_copy(
                   InputIterator  first,
                   InputIterator  last,
                   OutputIterator result,
                   const T&       old_value,
```

```
                            const T&        new_value);
    }
```

DESCRIPTION: Copies the sequence from `first` up to `last` to the location referenced by `result`. During copying, any values equal to `old_value` are replaced by `new_value`. The original sequence is left unchanged. The function returns an iterator that refers to the element one past the end of the result sequence.

SEE ALSO: replace, replace_if, replace_copy_if

replace_copy_if

TYPE: function   **HEADER:** <algorithm> [algo.h]
TIME: linear   **SPACE:** constant

```
namespace std{
    template <class Iterator, class OutputIterator,
        class Predicate, class T>
    OutputIterator replace_copy_if(
                            Iterator        first,
                            Iterator        last,
                            OutputIterator result,
                            Predicate       pred,
                            const T&        new_value);
}
```

DESCRIPTION: Copies the sequence from `first` up to `last` to the location referenced by `result`. During copying, any values that satisfy the predicate are replaced by `new_value`. The original sequence is left unchanged. The function returns an iterator that refers to the element one past the end of the result sequence.

SEE ALSO: replace, replace_if, replace_copy

replace_if

TYPE: function   **HEADER:** <algorithm> [algo.h]
TIME: linear   **SPACE:** constant

```
namespace std{
    template <class ForwardIterator, class Predicate,
        class T>
    void replace_if(ForwardIterator  first,
```

```
        ForwardIterator        last,
        Predicate              pred,
        const T&               new_value);
}
```

DESCRIPTION: Replaces all values in the range from `first` up to `last` that satisfy the predicate by `new_value`.

SEE ALSO: replace, replace_copy, replace_copy_if

---

reverse

TYPE: function   **HEADER:** <algorithm> [algo.h]
TIME: linear   **SPACE:** constant

```
namespace std{
    template <class BidirectionalIterator>
    void reverse(BidirectionalIterator    first,
             BidirectionalIterator    last);
}
```

DESCRIPTION: Reverses the order of the elements in the range from `first` up to `last`.

SEE ALSO: reverse_copy

---

reverse_copy

TYPE: function   **HEADER:** <algorithm> [algo.h]
TIME: linear   **SPACE:** constant

```
namespace std{
    template <class BidirectionalIterator,
        class OutputIterator>
    OutputIterator reverse_copy(
                BidirectionalIterator    first,
                BidirectionalIterator    last,
                OutputIterator           result);
}
```

DESCRIPTION: Copies the sequence from `first` up to `last` to the position referenced by `result`. During copying, the order of the elements is reversed, and the order of the original sequence is unchanged. The function returns an iterator that is one past the end of the result sequence.

SEE ALSO: reverse

---

reverse_iterator

TYPE: adaptor   **HEADER:** <iterator> [iterator.h]

```
namespace std {
  template <class Iterator>
  class reverse_iterator : public
  iterator<typename iterator_traits<Iterator>::
      iterator_category,
  iterator<typename iterator_traits<Iterator>::
      value_type,
  iterator<typename iterator_traits<Iterator>::
      iterator_category,
  iterator<typename iterator_traits<Iterator>::
      iterator_category,
  iterator<typename iterator_traits<Iterator>::
      iterator_category>;
}
```

DESCRIPTION: A reverse iterator adapts a forward iterator so that it traverses a container in the backward direction rather than the forward direction. The increment and decrement operators for reverse iterators have the opposite effect that the same operators have on a forward iterator. Thus, when a reverse iterator is incremented, it moves backward through the container.

Public Members:

```
reverse_iterator<Iterator>::difference_type;
```

A type that can represent the difference between any two iterators.

```
reverse_iterator<Iterator>::iterator_type;
```

The iterator adapted.

```
reverse_iterator<Iterator>::pointer;
```

The type of a pointer to the type referenced by the iterator.

```
reverse_iterator<Iterator>::reference;
```

The type of a reference to the type referenced by the iterator.

Public Methods:

```
reverse_iterator&
reverse_iterator<Iterator>::operator++();
reverse_iterator
reverse_iterator<Iterator>::operator++(int);
```

Moves the iterator one position backward.

```
reverse_iterator&
reverse_iterator<Iterator>::operator--();
reverse_iterator
reverse_iterator<Iterator>::operator--(int);
```

Moves the iterator one position forward.

```
reverse_iterator
reverse_iterator<Iterator>::operator+(
   difference_type n) const;
```

Adds n onto the value of the iterator and returns this. The value of the iterator itself is not changed.

```
reverse_iterator&
reverse_iterator<Iterator>::operator+=(
   difference_type n);
```

Moves the iterator backward n positions.

```
reverse_iterator
reverse_iterator<Iterator>::operator-(
   difference_type n) const;
```

Returns the value of the iterator minus n.

```
reverse_iterator&
reverse_iterator<Iterator>::operator-=(
   difference_type n);
```

Moves the iterator n positions forward.

```
reference reverse_iterator<Iterator>::operator*()
   const;
```

Dereferences the iterator to access the object referenced by the iterator.

```
pointer reverse_iterator<Iterator>::operator->()
   const;
```

Returns a pointer to the object referenced by the iterator.

```
reference reverse_iterator<Iterator>::operator[](
   difference_type n) const;
```

Returns a reference to the member n positions from the position of the iterator.

```
reverse_iterator<Iterator>::reverse_iterator();
explicit reverse_iterator<Iterator>::reverse_iterator(
   Iterator x);
template<class U>
reverse_iterator<Iterator>::reverse_iterator(
   const reverse_iterator<U>& u);
```

Constructors for an uninitialized reverse iterator and one initialized to x. The third form constructs an iterator to reference the same object as u.

Nonmember Functions:

```
template <class Iterator>
bool operator==(
   const reverse_iterator<Iterator>& x,
   const reverse_iterator<Iterator>& y);
```

Compares two reverse iterators for equality.

```
template <class Iterator>
bool operator<(
   const reverse_iterator<Iterator>& x,
   const reverse_iterator<Iterator>& y);
```

Returns true if iterator x is less than iterator y.

```
template <class Iterator>
bool operator!=(
   const reverse_iterator<Iterator>& x,
   const reverse_iterator<Iterator>& y);
```

Returns true if iterator x is not equal to iterator y.

```
template <class Iterator>
bool operator>(
   const reverse_iterator<Iterator>& x,
   const reverse_iterator<Iterator>& y);
```

Returns true if iterator x is greater than iterator y.

```
template <class Iterator>
bool operator<=(
   const reverse_iterator<Iterator>& x,
   const reverse_iterator<Iterator>& y);
```

Returns true if iterator x is less than or equal to iterator y.

```
template <class Iterator>
bool operator>=(
   const reverse_iterator<Iterator>& x,
   const reverse_iterator<Iterator>& y);
```

Returns true if iterator x is greater than or equal to iterator y.

```
template <class Iterator>
typename reverse_iterator<Iterator>::difference_type
operator-(
   const reverse_iterator<Iterator>& x,
   const reverse_iterator<Iterator>& y);
```

Subtracts one reverse iterator from another.

```
template <class Iterator>
reverse_iterator<Iterator>
operator+(typename
reverse_iterator<Iterator>::difference_type  n,
const reverse_iterator<Iterator>&                x);
```

Adds an arbitrary value and a reverse iterator.

rotate

TYPE: function   **HEADER:** <algorithm> [algo.h]
TIME: linear   **SPACE:** constant

```
namespace std{
   template <class ForwardIterator>
```

```
        void rotate(ForwardIterator  first,
                    ForwardIterator  middle,
                    ForwardIterator  last);
}
```

DESCRIPTION: Rotates the elements in the sequence first up to last of length n by a distance $n-m$, where m is the size of the sequence from first up to middle. The result is that each element x_i is moved to the location $x_{\mod_n (i+n-m)}$. Another way of saying this is that the sequence from first up to last will be rotated so that the element referred to by middle, within the sequence, will be rotated to the position referred to by first, and all other elements rotated appropriately.

SEE ALSO: rotate_copy

rotate_copy

TYPE: function   **HEADER:** <algorithm> [algo.h]
TIME: linear   **SPACE:** constant

```
namespace std{
  template <class ForwardIterator,
      class OutputIterator>
  OutputIterator rotate_copy(ForwardIterator first,
                             ForwardIterator  middle,
                             ForwardIterator  last,
                             OutputIterator   result);
}
```

DESCRIPTION: Performs the same operation as the function rotate, but places the rotated sequence at the position referred to by result, leaving the original sequence unchanged.

SEE ALSO: rotate

search

TYPE: function   **HEADER:** <algorithm> [algo.h]
TIME: quadratic   **SPACE:** constant

```
namespace std{
  template <class ForwardIterator1,
      class ForwardIterator2>
  ForwardIterator1 search(
```

```
                 ForwardIterator1    first1,
                 ForwardIterator1    last1,
                 ForwardIterator2    first2,
                 ForwardIterator2    last2);

template <class ForwardIterator1,
    class ForwardIterator2, class BinaryPredicate>
ForwardIterator1 search(
                 ForwardIterator1    first1,
                 ForwardIterator1    last1,
                 ForwardIterator2    first2,
                 ForwardIterator2    last2,
                 BinaryPredicate     binary_pred);

template<class ForwardIterator, class Size,
    class T>
ForwardIterator search_n(
                 ForwardIterator          first,
                 ForwardIterator          last,
                 Size                     n,
                 const T&                 value);


template<class ForwardIterator, class Size,
    class T, class BinaryPredicate>
ForwardIterator search_n(
                 ForwardIterator          first,
                 ForwardIterator          last,
                 const T&                 value,
                 Size                     n,
                 BinaryPredicate          pred);
}
```

DESCRIPTION: Searches the sequence from `first1` up to `last1` for the subsequence from `first2` up to `last2`. The function returns an iterator that references the first occurrence of the subsequence within the first sequence. If the subsequence does not occur within the first sequence, then `last1` is returned. The second form allows the specification of a predicate to determine element equality other than the default, `operator==`. The input sequence is not assumed to be sorted. `search_n()` searches for a subsequence of n copies of `value`.

set

TYPE: class   **HEADER:** <set> [set.h]

```
namespace std {
  template <class Key, class Compare = less<Key>,
  class Allocator = allocator<Key> >
  class set;
}
```

DESCRIPTION: This is an associative container and should not be confused with the mathematical concept of a set. It is well-suited to the implementation of mathematical sets, as it has fast insertion and retrieval times and stores its contents ordered. To use this as a mathematical set, you should use the set operations. The set allows you to insert objects and provides fast retrieval using a comparison function to determine the equality of objects. The objects are actually stored in a tree so that insertion and retrieval take logarithmic time. The set is useful for applications that require fast storage and retrieval of objects in random order. Internally, the objects in the set are always ordered so that an iterator will retrieve the objects in sorted order.

SEE ALSO: multiset, map, multimap

Public Members:

```
set<Key, Compare, Allocator>::allocator_type;
```

The type of the allocator.

```
set<Key, Compare, Allocator>::const_iterator;
```

A constant iterator for the container.

```
set<Key, Compare, Allocator>::const_pointer;
```

The type of a constant pointer to the content.

```
set<Key, Compare, Allocator>::const_reference;
```

The type of a constant reference to the content.

```
set<Key, Compare,
  Allocator>::const_reverse_iterator;
```

A constant reverse iterator for the container.

```
set<Key, Compare, Allocator>::difference_type;
```

Able to represent the difference between any two iterators.

```
set<Key, Compare, Allocator>::iterator;
```

An iterator for the container.

```
set<Key, Compare, Allocator>::key_compare;
```

The type of the Compare object.

```
set<Key, Compare, Allocator>::key_type;
```

The type of the key.

```
set<Key, Compare, Allocator>::pointer;
```

The type of a pointer to the content.

```
set<Key, Compare, Allocator>::reference;
```

The type of a reference to the content.

```
set<Key, Compare, Allocator>::reverse_iterator;
```

A reverse iterator for the container.

```
set<Key, Compare, Allocator>::size_type;
```

Able to represent any non-negative value of `difference_type`.

```
set<Key, Compare, Allocator>::value_compare;
```

The type of the Compare object.

```
set<Key, Compare, Allocator>::value_type;
```

The type of the key.

Public Methods:

```
iterator set<Key, Compare, Allocator>::begin() ;
const_iterator set<Key, Compare, Allocator>::begin()
  const;
```

Returns an iterator referencing the first value in the set.

```
void set<Key, Compare, Allocator>::clear();
```

Removes all elements from the container.

```
size_type set<Key, Compare, Allocator>::
  count(const key_type& x) const;
```

Returns a count of the number of objects equal to x. For a set, this will be 0 or
  1.

```
bool set<Key, Compare, Allocator>::empty() const;
```

Returns a Boolean indicating if the set is empty.

```
iterator set<Key, Compare, Allocator>::end();
const_iterator set<Key, Compare, Allocator>::end()
  const;
```

Returns a past-the-end iterator for the set.

```
void set<Key, Compare, Allocator>::
  erase(iterator position);
size_type set<Key, Compare, Allocator>::
  erase(const key_type& x);
void set<Key, Compare, Allocator>::erase(
                      iterator first,
                      iterator last);
```

The first form deletes the object referenced by the iterator position. The second form deletes all occurrences of the object x and returns the number of
  objects deleted. The third form deletes all the objects in the range from
  first up to last.

```
pair<iterator, iterator>
set<Key, Compare, Allocator>::equal_range(
  const key_type& x) const;
```

Returns a pair of iterators delimiting a range of values equal to x.

```
iterator set<Key, Compare, Allocator>::find(
  const key_type& x) const;
```

Finds the first object equal to x and returns an iterator referencing it. If not
found, it returns a past-the-end iterator.

```
allocator_type set<Key, Compare, Allocator>::
  get_allocator() const;
```

Returns the class allocator.

```
pair<iterator, bool> set<Key, Compare, Allocator>::
  insert(const value_type& value);
iterator set<Key, Compare, Allocator>::insert(
                 iterator           posn,
                 const value_type&  value);
template<class InputIterator>
void set<Key, Compare, Allocator>::insert(
                 InputIterator first,
                 InputIterator last);
```

Inserts a new value into the set. The first form returns a pair whose second
member is a bool indicating if the insertion was successful. An insertion
can fail if the object being inserted is already in the set. The first member is
an iterator referencing the newly inserted object or the existing object if the
object being inserted is a duplicate. The second form does the same, using
posn as a hint about where to start searching for the insertion position, and
returning an iterator referencing the element in the set equal to value. The
third form inserts the values from first up to last, provided they are not
already in the set.

```
key_compare set<Key, Compare, Allocator>::
  key_comp() const;
```

Returns the comparison function for the set.

```
iterator set<Key, Compare, Allocator>::lower_bound(
  const key_type& x) const;
```

Returns an iterator referencing the lower bound on a range of values equal to x.

```
size_type set<Key, Compare, Allocator>::
  max_size() const;
```

Returns the maximum size of the container.

```
set<Key, Compare, Allocator>&
set<Key, Compare, Allocator>::
  operator=(const set<Key, Compare>& x);
```

Assignment operator to assign the value of one set to another.

```
reverse_iterator set<Key, Compare, Allocator>::
  rbegin();
const_reverse_iterator set<Key, Compare, Allocator>::
  rbegin() const;
```

Returns a reverse iterator referencing the last object in the set.

```
reverse_iterator set<Key, Compare, Allocator>::
  rend() ;
const_reverse_iterator set<Key, Compare, Allocator>::
  rend() const;
```

Returns a past-the-end iterator for a reverse iteration.

```
set<Key, Compare, Allocator>::set(
  const Compare& comp = Compare(),
  const Allocator& = Allocator());

template<class InputIterator>
set<Key, Compare, Allocator>::set(
                InputIterator      first,
                InputIterator      last,
                const Compare&     comp = Compare(),
                const Allocator& = Allocator());

set<Key, Compare, Allocator>::
  set(const set<Key, Compare, Allocator>& x);
```

These are the set constructors. Two of these allow the specification of an alternate comparison function other than the one specified in the template parameters. The first form constructs an empty set, and the second constructs a set and inserts the values from the range of the interators first up to last. The third form is the copy constructor.

```
size_type set<Key, Compare, Allocator>::size() const;
```

Returns the current number of objects in the container.

```
void set<Key, Compare, Allocator>::
    swap(set<Key, Compare, Allocator>& x);
```

Swaps the contents of two sets.

```
iterator set<Key, Compare, Allocator>::upper_bound(
    const key_type& x) const;
```

Returns the upper bound on a range of values equal to x.

```
value_compare set<Key, Compare, Allocator>::
    value_comp();
```

Returns the value comparison object.

Nonmember Functions:

```
template <class Key, class Compare, class Allocator>
bool operator==(
        const set<Key, Compare, Allocator>&   x,
        const set<Key, Compare, Allocator>&   y);
```

Compares two sets for equality.

```
template <class Key, class Compare, class Allocator>
bool operator<(
        const set<Key, Compare, Allocator>&   x,
        const set<Key, Compare, Allocator>&   y);
```

Returns true if set x is lexicographically less than set y.

```
template <class Key, class Compare, class Allocator>
bool operator!=(
        const set<Key, Compare, Allocator>&   x,
        const set<Key, Compare, Allocator>&   y);
```

Returns true if set x is not equal to set y.

```
template <class Key, class Compare, class Allocator>
bool operator<=(
        const set<Key, Compare, Allocator>&   x,
        const set<Key, Compare, Allocator>&   y);
```

Returns true if set x is lexicographically less than or equal to set y.

```
template <class Key, class Compare, class Allocator>
bool operator>(
        const set<Key, Compare, Allocator>&   x,
        const set<Key, Compare, Allocator>&   y);
```

Returns true if set x is lexicographically greater than set y.

```
template <class Key, class Compare, class Allocator>
bool operator>=(
        const set<Key, Compare, Allocator>&   x,
        const set<Key, Compare, Allocator>&   y);
```

Returns true if set x is lexicographically greater than or equal to set y.

```
template <class Key, class Compare, class Allocator>
void swap(
        const set<Key, Compare, Allocator>&   x,
        const set<Key, Compare, Allocator>&   y);
```

Swaps the values in the sets x and y.

set_difference

TYPE: function   **HEADER:** <algorithm> [algo.h]
TIME: linear   **SPACE:** constant

```
namespace std{
  template <class InputIterator1,
      class InputIterator2, class OutputIterator>
  OutputIterator set_difference(
                      InputIterator1 first1,
                      InputIterator1 last1,
                      InputIterator2 first2,
                      InputIterator2 last2,
                      OutputIterator result);

    template <class InputIterator1,
        class InputIterator2, class OutputIterator,
        class Compare>
    OutputIterator set_difference(
                      InputIterator1    first1,
                      InputIterator1    last1,
                      InputIterator2    first2,
                      InputIterator2    last2,
                      OutputIterator    result,
```

```
                                Compare              comp);
}
```

DESCRIPTION: Both the first sequence from `first1` up to `last1` and the second sequence from `first2` up to `last2` are sets if they are in ascending order. The function computes the set difference of the two sets and places the resultant sequence at the position referenced by `result`. An iterator is returned that is one past the end of the resultant sequence. The second form of the function allows the specification of a comparison operator other than the default, `operator<`.

SEE ALSO: includes, set_union, set_intersection, set_symmetric_difference

set_intersection

TYPE: function   **HEADER:** <algorithm> [algo.h]
TIME: linear   **SPACE:** constant

```
namespace std{
  template <class InputIterator1,
      class InputIterator2, class OutputIterator>
  OutputIterator set_intersection(
                      InputIterator1     first1,
                      InputIterator1     last1,
                      InputIterator2     first2,
                      InputIterator2     last2,
                      OutputIterator     result);

  template <class InputIterator1,
      class InputIterator2, class OutputIterator,
      class Compare>
  OutputIterator set_intersection(
                      InputIterator1     first1,
                      InputIterator1     last1,
                      InputIterator2     first2,
                      InputIterator2     last2,
                      OutputIterator     result,
                      Compare            comp);
}
```

DESCRIPTION: Both the first sequence from `first1` up to `last1` and the second sequence from `first2` up to `last2` are sets if they are in ascending order. The function computes the intersection of the two sets and places the resultant sequence at the location referred to by `result`. The function returns an iterator that is one past the end of the resultant sequence. The second form of the function allows the specification of a comparison operator other than the default, `operator<`.

SEE ALSO: includes, set_difference, set_symmetric_difference, set_union

set_symmetric_difference

TYPE: function   **HEADER:** <algorithm> [algo.h]
TIME: linear   **SPACE:** constant

```
namespace std{
  template <class InputIterator1,
      class InputIterator2, class OutputIterator>
  OutputIterator set_symmetric_difference(
                InputIterator1      first1,
                InputIterator1      last1,
                InputIterator2      first2,
                InputIterator2      last2,
                OutputIterator      result);

  template <class InputIterator1,
      class InputIterator2, class OutputIterator,
      class Compare>
  OutputIterator set_symmetric_difference(
                InputIterator1      first1,
                InputIterator1      last1,
                InputIterator2      first2,
                InputIterator2      last2,
                OutputIterator      result,
                Compare             comp);
}
```

DESCRIPTION: Both the first sequence from `first1` up to `last1` and the second sequence from `first2` up to `last2` are sets if they are in ascending order. The function computes the symmetric set difference of the two sets and places the resultant sequence at the location referred to by `result`. The function returns an iterator that is one past the end of the resultant sequence. The second form of the function allows the specification of a comparison operator other than the default, `operator<`.

SEE ALSO: includes, set_difference, set_intersection, set_union

---

set_union

TYPE: function   HEADER: <algorithm> [algo.h]
TIME: linear   SPACE: constant

```
namespace std{
  template <class InputIterator1,
      class InputIterator2, class OutputIterator>
  OutputIterator set_union(
                    InputIterator1    first1,
                    InputIterator1    last1,
                    InputIterator2    first2,
                    InputIterator2    last2,
                    OutputIterator    result);

  template <class InputIterator1,
      class InputIterator2, class OutputIterator,
      class Compare>
  OutputIterator set_union(
                    InputIterator1    first1,
                    InputIterator1    last1,
                    InputIterator2    first2,
                    InputIterator2    last2,
                    OutputIterator    result,
                    Compare           comp);
}
```

DESCRIPTION: Both the first sequence from first1 up to last1 and the
second sequence from first2 up to last2 are sets if they are in ascending
order. The function computes the set union of the two sets and places the resultant sequence at the location referred to by result. The function returns
an iterator that is one past the end of the resultant sequence. The second
form of the function allows the specification of a comparison operator other
than the default, operator<.

SEE ALSO: includes, set_difference, set_intersection,
set_symmetric_difference

---

size_type

TYPE: typedef   REQUIRED BY: all containers

DESCRIPTION: A typedef provided by all containers that defines a type used to represent a number of elements, such as the number of elements in the container.

slice

TYPE: class   **HEADER:** <numeric> []

```
namespace std {
    class slice;
}
```

DESCRIPTION: The class slice represents a slice through an array. This is useful for generating the subscripts for a slice through a multi-dimensional array that is actually stored in a one-dimensional array.

Public Functions:

```
size_t slice::size() const;
```

Returns the number of subscripts to be generated.

```
slice::slice();
slice::slice(size_t   start,
             size_t   length,
             size_t   stride);
slice::slice(const slice&);
```

These are the slice constructors. The default constructor creates an empty slice and is used only to construct arrays of slices. The second form is the most commonly used and takes a starting index, the number of indices to generate, and a stride that is repeatedly added to the starting index to generate the subsequent indices. The third form is the copy constructor.

```
size_t slice::start() const;
```

Returns the starting index for the slice.

```
size_t slice::stride() const;
```

Returns the stride that is the increment added to the starting index to generate subsequent indices.

slice_array

TYPE: class   **HEADER:** <numeric> []

```
namespace std {
  template <class T>
      class slice_array;
}
```

DESCRIPTION: The slice_array is used internally by the class valarray to return the results of subscripting with a slice. It has no public constructors and can be instantiated only by using a slice to subscript a
valarray. It contains a reference to the valarray subscripted as well as
the subscripts to be referenced.

Public Members:

```
typedef T slice_array<T>::value_type;
```

The type referenced by the slice_array.

Public Methods:

```
void slice_array<T>::operator=(
                const valarray<T>& a) const;
slice_array& slice_array<T>::operator=(
                const slice_array& a);
```

The first form assigns the subscripted members of the valarray referenced by
*this the values in a. The second form is private and allows one
slice_array to be assigned to another.

```
void slice_array<T>::operator*=(
                const valarray<T>& a) const;
```

Multiplies the subscripted members of the valarray referenced by *this by
the values in a.

```
void slice_array<T>::operator/=(
                const valarray<T>& a) const;
```

Divides the subscripted members of the valarray referenced by *this by
the values in a.

```
void slice_array<T>::operator%=(
                  const valarray<T>& a) const;
```

Replaces the subscripted members of the `valarray` referenced by `*this` by the remainder upon division of these values by the values in a.

```
void slice_array<T>::operator+=(
                  const valarray<T>& a) const;
```

Adds the values in a onto the subscripted members of the `valarray` referenced by `*this`.

```
void slice_array<T>::operator-=(
                  const valarray<T>& a) const;
```

Subtracts the values in a from the subscripted members of the `valarray` referenced by `*this`.

```
void slice_array<T>::operator^=(
                  const valarray<T>& a) const;
```

Replaces each of the subscripted members of the `valarray` referenced by `*this` with itself, exclusive OR'ed with the corresponding value from a.

```
void slice_array<T>::operator&=(
                  const valarray<T>& a) const;
```

Replaces each of the subscripted members of the `valarray` referenced by `*this` with itself, bitwise AND'ed with the corresponding value from a.

```
void slice_array<T>::operator|=(
                  const valarray<T>& a) const;
```

Replaces each of the subscripted members of the `valarray` referenced by `*this` with itself, inclusive OR'ed with the corresponding value from a.

```
void slice_array<T>::operator<<=(
                  const valarray<T>& a) const;
```

Replaces each of the subscripted members of the `valarray` referenced by `*this` with itself, shifted left by the corresponding value from a.

```
void slice_array<T>::operator>>=(
                    const valarray<T>& a) const;
```

Replaces each of the subscripted members of the valarray referenced by
*this with itself, shifted right by the corresponding value from a.

```
void slice_array<T>::fill(const T& v);
```

Assigns the value v to the subscripted elements of the valarray referenced by
*this.

```
slice_array<T>::slice_array();
slice_array<T>::slice_array(const slice_array&);
```

These are the private constructors. The first is the default constructor and the
second is the copy constructor. These might not be defined by all
implementations.

```
slice_array<T>::~slice_array();
```

The class destructor.

slist

TYPE: class   **HEADER:** <> [] {slist.h}

```
namespace std{
  template<class T, class Allocator = allocator<T> >
  class slist;
}
```

DESCRIPTION: slist is a singly linked list that is implemented as part of
the SGI version of the STL. It is not included in the C++ standard and is unlikely to be found in other STL implementations. For this reason, the user is
cautioned against its use unless the SGI implementation will be available in
all environments to which the code will be ported. slist differs from
list in that each node has a pointer only to the next node in the list and
does not have the pointer to the previous node that list provides. This
means that an slist will consume less storage that a list. It also means
that the list can be traversed only in the forward direction; thus, a forward iterator is provided rather than the bidirectional iterator provided by the list.

SEE ALSO: list

Public Members:

```
slist<T, Allocator>::const_iterator;
```

A constant iterator which can iterate through the container.

```
slist<T, Allocator>::const_reference;
```

The type of a constant reference to the data stored in the container.

```
slist<T, Allocator>::difference_type;
```

A signed integral type used to represent the difference in iterators.

```
slist<T, Allocator>::iterator;
```

An iterator which can iterate through the container.

```
slist<T, Allocator>::pointer;
```

The type of a pointer to the data stored in the container.

```
slist<T, Allocator>::reference;
```

The type of a reference to the data stored in the container.

```
slist<T, Allocator>::size_type;
```

An unsigned integral type used to indicate sizes and positions.

```
slist<T, Allocator>::value_type;
```

The type stored in the container.

Public Methods:

```
iterator slist<T, Allocator>::begin();
const_iterator slist<T>::begin();
```

Returns an iterator referencing the first element in the list.

```
bool slist<T, Allocator>::empty();
```

Returns `true` if the list is empty.

```
iterator slist<T, Allocator>::end();
const_iterator slist<T>::end();
```

Returns a past-the-end iterator for the list.

```
iterator slist<T, Allocator>::erase(iterator it);
iterator slist<T, Allocator>::erase(iterator first,
                                    iterator last);
```

The first form deletes the element referenced by `it`, while the second form deletes the elements from `first` up to `last`.

```
iterator slist<T, Allocator>::erase_after(
                                iterator it);
iterator slist<T, Allocator>::erase_after(
                                iterator first,
                                iterator last);
```

The first form erases the element immediately after `it`. The second form erases all elements in the range `[first + 1, last)`.

```
reference slist<T, Allocator>::front();
const_reference slist<T, Allocator>::front();
```

Returns a reference to the first element in the list.

```
iterator slist<T, Allocator>::insert(
                                iterator  it,
                                const T&  t);
void slist<T, Allocator>::insert(
                                iterator      it,
                                InputIterator first,
                                InputIterator last);
void slist<T, Allocator>::insert(
                                iterator      it,
                                size_type     n,
                                const T&      t);
```

The first form inserts the value t immediately before the element referenced by it. It returns an iterator referencing the element inserted. The second form inserts the elements from first up to last immediately before the element referenced by it. The third form inserts n copies of the value t immediately before the element referenced by it.

```
iterator slist<T, Allocator>::insert_after(
                                 iterator  it);
iterator slist<T, Allocator>::insert_after(
                                 iterator  it,
                                 const T&  t);
void slist<T, Allocator>::insert_after(
                          iterator      it,
                          InputIterator first,
                          InputIterator last);
void slist<T, Allocator>::insert_after(
                          iterator      it,
                          size_type     n,
                          const T&      t);
```

The first form inserts T() immediately after it. The second inserts t immediately after it. Both of these forms return an iterator referencing the element inserted. The third form inserts the elements from first up to last immediately after it. The fourth form inserts n copies of t immediately after it.

```
size_type slist<T, Allocator>::max_size();
```

Returns the largest possible size of the list.

```
void slist<T, Allocator>::merge(slist<T>& l);
void slist<T, Allocator>::merge(
                slist<T, Allocator>&   l,
                BinaryPredicate        pred);
```

Performs a merge of the two sorted lists, *this and l, removing the elements from l as they are inserted in *this. *this and l must be separate lists. The second form uses a comparison function other than the default, operator<.

```
slist<T, Allocator>::operator=(
        const slist<T, Allocator>& l);
```

Assigns this list the contents of the list l.

```
void slist<T, Allocator>::pop_front();
```

Removes the first element in the list.

```
iterator slist<T, Allocator>::previous(iterator it);
const_iterator slist<T, Allocator>::previous(
        const_iterator it);
```

Returns the iterator previous to it.

```
void slist<T, Allocator>::push_front(const T& t);
```

Inserts the value t as the first element in the list.

```
void slist<T, Allocator>::remove(const T& val);
void slist<T, Allocator>::remove_if(Predicate pred);
```

Removes all elements equal to val or that satisfy the predicate pred.

```
size_type slist<T, Allocator>::size();
```

Returns the number of elements stored in the list.

```
slist<T, Allocator>::slist();
slist<T, Allocator>::slist(size_type n);
slist<T, Allocator>::slist(size_type n, const T& t);
slist<T, Allocator>::slist(const slist<T>& l);
slist<T, Allocator>::slist(InputIterator     first,
                           InputIterator     last);
```

These are the class constructors. The first constructor creates an empty list. The second creates a list with n members, each initialized with T(). The third also creates a list of length n, but each node is a copy of t. The fourth is the copy constructor. The final constructor creates a list whose contents are a copy of the elements from first up to last.

```
slist<T, Allocator>::~slist();
```

The class destructor.

```
void slist<T, Allocator>::sort();
void slist<T, Allocator>::sort(BinaryPredicate pred);
```

Performs a stable sort on the list using operator<. The second form uses a comparison function other than the default, operator<.

```
void slist<T, Allocator>::splice(
                iterator                      it,
                slist<T, Allocator>&          l);
void slist<T, Allocator>::splice(
                iterator                      it,
                slist<T, Allocator>&          l,
                iterator                      i);
void slist<T, Allocator>::splice(
                iterator                      it,
                slist<T, Allocator>&          l,
                iterator                      first,
                iterator                      last);
```

Inserts the elements of the list l immediately before the element referenced by it and removes the inserted elements from the list l. It is required that *this and l be different lists. The first form moves all elements of l. The second form moves only the element of l referenced by i. The third form moves the elements of l from first up to last.

```
void slist<T, Allocator>::splice_after(
                              iterator  it,
                              iterator  p);
void slist<T, Allocator>::splice_after(
                              iterator  it,
                              iterator  first,
                              iterator  last);
```

The first form inserts the element immediately after p so that it is immediately after it. The element immediately after p is removed from the container holding it. The second form moves the elements in the range from first + 1 up to last + 1 immediately after it.

```
void slist<T, Allocator>::swap(
        slist<T, Allocator>& l);
```

Swaps the contents of this list and the list l.

```
void slist<T, Allocator>::unique();
void slist<T, Allocator>::unique(
                        BinaryPredicate pred);
```

Removes adjacent duplicate elements so that only a single copy of each element remains. The second form uses a comparison function other than the default, `operator==`.

Nonmember Functions:

```
bool operator==(
        const slist<T, Allocator>&   l1,
        const slist<T, Allocator>&   l2);
```

Returns `true` if the two lists are element-wise equivalent.

```
bool operator<(
        const slist<T, Allocator>&   l1,
        const slist<T, Allocator>&   l2);
```

Returns `true` if `l1` is lexicographically less than `l2`.

---

sort

TYPE: function   **HEADER:** <algorithm> [algo.h]
TIME: n log n   **SPACE:** logarithmic

```
namespace std{
  template <class RandomAccessIterator>
  void sort(RandomAccessIterator      first,
            RandomAccessIterator      last);

  template <class RandomAccessIterator,
      class Compare>
  void sort(RandomAccessIterator      first,
            RandomAccessIterator      last,
            Compare                   comp);
}
```

DESCRIPTION: Sorts the sequence from `first` up to `last`. The first form of the function uses `operator<` to perform comparisons, while the second form uses the function object `comp` to perform the comparisons.

SEE ALSO: stable_sort, partial_sort, partial_sort_copy

sort_heap

TYPE: function   **HEADER:** <algorithm> [heap.h]
TIME: n log n   **SPACE:** constant

```
namespace std{
  template <class RandomAccessIterator>
  void sort_heap(RandomAccessIterator    first,
                 RandomAccessIterator    last);

  template <class RandomAccessIterator,
      class Compare>
  void sort_heap(RandomAccessIterator    first,
                 RandomAccessIterator    last,
                 Compare                 comp);
}
```

DESCRIPTION: Assumes that the sequence from first up to last is a valid heap created by the function make_heap(). This function repeatedly removes the top element from the heap and places it at the end of the heap until there are no elements left in the heap. The resulting sequence is sorted, although the heap property of the sequence has been destroyed. The speed of this sort is approximately equal to the quicksort algorithm used by the function sort.

SEE ALSO: make_heap, push_heap, pop_heap, sort

stable_partition

TYPE: function   **HEADER:** <algorithm> [algo.h]
TIME: n log n   **SPACE:** constant

```
namespace std{
  template <class BidirectionalIterator,
      class Predicate>
  BidirectionalIterator
  stable_partition(BidirectionalIterator    first,
                   BidirectionalIterator     last,
                   Predicate                 pred);
}
```

DESCRIPTION: Rearranges the elements in the sequence from `first` up to `last` so that all elements that satisfy the predicate are placed before all elements that do not satisfy the predicate. The function returns an iterator *i* such that all elements in the range from `first` up to *i* satisfy the predicate and all elements from *i* up to `last` do not satisfy the predicate. The relative order of the elements in each of the two subranges is guaranteed to be the same as it was in the original unpartitioned sequence. This stability of relative ordering is the difference between the `stable_partition()` function and the `partition()` function.

stable_sort

TYPE: function   **HEADER:** <algorithm> [algo.h]
TIME: n log₂ n   **SPACE:** logarithmic

```
namespace std{
   template <class RandomAccessIterator>
   void stable_sort(
       RandomAccessIterator    first,
       RandomAccessIterator    last);

   template <class RandomAccessIterator,
       class Compare>
   void stable_sort(
       RandomAccessIterator    first,
       RandomAccessIterator    last,
       Compare                 comp);
}
```

DESCRIPTION: Sorts the sequence from `first` up to `last` so that the relative order of equal elements is preserved. The first form of the function uses `operator<` to perform comparisons and results in a sequence in ascending order. The second form uses the function object `comp` to perform the comparison.

SEE ALSO: sort, partial_sort, partial_sort_copy

stack

TYPE: adaptor   **HEADER:** <stack> [stack.h]

```
namespace std{
   template <class T, class Container = deque<T> >
```

```
    class stack;
}
```

DESCRIPTION: The stack is a container adaptor that can use one of the sequence containers (vector, deque, list) to create a new container with a restricted set of operations. Stacks are characterized by allowing addition and deletion of elements at one end of the stack only. This means that the items on a stack emerge in the opposite of the order in which they were inserted. This capability is useful for a wide variety of applications. The class makes extensive use of the push_back() and pop_back() operations of the underlying class. Since all sequence containers implement these operations in constant time, the decision about which container the stack should be based on comes down to a question of efficiency of memory utilization.

SEE ALSO: vector, deque, list, queue

Public Members:

```
stack<T, Container>::container_type;
```

The type of the adapted container.

```
stack<T, Container>::size_type;
```

A type which can represent the number of values in the container.

```
stack<T, Container>::value_type;
```

The type stored in the container.

Public Methods:

```
bool stack<T, Container>::empty() const;
```

Returns true if the stack is empty, otherwise returns false.

```
void stack<T, Container>::pop();
```

Removes the value from the top of the stack but does not return the value.

```
void stack<T, Container>::push(const value_type& x);
```

Adds the value x to the top of the stack.

```
size_type stack<T, Container>::size() const;
```

Returns the number of elements stored in the stack.

```
explicit stack<T, Container>::stack(
    const Container& = Container());
```

Default constructor.

```
value_type& stack<T, Container>::top();
const value_type& stack<T, Container>::top() const;
```

Returns the value at the top of the stack without removing it from the stack.

Nonmember Functions:

```
template <class T, class Container>
bool operator==(const stack<T, Container>&    x,
                const stack<T, Container>&    y);
```

Compares two stacks by invoking operator== as defined for the class on which the stack is based.

```
template <class T, class Container>
bool operator<(const stack<T, Container>&    x,
               const stack<T, Container>&    y);
```

Compares two stacks by invoking operator< as defined for the class on which the stack is based.

```
template <class T, class Container>
bool operator!=(const stack<T, Container>&    x,
                const stack<T, Container>&    y);
```

Compares two stacks for inequality.

```
template <class T, class Container>
bool operator<=(const stack<T, Container>&    x,
                const stack<T, Container>&    y);
```

Returns true if the first stack is less than or equal to the second.

```
template <class T, class Container>
bool operator>(const stack<T, Container>&   x,
        const stack<T, Container>&   y);
```

Returns true if the first stack is greater than the second.

```
template <class T, class Container>
bool operator>=(const stack<T, Container>&   x,
        const stack<T, Container>&   y);
```

Returns true if the first stack is greater than or equal to the second.

swap

TYPE: function   **HEADER:** <algorithm> [algobase.h]
TIME: constant   **SPACE:** constant

```
namespace std{
  template <class T>
  void swap(T&   a,
      T&       b);
}
```

DESCRIPTION: Swaps the two values a and b.

SEE ALSO: iter_swap, swap_ranges

swap_ranges

TYPE: function   **HEADER:** <algorithm> [algo.h]
TIME: linear   **SPACE:** constant

```
namespace std{
  template <class ForwardIterator1,
      class ForwardIterator2>
  ForwardIterator2 swap_ranges(
            ForwardIterator1   first1,
            ForwardIterator1   last1,
            ForwardIterator2   first2);
}
```

DESCRIPTION: Swaps the *n* elements in the sequence from first1 up to last1 with the *n* elements in the sequence beginning at first2. The function returns an iterator that is one past the end of the second sequence.

SEE ALSO: swap, iter_swap

times

TYPE: function object   **HEADER:** <> [function.h]
TIME: constant   **SPACE:** constant

```
template <class T>
struct times: binary_function<T, T, T> {
    T operator()(const T& x, const T& y);
};
```

DESCRIPTION: A function object that can be passed to another function as a substitute for operator*. It applies operator* to its two parameters and returns the result. This function object has been replaced by multiplies in implementations conforming to the C++ standard.

SEE ALSO: minus, plus, divides, modulus, multiplies

transform

TYPE: function   **HEADER:** <algorithm> [algo.h]
TIME: linear   **SPACE:** constant

```
namespace std{
  template <class InputIterator,
      class OutputIterator, class UnaryOperation>
  OutputIterator transform(
                  InputIterator     first,
                  InputIterator     last,
                  OutputIterator    result,
                  UnaryOperation    op);

  template <class InputIterator1,
      class InputIterator2, class OutputIterator,
      class BinaryOperation>
  OutputIterator transform(
                  InputIterator1    first1,
                  InputIterator1    last1,
                  InputIterator2    first2,
                  OutputIterator    result,
                  BinaryOperation   binary_op);
}
```

DESCRIPTION: The first form of the function transforms the sequence from `first1` up to `last1` to a new sequence by applying the unary function object `op` to each element. The resultant sequence is placed at the location referred to by `result`. The second form of the function transforms the sequence from `first1` up to `last1` and the sequence from `first2` up to `last2` into a new sequence by applying the binary function object `op` to each pair of elements in turn. The resultant sequence is placed at the location referred to by `result`. Both functions return an iterator that is one past the end of the resultant sequence.

unary_function

TYPE: struct   **HEADER:** <functional> [function.h]

```
namespace std{
   template <class Arg, class Result>
   struct unary_function;
}
```

DESCRIPTION: This is a base struct used internally to derive function objects that are `unary_functions`. The class is intended to model a function that requires a single argument and returns a result. Any function conforming to the definition of a `unary_function` must define the types `argument_type` and `result_type`.

SEE ALSO: binary_function

Public Members:

```
unary_function<Arg, Result>::argument_type;
```

The type of the function argument.

```
unary_function<Arg, Result>::result_type;
```

The type of the function result.

unary_negate

TYPE: adaptor   **HEADER:** <functional> [function.h]

```
namespace std{
   template <class Predicate>
```

```
   class unary_negate
   : public unary_function<
   typename Predicate::argument_type,bool>;
}
```

DESCRIPTION: This is an adaptor that negates the result of a unary predicate. The predicate must satisfy the requirements of a unary_function. This is used by the adaptor not1, which is more convenient than this adaptor.

SEE ALSO: binary_negate, not1, unary_function

Public Methods:

```
explicit unary_negate<Predicate>::unary_negate(
                 const Predicate& pred);
```

This is the constructor that accepts the predicate to be negated.

```
bool unary_negate<Predicate>::operator()(
   const typename Predicate::argument_type& x) const;
```

Like all function adaptors, this defines operator(), which, when called, returns the logical negation of pred(x).

unique

TYPE: function   **HEADER:** <algorithm> [algo.h]
TIME: linear   **SPACE:** constant

```
namespace std{
   template <class ForwardIterator>
   ForwardIterator unique(ForwardIterator      first,
                          ForwardIterator      last);

   template <class ForwardIterator,
       class BinaryPredicate>
   ForwardIterator unique(
                   ForwardIterator      first,
                   ForwardIterator      last,
                   BinaryPredicate      binary_pred);
}
```

DESCRIPTION: Traverses the sequence from `first` up to `last`, removing all adjacent duplicate elements so that only a single copy of each element remains. The function returns an iterator that is one past the end of the possibly shorter resultant sequence. The second form of the function allows the specification of a comparison operation other than the default `operator==`. The input sequence is assumed to be sorted.

SEE ALSO: unique_copy

unique_copy

TYPE: function   **HEADER:** <algorithm> [algo.h]
TIME: linear   **SPACE:** constant

```
namespace std{
  template <class InputIterator,
      class OutputIterator>
  OutputIterator unique_copy(
                    InputIterator    first,
                    InputIterator    last,
                    OutputIterator   result);

  template <class InputIterator,
      class OutputIterator, class BinaryPredicate>
  OutputIterator unique_copy(
                    InputIterator    first,
                    InputIterator    last,
                    OutputIterator   result,
                    BinaryPredicate  binary_pred);
}
```

DESCRIPTION: Copies the sequence from `first` up to `last` to the location referenced by `result`. All adjacent duplicate elements are removed during the copy so that only a single copy of each element remains. The function returns an iterator that is one past the end of the sequence beginning at `result`. The second form of the function allows the specification of a comparison operation other than the default, `operator==`. The input sequence is assumed to be sorted.

SEE ALSO: unique

upper_bound

TYPE: function   **HEADER:** <algorithm> [algo.h]
TIME: logarithmic   **SPACE:** constant

```
namespace std{
  template <class ForwardIterator, class T>
  ForwardIterator upper_bound(
      ForwardIterator   first,
      ForwardIterator   last,
      const T&          value);

  template <class ForwardIterator, class T,
      class Compare>
  ForwardIterator upper_bound(
      ForwardIterator   first,
      ForwardIterator   last,
      const T&          value,
      Compare           comp);
}
```

DESCRIPTION: Returns an iterator that references the first element in the range from `first` up to `last` that is greater than `value`. If no such element exists, it returns `last`. The elements in the range `first` up to `last` are assumed to be sorted. The second form allows the specification of a comparison function other than the default, `operator<`.

SEE ALSO: lower_bound, equal_range

valarray

TYPE: class   **HEADER:** <numeric> []

```
namespace std {
  template<class T>
  class valarray;
}
```

DESCRIPTION: A `valarray` is a *smart* numeric array. It can be used to hold any type, not just numbers, but it is most useful for numbers. `valarray` provides array operations so that all members of an array can be operated upon at once. It also provides several subscripting options so that several members can be retrieved with a single subscript operation.

SEE ALSO: slice, slice_array, gslice, gslice_array, indirect_array

Public Members:

```
valarray<T>::value_type;
```

The type stored in the `valarray`.

Public Methods:

```
valarray<T> valarray<T>::apply(T func(T)) const;
valarray<T> valarray<T>::apply(T func(const T&))
  const;
```

Returns an array of the same length as the original whose members are the result
of applying the function `func` to each member of the original array.

```
valarray<T> valarray<T>::cshift(int n) const;
```

Returns a `valarray` equal to `*this` with the values circularly shifted by n
positions. A circular shift is defined such that when a value is shifted off one
end of the array, it appears at the other end of the array. Positive values of n
shift to the left and negative values to the right.

```
T valarray<T>::min() const;
```

Returns the minimum value in the `valarray` as determined by `operator<`.
The result is undefined for an array of length zero.

```
T valarray<T>::max() const;
```

Returns the maximum value in the `valarray` as determined by `operator<`.
The result is undefined for an array of length zero.

```
valarray<T> valarray<T>::operator+() const;
```

Applies unary + to each member of the array.

```
valarray<T> valarray<T>::operator-() const;
```

Applies unary – to each member of the array.

```
valarray<T> valarray<T>::operator~() const;
```

Applies unary ~ to each member of the array.

```
valarray<bool> valarray<T>::operator!() const;
```

Applies unary ! to each member of the array.

```
T              valarray<T>::operator[](size_t)
               const;
T&             valarray<T>::operator[](size_t);
valarray<T>    valarray<T>::operator[](slice) const;
slice_array<T> valarray<T>::operator[](slice);
valarray<T>    valarray<T>::operator[](
               const gslice&) const;
gslice_array<T> valarray<T>::operator[](
               const gslice&);
valarray<T>    valarray<T>::operator[](
               const valarray<bool>&) const;
mask_array<T>  valarray<T>::operator[](
               const valarray<bool>&);
valarray<T>    valarray<T>::operator[](
               const valarray<size_t>&) const;
indirect_array<T> valarray<T>::operator[](
               const valarray<size_t>&);
```

These are the subscript operators. The const versions return a `valarray` that can be used only as an r-value. The non-const versions return an instance of a class that has reference semantics to the original array and can be used as an l-value to reference the subscripted members.

```
valarray<T>& valarray<T>::operator=(const T& a);
valarray<T>& valarray<T>::operator=(
  const valarray<T>& a);
valarray<T>& valarray<T>::operator=(
  const slice_array<T>& a);
valarray<T>& valarray<T>::operator=(
  const gslice_array<T>& a);
valarray<T>& valarray<T>::operator=(
  const mask_array<T>& a);
valarray<T>& valarray<T>::operator=(
  const indirect_array<T>& a);
```

These are the assignment operators. The first assigns the value of the scalar argument to each member of the array. The second assigns each member of *this the value of the corresponding member of the argument array, which must be of the same size. The remaining operators assign the results of a generalized subscripting operation to the appropriate members of the array.

```
valarray<T>::valarray();
explicit valarray<T>::valarray(size_t n);
valarray<T>::valarray(const T& val, size_t n);
valarray<T>::valarray(const T* val,
                      size_t   n);
valarray<T>::valarray<T>::valarray(
                      const valarray<T>&);
valarray<T>::valarray(const slice_array<T>&);
valarray<T>::valarray(const gslice_array<T>&);
valarray<T>::valarray(const mask_array<T>&);
valarray<T>::valarray(const indirect_array<T>&);
```

These are the valarray constructors. The first constructs a valarray of zero length. The second constructs a valarray of length n whose members are initialized to T(). The third constructs an array of length n, each of whose members is initialized as T(val). The fourth constructs a valarray of length n, each of whose members are initialized with the corresponding member of the array val. This constructor is the recommended method for converting an array into a valarray. The fifth form is the copy constructor that produces a valarray identical to its argument. The remaining forms are conversion constructors that convert their arguments to valarrays.

```
valarray<T>& valarray<T>::operator*=(
  const valarray<T>& a);
```

Multiplies each member of *this by the corresponding member of a. *this and a must be of the same length. A reference to the modified array is returned.

```
valarray<T>& valarray<T>::operator/=(
  const valarray<T>& a);
```

Divides each member of *this by the corresponding member of a. *this and a must be of the same length. A reference to the modified array is returned.

```
valarray<T>& valarray<T>::operator%=(
  const valarray<T>& a);
```

Replaces each member of *this by itself modulo the corresponding member of a. *this and a must be of the same length. A reference to the modified array is returned.

```
valarray<T>& valarray<T>::operator+=(
  const valarray<T>& a);
```

Replaces each member of *this by adding the corresponding member of a.
*this and a must be of the same length. A reference to the modified array
is returned.

```
valarray<T>& valarray<T>::operator-=(
  const valarray<T>& a);
```

Replaces each member of *this by subtracting the corresponding member of
a. *this and a must be of the same length. A reference to the modified array is returned.

```
valarray<T>& valarray<T>::operator^=(
  const valarray<T>& a);
```

Replaces each member of *this by the bitwise exclusive OR of itself and the
corresponding member of a. *this and a must be of the same length. A
reference to the modified array is returned.

```
valarray<T>& valarray<T>::operator&=(
  const valarray<T>& a);
```

Replaces each member of *this by the bitwise AND of itself and the corresponding member of a. *this and a must be of the same length. A reference to the modified array is returned.

```
valarray<T>& valarray<T>::operator|=(
  const valarray<T>& a);
```

Replaces each member of *this by the bitwise inclusive OR of itself and the
corresponding member of a. *this and a must be of the same length. A
reference to the modified array is returned.

```
valarray<T>& valarray<T>::operator<<=(
  const valarray<T>& a);
```

Replaces each member of *this by itself, shifted left by the amount indicated
by the corresponding member of a. *this and a must be of the same
length. A reference to the modified array is returned.

```
valarray<T>& valarray<T>::operator>>=(
    const valarray<T>& a);
```

Replaces each member of *this by itself, shifted right by the amount indicated
by the corresponding member of a. *this and a must be of the same
length. A reference to the modified array is returned.

```
void valarray<T>::resize(size_t sz, T c = T());
```

This changes the size of the array to sz and assigns the value c to all of the
members. All iterators and references to members of the array are
invalidated.

```
valarray<T> valarray<T>::shift(int n) const;
```

Returns a valarray equal to *this but with the values in the array by n positions, filling in the positions vacated by the shifted elements with T(). Elements shifted off the end of the array are lost. Positive values of n shift to
the left and negative values to the right.

Nonmember Functions:

```
template<class T>
valarray<T> abs(const valarray<T>& a);
```

Returns an array containing the absolute value of every member of a.

```
template<class T>
valarray<T> acos(const valarray<T>& a);
```

Returns an array whose members are the arc cosine of the members of a.

```
template<class T>
valarray<T> asin(const valarray<T>& a);
```

Returns an array whose members are the arc sine of the members of a.

```
template<class T>
valarray<T> atan(const valarray<T>& a);
```

Returns an array whose members are the arc tangent of the members of a.

```
template<class T>
valarray<T> atan2(const    valarray<T>& x,
                  const    valarray<T>& y);
```

Returns the result of applying `atan2(x[i], y[i])`, where $0 \le i <$ `x.size()`.

```
template<class T>
valarray<T> atan2(const valarray<T>& x, const T& y);
```

Returns the result of applying `atan2(x[i], y)`, where $0 \le i <$ `x.size()`.

```
template<class T>
valarray<T> atan2(const T& x, const valarray<T>& y);
```

Returns the result of applying `atan2(x, y[i])`, where $0 \le i <$ `x.size()`.

```
template<class T>
valarray<T> cos(const valarray<T>& a);
```

Returns an array whose members are the cosine of the members of a.

```
template<class T>
valarray<T> cosh(const valarray<T>& a);
```

Returns an array whose members are the hyperbolic cosine of the members of a.

```
template<class T>
valarray<T> exp(const valarray<T>& a);
```

Returns an array whose members are *e* to the power of the members of a.

```
template<class T>
valarray<T> log(const valarray<T>& a);
```

Returns an array whose members are the natural logarithm of a.

```
template<class T>
valarray<T> log10(const valarray<T>& a);
```

Returns an array whose members are the base 10 logarithm of a.

```
template<class T>
valarray<T>
operator*(const valarray<T>&    a,
        const valarray<T>&      b);
```

Returns an array whose members are the members of a multiplied by the corresponding members of b.

```
template<class T>
valarray<T>
operator/(const valarray<T>&    a,
        const valarray<T>&      b);
```

Returns an array whose members are the members of a divided by the corresponding members of b.

```
template<class T>
valarray<T>
operator%(const valarray<T>&    a,
        const valarray<T>&      b);
```

Returns an array whose members are the members of a modulo the corresponding members of b.

```
template<class T>
valarray<T>
operator+(const valarray<T>&    a,
        const valarray<T>&      b);
```

Returns an array whose members are the members of a plus the corresponding members of b.

```
template<class T>
valarray<T>
operator-(const valarray<T>&    a,
        const valarray<T>&      b);
```

Returns an array whose members are the members of a minus the corresponding members of b.

```
template<class T>
valarray<T>
operator^(const valarray<T>&    a,
        const valarray<T>&      b);
```

Returns an array whose members are the members of a exclusive OR'ed with the corresponding members of b.

```
template<class T>
valarray<T>
operator&(const valarray<T>&   a,
        const valarray<T>&     b);
```

Returns an array whose members are the members of a bitwise AND'ed with the corresponding members of b.

```
template<class T>
valarray<T>
operator|(const valarray<T>&   a,
        const valarray<T>&     b);
```

Returns an array whose members are the members of a inclusive OR'ed with the corresponding members of b.

```
template<class T>
valarray<T>
operator<<(const valarray<T>&   a,
        const valarray<T>&     b);
```

Returns an array whose members are the members of a shifted left by the corresponding members of b.

```
template<class T>
valarray<T>
operator>>(const valarray<T>&   a,
        const valarray<T>&     b);
```

Returns an array whose members are the members of a shifted right by the corresponding members of b.

```
template<class T>
valarray<T>
operator*(const valarray<T>&   a,
            const T&            v);
```

Returns an array whose members are the members of a multiplied by v.

```
template<class T>
valarray<T>
```

```
operator*(const T&           v,
        const valarray<T>& a);
```

Returns an array whose members are the members of a multiplied by v.

```
template<class T>
valarray<T>
operator/(const valarray<T>& a,
            const T&           v);
```

Returns an array whose members are the members of a divided by v.

```
template<class T>
valarray<T>
operator/(const T&           v,
        const valarray<T>& a);
```

Returns an array whose members are v divided by the members of a.

```
template<class T>
valarray<T>
operator%(const valarray<T>& a,
            const T&           v);
```

Returns an array whose members are the members of a modulo v.

```
template<class T>
valarray<T>
operator%(const T&           v,
        const valarray<T>& a);
```

Returns an array whose members are v modulo the members of a.

```
template<class T>
valarray<T>
operator+(const valarray<T>& a,
            const T&           v);
```

Returns an array whose members are the members of a plus v.

```
template<class T>
valarray<T>
operator+(const T&           v,
        const valarray<T>& a);
```

Returns an array whose members are the members of a plus v.

```
template<class T>
valarray<T>
operator-(const valarray<T>&    a,
          const T&               v);
```

Returns an array whose members are the members of a minus v.

```
template<class T>
valarray<T>
operator-(const T&           v,
      const valarray<T>& a);
```

Returns an array whose members are v minus the members of a.

```
template<class T>
valarray<T>
operator^(const valarray<T>&    a,
          const T&               v);
```

Returns an array whose members are the members of a exclusive OR'ed with v.

```
template<class T>
valarray<T>
operator^(const T&           v,
      const valarray<T>& a);
```

Returns an array whose members are v exclusive OR'ed with the members of a.

```
template<class T>
valarray<T>
operator&(const valarray<T>&    a,
          const T&               v);
```

Returns an array whose members are the members of a bitwise AND'ed with v.

```
template<class T>
valarray<T>
operator&(const T&           v,
      const valarray<T>& a);
```

Returns an array whose members are v bitwise AND'ed with the members of a.

```
template<class T>
valarray<T>
operator|(const valarray<T>    a&,
          const T&             v);
```

Returns an array whose members are the members of a bitwise OR'ed with v.

```
template<class T>
valarray<T>
operator|(const T&         v,
      const valarray<T>& a);
```

Returns an array whose members are v bitwise OR'ed with the members of a.

```
template<class T>
valarray<T>
operator<<(const valarray<T>&  a,
           const T&            v);
```

Returns an array whose members are the members of a shifted left by v.

```
template<class T>
valarray<T>
operator<<(const T&         v,
      const valarray<T>& a);
```

Returns an array whose members are v shifted left by the members of a.

```
template<class T>
valarray<T>
operator>>(const valarray<T>&  a,
           const T&            v);
```

Returns an array whose members are the members of a shifted right by v.

```
template<class T>
valarray<T>
operator>>(const T&         v,
      const valarray<T>& a);
```

Returns an array whose members are v shifted right by the members of a.

```
template<class T>
valarray<bool>
```

```
operator==(const valarray<T>&  a,
           const valarray<T>& b);
```

Returns a Boolean array containing the result of applying `operator==` to the corresponding elements of a and b. a and b must be of the same length.

```
template<class T>
valarray<bool>
operator!=(const valarray<T>&  a,
           const valarray<T>& b);
```

Returns a Boolean array containing the result of applying `operator!=` to the corresponding elements of a and b. a and b must be of the same length.

```
template<class T>
valarray<bool>
operator<(const valarray<T>&   a,
          const valarray<T>& b);
```

Returns a Boolean array containing the result of applying `operator<` to the corresponding elements of a and b. a and b must be of the same length.

```
template<class T>
valarray<bool>
operator>(const valarray<T>&   a,
          const valarray<T>& b);
```

Returns a Boolean array containing the result of applying `operator>` to the corresponding elements of a and b. a and b must be of the same length.

```
template<class T>
valarray<bool>
operator<=(const valarray<T>&  a,
           const valarray<T>& b);
```

Returns a Boolean array containing the result of applying `operator<=` to the corresponding elements of a and b. a and b must be of the same length.

```
template<class T>
valarray<bool>
operator>=(const valarray<T>&  a,
           const valarray<T>& b);
```

Returns a Boolean array containing the result of applying `operator>=` to the corresponding elements of a and b. a and b must be of the same length.

```
template<class T>
valarray<bool>
operator&&(const valarray<T>&  a,
           const valarray<T>& b);
```

Returns a Boolean array containing the logical AND of the corresponding elements of a and b. a and b must be of the same length.

```
template<class T>
valarray<bool>
operator||(const valarray<T>&  a,
           const valarray<T>& b);
```

Returns a Boolean array containing the logical OR of the corresponding elements of a and b. a and b must be of the same length.

```
template<class T>
valarray<T> pow(const       valarray<T>& a,
                const       valarray<T>& b);
```

Returns a `valarray` whose members are the members of a to the power of the corresponding members of b. a and b must be of the same length.

```
template<class T>
valarray<T> pow(const valarray<T>& a, const T& j);
```

Returns a `valarray` whose members are the members of a to the power of j.

```
template<class T>
valarray<T> pow(const T& j, const valarray<T>& a);
```

Returns a `valarray` whose members are each j to the power of the corresponding member of a.

```
template<class T>
valarray<T> sin(const valarray<T>& a);
```

Returns a `valarray` whose members are the sine of the members of a.

```
template<class T>
valarray<T> sinh(const valarray<T>& a);
```

Returns a `valarray` whose members are the hyperbolic sine of the members of
a.

```
template<class T>
valarray<T> sqrt(const valarray<T>& a);
```

Returns a `valarray` whose members are the square root of the members of a.

```
template<class T>
valarray<T> tan(const valarray<T>& a);
```

Returns a `valarray` whose members are the tangent of the members of a.

```
template<class T>
valarray<T> tanh(const valarray<T>& a);
```

Returns a `valarray` whose members are the hyperbolic tangent of the members of a.

value_compare

TYPE: typedef   **REQUIRED BY:** associative containers

DESCRIPTION: A typedef defined by all associative containers that returns a
function object used to compare values within the container.

SEE ALSO: key_compare, value_type

value_type

TYPE: function   **HEADER:** <> [iterator.h]
TIME: constant   **SPACE:** constant

```
template <class T, class Distance>
T* value_type(
   const input_iterator<T, Distance>&);
```

```
template <class T, class Distance>
inline T* value_type(
   const forward_iterator<T, Distance>&);
```

```
template <class T, class Distance>
```

```
inline T* value_type(
  const bidirectional_iterator<T, Distance>&);

template <class T, class Distance>
inline T* value_type(
  const random_access_iterator<T, Distance>&);

template <class T>inline T* value_type(const T*);
```

DESCRIPTION: An iterator is passed to this function, which then returns a pointer to the type stored in the container with which the iterator is associated. The value of this pointer is zero and can be ignored; only the type is important. This function is used to specialize algorithms to take advantage of the capabilities of specific iterator categories. This function has been removed from the C++ standard and replaced by the expression `iterator_type<iter>::value_type`.

SEE ALSO: iterator_category, distance_type

value_type

TYPE: typedef   **REQUIRED BY:** all containers

DESCRIPTION: a typedef that represents the type of the value stored in the container.

SEE ALSO: key_type, value_compare

vector

TYPE: class   **HEADER:** <vector> [vector.h]

```
namespace std{
  template <class T, class Allocator = allocator<T> >
  class vector;
}
```

DESCRIPTION: A vector is similar to an array, represents a sequence of elements, and can be subscripted to retrieve values stored in the vector, or to modify existing values. A vector must be extended using one of the methods push_front(), push_back(), or insert(). You cannot subscript a nonexistent member of a vector. Subscripting of existing elements is a constant time operation. Vectors are inherently less efficient for many operations than lists, and the programmer should have an understanding of how a vector works. A vector allocates a block of memory large enough to hold the data. If the amount of data becomes larger than the allocated storage, then a larger block is allocated, and the data are copied to the new block. Data are also copied during insertion and deletion of elements in the vector, other than at the end. Such operations can be very expensive and should be used infrequently. Insertion and deletion at the end of a vector can take constant time, assuming additional space does not have to be allocated, whereas insertion and deletion at any other point take linear time. A vector should be used when there are few insertions or deletions, except at the end, and when direct access to the elements is required.

SEE ALSO: deque, list

Public Members:

```
vector<T, Allocator>::allocator_type;
```

The type of the allocator.

```
vector<T, Allocator>::const_iterator;
```

A constant iterator for the container.

```
vector<T, Allocator>::const_pointer;
```

The type of a constant pointer to the content.

```
vector<T, Allocator>::const_reference;
```

The type of a constant reference to the content.

```
vector<T, Allocator>::const_reverse_iterator;
```

A constant reverse iterator for the container.

```
vector<T, Allocator>::difference_type;
```

Able to represent the difference between any two iterators.

```
vector<T, Allocator>::iterator;
```

An iterator for the container.

```
vector<T, Allocator>::pointer;
```

The type of a pointer to the content.

```
vector<T, Allocator>::reference;
```

The type of a reference to the content.

```
vector<T, Allocator>::reverse_iterator;
```

A reverse iterator for the container.

```
vector<T, Allocator>::size_type;
```

Able to represent any non-negative value of difference_type.

```
vector<T, Allocator>::value_type;
```

The type stored in the container.

Public Methods:

```
void vector<T, Allocator>::assign(
            size_type    n,
            const T&     value);

template<class InputIterator>
void vector<T, Allocator>::assign(
            InputIterator first,
            InputIterator last);
```

These methods erase the content of the vector and replace it with new values specified by the parameters. The first form fills the vector with n copies of value. The second form inserts the values from first up to last.

```
reference vector<T, Allocator>::at(size_type n);
const_reference vector<T, Allocator>::at(
    size_type n) const;
```

Returns a reference to the nth element of the vector. n must be less than `size()`.

```
reference vector<T, Allocator>::back();
const_reference vector<T, Allocator>::back() const;
```

Returns the last element in the vector.

```
iterator vector<T, Allocator>::begin();
const_iterator vector<T, Allocator>::begin() const;
```

Returns an iterator that references the first element in the vector.

```
size_type vector<T, Allocator>::capacity() const;
```

Returns the number of elements that can be stored in the currently allocated block of memory in which the vector is stored.

```
void vector<T, Allocator>::clear();
```

Removes all elements from the vector.

```
bool vector<T, Allocator>::empty() const;
```

Returns a Boolean value indicating if the vector is empty.

```
iterator vector<T, Allocator>::end();
const_iterator vector<T, Allocator>::end() const;
```

Returns an iterator that is one past the last element in the vector.

```
iterator vector<T, Allocator>::erase(
   iterator position);
iterator vector<T, Allocator>::erase(
                             iterator first,
                             iterator last);
```

Deletes the element at the indicated position from the vector. The second form deletes all elements in the range from `first` up to `last`. Returns an iterator referencing the element after the last element deleted.

```
reference vector<T, Allocator>::front();
const_reference vector<T, Allocator>::front() const;
```

Returns the first element in the vector.

```
allocator_type vector<T, Allocator>::get_allocator()
    const;
```

Returns the allocator for the container.

```
iterator vector<T, Allocator>::insert(
                    iterator     position,
                    const T&     x);
template<class InputIterator>
void vector<T, Allocator>::insert(
        iterator         position,
        InputIterator    first,
        InputIterator    last);
void vector<T, Allocator>::insert(
        iterator    position,
        size_type   n,
        const T&    x);
```

Inserts the element x just before position. The first form returns an iterator that refers to the element inserted. The second form inserts the elements from first up to last so that they are placed just before position. The third form inserts n copies of the element x just before position.

```
size_type vector<T, Allocator>::max_size() const;
```

Returns the maximum number of elements that can be stored in the vector. This usually corresponds to a system-imposed limit on the amount of memory available for a contiguous block.

```
vector<T, Allocator>& operator=(
    const vector<T, Allocator>& x);
```

Assigns the value of the vector x to the object, adjusting the allocated space as necessary.

```
reference operator[](size_type n);
const_reference operator[](size_type n) const;
```

A subscript operation that returns the nth element of the vector. The nth element of the vector must exist, as this operator cannot be used to extend the limits of the vector.

```
void vector<T, Allocator>::pop_back();
```

Deletes the last element in the vector.

```
void vector<T, Allocator>::push_back(const T& x);
```

Appends the element x to the end of the vector.

```
reverse_iterator vector<T, Allocator>::rbegin();
const_reverse_iterator vector<T, Allocator>::rbegin()
  const;
```

Returns an iterator that can be used as the starting value for a reverse iterator.

```
void vector<T, Allocator>::remove(const T& value);
```

Removes all elements equal to value from the vector.

```
reverse_iterator vector<T, Allocator>::rend();
const_reverse_iterator vector<T, Allocator>::rend()
  const;
```

Returns a past-the-end iterator for a reverse iteration.

```
void vector<T, Allocator>::reserve(size_type n);
```

Alters the size of the vector so that it is greater than or equal to n. This might result in storage reallocation.

```
void vector<T, Allocator>::resize(
                          size_type size,
                          T         value = T());
```

Changes the size of the vector so that it contains size members. If the vector has less than size elements, new elements are appended to make it the desired length, with the new elements assigned value. If the vector has more than size elements, elements are removed from the end to make it the desired length. If the vector is the desired length, nothing is done.

```
size_type vector<T, Allocator>::size() const;
```

Returns the number of elements currently stored in the vector.

```
void vector<T, Allocator>::swap(
  vector<T, Allocator>& x);
```

Swaps the contents of this vector with the vector x so that each has the contents
of the other.

```
explicit vector<T, Allocator>::vector(
  const Allocator& = Allocator());
```

```
explicit vector<T, Allocator>::vector(
                     size_type n,
                     const T& value = T(),
                     const Allocator& = Allocator());
```

```
template<class InputIterator>
vector<T, Allocator>::vector(
      InputIterator first,
      InputIterator last,
      const Allocator& = Allocator());
```

```
vector<T, Allocator>::vector(
      const vector<T, Allocator>& x);
```

Constructors to create a new vector. The first form constructs a vector and allocates a buffer of default size to hold the elements. The second form allocates
a buffer large enough to hold n elements and initializes each of them to
value. The third form allocates a buffer large enough to hold the elements
from first up to last and then copies these elements into the newly allocated space. The fourth form is the copy constructor.

```
vector<T, Allocator>::~vector();
```

Deletes all the elements stored in the vector and then deallocates the buffer in
which they were stored.

Nonmember Functions:

```
template <class T, class Allocator>
bool operator==(const vector<T, Allocator>& x,
                const vector<T, Allocator>& y);
```

Returns a Boolean indicating if the two vectors are equal.

```
template <class T, class Allocator>
bool operator<(const vector<T, Allocator>& x,
               const vector<T, Allocator>& y);
```

Returns true if the first vector is less than the second.

```
template <class T, class Allocator>
bool operator!=(const vector<T, Allocator>& x,
                const vector<T, Allocator>& y);
```

Returns true if the first vector is not equal to the second.

```
template <class T, class Allocator>
bool operator<=(const vector<T, Allocator>& x,
                const vector<T, Allocator>& y);
```

Returns true if the first vector is less than or equal to the second.

```
template <class T, class Allocator>
bool operator>(const vector<T, Allocator>& x,
               const vector<T, Allocator>& y);
```

Returns true if the first vector is greater than the second.

```
template <class T, class Allocator>
bool operator>=(const vector<T, Allocator>& x,
                const vector<T, Allocator>& y);
```

Returns true if the first vector is greater than or equal to the second.

```
template <class T, class Allocator>
void swap(const vector<T, Allocator>& x,
          const vector<T, Allocator>& y);
```

Swaps the contents of the two vectors.

vector<bool>

TYPE: class   **HEADER:** <vector> [vector.h]

```
namespace std{
  template <class Allocator>
  class vector<bool, Allocator>;
}
```

DESCRIPTION: This is a specialization of the vector. It works the same as a vector but adds the method `flip()` and no longer supports `remove()`.

SEE ALSO: vector, bitset

Public Members:

```
vector<bool, Allocator>::allocator_type;
```

The type of the allocator.

```
vector<bool, Allocator>::const_iterator;
```

A constant iterator for the container.

```
vector<bool, Allocator>::const_pointer;
```

The type of a constant pointer to the content.

```
vector<bool, Allocator>::const_reference;
```

The type of a constant reference to the content.

```
vector<bool, Allocator>::const_reverse_iterator;
```

A constant reverse iterator for the container.

```
vector<bool, Allocator>::difference_type;
```

Able to represent the difference between any two iterators.

```
vector<bool, Allocator>::iterator;
```

An iterator for the container.

```
vector<bool, Allocator>::pointer;
```

The type of a pointer to the content.

```
vector<bool, Allocator>::reference;
```

The type of a reference to the content.

```
vector<bool, Allocator>::reverse_iterator;
```

A reverse iterator for the container.

```
vector<bool, Allocator>::size_type;
```

Able to represent any non-negative value of difference_type.

```
vector<bool, Allocator>::value_type;
```

The type stored in the container.

Public Methods:

```
void vector<bool, Allocator>::assign(
            size_type    n,
            const T&     value);

template<class InputIterator>
void vector<bool, Allocator>::assign(
            InputIterator first,
            InputIterator last);
```

These methods erase the content of the vector and replace it with new values
specified by the parameters. The first form fills the vector with n copies of
value. The second form inserts the values from first up to last.

```
reference vector<bool, Allocator>::at(size_type n);
const_reference vector<bool, Allocator>::at(
  size_type n) const;
```

Returns a reference to the nth element of the vector. n must be less than
size().

```
reference vector<bool, Allocator>::back();
const_reference vector<bool, Allocator>::back() const;
```

Returns the last element in the vector.

```
iterator vector<bool, Allocator>::begin();
const_iterator vector<bool, Allocator>::begin() const;
```

Returns an iterator that references the first element in the vector.

```
size_type vector<bool, Allocator>::capacity() const;
```

Returns the number of elements that can be stored in the currently allocated block of memory in which the vector is stored.

```
void vector<bool, Allocator>::clear();
```

Removes all elements from the vector.

```
bool vector<bool, Allocator>::empty() const;
```

Returns a Boolean value indicating if the vector is empty.

```
iterator vector<bool, Allocator>::end();
const_iterator vector<bool, Allocator>::end() const;
```

Returns an iterator that is one past the last element in the vector.

```
iterator vector<bool, Allocator>::erase(
   iterator position);
iterator vector<bool, Allocator>::erase(
                              iterator  first,
                              iterator  last);
```

Deletes the element at the indicated position from the vector. The second form deletes all elements in the range from first up to last. Returns an iterator referencing the element after the last element deleted.

```
void vector<bool, Allocator>::flip();
```

Flips all the bits.

```
reference vector<bool, Allocator>::front();
const_reference vector<bool, Allocator>::front()
const;
```

Returns the first element in the vector.

```
allocator_type vector<bool,Allocator>::
   get_allocator() const;
```

Returns the allocator for the container.

```
iterator vector<bool, Allocator>::insert(
                    iterator       position,
                    const bool&       x);
template<class InputIterator>
void vector<bool, Allocator>::insert(
        iterator          position,
        InputIterator     first,
        InputIterator     last);
void vector<bool, Allocator>::insert(
        iterator    position,
        size_type   n,
        const bool&    x);
```

Inserts the element x just before position. The first form returns an iterator that refers to the element inserted. The second form inserts the elements from first up to last so that they are placed just before position. The third form inserts n copies of the element x just before position.

```
size_type vector<bool, Allocator>::max_size() const;
```

Returns the maximum number of elements that can be stored in the vector. This usually corresponds to a system-imposed limit on the amount of memory available for a contiguous block.

```
vector<bool, Allocator>& operator=(
    const vector<bool, Allocator>& x);
```

Assigns the value of the vector x to the object, adjusting the allocated space as necessary.

```
reference operator[](size_type n);
const_reference operator[](size_type n) const;
```

A subscript operation that returns the nth element of the vector. The nth element of the vector must exist, as this operator cannot be used to extend the limits of the vector.

```
void vector<bool, Allocator>::pop_back();
```

Deletes the last element in the vector.

```
void vector<bool, Allocator>::push_back(const bool&
x);
```

Appends the element x to the end of the vector.

```
reverse_iterator vector<bool, Allocator>::rbegin();
const_reverse_iterator vector<bool,
Allocator>::rbegin()
    const;
```

Returns an iterator that can be used as the starting value for a reverse iterator.

```
reverse_iterator vector<bool, Allocator>::rend();
const_reverse_iterator vector<bool, Allocator>::rend()
    const;
```

Returns a past-the-end iterator for a reverse iteration.

```
void vector<bool, Allocator>::reserve(size_type n);
```

Alters the size of the vector so that it is greater than or equal to n. This might result in storage reallocation.

```
void vector<bool, Allocator>::resize(
                        size_type size,
                        bool      value = bool());
```

Changes the size of the vector so that it contains size members. If the vector has less than size elements, new elements are appended to make it the desired length, with the new elements assigned value. If the vector has more than size elements, elements are removed from the end to make it the desired length. If the vector is the desired length, nothing is done.

```
size_type vector<bool, Allocator>::size() const;
```

Returns the number of elements currently stored in the vector.

```
void vector<bool, Allocator>::swap(
    vector<bool, Allocator>& x);
static void vector<bool, Allocator>::swap(
                reference    x,
                reference    y);
```

The first form swaps the contents of this vector with the vector x so that each has the contents of the other. The second form swaps the values of x and y.

```
explicit vector<bool, Allocator>::vector(
   const Allocator& = Allocator());

explicit vector<bool, Allocator>::vector(
                      size_type n,
                      const bool&   value = bool(),
                      const Allocator& = Allocator());

template<class InputIterator>
vector<bool, Allocator>::vector(
        InputIterator first,
        InputIterator last,
        const Allocator& = Allocator());

vector<bool, Allocator>::vector(
        const vector<bool, Allocator>& x);
```

Constructors to create a new vector. The first form constructs a vector and allocates a buffer of default size to hold the elements. The second form allocates a buffer large enough to hold n elements and initializes each of them to value. The third form allocates a buffer large enough to hold the elements from first up to last and then copies these elements into the newly allocated space. The fourth form is the copy constructor.

```
vector<bool, Allocator>::~vector();
```

Deletes all the elements stored in the vector and then deallocates the buffer in which they were stored.

Nonmember Functions:

```
template <class bool, class Allocator>
bool operator==(const vector<bool, Allocator>& x,
                const vector<bool, Allocator>& y);
```

Returns a Boolean indicating if the two vectors are equal.

```
template <class bool, class Allocator>
bool operator<(const vector<bool, Allocator>& x,
                const vector<bool, Allocator>& y);
```

Returns true if the first vector is less than the second.

```
template <class bool, class Allocator>
bool operator!=(const vector<bool, Allocator>& x,
                const vector<bool, Allocator>& y);
```

Returns true if the first vector is not equal to the second.

```
template <class bool, class Allocator>
bool operator<=(const vector<bool, Allocator>& x,
                const vector<bool, Allocator>& y);
```

Returns true if the first vector is less than or equal to the second.

```
template <class bool, class Allocator>
bool operator>(const vector<bool, Allocator>& x,
               const vector<bool, Allocator>& y);
```

Returns true if the first vector is greater than the second.

```
template <class bool, class Allocator>
bool operator>=(const vector<bool, Allocator>& x,
                const vector<bool, Allocator>& y);
```

Returns true if the first vector is greater than or equal to the second.

```
template <class bool, class Allocator>
void swap(const vector<bool, Allocator>& x,
          const vector<bool, Allocator>& y);
```

Swaps the contents of the two vectors.

References

BM95   J. Barreiro and D. Musser, *An STL Hash Table Implementation with Gradual Resizing*, Computer Science Dept., Rensselaer Polytechnic Institute, Troy, NY, 1995, included in HP distribution [STE95].

BFM95   J. Barreiro, R. Fraley, and D. Musser, *Hash Tables for the Standard Template Library*, Doc. No. X3J16/94-0218 WG21/N0605, included in HP distribution [STE95].

GLA96   G. Glass, "STL in Action: Helper Algorithms," *C++ Report*, Vol. 8, No. 1, January 1996, pp. 18–21.

HOR95   C. Horstmann, *Safe STL*, http://www.mathcs.sjsu.edu/faculty/horstman/safestl.html.

IG98   S. Ignatchenko, "STL Implementations and Thread Safety," *C++ Report*, July/August 1998.

KAS96   L. Kasparek, "Processing Variant Records with STL," *C/C++ Users Journal*, Vol. 14, No. 9, September 1996, pp. 19–27.

KEF95   T. Keffer, "Programming with the Standard Template Library," *Dr. Dobb's Sourcebook*, Vol. 20, No. 15, July/August 1995, pp. 7–11.

KOE94a   A. Koenig, "Templates and Generic Algorithms," *Journal of Object-Oriented Programming*, June 1994, pp. 45–47.

KOE94b   A. Koenig, "Generic Iterators," *Journal of Object-Oriented Programming*, September 1994, pp. 69–72.

KOE94c   A. Koenig, "File Iterators," *Journal of Object-Oriented Programming*, November/December 1994, pp. 59–62.

LAR88   P. Larson, "Dynamic Hash Tables," *Communications of the ACM*, Vol. 31, No. 4, April 1988, pp. 446–457.

LINK   A collection of STL-related links on the internet. http://www.geocities.com/SiliconValley/hills/6191/STL_LINK.HTML.

MUS87   D. Musser and A. Stepanov, "A Library of Generic Algorithms in Ada," in *Proc. ACM SigAda International Conference*, Boston, December 1987.

MUS88   D. Musser and A. Stepanov, "Generic Programming," *First International Joint Conference of ISSAC-88 and AAECC-6*, Rome, Italy, July 4–8, 1988.

MUS89   D. Musser and A. Stepanov, *The Ada Generic Library: Linear List Processing Packages*, Springer-Verlag, 1989.

MUS89a   D. Musser and A. Stepanov, "Generic Programming," in *Symbolic and Algebraic Computation Proceedings,* P. Gianni (ed.), Lecture Notes in Computer Science, Springer-Verlag, 1989.

MUS94   D. Musser and A. Stepanov, "Algorithm-oriented Generic Libraries," *Software — Practice and Experience*, Vol. 24, No. 7, July 1994, pp. 623–642.

MUS95a   D. Musser, *Rationale for Adding Hash Tables to the C++ Standard Template Library*, Computer Science Dept., Rensselaer Polytechnic Institute, Troy, NY, 1995, included in HP distribution [STE95].

PLA96   P. J. Plauger, "Standard C/C++: Introduction to <algorithm>," *C/C++ Users Journal*, Vol. 14, No. 9, September 1996, pp. 8–17.

RI99   E. Richards, "Adding Level-2 Thread Safety to Existing Objects," *C/C++ Users Journal*, February 1999.

SG86   R. Scheifler and J. Gettys, "The X Window System," *ACM Transactions on Graphics*, Vol. 5, No. 2, April 1986, pp. 79–109.

STD98   International Standard, ISO/IEC 14882, *Programming Languages—C++*, American National Standards Institute, September 1998.

STE95   A. Stepanov and M. Lee, *The Standard Template Library*, Hewlett-Packard Laboratories, Palo Alto, CA, 1995, ftp://butler.hpl.hp.com/stl.

STE95a   A. Stevens, "Alexander Stepanov and STL," *Dr. Dobb's Journal*, Vol. 20, No. 3, March 1995, pp. 115–123.

STE95b   A. Stepanov, "The Standard Template Library," *Byte*, Vol. 20, No. 10, Oct. 1995, pp. 177–178.

STR91   B. Stroustrop, *The C++ Programming Language,* Second Edition, Addison-Wesley, Reading, MA, 1991.

STR94   B. Stroustrop, *The Design and Evolution of C++*, Addison-Wesley, Reading, MA, 1994.

STR94a   B. Stroustrop, "Making a Vector Fit for a Standard," *C++ Report*, Vol. 6, No. 8, October 1994, pp. 30–34.

VIL94   M. Vilot, "An Introduction to the Standard Template Library," *C++ Report*, Vol. 6, No. 8, October 1994, pp. 22–35.

VIL95   M. Vilot, "The C++ Standard Library," *Dr. Dobb's Journal*, Vol. 20, No. 8, August 1995, pp. 111–113.

VWY90   C. Van Wyk, *Data Structures and C Programs*, Addison Wesley, 1990.

ZIG95   D. Zigmond, "Generic Programming and the C++ STL," *Dr. Dobb's Journal*, Vol. 20, No. 8, August 1995, pp. 18–24.

Index